Modern Slavery and the Governance of Global Value Chains

Modern Slavery and the Governance of Global Value Chains provides an interdisciplinary analysis of the links between global value chain (GVC) governance, regulation, and vulnerability to severe forms of labour market exploitation by focusing on initiatives that seek to induce corporate action to end or mitigate modern slavery. The book brings together chapters by scholars from developed, developing, and emerging economies and from various disciplines to explore the complex relationship between global and local patterns of production and consumption, and severe forms of labour market exploitation.

Hila Shamir is Professor of Law at Tel Aviv University. She teaches and researches in the fields of employment, labour, immigration, and welfare law with a focus on issues of labour trafficking and feminist legal thought. Shamir was the Principal Investigator (PI) of the research group TraffLab: Labor Approach to Human Trafficking (ERC StG), 2018–23, and is the PI of the research group ChainGE Lab (ERC COG), www.chaingelab.org, 2024–29.

The late **Bimal Arora** was Professor at Manchester Metropolitan University and the founding CEO and Director of the Centre for Responsible Business, New Delhi, which he established to facilitate participation of Indian actors in voluntary global governance for sustainability.

Shilpi Banerjee is senior research fellow at Hult Impact Labs, Hult International Business School, Dubai. Her research explores new ways of thinking about the social, ethical, and environmental dimensions of business.

Tamar Barkay is senior lecturer and the head of the Sociology and Anthropology Programme in the Department of Multidisciplinary Studies at Tel-Hai College. She is also affiliated with ChainGE Lab (ERC) at Tel Aviv University. Her research focuses on economic sociology, particularly the social and political implications of CSR and labour governance in supply chains.

Development Trajectories in Global Value Chains

A feature of the current phase of globalization is the outsourcing of production tasks and services across borders, and the increasing organization of production and trade through global value chains (GVCs), global commodity chains (GCCs), and global production networks (GPNs). With a large and growing literature on GVCs, GCCs, and GPNs, this series is distinguished by its focus on the implications of these new production systems for economic, social, and regional development.

This series publishes a wide range of theoretical, methodological, and empirical works, both research monographs and edited volumes, dealing with crucial issues of transformation in the global economy. How do GVCs change the ways in which lead and supplier firms shape regional and international economies? How do they affect local and regional development trajectories, and what implications do they have for workers and their communities? How is the organization of value chains changing and how are these emerging forms contested as more traditional structures of North–South trade complemented and transformed by emerging South–South lead firms, investments, and trading links? How does the large-scale entry of women into value-chain production impact on gender relations? What opportunities and limits do GVCs create for economic and social upgrading and innovation? In what ways are GVCs changing the nature of work and the role of labor in the global economy? And how might the increasing focus on logistics management, financialization, or social standards and compliance portend important developments in the structure of regional economies?

This series includes contributions from all disciplines and interdisciplinary fields and approaches related to GVC analysis, including GCCs and GPNs, and is particularly focused on theoretically innovative and informed works that are grounded in the empirics of development related to these approaches. Through their focus on changing organizational forms, governance systems, and production relations, volumes in this series contribute to on-going conversations about theories of development and development policy in the contemporary era of globalization.

Titles in the Series

1. Labour in Global Value Chains in Asia
   Edited by *Dev Nathan, Meenu Tewari and Sandip Sarkar*
2. The Sweatshop Regime: Laboring Bodies, Exploitation and Garments Made in India
   Alessandra Mezzadri
3. The Intangible Economy: How Services Shape Global Production and Consumption
   Edited by *Deborah K. Elms, Arian Hassani and Patrick Low*
4. Making Cars in the New India: Industry, Precarity and Informality
   Tom Barnes
5. Development with Global Value Chains: Upgrading and Innovation in Asia
   Edited by *Dev Nathan, Meenu Tewari and Sandip Sarkar*
6. Global Value Chains and Development: Redefining the Contours of 21st Century Capitalism
   Gary Gereffi
7. Capturing the Gains? Gender and Work in Global Value Chains
   Stephanie Barrientos
8. Monopsony Capitalism: Power and Production in the Twilight of the Sweatshop Age
   Ashok Kumar
9. Reverse Subsidies in Global Monopsony Capitalism: Gender, Labour, and Environmental Injustice in Garment Value Chains
   Dev Nathan, Shikha Silliman Bhattacharjee, S. Rahul, Purushottam Kumar, Immanuel Dahaghani, Sukhpal Singh and Padmini Swaminathan
10. Television in the Streaming Era: The Global Shift
    Jean K. Chalaby
11. At the Margins of the Global Market: Making Commodities, Workers, and Crisis in Rural Colombia
    Phillip A. Hough
12. Europe's Auto Industry: Global Production Networks and Spatial Change
    Petr Pavlínek

Modern Slavery and the Governance of Global Value Chains

Edited by

Hila Shamir

Bimal Arora

Shilpi Banerjee

Tamar Barkay

CAMBRIDGE
UNIVERSITY PRESS

CAMBRIDGE
UNIVERSITY PRESS

Shaftesbury Road, Cambridge CB2 8EA, United Kingdom

One Liberty Plaza, 20th Floor, New York, NY 10006, USA

477 Williamstown Road, Port Melbourne, VIC 3207, Australia

314–321, 3rd Floor, Plot 3, Splendor Forum, Jasola District Centre, New Delhi – 110025, India

103 Penang Road, #05–06/07, Visioncrest Commercial, Singapore 238467

Cambridge University Press is part of Cambridge University Press & Assessment, a department of the University of Cambridge.

We share the University's mission to contribute to society through the pursuit of education, learning and research at the highest international levels of excellence.

www.cambridge.org
Information on this title: www.cambridge.org/9781009591089

DOI: 10.1017/9781009591102

When citing this work, please include a reference to the DOI 10.1017/9781009591102

First published 2025

Printed in India by Avantika Printers Pvt. Ltd.

Cover image: 'Highway and Byways' – Paul Klee, 1929. Image credit: Historisches Archiv mit Rheinischem Bildarchiv, Sabrina Walz, rba_d039386_01 Museum Ludwig Köln, Paul Klee, Hauptweg und Nebenwege, ML 76/3253.

A catalogue record for this publication is available from the British Library

ISBN 978-1-009-59108-9 Hardback

In memory of our dear friend, collaborator, and
mentor Bimal Arora and our inspiring
colleague Varsha Joshi

This work has received support from ERC StG grant agreement No. 756672, TraffLab: Labor Perspective to Human Trafficking, PI Prof. Hila Shamir/Tel Aviv University, as well as from ChainGE Lab (ERC) funded by the European Union, Horizon ERC grant ERC-2022-COG (Project No. 101088188, PI Prof. Hila Shamir). Views and opinions expressed are, however, those of the author(s) only and do not necessarily reflect those of the European Union or the European Research Council Executive Agency (ERCEA) (the 'granting authority'). Neither the European Union nor the granting authority can be held responsible for them. This work has received further funding from the Israel Science Foundation (ISF) grant no. 1866/20.

Contents

Part II Actors

Part III Sectors

Foreword

Kailash Satyarthi*

This book is a much-needed contribution to our understanding of labour exploitation in global value chains (GVCs). It brings together diverse voices that illuminate the invisible realities behind the products we use daily. This is a necessary step towards business grounded in dignity and justice. Only through informed study of lived experiences can we understand the full scope of the problem.

In my experience with children who have survived the worst forms of labour, I have witnessed first-hand the cost of unchecked greed. In the late 1980s, a few years after my colleagues and I began rescue work, we witnessed an alarming rise in the number of child labourers in South Asia's carpet industry, driven by growing demand for cheaper carpets in the West. I proposed a first-of-its-kind consumer campaign, which eventually led to the creation of Rugmark (now GoodWeave), a child-labour-free certification label, and helped reduce child labour in the regional carpet industry by 80 per cent.

This is the impact we can create when every person in the GVC – from board members to buyers – acts with compassion. Compassion is not a weak emotion;

* Mr Kailash Satyarthi was awarded the Nobel Peace Prize in 2014 for his 'struggle against the suppression of children and young people and for the right of all children to education'. He has established several initiatives to advance child and human rights, including the Save the Childhood Movement, Global Campaign for Education, and, most recently, the Satyarthi Movement for Global Compassion (SMGC). Through SMGC, Mr Satyarthi aims to globalize compassion to promote a more just, peaceful, and sustainable world.

it is a powerful force, born from feeling others' suffering as our own and taking mindful action to end that suffering.

Too often, I have seen the price children pay so the world can live in luxury. I have met mothers who sold everything to buy freedom, and fathers who broke chains with bare hands. Their stories are not peripheral; they are central to the hidden engine that powers global trade.

I have said time and again that businesses cannot sustain without human rights, and human rights cannot be protected without effective business leadership. Many governments have failed to safeguard the rights of the vulnerable, while the influence of businesses has grown. This places a moral responsibility on corporates to lead the way.

I know what becomes possible when businesses act with moral courage. We have made meaningful strides in industries like carpets, sports goods, and mica. But progress remains slow and selective. Slavery persists because global systems allow it to. Laws that protect children in wealthy economies shift the burden to poorer ones. Corporates that commit to ethical practices at headquarters ignore what happens at the end of their supply chains. And most of us, as consumers, remain unaware that our choices fuel this injustice. This is unacceptable. Freedom is universal and indivisible.

In June 2021, the International Labour Organization (ILO) and the United Nations Children's Fund (UNICEF) reported the first increase in child labour in two decades. While their 2025 data confirms a reversal of this trend, this crisis reminds us that our everyday choices impact the freedom and future of millions. If this is not a wake-up call, what is?

Investing in compassionate leadership is investing in our collective future. The future of corporates rests on their ability to follow a compassionate intelligence framework. When those in power lead with compassion, they are seen as authentic and accountable. Only compassionate leaders can build sustainable supply chains that protect children and uphold human dignity. The Environmental, Social, and Governance (ESG) framework reflects elements of compassionate leadership, but it must be a moral resolve and lasting commitment.

The insights herein reveal the urgent need for ethical supply chains, corporate accountability, and global compassion. I thank Bimal, Hila, Shilpi, and Tamar for putting together this crucial academic contribution, and urge readers to engage with this book critically to push the narrative forward. Let the governance of GVCs begin and end with those who create value: people.

Introduction

Hila Shamir, Bimal Arora, Shilpi Banerjee, and Tamar Barkay*

There is growing awareness of the role that multinational corporations (MNCs) play in contributing to modern slavery down their supply chains (8.7 Alliance, 2023). According to *Global Estimates of Modern Slavery*, published by the International Labour Organization (ILO), in 2021 there were 27.6 million people trapped in situations of forced labour around the world, with 17.3 million individuals being exploited in the private sector (ILO, 2022). Sectoral analysis of this finding suggests that a third of exploited workers are employed in export-related sectors and are, presumably, part of global value chains (GVCs) (ILO, 2022). The increasing realization, in the last decade or so, that MNCs' profits are linked to modern slavery has driven workers, their representatives, global

* The research has received support from ERC StG grant agreement No. 756672, TraffLab: Labor Perspective to Human Trafficking, PI Prof. Hila Shamir/Tel Aviv University, as well as from ChainGE Lab (ERC) funded by the European Union, Horizon ERC grant ERC-2022-COG (Project No. 101088188, PI Hila Shamir). Views and opinions expressed are, however, those of the author(s) only and do not necessarily reflect those of the European Union or the European Research Council Executive Agency (ERCEA) (the 'granting authority'). Neither the European Union nor the granting authority can be held responsible for them. It received further funding from the Israel Science Foundation (ISF) grant no. 1866/20.

We are deeply grateful to Debbie Siton for her meticulous work on editing this introduction and for editing and expertly managing the publication of this book. We also thank Jade Kosche for her valuable help with editing and project management in the early stages of the book.

and local activists, consumer organizations, and unions, as well as legislators and policymakers at various levels (local, national, regional, and international), to seek innovative and effective ways to hold MNCs accountable and assign them responsibility (LeBaron, 2020; ITUC, 2020; Trautrims et al., 2021).

This trend suggests a shift in policy responses to modern slavery. Since the adoption of the United Nations Office on Drugs and Crime (UNODC) Trafficking Protocol in 2000,[1] there has been a predominant view that human trafficking and modern slavery primarily result from the operation of organized crime (H. Shamir, 2012). The expansion of the anti-trafficking and modern slavery policy response towards addressing the role of mainstream business entities, and particularly MNCs, raises multiple complex questions for scholars, policymakers, and activists. These relate to the exact role of MNCs in modern slavery and the practices they adopt, and MNC and supplier compliance (Han et al., 2022); the causes and drivers of modern slavery; the reality of work on the factory floor (and wherever work takes place); and effective policy solutions to change corporate patterns of purchasing, supply chain management, and engagement with suppliers, as well as with workers and their communities.

The aim of this book is to provide an interdisciplinary and multifaceted analysis of the links between the governance and regulation of GVCs and modern slavery. The book focuses on the role of business enterprises in modern slavery. In particular, it centres on governance initiatives that seek to induce corporate action to end or mitigate modern slavery in their global, regional, and domestic value chains, and the impact, potential, challenges, and limitations of such initiatives. The book, organized into three parts, explores the main regulatory tools currently used to address modern slavery and GVCs along the spectrum between private (voluntary) and public (at times, legislative) governance initiatives (Part I: Law and Governance); key actors attempting to address modern slavery in GVCs, most notably states, MNCs, workers and their representatives, non-governmental organizations (NGOs), recruiters, and migration intermediaries (Part II: Actors); and, finally, modern slavery and severe forms of exploitation, applying a sectoral, contextual analysis (Part III: Sectors).

In this Introduction, we first address and define the term 'modern slavery'. Second, we explain the two main critical approaches to the topic addressed through this book's structural analysis: the labour and development approaches to human trafficking and modern slavery. Third, we introduce and contextualize the academic literature, activism, and policy shifts at the centre of this book, specifically looking at different attempts to contend with modern slavery by focusing on the role of corporations and the operation of GVCs. Finally, we describe the book's contributions to the literature on modern slavery and GVCs and provide an overview of its structure and chapters to guide readers.

Defining 'Modern Slavery'

The term *modern slavery* is currently undefined in international law. It was developed in several national contexts in Organisation for Economic Co-operation and Development (OECD) countries (particularly the UK and Australian Modern Slavery Acts of 2015 and 2018, respectively) in response to the definitional debates around the meaning and scope of the term 'human trafficking' (Fudge, 2018a; Broad and Turnbull, 2018; Plant, 2014). Accordingly, we will first address the 'human trafficking' label and then explain the turn to the language of modern slavery.

Human trafficking has garnered renewed national and international attention in the last three decades. The legal interest in trafficking is by no means a new trend. In 1904, an international treaty on trafficking was adopted, followed by conventions signed in 1910, 1921, 1933, and 1950.[2] This first generation of anti-trafficking conventions reflected an understanding of trafficking that differs from the term's contemporary application. Albeit refraining from an explicit definition of human trafficking, these instruments sought to address what was known at the time as the 'white slave trade' (Doezema, 2000), referring to the forced movement of women and girls across borders for the purpose of prostitution. The second, contemporary, wave of anti-trafficking instruments began in the 1990s, culminating in the introduction of the aforementioned Trafficking Protocol, in which human trafficking was first defined in international law. Under Article 3, trafficking comprises three components: (*a*) a particular *action* – 'the recruitment, transportation, transfer, harbouring or receipt of persons'; (*b*) certain *means* for carrying out the action – 'the threat or use of force or other forms of coercion, of abduction, of fraud, of deception, of the abuse of power or of a position of vulnerability or of the giving or receiving of payments or benefits to achieve the consent of a person having control over another person'; and (*c*) the end *purpose* of exploitation. The Protocol defines 'exploitation' sweepingly to include, at a minimum, 'the exploitation of the prostitution of others or other forms of sexual exploitation, forced labour or services, slavery or practices similar to slavery, servitude or the removal of organs'. This broad definition marked a new understanding of human trafficking: it is gender-neutral and extends beyond sex trafficking to include multiple types of labour market exploitation, even when within the borders of the victim's own country (H. Shamir, 2017).

Although the Protocol's definition of trafficking attempted to clarify the forms that this practice can take, there remained some ambiguity regarding the 'purpose' and 'means' components of the definition. First of all, the crucial term 'exploitation' was not defined in the Protocol, creating uncertainty as to the conditions under which exploitation amounts to trafficking. Likewise, the elements listed under the 'means' component are not defined, raising the question of the level of coercion and abuse of power required to satisfy this factor of the definition. Where, then, to draw the line? As Gallagher (2010: 49) observes: 'There is general agreement that not all undesirable practices involving the exploitation of individuals could or should be identified as trafficking. Most activists and scholars appear to accept the validity of some kind of a "seriousness" threshold.' In so far as the precise contours of this threshold are left unclear, uncertainty remains as to what exactly constitutes trafficking (UNODC, 2015).

Notwithstanding this definitional vagueness, national and global experience with applying the international definition has provided its 'means' element with content. For example, it has become quite clear that physical coercion is not required for a practice to constitute trafficking and that relatively subtle forms of intimidation suffice. Indeed, practices such as withholding wages or identification papers, continually threatening to expose a worker's undocumented status to authorities, or using indebted labour are all understood to satisfy the 'means' element (ILO, 2009: 1). Moreover, it is now broadly understood that abduction and deception regarding the nature of a job, such as a false promise of waitressing or care work that, upon arrival, is revealed to be forced prostitution, are not the only behaviours that may lead to human trafficking. In fact, many migrant workers who were trafficked appear to have voluntarily embarked on their journeys, seeking paid employment in a line of work they had agreed to in advance (Richards, 2004: 154). Trafficking today is often recognized not only in circumstances of exploitation and manipulation that relate to the type of work one is made to engage in but also in the working conditions attached to an *agreed* type of work. This includes situations in which a worker agrees to perform a certain job yet finds themselves being forced to consent to certain detrimental working conditions, such as restrictions on freedom of movement, inhumane working hours, excessive wage deductions, delayed payment, an abusive and dangerous work environment, or low wages. Human trafficking has emerged, therefore, as comprising a series of labour rights violations. While each one, individually, might not amount to trafficking, when combined they constitute this practice (H. Shamir, 2012).

Despite this wide breadth of contexts and the manifold manifestations of trafficking, in the years since the Trafficking Protocol's introduction and incorporation into regional and domestic law, global attention and enforcement efforts have focused largely on the movement of women and girls across borders into the sex industry (UNODC, 2018; 2022). National and international responses paid less attention to the far more common problem of labour trafficking – the trafficking of persons for the purpose of exploitative employment in a range of sectors (Chuang, 2010). Indeed, the term 'trafficking' was often conflated with prostitution, and anti-trafficking efforts were (and are) conceived as a project concerned with an exceptional social failure that has to do with criminal behaviour, gender disparities, and/or sexual morality (Vance, 2011; Peters, 2015). In addition, institutions and scholars were locked in deep disagreement about the relationship between the different elements of 'exploitation' in the Protocol and about who can be considered a 'trafficked individual'. This led to diverse measurement models and policy solutions being in circulation simultaneously (Engle Merry, 2016).

Attempting to address this unhelpful heterogeneity, anthropologist Sally Engle Merry (2017) demonstrated that the ILO views trafficked victims as a subset of forced labour and, accordingly, proposed that this issue be addressed through enhanced protection of labour rights and the prosecution of employers and individuals involved in profiting from such exploitative labour practices. At the same time, the International Organization for Migration (IOM) discussed trafficking as resulting from the exploitation of 'irregular' migrants and focused its best practices and prevention recommendations on recruitment and border control practices. Engle Merry (2017) also noted that the US Department of State, in its *Trafficking in Persons Report*, framed trafficking as the action of organized criminals whose deception and coercion of victims must be addressed through a firm criminal justice response. And, in yet another response, the influential NGO 'Walk Free', in its Global Slavery Index, positioned slavery as bondage embedded in local social relationships. Therefore, the solutions it pointed to focused on the criminalization of traffickers and the rescue of victims (Engle Merry, 2017).

Against this backdrop – and to minimize further definitional traps, ambiguities, and unproductive disagreements around trafficking – scholars, activists, and policymakers gradually shifted towards using the umbrella term *modern slavery* to refer to various forms of severe labour market exploitation in the global economy, including human trafficking, forced labour, debt bondage, and servitude (Broad and Turnbull, 2018; for example, US Department of State, 2023).

The term *modern slavery* is generally adopted throughout this book, despite some of its ideological baggage, because this terminology has most recently been incorporated into the laws of several countries in different parts of the world and is increasingly accepted by UN bodies. The UK Modern Slavery Act 2015 was the first national legislation to use the term. Yet this terminological change has not escaped criticism – as reflected in some of the contributions to this book (see Gill, Chapter 7, and Arocha et al., Chapter 8). Scholars have argued against the use of 'modern slavery' language because of the imagery of chattel slavery the term may invoke, which does not fit the much more capacious definition of trafficking. Chuang (2014), for example, suggested that such an 'exploitation creep' would move the debate away from the more nuanced understanding of consent and compulsion that developed in the legal discussion around trafficking. Instead, Chuang argued, it may lead to a binary discussion that assumes there is either full consent or full coercion, thereby overlooking the complicated spectrum between the two extremes in which many workers find themselves. Fudge (2018b: 415), along similar lines, argued that

> the modern slavery paradigm tends to reinforce the view that labour exploitation and unfreedom are the result of morally culpable individuals who should be publicly vilified, rather than systemic and institutional features of state policies and practices relating to immigration and labour regulation combined with the 'free market' behaviour of employers.

We share the concern that the term may limit what is necessarily a complex understanding of the continuum of exploitation and the nuances of coercion it entails (Dottridge, 2018). Yet, given that it has been increasingly incorporated into public, legal, and academic discourses and is now commonly used, we have decided to use the term here while paying heed to the pitfalls pointed out by its many critics. We turn now to the structural–analytical framework we adopt to address modern slavery.

The Labour and Development Approaches to Modern Slavery: A Structural Analysis

Drawing from the principles of the Trafficking Protocol and the influential US Victims of Trafficking and Violence Protection Act (TVPA),[3] both enacted in 2000, the global regulatory response to modern slavery centres around what is known as the '3Ps approach': *prevention* of trafficking, *protection* of victims, and *prosecution* of traffickers (UNODC, 2022; US Department of State, 2023).

Regulators across various contexts have emphasized the implementation of these 3Ps, encompassing the criminalization of offenders and enforcement of criminal law (prosecution), strict border control as the primary tool in thwarting exploitation (prevention), and ex-post human rights assistance for identified victims (protection). This is an individualistic, victim-centred approach to addressing modern slavery that treats it as an exceptional crime (H. Shamir, 2012; Quirk and Bunting, 2015). Its objective is to extricate individuals from harmful work environments and ensure ex-post aid, with victims playing a relatively passive role in the process of their rescue, rehabilitation, and repatriation. While the 3Ps framework certainly extends some assistance to identified victims, there is a growing consensus that it fails to tackle the economic, social, and legal conditions that create workers' vulnerability to exploitation in the first place and is, therefore, mostly ineffective in curbing human trafficking (H. Shamir, 2012, Thiemann, 2016, 2019; Fudge, 2024; Mantouvalou, 2023; Thibos, 2020).

An astounding total of 168 countries around the world have legislated or amended laws to reflect their commitment to end modern slavery (UNODC, 2018: 45). In addition, significant resources have been dedicated to combatting and reducing modern slavery globally. Dottridge (2014) provided a (modest) estimate that, at the time, more than USD 120 million had been invested annually by OECD countries in anti-trafficking activities. Yet, despite impressive-looking commitments and significant resources devoted to the issue, there are no indications that instances of modern slavery have decreased globally. On the contrary, the ILO's 2022 *Global Estimates of Modern Slavery* found an increase of 10 million people in modern slavery from 2016 to 2021 (ILO, 2022: 2). In addition, according to figures reported in the 2023 US *Trafficking in Persons Report*, of the estimated 50 million people in situations of modern slavery (ILO, 2022), a mere 115,322 were identified as trafficked persons worldwide in 2022; and, of these, just 24,340 were identified as victims of labour trafficking (US Department of State, 2023: 76). Furthermore, the numbers of prosecutions and convictions were even lower – as of 2022, there were only 15,159 prosecutions relating to human trafficking worldwide (of which 2,670 were for labour trafficking) and 5,577 convictions (of which 528 were for labour trafficking) (ILO, 2022). The pitifully low rates of prosecutions, convictions, and victim identification reveal that, despite significant efforts and resources, the assistance provided under this traditional paradigm reaches an alarmingly minute percentage of the world's severely exploited individuals.

Indeed, scholars and policymakers alike are starting to reach a consensus that the methods employed thus far to combat human trafficking, forced labour, and modern slavery are inadequate in addressing this complex issue. Research indicates that such methods fail to address the structural conditions present in contemporary local labour markets and GVCs, which are frequently influenced, endorsed, or perpetuated by governmental policies (Mantouvalou, 2023; Fudge, 2020; Niezna, 2022; Jovanovic, 2023; Shamir and Niezna 2022; LeBaron, 2020; Kenway, 2021; Quirk and Bunting, 2015). Together, the authors in this book expand on two structural approaches to modern slavery that have developed, in the literature and in practice, in response to these recognized shortcomings: the labour approach (H. Shamir, 2012, 2021; Niezna et al., 2021) and the development approach (Kotiswaran, 2019).

On the one hand, the labour approach to modern slavery seeks to address those structures that create and enable workers' vulnerability to severe forms of exploitation. Its goal is not only to assist victims of trafficking after they are removed from the exploitative environment but also to transform the structure of labour markets that create and sustain that very vulnerability. Adopting a labour approach shifts the focus away from individual harms to the crucial power disparities between victims and exploiters and the economic and social conditions that make exploitation possible. Understanding workers as *agents*, this approach is grounded in an assumption that, if given the legal and associational tools, workers can resist exploitative working conditions in a manner that does not signal the end of their employment relationships but *transforms* them – bearing in mind that 'rescuing' the workers may, in fact, worsen their life conditions overall. This understanding thus acknowledges that bottom-up change is essential if we are to remedy the structural causes of power disparities. A labour approach focuses on using agentic strategies such as collective action and bargaining, protective employment legislation, contextual standard-setting, and restructuring of economic institutions and corporate governance to address the unequal power relations in labour sectors that are particularly susceptible to trafficking and modern slavery (H. Shamir, 2012).

On the other hand, the critical perspective adopted by contributors to this volume further complements the labour approach to modern slavery with the development-oriented approach. The development approach, first articulated by Prabha Kotiswaran (2019), recognizes the paradox of a developmental state operating in neoliberal times and highlights the importance of policies and programmes aimed at reducing inequality and providing social protections. This paradigm questions the logic of the global economy, which encourages poor workers from developing countries to immigrate to the Global North to secure employment, and suggests a change in perspective. Instead of accepting the economic disparity in the developing world as the root cause of modern slavery and concentrating on working conditions in the receiving countries of the Global North, it emphasizes the need to enhance *domestic* development in Global South countries. The development approach provides a framework for addressing the socio-economic conditions that often underlie labour exploitation of workers coming from the Global South. This includes efforts to reduce poverty, improve education, and expand social safety nets, based on the logic that this will decrease vulnerabilities to modern slavery. According to Kotiswaran, while a labour approach that improves working conditions is important, it will not suffice to address modern slavery.

She takes the case of India to demonstrate the insufficiency of simply improving labour regulations, since these do not apply to the most severe cases of exploitation – workers who are employed illegally and unregistered. In contrast, she prioritizes investment in India's economy and enhancement of public funding to impact the country's overall development and increase the economic well-being and (decent) employment opportunities available to workers (Kotiswaran, 2019).

Both of these two critical approaches share the view that modern slavery is the result of wider socio-economic conditions, legal rules, and institutions that limit workers' bargaining power and choice, potentially placing them (and keeping them) in conditions of vulnerability (see Mantouvalou, 2020; 2023; Niezna, 2022; Fudge, 2020). Under both perspectives, modern slavery predominantly results from systemic, structural conditions that enable exploitation, rather than from isolated instances of criminal activity.

One useful framing that reflects the understanding of both approaches, as well as other critical approaches to the dominant carceral modern slavery policy, is that of a continuum of vulnerability to exploitation (Skrivankova, 2010; Strauss and Fudge, 2013; Scott, 2017; Waite et al., 2015; Phillips, 2013; Costello, 2015; Fudge, 2018b; Davies, 2018). Under this view, modern slavery should be understood not as resulting from a stark binary between slavery and freedom (O'Connell Davidson, 2013) but, rather, in terms of 'stages – or degrees of freedom – varying from enslaved to fully free' (Boucher, 2022: 633). At one end of the continuum are the most empowered workers – those with a work contract based on negotiated terms reflecting their choice and consent (the classic liberal conception of the contract). At the other end of the continuum are the most deeply disempowered and vulnerable workers. Here, workers' weak bargaining power – caused by market dynamics as well as structural and legal elements and often compounded by identity-based vulnerabilities – leads to substandard working conditions, rights violations, and, at its most extreme end, modern slavery (Niezna et al., 2021). This conception of modern slavery as escalated exploitation of worker vulnerability looks to the pervasive political economy and labour market dynamics that enable the exploitation and objectification of the most socially and economically vulnerable workers.

However, not even the labour and development approaches, at least in their original formulations, address corporate patterns of capital ownership and the impact of multi-tiered supply and production, as well as international trade and international labour governance policies. The collection of articles in this volume seeks to add these important perspectives to the engagement of critical modern slavery literature with law and policy, aiming to address structural causes of vulnerabilities. We turn next to discuss the intersection of labour governance in GVCs and modern slavery law and policy.

Modern Slavery in GVCs

Despite growing recognition and criticism of the failures of the paradigmatic modern slavery policy response, as we have seen, there have been very few alternatives added to the 'classic' policy toolbox to address this issue. One notable exception has been the emphasis on the role of MNCs in modern slavery and the potential of labour governance in GVCs to combat it (Crane, 2013; New, 2015). The trajectory of modern slavery policy and activism towards addressing the involvement of large businesses, particularly through their governance of GVCs, has brought together two thriving human rights agendas seeking to transform global markets: international and national efforts by public actors to address modern slavery and the private and voluntary regulatory nature of multi-stakeholder initiatives (MSIs). The convergence of the two agendas has led to an exponential proliferation of business and human rights initiatives aimed at tackling modern slavery in GVCs (McGaughey et al., 2021). These policies and practices view MNCs as key actors that, due to their strong bargaining power in the chain, can often drive certain contractual conditions in their relations with suppliers that may cause or contribute to modern slavery, or, equally, can facilitate its prevention (Lipson, 2019).

The turn to the governance of GVCs and the role of MNCs in addressing modern slavery derives, in part, from research showing that despite the distributive potential of GVCs to support development in emerging economies and improve workers' incomes, such 'economic upgrading' is not inherent in GVCs and that some GVCs may be characterized by misdistribution of power and profit along the chain (Nathan, 2019; Gereffi, 2018; LeBaron and Lister, 2021; Ponte et al., 2023). Furthermore, some GVC scholars have raised concerns about 'social upgrading' and distributive injustice along the value chain in relation to local communities and, particularly, workers (Rossi, 2019). Indeed, a growing body of GVC and labour literature highlights the often exploitative working conditions of workers in the lower tiers of GVCs. It suggests that MNCs, despite being contractually removed from the workers, may have significant power and control over their working conditions and income through the contractual conditions they impose on suppliers, such as short production timelines and price (Eller, 2020; Salminen, 2020).

Scholars show, for example, that in some buyer-driven GVCs, cost squeezes on the supply side, predatory purchasing practices, and increased demand for work intensity, and quick production rates may contribute to workers' exploitation, as well as to verbal and physical abuse and gender-based violence (Campling and Quentin, 2021; Anner, 2020; 2019; Bartley, 2018). Building on such findings, anti-modern-slavery-in-GVC initiatives often begin with an acknowledgement that a substantial portion of today's corporate revenues can likely be traced back to severe forms of labour exploitation, including trafficking, forced labour, and modern slavery (Faure, 2015; ITUC, 2016). If modern slavery is generated and sustained, then, by the very structural conditions under which GVCs are free to operate – plagued by gaps and loopholes in governance – it must be tackled by addressing GVC governance (Bair and Palpacuer, 2015; Raigrodski, 2016). Yet, attempts to govern various features of GVCs, including modern slavery, have, to date, met with the challenge of attributing liability – contractual or otherwise – to the lead firms at the top of the chains (Dahan et al., 2016).

There is a wide array of human rights and labour governance initiatives related to modern slavery in GVCs (Gómez-Mera, 2017). Elsewhere, two of the authors of this Introduction (Shamir and Barkay, forthcoming) have suggested that such initiatives can be categorized, according to the actors that lead them, as corporate-driven, worker-driven, or state-driven (see also Haipeter et al., 2021). While such initiatives are led by different stakeholders, many are MSIs that involve global and local actors and are characterized by the proactive role taken by non-state actors in setting (private) standards to end severe forms of labour market exploitation (Locke, 2013; LeBaron and Lister, 2021; Shih et al., 2021).

Beginning in the early 1990s, under conditions of a global governance deficit, exploitative working conditions in MNCs' supply chains and MNCs' lack of accountability became prime targets for consumer and political pressures (Locke, 2013; Bartley, 2018). Consumer boycotts, tort litigations, and the threat of new regulatory demands prompted lead firms that were found to have severely exploited workers in their supply chains to develop corporate social responsibility (CSR) strategies and join MSIs (Carrington et al., 2021a). These corporate-led initiatives developed in the ensuing years into a dynamic 'industrial complex' involving a range of private, public, and civil society actors that developed and deployed numerous self-regulatory and social performance measurement tools (O'Rourke, 2006; R. Shamir, 2010; Bartley, 2011; Gereffi and Lee, 2016).

The business management and governance and regulation literatures commonly treat CSR as a 'beyond compliance' tool located at the voluntary end of a wide regulatory spectrum that has been broadened in the last few decades to include other self-regulatory, soft law, public–private, and other soft public regulation tools and mechanisms (Bernstein and Cashore, 2007; Choudhury, 2018). Within this literature, the state is depicted as either a passive bystander or an active facilitator of soft regulation, nudging corporations to take responsibility for their impact on society (Rühmkorf, 2018). In contrast, critical socio-legal and political sociology literatures treat CSR as a contested battleground shaped by, and adapted to, transformations in power relations within the contemporary global economy (R. Shamir, 2010; Djelic and Etchanchu, 2017). Accordingly, in these literatures, the voluntary nature of CSR is theorized as a constructed outcome of institutionalization and mainstreaming processes fuelled by corporate anti-regulatory interests (Rowe, 2005; Kinderman, 2016). While scholars diverge in their evaluations of the actual and potential implications of CSR, a growing body of critical literature questions CSR's ability to transform corporate action (Locke, 2013; Bartley, 2018; Kuruvilla and Bae, 2021; Kuruvilla and Fischer-Daly, 2021). Whatever their assessment, however, scholars appear to share the common understanding that the growth of such soft, self-regulatory forms of governance has become a main feature of governance in the current order (Levi-Faur, 2011; Kolben, 2014).

Clearly, policies in relation to modern slavery in GVCs *have* impacted aspects of corporate policies and behaviour, yet there is ample empirical research showing that many initiatives have done little to secure labour rights and human rights on any significant scale (Locke, 2013; Lee, 2016; Rossi, 2014). This is the case either because they are only partial in their reach and impact, or because the costs associated with ensuring labour rights are pushed down the supply chains.

This may result in cascading exploitative labour practices down the chain, usually to more unorganized and informal segments of the market, rendering them even more invisible and harder to trace and eradicate.

Amid growing awareness that CSR was not leading to the required change in corporate practices, starting in the early 2010s, UN agencies, supranational organizations, and governments began to take action, and a number of state-driven initiatives were developed. Legislators on the international, national, and regional levels began enacting new laws requiring corporations to disclose their actions to protect workers' rights down their supply chains (known as 'transparency legislation') (Fudge, 2018a; Barkay et al., 2024). Such measures were adopted, for example, in the US state of California (2010), the UK (2015), and Australia (2018). Other laws required firms to implement a Human Rights Due Diligence (HRDD) process to identify, prevent, mitigate, and account for how they manage potential adverse human rights impacts in their supply chains, including protection of workers' rights (Landau, 2019; Sarfaty, 2020; LeBaron and Rühmkorf, 2019; Landau, 2023; Landau and Marshall, Chapter 4 of this volume). First introduced through the UN Guiding Principles on Business and Human Rights in 2011, HRDD laws have since been legislated in France (2017), the Netherlands (2019), Norway (2021), Germany (2021), and Canada (2023) and are being considered in other OECD countries. In its most recent iteration, in 2024, the European Parliament passed the Corporate Sustainability Due Diligence Directive (see Shift, 2022; Marshall et al., 2023; Zumbansen, 2024). However, it should be noted that both HRDD and Transparency Acts, despite being state-driven and legislation-based, are concerned with enhancing market-based forms of supply chain governance and predominantly rely on consumer sanctions for compliance. As such, they should not be understood as 'hard law' (see Barkay and Shamir, Chapter 6 of this volume).

Another emerging state-driven innovation has been the introduction of trade-related tools and, specifically, forced labour import bans (see Ebert et al., Chapter 3 of this volume). These are measures to prevent the entry of imported goods into a country if it is suspected that those goods were produced under conditions of forced labour or modern slavery (Pietropaoli et al., 2021; A. Brudney, 2020; LaFianza, 2022). While, to date, very few countries have imposed such bans – notably, the US and Canada – there is increasing interest in the effectiveness of this tool as hard regulation accompanied by significant economic sanctions, unlike the 'soft' regulation adopted in this field so far (Kolben, 2023; Polaski et al., 2022).

Despite what may seem like encouraging developments, current research indicates that the transparency and HRDD legislation, along with trade bans as presently formulated, is continuing to prove inadequate to bring about transformative improvements in working conditions within GVCs (McCorquodale and Nolan, 2021; LeBaron, 2020; LeClercq, 2022; Vogt et al., 2022; Marshall et al., 2023). Attempts to demand that corporations fulfil their commitments regarding labour conditions through litigation have also mostly failed (Fudge and Mundlak, 2023). Moreover, research suggests that voluntary commitments and self-regulation by corporations – including those originating in transparency and HRDD legislation – have not mitigated corporate institutional antagonism to unionizing and collective bargaining (Kuruvilla and Li, 2021; Vogt et al., 2022). In addition, mounting evidence of the ineffectiveness of such regulatory mechanisms reveals major gaps in the regulation of labour standards in GVCs. These gaps can be attributed to various factors, including the reluctance of corporations to monitor and enforce their commitments (Lee, 2016; Lim and Prakash, 2017); the insufficiency of private accreditation and enforcement mechanisms (LeBaron, 2018); the limited power of consumers to economically sanction corporations in many contexts (Carrington et al., 2021b); the unwillingness of states to supervise and enforce corporate commitments and to create state-backed sanction mechanisms (LeBaron, 2020); and the lack of workers' input in defining, enforcing, and monitoring standards (Lee, 2016; Lim and Prakash, 2017; Brooks, 2007; Rende-Taylor and Shih, 2019). As a result, concerns have been raised in academic and policy circles over the effectiveness of *voluntary* corporate commitments to protect workers' rights in GVCs (Allain et al., 2013; Anner et al., 2013; Kuruvilla and Li, 2021).

A more promising alternative, hailed by activists and scholars, is the worker-driven social responsibility (WSR) model (Mieres and McGrath, 2021; Asbed and Hitov, 2017; Fine and Bartley, 2019; Sellers, 2021). WSR is a supply chain governance scheme that originated from workers and their communities and involves both suppliers and lead firms. WSR was conceived to address the identified failures of CSR, HRDD, and transparency legislation, in that it is premised on worker agency and, specifically, the exercise of that agency through new forms of supply chain collective bargaining (Dias-Abey, 2018; Donaghey and Reinecke, 2018; see also Barkay and Shamir, Chapter 6 of this volume). Some of the foundational features of the WSR model distinguish it from traditional CSR initiatives: the process is *worker-driven*, it is based on *effective* monitoring and enforcement, and it requires *legally binding* commitments (WSR, 2017). Indeed, the 'worker-related' term was chosen by the model's architects to mark it as an alternative to CSR structures, both unilateral corporate-led codes and MSIs. As its name suggests, WSR's key advancement over – and criticism of – existing

CSR frameworks is the absence of workers' voice and power therein. As Gordon (2017: 4) writes, 'frequently, the parties most affected by labour codes and MSIs – the workers whose lives are affected by the standards being negotiated – have no say in any part of their design or implementation'.

While acknowledging the great promise of WSR, the major successful example of this model, the Fair Food Program (FFP) in Florida, has proven very difficult to replicate and sustain in other environments (Babineau and Bair, 2020). First, WSR has been implemented in only four additional contexts so far: the Accord on Fire and Building Safety in the Bangladeshi garment sector; the Milk with Dignity programme, led by the organization Migrant Justice in the dairy sector in Vermont (US); the 2019 agreement in Lesotho's apparel industry; and the Dindigul Agreement on caste discrimination and gender-based violence signed between various international NGOs, local unions, and global brands with Eastman Exports, a major clothing and textile manufacturer in Tamil Nadu, India, in 2022 (Fudge and LeBaron, 2024). Of these four WSR examples, the latter two represent adaptations of a narrower example of the model because both are geared specifically to address specific harms, focusing on sexual harassment and gender-based violence (Mieres and McGrath, 2021). Yet even these few examples of WSR implementation are struggling to thrive. A case in point is the weakening of the Bangladesh Accord, the future of which looks uncertain due to external and internal challenges in recent years (Bair et al., 2020; Kang, 2021; Champagne, 2021). Indeed, the WSR model is facing the dual challenge of scalability and sustainability in global – as opposed to local – long and complex supply chains (J. Brudney, 2021).

As this brief review suggests, despite the proliferation of initiatives on the international, regional, national, and local levels, and the enormous efforts made, none has brought about effective, wide-reaching change, and modern slavery continues to pose an increasingly urgent global problem. Regrettably, there is little evidence of effective sustainable change on the ground resulting from lead firms' responses to the policy trends outlined in this Introduction. While certain civil society organizations, unions, and corporations have developed some promising best practices, including the WSR model, it remains widely acknowledged that the much-needed systemic change required to improve working conditions in the lower tiers of GVCs has yet to occur.

The emphasis on the importance of transforming labour market structures that enable and sustain modern slavery in GVCs resonates with both the 'labour' and 'development' perspectives. However, while the latter focuses on enhancing workers' agency, politicization, and bargaining power, the former promotes the construction of corporations as private sources of governance and as de-politicized agents of change (Todres, 2012; Barkay et al., 2024). Indeed, so far, there has been little evidence that these regulatory developments and innovations have promoted effective and impactful collective worker mobilization (Kuruvilla and Li, 2021; Donaghey and Reinecke, 2018; Marshall et al., 2023; Kuruvilla et al., 2021) or systematically improved workers' rights (MSI Integrity, 2020; Kuruvilla and Bae, 2021).

Arguably, the fundamental characteristics of common forms of MNC activity around modern slavery in GVCs still appear to be driven by a mindset of preserving business benefits, rather than a genuine commitment to transforming exploitative structures and labour practices. And the large majority of state- and industry-driven initiatives (including trade bans, as Ebert et al. show in Chapter 3 of this volume) still largely depend on goodwill and collaborative gestures on the part of MNCs and their suppliers to insist on workers' rights protections. Traditionally, such transformations have occurred only following long struggles and strong collective action by unions and other civil society organizations. Improvements in workers' rights tend to increase labour costs throughout the supply chain, and, accordingly, increase the costs of production and business operations overall. Absent the countervailing power of workers and unions, the financial costs associated with securing workers' rights – at best, accompanied by enhanced workers' voice and intensification of monitoring and inspections of working conditions – pose a significant challenge for businesses to bring about transformational change (Vaughan-Whitehead, 2014; Crane et al., 2019; LeBaron, 2021; LeBaron et al., 2018; Anner et al., 2023).

Together, the different chapters in this volume aim to enhance our understanding of the rapid developments in the field of modern slavery in GVCs, and, in particular, the possibilities and limitations of existing regulatory tools. It accomplishes this by amalgamating insights from scholarship that critically examines modern slavery law, policy, and research, along with literature on GVC regulation.

Contributions of This Book: Chapter Overview

The chapters collected in this volume employ a multidisciplinary perspective, by scholars from the developed and developing world, on the intricate relationships between business models, production and consumption patterns, workers' rights, and modern slavery within GVCs. From a range of angles, they offer an in-depth, panoramic account of the power dynamics, structural gaps, and governance challenges that shape the impact of the contemporary anti-modern-slavery field of action. The book seeks to intervene in, extend, and develop GVC analysis and modern slavery literature by bringing the two realms of research into direct conversation. To do so, it applies the methodological and analytical traditions and insights of different academic disciplines – law, sociology, economics, geography, and anthropology – to enrich, deepen, and challenge our understanding of the potential and limits of various governance modes – state-, industry-, and worker-driven – in relation to modern slavery in GVCs. We now turn to the four main strands of insight that run through the chapters and form the broad structure of the volume as a whole.

The Role of Law in Enabling and Sustaining Current Patterns of GVCs

First, the book contributes to better understanding how the law manifests in GVC structures and functionalities, and how it ultimately influences the distributive outcomes of these value chains. As Danielson and Bair (2019) observe, the role of law remains 'significantly undertheorized in the burgeoning social science and policy literatures on GVCs' (see also IGLP, 2016). This book seeks to remedy that under-theorization by analysing the legal scaffoldings of GVCs to discern the role of law in *enabling* modern slavery in supply chains (Jovanovic, 2023; Webb and Garciandia, 2019; H. Shamir, 2017; Mantouvalou, 2023), as well as law's potential to transform GVCs and prevent modern slavery. As such, the book offers a multi-faceted discussion of GVCs and law, including an exploration of private and public governance mechanisms, and legal interactions and spillovers (Ashwin et al., 2020) between the two, in the context of modern slavery (Horner, 2017; Smith, 2015; Mayer and Philips, 2017). These contributions are presented mainly, but not exclusively, in Part I, 'Law and Governance'.

By employing critical approaches to the analysis of current developments in the regulation and governance of GVCs, the four chapters in this part expose the role of law – understood as multiple normative sources and regulatory layers, on different scales – in shaping, constituting, and transforming labour practices in GVCs and developing directions for effective regulatory interventions. Sharing the understanding that modern slavery legislation (including international, regional, and domestic norms) and voluntary CSR initiatives have, so far, made limited demonstrable impact, the authors of these chapters offer analyses of the role of law in the governance of GVCs, concerning working conditions and modern slavery.

Chapters 1 and 2 focus on the centrality of the transparency ideal in CSR and modern-slavery reporting legislation and critically examine their assumptions and possible implications. In Chapter 1, Klaas Hendrik Eller explores the complex interplay between legal mechanisms, reporting regulations, and corporate governance in the governance of GVCs. The chapter highlights the limitations of the linear narrative of CSR evolving from voluntary to mandatory instruments, pointing out shared structural deficits and the political dynamics at play. The author delves into the role of reporting regulations in addressing corporate responsibility, particularly regarding modern slavery, and suggests a shift in perspective from merely informing stakeholders to altering the very information architecture of GVCs. This involves examining the internal communication and knowledge-building processes among chain actors, in an attempt to enhance transparency and accountability in corporate practices. In Chapter 2, Ioannis Kampourakis critically examines transparency legislation from a different perspective. He argues that transparency legislation, while promoting accountability through market and civil society pressures, often reinforces existing power imbalances and fails to deliver substantive regulatory outcomes. His analysis highlights the need for stronger public regulatory frameworks to complement transparency measures and ensure genuine accountability and sustainability in GVCs.

Chapters 3 and 4 address two additional state-led regulatory tools, HRDD legislation and trade bans, and their interactions with corporate-led and worker-led initiatives. In Chapter 3, Franz Christian Ebert, Francesca Francavilla, and Lorenzo Guarcello analyse the integration of forced labour considerations into trade instruments, and their practical implications for GVCs. The chapter highlights the potential of these trade instruments to foster long-term improvements and address forced labour effectively. Through a case study of the Malaysian rubber glove industry, the research presented in the chapter illustrates how, under certain circumstances, import bans and other trade-related measures can generate significant changes on both the company and the sectoral levels, promoting broader policy efforts to combat forced labour. This analysis explores the scope of trade bans to address forced labour (and their limitations) and highlights their interaction with and spillover effects on corporate-led MSIs to enhance labour standards in GVCs. In Chapter 4, Ingrid Landau and Shelly Marshall examine the potential of mandatory human rights due diligence laws in Europe to improve access to remedy for victims of modern slavery within GVCs. It evaluates the effectiveness of legislation from France, Germany, Norway, and the European Union's Corporate Sustainability Due Diligence

Directive (CSDDD). While acknowledging that these laws mark significant progress in corporate accountability, the chapter identifies gaps in their ability to deliver meaningful remedies and calls for more robust mechanisms to address the legal and practical barriers faced by victims seeking redress.

Together, the four chapters in this part reveal the challenges faced by legal doctrine and by tools attempting to impact corporate processes and action – and to leverage lead-firm and importing-country power – to drive positive change in working conditions throughout the value chains. They critically examine how, by using private law, corporate law, and trade law, state-driven modern slavery efforts – by activists, workers and their representatives, corporations, and policymakers – might 'use the master's tools to dismantle the master's house' (to paraphrase Audre Lord's provocation) (Lorde, 1984).

Understanding the Roles of Different Actors in Addressing Modern Slavery in GVCs

By considering the complexities of modern slavery as a rich case study, Part II of the volume focuses on the respective roles, capacities, and perspectives of different actors and stakeholders engaged in combating modern slavery in supply chains. Broadly speaking, accounts of the logic driving commodity and value chains within capitalist production and distribution systems tend to apply a lead-firm-centred conceptualization of governance (Gereffi, 2014). Seeking to complicate this view, the authors in this volume demonstrate how adopting the lens of modern slavery provides an opportunity to identify and typify some of the characteristic shortcomings found in lead-firm-centred analyses of GVC regulation and governance and offer a prism through which to analyse the triadic relationship between power, governance, and inequality (Ponte et al., 2023). Taken as a whole, the chapters facilitate a more nuanced understanding of the imbalanced power dynamics involved in GVCs' labour governance. Part II of the book is therefore devoted to 'Actors', both inside and beyond lead firms. The three chapters in this part closely study how various actors involved in modern slavery initiatives can and do interact with, against, and around the law and governance of modern slavery in GVCs. Such actors include corporations, workers, unions and workers' organizations, civil society, and for-profit and non-profit organizations, as well as recruitment agencies and contractors (middlemen).

Roseanne Russell, in Chapter 5, opens this part of the book by exploring the promise and the shortcomings of corporate governance in regulating modern slavery within GVCs. She critiques the ideology of shareholder primacy, which prioritizes investor returns at the expense of labour rights, and argues that this focus facilitates exploitative labour practices. The chapter proposes integrating proportionality principles into boardroom decisions to balance the interests of diverse stakeholders and prevent the worst forms of labour abuses.

In Chapter 6, Tamar Barkay and Hila Shamir apply the notion of 'anti-trafficking chains', referring to the dynamic web of anti-trafficking actors, initiatives, and activities in GVCs, to comparatively explore the structural conditions that shape the impact of modern slavery transparency legislation and the worker social responsibility (WSR) model. They argue that transparency laws, while increasing awareness and compliance, often fail to drive substantial corporate change due to their reliance on market-based mechanisms and minimal legal requirements. In contrast, the WSR model, exemplified by the FFP, demonstrates greater potential for systemic change by empowering workers, enforcing strict standards, and leveraging consumer pressure. The chapter suggests that, of the two approaches, WSR has the greater potential to impact GVCs' labour governance, as it can help create a 'bottom-up' anti-trafficking chain that manages to break away from the 'top-down' supply chain dynamics.

Following chapters that explore corporate boards, workers' organizations, and private and public anti-trafficking service providers, in Chapter 7, Sahiba Gill turns to examine the 'human supply chain', specifically focusing on labour migration and the significant influence wielded by recruiters. Utilizing empirical qualitative research on the recruitment of low-wage migrant workers from Nepal to the Gulf Cooperation Council (GCC) countries, Gill identifies how GCC employers exert control over recruitment, creating employer-driven human supply chains. The chapter highlights that this control perpetuates recruitment abuses, emphasizing the need for stronger regulatory frameworks to address the power imbalances that are inherent to these chains and prevent modern slavery within these migration corridors. As such, this chapter aligns with other studies in the book that highlight the role of lead firms in global economic governance while also underlining the importance of structural changes that empower and enable other actors – whether workers' organizations, NGOs, or states, but also suppliers and recruiters, for instance – to disrupt the prevailing supply chain logic.

Overall, the chapters in this part offer a comprehensive examination of key actors and their involvement with labour governance in GVCs, particularly in terms of the power dynamics that fuel exploitation in these chains.

Using GVC Analysis to Expand the Modern Slavery Normative and Policy Toolkit: Contextual and Sectoral Analysis

This book employs GVC analysis as a method to expand the normative and policy toolkit for addressing modern slavery. As noted earlier in this Introduction, the anti-modern-slavery field is still in search of constructive tools, with critical voices gesturing towards the 'development' and 'labour' approaches to the issue. Part III, entitled 'Sectors', shows how certain analytical tools that evolved in the GVC governance literature understand the root causes of severe forms of labour market exploitation – tools that are being developed in some promising new directions. The chapters in this part manifest how spotlighting GVC governance frameworks enables us to discern the regulatory and economic conditions that render modern slavery possible. Further, GVC analysis opens up space for critical engagement with the role of law and businesses – lead firms as well as suppliers – in suppressing, disregarding, enabling, creating, or transforming modern slavery.

Taken as a whole, this part provides a nuanced and sophisticated analysis of the operation of the law and governance of modern slavery (and sometimes the lack thereof) by looking at four distinct sectors in India: sugarcane cutting, sex work, construction, and garment production. Myriad actors are viewed here through the close study of the lower tiers and informal 'loose ends' of particular value chains. Within the single national context of India, this part's focus on different labour sectors – and the GVCs in which they participate – captures the way in which social and economic factors influence working conditions in the lower tiers of GVCs.

In Chapter 8, Lorena Arocha, Bindhulakshmi Pattadath, Meena Gopal, and Roshni Chattopadhyay address the informal and precarious ends of domestic and GVCs in the Indian context, focusing on the sectors of sugarcane cutting and sex work. Through detailed empirical research from the state of Maharashtra, they critique the application of the 'modern slavery' discourse, arguing that this framing oversimplifies and obscures the complex and historically rooted caste, gendered, and class power dynamics at play. The authors signal the need for a nuanced understanding of local contexts and histories to effectively address the exploitative conditions faced by workers in these sectors and value chains. Specifically, they explore how worker mobilization among informal workers in India offers a challenge to exploitative working conditions while simultaneously ensuring livelihoods.

In Chapter 9, Saie Shetye and Divya Priyadarshini offer a detailed analysis of the human supply chain and working conditions in the Indian construction sector, exposing the legal infrastructure of construction value chains and the vulnerabilities to exploitation they create. The chapter highlights how the lack of formal employment contracts and regulatory oversight in the construction sector exacerbates abusive working conditions. The authors argue that severe forms of labour exploitation in this sector should not be treated as an exceptional, individualized phenomenon but, rather, understood within the larger context of agricultural distress and land dispossession in Indian villages. Like Chapter 8, this chapter demonstrates the crucial importance of understanding local conditions and the characteristics of informal labour relations if effective governance intervention in supply chains is to be achieved.

In Chapter 10, Dev Nathan and the late Varsha Joshi investigate the factors contributing to the reduction of child labour in India and the challenges that render it difficult to detect. They highlight the roles played by low adult wages, poverty, and lack of access to quality education as key drivers of this phenomenon. Their analysis also contemplates how informal labour practices, particularly within family-based and caste-based divisions of labour, contribute to its persistence. Drawing on experiences from various production sectors, including garment, accessory, and jewellery manufacturing, the authors argue that the most impactful corporate strategies have been automation, which eliminates the possibility of child labour, and the relocation of production processes from home-based settings to factories. However, they note that this relocation is not always straightforward, as some child labour is simply shifted to less regulated environments, such as remote villages. The chapter emphasizes that, while legal and development interventions are crucial, addressing the underlying socio-economic conditions is equally essential for the effective eradication of child labour in India.

Overall, the three chapters in this part discuss how actors respond to, shape, and circumvent governance tools in specific sectors within India in which informal labour is widespread. The prevalence of informality in each of the contexts studied highlights the challenges and opportunities inherent in any attempt to undertake GVC analysis – or apply GVC regulation – at the informal ends of supply chains. As a result, the sectoral analysis developed in this part illustrates why 'one size fits all' solutions, common in the modern slavery policy realm (Chuang, 2006), are insufficient for the complex realities of many GVCs.

The Interaction between Formal and Informal Economy within GVCs

The fourth strand of insight that runs throughout the book is concerned with the interaction between formal and informal economy within GVCs, and here it joins the nascent body of literature directing an analytical gaze towards this issue. Despite the significant impact of informality on GVCs, scholars have observed that research tends to be inattentive to this issue (Pickles et al., 2016; Phillips, 2011; Selwyn, 2019). For example, many diagrams and conceptual models depicting these chains often oversimplify the complexities of informal labour arrangements. They frequently portray clear-cut, linear connections between corporations, suppliers, and workers, neglecting the intricate web of informal actors and the myriad non-standard contractual relationships that actually characterize many GVCs. The omission of informality in GVC literature is concerning because informal, non-transparent labour practices play a pivotal role in shaping working conditions, wages, and overall labour governance within these chains. Informal workers, who are often excluded from state protections and social safety nets, face acute vulnerabilities, such as abusive working hours, low pay, and inadequate working conditions. Ignoring the realities of informal labour hinders a comprehensive, accurate understanding of power dynamics and social implications within GVCs (Marshall, 2019).

Addressing informality requires scholars to explore the involvement of diverse actors, the informal networks operating alongside formal structures, and the interactions between formal and informal practices. Despite the value of this research area, only a limited number of recent studies have contributed to it. Among the exceptions to this scant attention, Barrientos (2019), Nathan et al. (2023), and Marshall (2019) foreground the role of home-workers, household labour, and other non-standard workers in the informal economy, prevalent in many countries of the Global South, in their recent books. Similarly, this volume aims to enhance GVC analysis by addressing the reliance of formal supply chains on the labour of informal workers. Several chapters in the book delve into the significant, yet often overlooked or denied, role of informal work in GVCs. They offer methods to reincorporate the informal sector into GVC analysis and propose innovative ways to regulate and govern GVCs that extend even to their 'fuzzy ends' at the bottom of value chains.

In examining the presence of modern slavery within GVCs from a multidisciplinary perspective, this book underscores the undeniable gravity of this complex issue, urging us to address its profound impact and collaborate on finding effective solutions. By fostering constructive dialogue between modern slavery scholars and GVC researchers, the authors of this book seek to shed light on blind spots in each analysis, leading to a thicker understanding and actionable insights to combat this pressing global challenge.

The genesis of this book lies in a process of knowledge-sharing and deliberation that commenced during a multidisciplinary international conference held at the National Law University, New Delhi, in November 2019. Subsequently, the process continued in an online workshop in September 2021. These events brought together scholars from the Global North and South, representing diverse social science disciplines. Tragically, in 2022, we mourned the loss of our dear friend, collaborator, and co-editor of this book Bimal Arora. His passing left his family, friends, and colleagues heartbroken and grieving. To honour his memory, we dedicate this book to him and to the late Varsha Joshi, an exceptional scholar and activist who also contributed to this book and sadly passed away in 2020. May their contributions and dedication to combatting modern slavery continue to inspire and drive progress towards improving workers' rights in GVCs.

Notes

1. Protocol to Prevent, Suppress and Punish Trafficking in Persons, Especially Women and Children, Supplementing the United Nations Convention against Transnational Organized Crime, 15 November 2000, 2237 U.N.T.S. 319 (the Trafficking Protocol).
2. International Agreement for the Suppression of the White Slave Traffic, 18 May 1904, 35 Stat. 1979, 1 L.N.T.S. 83. Later international instruments dealing with trafficking include the following: International Convention for the Suppression of the White Slave Traffic, 4 May 1910, 98 U.N.T.S. 101; International Convention for the Suppression of the Traffic in Women and Children, 30 September 1921, 53 U.N.T.S. 39; International Convention for the Suppression of the Traffic in Women of Full Age, 11 October 1933, 150 L.N.T.S. 431; Convention for the Suppression of the Traffic in Persons and of the Exploitation of the Prostitution of Others, 2 December 1949, *opened for signature* 21 March 1950, 96 U.N.T.S. 271.
3. Victims of Trafficking and Violence Protection Act of 2000, Pub. L. No. 106–386, 114 Stat. 1464 (2000).

References

8.7 Alliance (ILO, IOM, OECD, UNICEF) (2023). *Ending Child Labour, Forced Labour and Human Trafficking in Global Supply Chains*. Available at: www.ilo.org/media/405766/download.

Allain, J., A. Crane, G. LeBaron, and L. Behbahani (2013). *Forced Labour's Business Models and Supply Chains*. Belfast: Joseph Rowntree Foundation and Queen's University.

Anner, M. (2019). 'Predatory Purchasing Practices in Global Apparel Supply Chains and the Employment Relations Squeeze in the Indian Garment Export Industry'. *International Labour Review* 158(4): 705–27.

——— (2020). 'Squeezing Workers' Rights in Global Supply Chains: Purchasing Practices in the Bangladesh Garment Export Sector in Comparative Perspective'. *Review of International Political Economy* 27(2): 320–47.

Anner, M. and M. Fischer-Daly (2023). 'Worker Voice: What It Is, What It Is Not, and Why It Matters'. U.S. Department of Labor. Available at www.dol.gov/sites/dolgov/files/ILAB/Worker-Voice-Report-Final-3-6-24.pdf.

Anner, M., J. Bair, and J. Blasi (2013). 'Toward Joint Liability in Global Supply Chains: Addressing the Root Causes of Labor Violations in International Subcontracting Networks'. *Comparative Labour Law and Policy Journal* 35(1): 1–43.

Asbed, G. and S. Hitov (2017). 'Preventing Forced Labor in Corporate Supply Chains: The Fair Food Program and Worker-driven Social Responsibility'. *Wake Forest Law Review* 52(2): 497–531.

Ashwin, S., C. Oka, E. Schuessler, R. Alexander, and N. Lohmeyer (2020). 'Spillover Effects Across Transnational Industrial Relations Agreements: The Potential and Limits of Collective Action in Global Supply Chains'. *ILR Review* 73(4): 995–1020.

Babineau, K. and J. Bair (2020). 'The Art of Using Supply Chains to Defend Worker Rights'. *Open Democracy*, 14 December. Available at: https://tinyurl.com/2aka25pk.

Bair, J. and F. Palpacuer (2015). 'CSR beyond the Corporation: Contested Governance in Global Value Chains'. *Global Networks* 15(s1): S1–S19.

Bair, J., M. Anner, and J. Blasi (2020). 'The Political Economy of Private and Public Regulation in Post-Rana Plaza Bangladesh'. *ILR Review* 73(4): 969–94.

Barkay, T., J. Davies, I. Pietropaoli, and H. Shamir (2024). 'Anti-trafficking Chains: Analyzing the Impact of Transparency Legislation in the UK Construction Sector'. *Law and Social Inquiry* 49(4): 2152–83.

Barrientos, S. (2019). *Gender and Work in Global Value Chains: Capturing the Gains?* Cambridge, UK: Cambridge University Press.

Bartley, T. (2011). 'Transnational Governance as the Layering of Rules: Intersections of Public and Private Standards', *Theoretical Inquiries in Law* 12(2): 517–42.

——— (2018). *Rules without Rights: Land, Labor, and Private Authority in the Global Economy*. Oxford, UK: Oxford University Press.

Bernstein, S. and B. Cashore (2007). 'Can Non-state Global Governance Be Legitimate? An Analytical Framework'. *Regulation and Governance* 1(4): 347–71.

Boucher, A. (2022). '"What Is Exploitation and Workplace Abuse?" A Classification Schema to Understand Exploitative Workplace Behaviour towards Migrant Workers'. *New Political Economy* 27(4): 629–45.

Broad, R. and N. Turnbull (2018). 'From Human Trafficking to Modern Slavery: The Development of Anti-trafficking Policy in the UK'. *European Journal on Criminal Policy and Research* 25(2): 119–33.

Brooks, E. (2007). *Unravelling the Garment Industry: Transnational Organizing and Women's Work*. Minneapolis, MN: University of Minnesota Press.

Brudney, A. (2020). 'Using the Master's Tools to Dismantle the Master's House: 307 Petitions as a Human Rights Tool'. Corporate Accountability Lab, 31 August. Available at https://corpaccountabilitylab.org/calblog/2020/8/28/using-the-masters-tools-to-dismantle-the-masters-house-307-petitions-as-a-human-rights-tool.

Brudney, J. (2021). 'Reflections on Labor Standards in Global Supply Chains: Innovation and Scalability'. In *Power, Participation, and Private Regulatory Initiatives: Human Rights under Supply Chain Capitalism*, edited by D. Brinks, J. Dehm, K. Engle, and K. Taylor, 205–23. Philadelphia, PA: University of Pennsylvania Press.

Campling, L. and C. Quentin (2021). 'Global Inequality Chains: How Global Value Chains and Wealth Chains (Re)Produce Inequalities of Wealth'. In *Rethinking Value Chains: Tackling the Challenge of Global Capitalism*, edited by F. Palpacuer and A. Smith, 26–55. Bristol, UK: Policy Press.

Carrington, M., A. Chatzidakis, and D. Shaw (2021a). 'Consuming Worker Exploitation? Accounts and Justifications for Consumer (In)action to Modern Slavery'. *Work, Employment and Society* 35(3): 432–50.

——— (2021b). *Addressing Consumer Awareness and (In)Action Towards Modern Slavery – Rapid Research Report: Review of Existing Evidence*. London: Modern Slavery and Human Rights Policy and Evidence Center. Available at https://eprints.gla.ac.uk/255488/1/255488.pdf.

Champagne, J. (2021). 'From Public Relations to Enforceable Agreements: The Bangladesh Accord as a Model for Supply Chain Accountability'. In *Power, Participation, and Private Regulatory Initiatives: Human Rights under Supply Chain Capitalism*, edited by D. Brinks, J. Dehm, K. Engle, and K. Taylor, 154–79. Philadelphia, PA: University of Pennsylvania Press.

Choudhury, B. (2018). 'Balancing Soft and Hard Law for Business and Human Rights'. *International and Comparative Law Quarterly* 67(4): 961–86.

Chuang, J. (2006). 'Beyond a Snapshot: Preventing Human Trafficking in the Global Economy'. *Indiana Journal of Global Legal Studies* 13(1): 137–63.

——— (2010). 'Rescuing Trafficking from Ideological Capture: Prostitution Reform and Anti-trafficking Law and Policy'. *University of Pennsylvania Law Review* 158(6): 1655–728.

——— (2014). 'Exploitation Creep and the Unmaking of Human Trafficking Law'. *American Journal of International Law* 108(4): 609–49.

Costello, C. (2015). 'Migrants and Forced Labour: A Labour Law Response'. In *The Autonomy of Labour Law*, edited by A. Bogg, C. Costello, A. Davies, and J. Prassi, 189–228. Oxford, UK: Hart.

Crane, A. (2013). 'Modern Slavery as a Management Practice: Exploring the Conditions and Capabilities for Human Exploitation'. *Academy of Management Review* 38(1): 49–69.

Crane, A., G. LeBaron, J. Allain, and L. Behbahani (2017). 'Governance Gaps in Eradicating Forced Labor: From Global to Domestic Supply Chains'. *Regulation & Governance* 13(1): 86–106.

Dahan, Y., H. Lerner, and F. Milman-Sivan (2016). Global Labor Rights as Duties of Justice. In *Global Justice and International Labour Rights*, edited by Y. Dahan, H. Lerner, and F. Milman-Sivan, 53–91. Cambridge, UK: Cambridge University Press.

Danielson, D. and J. Bair (2019). 'The Role of Law in Global Value Chains: A Window into Law and Global Political Economy'. Law and Political Economy Blog, 16 December. Available at: https://lpeblog.org/2019/12/16/the-role-of-law-in-global-value-chains-a-window-into-law-and-global-political-economy.

Davies, J. (2018). 'From Severe to Routine Labour Exploitation: The Case of Migrant Workers in the UK Food Industry'. *Criminology and Criminal Justice* 19(3): 1–17.

Dias-Abey, M. (2018). 'Justice on Our Fields: Can "Alt-labor" Organizations Improve Migrant Farm Workers' Conditions?' *Harvard Civil Rights–Civil Liberties Law Review* 53(1): 167–211.

Djelic, M. L. and H. Etchanchu (2017). 'Contextualizing Corporate Political Responsibilities: Neoliberal CSR in Historical Perspective'. *Journal of Business Ethics* 142(4): 641–61.

Doezema, J. (2000). 'Loose Women or Lost Women? The Re-emergence of the Myth of White Slavery in Contemporary Discourses of Trafficking in Women'. *Gender Issues* 18(1): 23–50.

Donaghey, J. and J. Reinecke (2018). 'When Industrial Democracy Meets Corporate Social Responsibility: A Comparison of the Bangladesh Accord and Alliance as

Responses to the Rana Plaza Disaster'. *British Journal of Industrial Relations* 56(1): 14–42.

Dottridge, M. (2014). 'Editorial: How Is the Money to Combat Human Trafficking Spent?' *Anti Trafficking Review* 3: 1–14.

——— (2017). 'Eight Reasons Why We Shouldn't Use the Term "Modern Slavery"'. *Open Democracy*, 17 October. Available at: www.opendemocracy.net/en/beyond-trafficking-and-slavery/eight-reasons-why-we-shouldn-t-use-term-modern-slavery.

Eller, K. H (2020). 'Is "Global Value Chain" A Legal Concept?' *European Review of Contract Law* 16(1): 3–24.

Engle Merry, S. (2016). *The Seductions of Quantification: Measuring Human Rights, Gender Violence, and Sex Trafficking*. Chicago, IL: University of Chicago Press.

——— (2017). 'Counting the Uncountable: Constructing Trafficking through Measurement'. In *Revisiting the Law and Governance of Trafficking, Forced Labor and Modern Slavery*, edited by P. Kotiswaran, 273–304. Cambridge, UK: Cambridge University Press.

Faure, J. (2015). 'Forced Labour: Does It Make Economic Sense?' UNU/SIPA Junior Research Fellow Paper Series, United Nations University and Columbia University, New York. Available at: https://collections.unu.edu/eserv/UNU:3293/JRF01_ForcedLabour.pdf.

Fine, J. and T. Bartley (2019). 'Raising the Floor: New Directions in Public And Private Enforcement of Labor Standards in the United States'. *Journal of Industrial Relations* 61(2): 252–76.

Fudge J. (2018a). 'Slavery and Unfree Labour: The Politics of Naming, Framing, and Blaming'. *Labour/Le Travail* 82: 227–44.

——— (2018b). 'Modern Slavery, Unfree Labour and the Labour Market: The Social Dynamics of Legal Characterization'. *Social and Legal Studies* 27(4): 414–34.

——— (2020). 'Twenty Years after Palermo, Can We Stop Discussing Labour Exploitation and Start Fixing It?' *Open Democracy*, 19 November. Available at: https://tinyurl.com/yfxmckwj.

——— (2024). *Constructing Modern Slavery: Law, Capitalism and Unfree Labour*. Cambridge, UK: Cambridge University Press.

Fudge, J. and G. Mundlak (2023). 'Peeling the Onion: On Choices Judges Make in Transnational Labour Litigation'. In *Social Justice and the World of Work: Possible Global Futures Essays in Honour of Francis Maupain*, edited by B. Langille and A. Trebilcock, 249–60. Oxford, UK: Hart Publishing.

Fudge, J. and G. LeBaron (2024). 'Regulatory Design and Interactions in Worker-Driven Social Responsibility Initiatives: The Dindigul Agreement'. *International Labour Review* 163(4): 575–98.

Gallagher, A. T. (2010). *The International Law of Human Trafficking*. Cambridge, UK: Cambridge University Press.

Gereffi, G. (2014). 'Global Value Chains in a Post-Washington Consensus World'. *Review of International Political Economy* 21(1): 9–37.

——— (2018). *Global Value Chains and Development: Redefining the Contours of 21st Century Capitalism*. Cambridge, UK: Cambridge University Press.

Gereffi, G. and J. Lee (2016). 'Economic and Social Upgrading in Global Value Chains and Industrial Clusters: Why Governance Matters'. *Journal of Business Ethics* 133(1): 25–38.

Gibbon, P., J. Bair, and S. Ponte (2008). 'Governing Global Value Chains'. *Economy and Society* 37(3): 315–38.

Gómez-Mera, L. (2017). 'The Global Governance of Trafficking in Persons: Toward a Transnational Regime Complex'. *Journal of Human Trafficking* 3(4): 303–26.

Gordon, J. (2017). 'The Problem with Corporate Social Responsibility'. Worker-Driven Social Responsibility Network, 11 July. Available at: https://wsr-network.org/resource/the-problem-with-corporate-social-responsibility.

Han, C., M. Jia, Jiang, and L. Chen (2022). 'Modern Slavery in Supply Chains: A Systematic Literature Review'. *International Journal of Logistics Research and Applications* 27(7): 1–22. Available at: https://doi.org/10.1080/13675567.2022.2118696.

Horner, R. (2017). 'Beyond Facilitator? State Roles in Global Value Chains and Global Production Networks'. *Geography Compass* 11(2): 1–13.

Haipeter, T., M. Helfen, A. Kirsch, S. Rosenbohm, and C. Üyük (2021). 'Industrial Relations at Centre Stage: Efficiency, Equity and Voice in the Governance of Global Labour Standards'. *Industrielle Beziehungen* 28(2): 148–71.

IGLP Law and Global Production Working Group (2016). 'The Role of Law in Global Value Chains: A Research Manifesto'. *London Review of International Law* 4(1): 57–79.

International Labour Organization (ILO) (2009). *The Cost of Coercion: Global Report under the Follow-up to the ILO Declaration on Fundamental Principles and Rights at Work*. Available at: www.ilo.org/wcmsp5/groups/public/---ed_norm/---declaration/documents/publication/wcms_106268.pdf.

——— (2022). *Global Estimates of Modern Slavery: Forced Labour and Forced Marriage*. Available at: www.ilo.org/wcmsp5/groups/public/---ed_norm/---ipec/documents/publication/wcms_854733.pdf.

International Trade Union Confederation (ITUC) (2016). *Scandal: Inside the Global Supply Chains of 50 Top Companies*. ITUC Frontlines Report. Available at: www.ituc-csi.org/IMG/pdf/pdffrontlines_scandal_en-2.pdf.

——— (2020). *Towards Mandatory Due Diligence in Global Supply Chains*. Available at: www.ituc-csi.org/towards_mandatory_due_diligence.

Jovanovic, M. (2023). *State Responsibility for 'Modern Slavery' in Human Rights Law: A Right Not to Be Trafficked*. Oxford, UK: Oxford University Press.

Kang, Y. (2021). 'The Rise, Demise and Replacement of the Bangladesh Experiment in Transnational Labour Regulation'. *International Labour Review* 160(3): 407–30.

Kenway, E. (2021). *The Truth About Modern Slavery*. London: Pluto Press.

Kinderman, D. (2016). 'Time for a Reality Check: Is Business Willing to Support a Smart Mix of Complementary Regulation in Private Governance?' *Policy and Society* 35(1): 29–42.

Kolben, K. (2014). 'Dialogic Labor Regulation in the Global Supply Chain'. *Michigan Journal of International Law* 36(30): 425–65.

——— (2023). 'Labor Chapters Improve Supply Chain Resilience: The Case of the USMCA'. In *USMC Forward 2023: Building More Integrated, Resilient, and Secure Supply Chains in North America*, edited by J. P. Meltzer and B. S. Coulibaly, 105–11. Washington, DC: Brookings Institution. Available at: www.brookings.edu/wp-content/uploads/2023/03/USMCA-Forward-2023.pdf.

Kotiswaran, P. (2019). 'Trafficking: A Development Approach'. *Current Legal Problems* 72(1): 375–416.

Kuruvilla, S. and J. Bae (2021). 'Has Private Regulation Improved Labor Practices in Global Supply Chains? An Empirical Examination'. In *Private Regulation of Labor Standards in Global Supply Chains: Problems, Progress, and Prospects*, edited by S. Kuruvilla, 79–111. Ithaca, NY: Cornell University Press.

Kuruvilla, S. and M. Fischer-Daly (2021). 'Are Changes in Corporate Governance an Answer?' In *Private Regulation of Labor Standards in Global Supply Chains: Problems, Progress, and Prospects*, edited by S. Kuruvilla, 189–213. Ithaca, NY: Cornell University Press.

Kuruvilla, S., M. Fischer-Daly, and C. Raymond (2021). 'Freedom of Association and Collective Bargaining in Global Supply Chains'. In *Private Regulation of Labor Standards in Global Supply Chains: Problems, Progress, and Prospects*, edited by S. Kuruvilla, 148–80. Ithaca, NY: Cornell University Press.

Kuruvilla, S. and C. Li (2021). 'Freedom of Association and Collective Bargaining in Global Supply Chains: A Research Agenda'. *Journal of Supply Chain Management* 57(2): 43–57.

LaFianza, J. (2022). 'Threatening Ill-Gotten Gains: Analyzing the Effectiveness of a Forced Labor Import Ban in the European Union'. EU Law Working Paper No. 60, Stanford–Vienna Transatlantic Technology Law Forum. Available at: https://law.stanford.edu/wp-content/uploads/2022/05/EU-Law-WP-60-LaFianza.pdf.

Landau, I. (2019). 'Human Rights Due Diligence and the Risk of Cosmetic Compliance'. *Melbourne Journal of International Law* 20(1): 2–26.

——— (2023). *Human Rights Due Diligence and Labour Governance.* Oxford, UK: Oxford University Press.

LeBaron, G. (2018). *The Global Business of Forced Labor: Report of Findings.* SPERI and University of Sheffield. Available at: https://tinyurl.com/4pd57fer.

——— (2020). *Combatting Modern Slavery: Why Labour Governance Is Failing and What We Can Do About It.* Cambridge, UK: Polity Press.

——— (2021). 'The Role of Supply Chains in the Global Business of Forced Labour'. *Journal of Supply Chain Management* 57(2): 29–42.

LeBaron, G., N. Howard, C. Thibos, and P. Kyritsis (2018). *Confronting Root Causes: Forced Labour in Global Supply Chains.* OpenDemocracy and SPERI. Available at: https://tinyurl.com/tabzn4yf.

LeBaron, G. and J. Lister (2022). 'The Hidden Costs of Global Supply Chain Solutions'. *Review of International Political Economy* 29(3): 669–95.

LeBaron, G. and N. Phillips (2019). States and the Political Economy of Unfree Labour. *New Political Economy* 24(1): 1–21.

LeBaron, G. and A. Rühmkorf (2019). 'The Domestic Politics of Corporate Accountability Legislation: Struggles over the 2015 UK Modern Slavery Act'. *Socio-Economic Review* 17(3): 709–43.

LeClercq, D. (2022). 'Invisible Workers'. *AJIL Unbound* 116: 107–12.

Lee, J. (2016). 'Global Supply Chain Dynamics and Labour Governance: Implications for Social Upgrading'. ILO Research Paper No. 14, International Labour Office, Geneva.

Levi-Faur, D. (2011). 'The Regulatory State and Regulatory Capitalism: An Institutional Perspective'. In *Handbook on the Politics of Regulation*, edited by D. Levi-Faur, 662–72. Northampton, UK: Edward Elgar.

Lim, S. and A. Prakash (2017). 'From Quality Control to Labor Protection: ISO 9001 and Workplace Safety, 1993–2012'. *Global Policy* 8(3): 66–77.

Lipson. J. (2019). 'Promising Justice: Contract (As) Social Responsibility'. *Wisconsin Law Review* 2019(5): 1109–60.

Locke, R. (2013). *The Promise and Limits of Private Power: Promoting Labour Standards in a Global Economy.* Cambridge, UK: Cambridge University Press.

Lorde, A. (1984). 'The Master's Tools Will Never Dismantle the Master's House'. In *Sister Outsider: Essays and Speeches* (2017), edited by A. Lorde, 110–13. Berkeley, CA: Crossing Press.

Mantouvalou, V. (2020). 'Structural Injustice and the Human Rights of Workers'. *Current Legal Problems* 73(1): 59–87.

——— (2023). *Structural Injustice and Workers' Rights*. Oxford, UK: Oxford University Press.

Marshall, S. (2019). *Living Wage: Regulatory Solutions to Informal and Precarious Work in Global Supply Chains*. Oxford, UK: Oxford University Press.

Marshall, S., I. Landau, H. Shamir, T. Barkay, J. Fudge, and A. van Heerden (2023). *Mandatory Human Rights Due Diligence: Risks and Opportunities for Workers and Unions*. RMIT University Business and Human Rights Centre; TraffLab ERC; and Labour, Equality and Human Rights (LEAH) research group, Monash Business School. Available at: www.trafflab.org/_files/ugd/11e1f0_e1db27f1ec7f41459ac357d021f6011c.pdf.

Mayer, F. W. and N. Phillips (2017). 'Outsourcing Governance: States and the Politics of a "Global Value Chain World"'. *New Political Economy* 22(2): 134–52.

Mayer, F. W., N. Phillips, and A. C. Posthuma (2017). 'The Political Economy of Governance in a "Global Value Chain World"'. *New Political Economy* 22(2): 129–33.

McCorquodale, R. and J. Nolan (2021). 'The Effectiveness of Human Rights Due Diligence for Preventing Business Human Rights Abuses'. *Netherlands International Law Review* 68(3): 455–78.

McGaughey, F., H. Voss, H. Cullen, and M. Davis (2022). 'Corporate Responses to Tackling Modern Slavery: A Comparative Analysis of Australia, France and the United Kingdom'. *Business and Human Rights Journal* 7(2): 249–70.

Mieres, F. and S. McGrath (2021). 'Ripe to Be Heard: Workers' Voice in the Fair Food Programme'. *International Labour Review* 160(4): 631–47.

MSI Integrity (2020). *Not Fit-for-Purpose: The Grand Experiment of Multi-Stakeholder Initiatives in Corporate Accountability, Human Rights and Global Governance: Summary Report*. Available at: www.msi-integrity.org/not-fit-for-purpose.

Nathan, D. (2019). 'Labour in GVCs: An Analytical Framework'. In *Perspectives on Neoliberalism, Labour and Globalization in India*, edited by K. R. Sundar, 255–71. London: Palgrave Macmillan.

Nathan, D., S. S. Bhattacharjee, S. Rahul, P. Kumar, I. Dhagani, S. Singh, and P. Swaminathan (2022). *Reverse Subsidies in Global Monopsony Capitalism: Gender, Labour, and Environmental Injustice in Garment Value Chains*. Cambridge, UK: Cambridge University Press.

New, S. J. (2015). 'Modern Slavery and the Supply Chain: The Limits of Corporate Social Responsibility?' *Supply Chain Management: An International Journal* 20(6): 697–707.

Niezna, M. (2022). 'Paper Chains: Tied Visas, Migration Policies, and Legal Coercion'. *Journal of Law and Society* 49(2): 362–84.

Niezna, M., Y. Kurlander, and H. Shamir (2021). 'Underlying Conditions: The Increased Vulnerability of Migrant Workers under COVID-19 in Israel'. *Journal of Modern Slavery* 6(2): 133–58.

O'Connell Davidson, J. (2013). 'Troubling Freedom: Migration, Debt, and Modern Slavery'. *Migration Studies* 1(2): 176–95.

O'Rourke, D. (2006). 'Multi-stakeholder Regulation: Privatizing or Socializing Global Labor Standards?' *World Development* 34(5): 899–918.

Peters, A. W. (2015). *Responding to Human Trafficking: Sex, Gender, and Culture in the Law*. Philadelphia, PA: University of Pennsylvania Press.

Phillips, N. (2011). 'Informality, Global Production Networks and the Dynamics of Adverse Incorporation'. *Global Networks* 11(3): 380–97.

——— (2013). 'Unfree Labour and Adverse Incorporation in the Global Economy: Comparative Perspectives on Brazil and India'. *Economy and Society* 42(2): 171–96.

Pickles, J., A. Smith et al. (2016). *Articulations of Capital: Global Production Networks and Regional Transformations*. Malden, MA: Wiley-Blackwell.

Pietropaoli, I., O. Johnstone, and A. Balch (2021). *Effectiveness of Forced Labour Import Bans*. Policy Brief. London: Modern Slavery and Human Rights Policy and Evidence Centre. Available at: https://tinyurl.com/57j35cpv.

Plant, R. (2014). 'Modern Slavery: The Concepts and Their Practical Implications'. Paper presented at the 'Shaping the Definition of Human Trafficking' Conference, Dickson Poon School of Law, King's College, London (14 May). ILO. Available at: www.ilo.org/sites/default/files/wcmsp5/groups/public/%40ed_norm/%0declaration/documents/publication/wcms_355052.pdf.

Polaski, S., K. A. Nolan García, and M. Rioux (2022). 'The USMCA: A "New Model" for Labor Governance in North America?' In *NAFTA 2.0: From the First NAFTA to the United States-Mexico-Canada Agreement*, edited by G. Gagné and M. Rioux, 139–56. Basingstoke, UK: Palgrave Macmillan.

Ponte, S., J. Bair, and M. Dallas (2023). 'Power and Inequality in Global Value Chains: Advancing the Research Agenda'. *Global Networks* 23(4): 679–86.

Quirk, J. and A. Bunting (2015). 'The Politics of Exception: The Bipartisan Appeal of Human Trafficking'. In *Popular and Political Representations: Beyond*

Trafficking and Slavery Short Course Volume One (e-book), edited by J. Quirk and J. O'Connell Davidson, 64–68. Available at: https://cdn2.opendemocracy.net/media/documents/BTS-1-Representations.pdf.

Raigrodski. D. (2016). 'Creative Capitalism and Human Trafficking: The Business Case for Eliminating Forced Labor and Human Trafficking from Global Supply Chains'. *William and Mary Business Law Review* 8(1): 71–134.

Rende-Taylor, L. and E. Shih (2019). 'Worker Feedback Technologies and Combatting Modern Slavery in Global Supply Chains: Examining the Effectiveness of Remediation-Oriented and Due-Diligence-Oriented Technologies in Identifying and Addressing Forced Labour and Human Trafficking'. *Journal of the British Academy* 7(s1): 131–65.

Richards, K. (2004). 'The Trafficking of Migrant Workers: What Are the Links between Labour Trafficking and Corruption?' *International Migration* 42(5): 147–68.

Rossi, A., A. Luinstra, and J. Pickles (2014). *Towards Better Work: Advances in Labour Studies*. Basingstoke, UK: Palgrave Macmillan.

Rowe, J. K. (2005). 'Corporate Social Responsibility as Business Strategy'. In *Globalization, Governmentality and Global Politics*, edited by R. D. Lipschutz and J. K. Rowe, 122–60. Oxford, UK, and New York: Routledge.

Rühmkorf, A. (2018). 'From Transparency to Due Diligence Laws? Variations in Stringency of CSR Regulation in Global Supply Chains in the "Home State" of Multinational Enterprises'. In *Globalisation of Corporate Social Responsibility and Its Impact on Corporate Governance*, edited by J. Plessis, U. Varottil, and J. Veldman, 177–201. Cham, Switzerland: Springer.

Salminen, J. (2020). 'Towards a Genealogy and Typology of Governance through Contract Beyond Privity'. *European Review of Contract Law* 16(1): 25–43.

Sarfaty, G. (2020). 'Translating Modern Slavery into Management Practice'. *Law and Social Inquiry* 45(4): 1027–51.

Scott, S. (2017). *Labour Exploitation and Work-Based Harm*. Bristol, UK: Policy Press.

Selwyn, B. (2019). Poverty Chains and Global Capitalism. *Competition and Change* 23(1): 71–97.

Shamir, H. (2012). 'A Labor Paradigm for Human Trafficking'. *UCLA Law Review* 60(1): 76–136.

——— (2017). 'The Paradox of "Legality": Temporary Migrant Worker Programs and Vulnerability to Trafficking'. In *Revisiting the Law and Governance of Trafficking, Forced Labor and Modern Slavery*, edited by P. Kotiswaran, 471–502. Cambridge, UK: Cambridge University Press.

——— (2021). 'A Labor Approach to Human Trafficking: 20 Years to the International Attempt to Address Human Trafficking'. *Iyunei Mishpat – Tel Aviv University Law Review* 44: 377–482.

Shamir, H. and M. Niezna (eds.) (2022). 'An Alternative Anti-Trafficking Action Plan: A Proposed Model Based on a Labor Approach to Trafficking'. TraffLab Research Group Policy Paper, Tel Aviv University, Tel Aviv. Available at: www.trafflab.org/_files/ugd/11e1f0_861945c9ea904d57a359c89d44424869.pdf.

Shamir, H. and T. Barkay (forthcoming). 'Labor Governance Chains: A Comparative Structural Analysis'. *ILR Review*.

Shamir, R. (2010). 'Capitalism, Governance, and Authority: The Case of Corporate Social Responsibility'. *Annual Review of Law and Social Science* 6: 531–53.

Shift Project (2022). *The EU Commission's Proposal for a Corporate Sustainability Due Diligence Directive: Shift's Analysis*. Available at: https://shiftproject.org/resource/eu-csdd-proposal/shifts-analysis/.

Shih, E., J. Rosenbaum, and P. Kyritsis (2021). 'Undermining Labor Power: The False Promise of the Industry-Led Antislavery Initiatives'. In *Fighting Modern Slavery and Human Trafficking: History and Contemporary Policy*, Slaveries since Emancipation, edited by G. LeBaron, J. Pliley, and D. Blight, 141–55. Cambridge, UK: Cambridge University Press.

Skrivankova, K. (2010). 'Between Decent Work and Forced Labour: Examining the Continuum of Exploitation'. JRF programme paper, Joseph Rowntree Foundation, York, UK. Available at: www.jrf.org.uk/sites/default/files/migrated/migrated/files/forced-labour-exploitation-full.pdf.

Smith, A. (2015). 'The State, Institutional Frameworks and the Dynamics of Capital in Global Production Networks'. *Progress in Human Geography* 39(3): 290–315.

Strauss, K. and J. Fudge (2013). 'Temporary Work, Agencies and Unfree Labour: Insecurity in the New World of Work'. In *Temporary Work, Agencies and Unfree Labour: Insecurity in the New World of Work*, edited by J. Fudge and K. Strauss, 1–25. New York and London: Routledge.

Thibos, C. (2020). 'Twenty Years of Trafficking: Taking Stock of the World the Palermo Protocol Built'. Beyond Trafficking and Slavery Blog. *Open Democracy*, 15 November. Available at: www.opendemocracy.net/en/beyond-trafficking-and-slavery/twenty-years-trafficking-taking-stock-world-palermo-protocol-built.

Thiemann, I. (2016). 'Villains and Victims, But No Workers: Why a Prosecution-Focussed Approach to Human Trafficking Fails Trafficked Persons'. *Anti-Trafficking Review* 6: 126–29.

——— (2019). 'Beyond Victimhood *and* beyond Employment? Exploring Avenues for Labour Law to Empower Women Trafficked into the Sex Industry'. *Industrial Law Journal* 48(2): 199–224.

Todres, J. (2012). 'The Private Sector's Pivotal Role in Combating Human Trafficking'. *California Law Review Circuit* 3: 80–98.

Trautrims, A., S. Gold, A. Touboulic, C. Emberson, and H. Carter (2021). 'The UK Construction and Facilities Management Sector's Response to the Modern Slavery Act: An Intra-industry Initiative against Modern Slavery'. *Business Strategy and Development* 4(3): 279–93.

United Nations Office on Drugs and Crime (UNODC) (2015). 'The Concept of "Exploitation" in the Trafficking in Persons Protocol'. Available at: www.unodc.org/documents/congress/background-information/Human_Trafficking/UNODC_2015_Issue_Paper_Exploitation.pdf.

——— (2018). *Global Report on Trafficking in Persons 2018*. Available at: www.unodc.org/documents/data-and-analysis/glotip/2018/GLOTiP_2018_BOOK_web_small.pdf.

——— (2022). *Global Report on Trafficking in Persons 2022*. Available at: www.unodc.org/documents/data-and-analysis/glotip/2022/GLOTiP_2022_web.pdf.

US Department of State (2023). *Trafficking in Persons Report, June 2023*. Available at: www.state.gov/wp-content/uploads/2023/06/Trafficking-in-Persons-Report-2023.pdf.

Vance, C. (2011). 'States of Contradiction: Twelve Ways to Do Nothing about Trafficking while Pretending To'. *Social Research* 78(3): 933–48.

Vaughan-Whitehead, D. (2014). 'How "Fair" Are Wage Practices along the Supply Chain? A Global Assessment'. In *Towards Better Work: Advances in Labour Studies*, edited by A. Rossi, A. Luinstra, and J. Pickles, 68–102. Basingstoke, UK: Palgrave Macmillan.

Vogt, J., R. Subasinghe, and P. Danquah (2022). 'A Missed Opportunity to Improve Workers' Rights in Global Supply Chains'. Online post. OpinioJuris, 18 March. Available at: https://opiniojuris.org/2022/03/18/a-missed-opportunity-to-improve-workers-rights-in-global-supply-chains.

Waite, L., G. Craig, H. Lewis, and K. Skrivankova (2015). 'Introduction'. In *Vulnerability, Exploitation and Migrants*, edited by L. Waite, G. Craig, H. Lewis, and K. Skrivankova, 1–12. Basingstoke, UK: Palgrave Macmillan.

Webb, P. and R. Garciandia (2019). 'State Responsibility for Modern Slavery: Uncovering and Bridging the Gap'. *International and Comparative Law Quarterly* 68(3): 539–71.

Worker-Driven Social Responsibility Network (WSR) (2017). 'Factsheet: What Is WSR?' Available at: https://wsr-network.org/wp-content/uploads/2017/10/What_is_WSR_web.pdf.

Zumbansen, Peer C. (2024). 'Global Value Chain Legislation, Modern Slavery, Climate Change and Finance: Lessons from the European Corporate Sustainability Due Diligence Directive ("CSDDD")'. McGill SGI Research Papers in Business, Finance, Law and Society Research Paper No. 2024–08. Available at: https://ssrn.com/abstract=4784608.

Part I

Law and Governance

1

The Information Architecture of Corporate Accountability

Inside Corporate Reporting Regimes in Global Value Chains

Klaas Hendrik Eller*

What Trajectory for the Regulation of Transnational Corporate Responsibility?

The framework for transnational corporate responsibility along global value chains (GVCs) is in flux. While the legal mechanisms have generally become tighter in recent years, the development follows no uniform trajectory. With scattered, disparate, and overlapping initiatives and regulatory regimes currently coexisting, it seems an open political question which regulatory paradigm will prevail in the medium and longer term. This chapter zooms in on specific transitional moments in the regulatory evolution of corporate responsibility. The dominant narrative portrays this evolution as roughly two decades of linear progress from 'voluntary' (deemed 'ineffective') corporate social responsibility to 'mandatory' (and hence deemed more 'effective') instruments, with each stage reacting to deficits of the previous one by imposing tighter standards, leaving fewer gaps, and allowing stricter enforcement. While this sequential

---

* This chapter has benefited from generous comments by the late Bimal Arora, Meredith Dost, Luis Eslava, Ioannis Kampourakis, Galit Sarfaty, and Hila Shamir, as well as from seminar groups and conference audiences at Tel Aviv University, the University of Amsterdam, Harvard University, the Geneva Graduate Institute, and Bar-Ilan University. The research has received support from the ERC (grant agreement No 756672, TraffLab: Labor Perspective on Human Trafficking, PI Prof. Hila Shamir/Tel Aviv University) and the NWO (grant agreement VI.Veni.211R.058, 'Recoding Global Production').

understanding of corporate responsibility with each stage implementing selective improvements indeed captures an important dynamic within corporate responsibility, it paints an incomplete picture. First, it stresses rupture over continuity and thereby distracts attention from shared and structural deficits of the regulation of corporate responsibility across its different 'stages'. Second, it assumes regulatory discourses of corporate responsibility to be largely self-referential and isolated from broader regulatory developments in other fields. These two limitations have deflected the debate from exposing certain structural difficulties in regulating complex value chains, as well as the deeper political dynamics at play in framing regulatory 'innovations'.

Against this background, this chapter examines the example of reporting regulation as deployed to address different dimensions of corporate responsibility, including modern slavery. Among the substantive goals on the agenda of corporate responsibility, curbing modern slavery is arguably the most intricate. Intrinsically linked to and sustained by the business model of offshore capitalism, modern slavery forms a 'viable management practice for many enterprises' (Crane, 2013: 49). Its prevalence in the global economy results from an amalgam of reasons at the micro and macro levels (LeBaron, 2021). It is not the absence of regulations and sanctions per se – unlike many other corporate wrongs, modern slavery is criminalized under national and international law (Jeßberger, 2016) – but a certain elusiveness that defies regulatory responses. It is precisely the ubiquity of practices of modern slavery that makes them so difficult to pin down and has made them a litmus test for any regulation of corporate responsibility. Keeping in mind how entrenched modern slavery is, it seems almost surprising that regulators around the globe saw, and still see, reporting rules as a regulatory response that matches the dimension of the problem (Salminen and Rajavuori, 2019; Bartley, 2018; Mares, 2018). Starting with early examples, such as Section 1502 of the Dodd–Frank Act (2010), the California Transparency in Supply Chains Act (2010), and the UK Modern Slavery Act (2015), reporting obligations have become an integral part of the regulatory toolkit. This is further illustrated by the French Duty of Vigilance Law (2017),[1] the German Supply Chain Act (2021),[2] and the updated EU Corporate Sustainability Reporting Directive (2022).[3] The titles of these legislative acts suggest a certain terminological disparity that requires a word of clarification for the purpose of this chapter. Policy debates often employ the terms 'transparency', 'disclosure', and 'reporting' regulation interchangeably. In this chapter, I will use 'reporting' (regulation) to denote the regulatory mechanism, since it captures better the active construction of reported information for that purpose than the term 'disclosure'. 'Transparency', in turn, refers to the normative agenda – it is the allure of transparency as a legitimizing political ideal that serves as a normative and metaphorical substratum, despite (or, because of) its unclear contours and ambivalences (Koivisto, 2022). Reporting regulations thus claim to increase transparency and are also referred to as 'transparency regulations'.

I argue that one contributing factor to an overestimation of such regulation is that reporting regulation is an unacknowledged and ill-fitted 'legal transplant' (Watson, 1993; Goldbach, 2019) to the field of corporate responsibility. It is sustained by its prominence in other fields, notably freedom of information as a central pillar of governmental accountability, and a schematic understanding of information economics. The metaphorical openness of the concept of 'transparency' served to mystify this regulatory paradigm while at the same time obscuring the frictions that arise when introducing it to the realm of corporate responsibility.

Once demystified, the rather marginal effects that reporting regulation has had in practice can barely come as a surprise. A broad stream of literature has convincingly documented the relative absence of tangible improvements for affected communities (Monciardini et al., 2021; Phillips et al., 2018). My intention here is not to add to this critique of ineffectiveness but rather to ask what we can learn from it for both the legal-political debate, which embraces such regulation, and our regulatory conception of value chains. I argue that the shortcomings of reporting regulation are partly intrinsic to the functioning of 'transparency' as a regulatory aspiration and partly due to the complexity, design, and political economy of current value chains. As the debate presses to move to regulatory paradigms 'beyond transparency' (Rühmkorf, 2018) in the sequential understanding of corporate responsibility described earlier, the practice of 'transparency' regulation provides important insights on corporate compliance strategies in value chains – especially on lead firms' use of private governance as means of compliance. This is particularly revealing for a legal debate that still treats the 'inside' of value chains and its day-to-day operations as a 'black box', that is, that hardly investigates how value chains operate as a legal and managerial field in reaction to new regulations. Legal scholarship on governance within GVCs discusses contracting across multiple tiers (Salminen, 2020) and for flexible business models (Cafaggi, 2016). Incorporating bargaining power into contractual analysis, these works explore how lead firms can impose conditions on lower tiers in the chain. Little, in turn, is known about how lead firms react to public regulation of corporate responsibility in their actual operations and where exactly these regulations do (or do not) gain traction. What are the concrete legal strategies by which lead firms distance themselves from rights violations and the knowledge thereof, and what role does law play in enabling such violations? Even regulatory types which – in the move from 'soft' to 'hard' law – would be labelled 'harder' because of their public origins and possible sanctions, such as due diligence and civil liability, will face similar strategies of deflection and watering down. Methodologically, the chapter suggests studying corporate responsibility as shifting from 'norms' to 'practices' (Michaels and Riles, 2020) in order to capture the micro- and firm-level dynamics and technicalities (Valverde, 2009; Riles, 2005) of corporate and value chain operations and develop more tailored and original legal tools. This also shifts the focus of legal analysis and requires a holistic perspective at the various ways in which law and legal practices 'code' value chains, that is, structure them and shield them from legal and other contestation. This perspective also foregrounds the intrinsic connection that exists in value chain capitalism between the information architecture within GVCs as affected by reporting rules and material conditions for workers. How does information on labour right infringements travel upwards in the chain, and who gets to initiate, shape, and decide on the salience of such information flow? It overcomes the dominant binary of 'promise versus pitfalls' of transparency – a binary which 'pre-empt(s) the exploration of transparency as a dynamic, situated, and sometimes paradoxical phenomenon' (Albu and Flyverbom, 2016: 2).

The remainder of the chapter will proceed as follows. In the next section, I will chart the rise of 'transparency' as a regulatory paradigm in various contexts. The subsequent section will demonstrate how regulation that draws on 'transparency' has built a legacy in other contexts whose regulatory assumptions cannot easily be translated to (transnational) corporate responsibility, especially in the context of modern slavery. Turning then to GVCs, I argue that reporting rules at present leave the operational dynamics of value chains mostly unaffected. Understanding value chains as driven by complex strategies of governance and dissociation by lead firms, I suggest that the ineffectiveness of reporting rules requires a more granular study of the manifestation of governance, in particular of the flow of information, in GVCs. The next section provides a preliminary methodological framework for such a turn. The final section concludes.

The Rise of 'Transparency' as Paradigm in Transnational Regulation

'Transparency' is a concept of the hour in many cultural, political, and legal discourses. It finds endorsement across various contexts and is at times idealized as panacea (Han, 2015), ranging from transparency as personal virtue to transparency as a maxim of organizational conduct. As a regulatory paradigm, transparency is often hailed as a solution to misconduct in complex organizations, including governmental bodies, business entities, and transnational regimes. It represents the normative vantage point behind a shift to governance of and through information as a recurrent theme of regulatory discourses, implemented through reporting duties. As a political ideal, transparency rests on the assumption of access to information as a basic feature for reason-driven public debate and as a precondition for accountability (Berliner, 2014). Recent movements around 'open data', such as WikiLeaks and related cases of 'radical transparency',[4] may serve as illustrations.

In a preliminary definitional approach, transparency can be understood as 'the degree to which corporate decisions, policies, activities, and impacts are acknowledged and made visible to relevant stakeholders' (Crane and Matten, 2010: 71). Much of the appeal of transparency as a regulatory technique comes from an abstract yet intuitive plausibility of its presumed operating logic. Once a discloser, such as a company, publicizes information (such as its initiatives undertaken to prevent modern slavery) that is deemed relevant by addressees (such as consumers or investors), these addressees will act in response to it and in return trigger a constructive response by the discloser. It is the self-justificatory impetus of this 'transparency action cycle' (Fung et al., 2007) that has allowed it to expand across so many fields and domains of regulation (Koivisto, 2022; Flyverbom, 2015). A change in behaviour of the discloser is expected based on a combination of external (market pressure and public scrutiny) and internal factors (self-reflection). Each of these factors rests on multiple conceptual and factual assumptions. Market pressure, for instance, requires a certain public sensitivity, the ability to process revelations of corporate misconduct, and the determination to react to them in purchasing decisions. Each of these elements is highly demanding in itself and adds new practical constraints and provisos to the seemingly straightforward instrumental power of transparency as a regulatory technique.

Regulation aiming at 'transparency' through reporting is particularly on the rise in transnational contexts, where it has the comparative advantage of being less restricted to jurisdictional boundaries. Reporting requirements are employed to respond to accountability deficits of public, private, and hybrid entities alike (Schleifer et al., 2019; Auld and Gulbrandsen, 2010; Hale, 2008). Requiring, for instance, corporations to report on value chain operations confers an indirect transnational scope to this regulation without dependence on a law-enforcement apparatus in each of the affected jurisdictions (and at comparatively little costs).

In the value chain context, reporting regulation was first introduced in Section 1502 of the Dodd–Frank Act (2010) and the California Transparency in Supply Chains Act (2010). It then found its way into the toolkit of European regulators, starting with the EU Corporate Social Responsibility (CSR) Directive (2014), the UK Modern Slavery Act (2015), the EU Conflict Minerals Regulation (2017) and related national legislation, and, most recently, the EU Commission's 'Financing Sustainable Growth Action Plan', with its pillars of the Sustainable Financial Disclosure Regulation (SFDR, 2019), the Taxonomy Regulation (2020), and the Corporate Sustainability Reporting Directive (2022). Reporting also remains an element of due diligence legislations, such as in the French and German national value chain laws.[5] This is not the place to discuss the specifics of each regulation, which has been done elsewhere (Nolan and Bott, 2018; LeBaron and Rühmkorf, 2017; Steuer and Tröger, 2022). As a general feature, transparency regulation departs from previous generations of CSR by shifting from corporate self-regulatory norm-setting and communication of corporate 'values' (Groddeck, 2011) to reporting on corporate 'practices'. They require companies of a certain size (by turnover or number of employees) or with activities in a specific sector to report on their efforts related to their human rights and environmental impacts, often including at least parts of their value chain. With some variations between the different laws, sanctions for non-compliance generally played a secondary role in the earlier examples and are slowly becoming a more central feature. The California Transparency in Supply Chains Act (2010) requires companies to disclose 'to what extent, if any', they have taken steps towards the eradication of slavery and trafficking. Similarly, under the UK Modern Slavery Act (2015), a company is deemed compliant if it issues a statement of the steps it has taken regarding slavery and human trafficking – or by stating that it has *not* taken any such steps. More recently, this approach has been replaced by a 'comply or explain' mechanism that asks companies to lay out the motivations for not taking such measures (Harper Ho, 2017). Coupled with this is an increase of fines in case of failure to report. The substance of reports remains, however, largely beyond regulatory control and is hence left to civil society and other intermediaries that provide a second-order assessment (Mantouvalou, 2018). This problem runs through to due diligence legislation, where the openness of the due diligence process inhibits effective checks on the adequacy of diligence – suggesting a considerably larger continuity between reporting and due diligence than is commonly acknowledged.

Already as a first approximation, we see that reporting obligations leave a broad leeway to corporate compliance through multiple mechanisms that make reporting requirements at best a peephole into a constructed corporate reality.

Transparency Regulation as a Legal Transplant

Even if the promise of 'transparency' as readily fostering integrity has been dampened, reporting is still on the rise. In the realm of corporate responsibility and the turn to sustainability, it has emerged as the primary legislative go-to mode of regulation (LeBaron and Rühmkorf, 2019). In the EU, for instance, reporting obligations form the cornerstone of the 'Green Deal', a recent set of policies envisioning a growth strategy in light of climate and environmental crises (Zeben, 2020). The reason for the ongoing policy support can be seen as twofold. It stems from the persistence of the conceptual abstractions of neo-classical and information economics in our collective imaginary, coupled with the positive legacy that reporting rules have gained in other fields. It is only by putting the suggestive power of 'transparency' into perspective that we can get a clearer view of how 'transparency itself can be a technique for creating opacity' (Riles, 2011: 187).

The Intuitions of Market-Based Regulation of Corporate Responsibility

The quest for 'transparency' owes its success to transparency's 'metaphorical authority' (Koivisto, 2016: 2). Its suggestive power as an easy 'fix' (Fenster, 2017) to complex problems of accountability has a long history, as illustrated by Justice Brandeis's famous account that 'Sunlight is said to be the best of disinfectants' (Brandeis, 1913). Historically, reporting rules aiming at transparency have been both a source of accountability for public administration, often associated with the rule of law, and, at least in the past 40 years, a tool for regulating markets and private economic relationships. In the private realm, reporting takes Hayek's ground-breaking insight into the role of information and its circulation as a coordinating device for markets as a starting point (Hayek, 1945). While departing thus from the premise of complete information, reporting remains otherwise calibrated on the assumptions of neo-classical economics, that is, individual rationality, free choice, and marginal utility. In the traditional picture, reporting seeks to remedy information asymmetries between parties or within markets that would otherwise trigger adverse effects by sustaining dishonesty, as in Akerlof's 'market for lemons' (Akerlof, 1970; Coffee, 1984). This ties in with the prominent conception of earlier CSR mechanisms as being adopted only if there is the 'business case' of a reputational gain for them. Regulators like the European Union have internalized this perspective – cultivated among business – and long insisted that an economic 'win-win' scenario, not the imposition of public policies, should guide regulation of corporate responsibility (Amstutz, 2015). Even as this is gradually changing, a market-based approach prevails.

To this day, reporting has managed to maintain, at least in the dominant narrative, the facade of its neutrality and effectiveness. It has withstood both the insights from economic sociology and behavioural economics. Placing each of the neo-classical assumptions into its social context, scholars in economic sociology have shown how economic activity is embedded in social relations, institutions, and rules (White, 1981). This impacts the way signalling within markets is practiced and understood. For instance, such perspectives highlight that the exclusively positive signalling that is common for highly curated CSR reports gradually creates an overly favourable perception of corporate responsibility. In this sense, transparency comes with an angle and an interest (Hansen et al., 2015). Behavioural economics has provided challenges to the addressees' ability to identify, understand, and act upon reported information. Scenarios of information overload (Ben-Shahar and Schneider, 2014) and intelligibility of information are exacerbated in the context of corporate responsibility (Chilton and Sarfaty, 2017). The factual and organizational complexity of corporate involvement in, for example, modern slavery makes it difficult to trace concrete effects of individual corporate policies and often leads to overly general reports. Further abstraction is added by the fact that entire companies are subject to reports – not specific consumer goods or value chains as in the case of product certification. As a result, reports are crafted from a headquarters perspective that is far removed from on-the-ground factors, local dynamics, and the voice of those most affected.

Relatedly, reporting rules do not properly acknowledge the heterogeneity of reports' addressees, their diverging interests, pre-existing knowledge, and capacity of understanding. As such, they adhere to a growingly fictitious idea of a holistic, homogenous public sphere. Such a concept enjoys lasting prominence because of its role for modern conceptions of democracy (Fraser, 1990; Habermas, 1989). Habermas, for instance, develops the public sphere as a discursive arena distinct from both the state and market rationality in which political participation materializes through the medium of talk (Habermas, 1987). As a representation of the whole of society, the 'public sphere' provides the forum for deliberations on the common good. The assumption is a shared language and involvement of various societal groups. The cohesion and good-naturedness conveyed by such an image of a 'public sphere' have become problematic in a society marked by social and epistemic fragmentation (Ladeur, 2015) and a 'network of publics' (Bruns, 2023) that also challenges the idea of equal communicative standards within and across the whole of society. Different societal groups, systems, and communities of knowledge have reached high levels of specialization that are reflected in their own vocabulary. Under systems theory (Luhmann, 2012), this is highlighted by the fact that each functional system observes its environment pursuant to its own conditions and 'code'. In contrast, the current regime of reporting rules assumes similar modes of reception across all receivers,[6] thereby inviting a standard of reporting that is either mundane and irrelevant or too complex for many receivers.

Misleading Legacies: Freedom of Information Laws and Financial Accounting

We have seen that transparency regulation builds on a model of information economics whose translation into an effective tool for corporate responsibility is more demanding than is commonly assumed. Next to this, such regulation has been 'transplanted' to the context of corporate responsibility based on certain merit acquired in other contexts, with insufficient attention paid to the peculiarities of this new domain of application. This, again, has led to an overestimation of the potential of reporting and to a lack of engagement with the way information about adverse impacts on, for example, labour conditions along value chains is generated and transmitted in the corporate sphere. Transparency regulation is seen in plain instrumentalist terms, rather than by unpacking the many preconditions it relies upon to serve as means to an end in corporate reality.

The first field of reference for which transparency regulation is being attributed merit is 'open government' laws. In the realm of public administration, transparency is deemed to enhance the acceptance of power by adding to its legitimacy. This, to be sure, has not remained unquestioned both conceptually and in political praxis. Some have noted that transparency works best as a rhetorical claim, while upon closer look, its contribution to legitimacy appears more ambivalent, both in its conceptual underpinnings and its social practice (Curtin and Meijer, 2006). Others have criticized that 'transparency' embodies an overly harmonious, consensual, and ultimately 'post-political' narrative of conflicts of interest, mitigating diverging positions to win-win terms (Garsten and Jacobsson, 2011). Riles (2011) argues that freedom of information laws can be read as a neo-liberal 'assault on the character of technocratic knowledge' as 'constitutive of the regulatory state' (2011: 113). Pozen (2018) has coined this 'transparency's ideological drift', from a progressive tool with aspirations towards social justice, trust in public institutions, and civic empowerment to a tool geared towards a neoliberal and libertarian agenda, restricting the scope of government to the benefit of private governance. Pozen describes with a view to the US how legal developments surrounding transparency-inspired legislation together with shifts in the political climate have generated an anti-public-sector bias in how transparency rules function – a phenomenon he describes as 'at least partly … transnational' (Pozen, 2018: 124).

Landmark US legislation such as the Freedom of Information Act (FOIA),[7] the Truth in Lending Act,[8] and the National Environmental Policy Act of 1969 (NEPA)[9] pioneered the implementation of individual access to information about government documentation and policies, as well as administrative reporting duties. These laws have been copied in multiple jurisdictions and inspired other mechanisms of public accountability (Aaken, 2010), including in the EU.[10] However, rules on corporate reporting cannot be seen in direct continuation of this line, for they are ridden with additional prerequisites. While FOIA grants immediate access to *primary sources* (provided none of the exemptions related to sensitivity and personal rights apply, 5 U.S.C. § 552), corporate reporting regulations require (or allow) companies to *produce* specific reports. Reports are *secondary sources*, curated for the purpose of reporting and for an intended audience. This degree of intermediation is extended further by the fact that corporate files are less likely to contain positive documentation of malicious intentions behind corporate wrongs, simply because they can remain in the subtext of business decisions and be concealed by the economic rationality of inter-firm communication. Communication in the administrative sphere, on the other hand, is pluralistic in its ends and hence needs to specify ends and means (see Graeber, 2016; Weber, 2013), making it more significant and revealing for outsiders. Take the example of the notorious 'Torture Memos' of 2002 advising the US government and security apparatus on certain interrogation techniques and providing explicit documentation of the readiness and alleged legality to recur to such practices (Johns, 2013: 32 et seq.). While in this case, the administrative documents show how possible state involvement in torture was actively weighed, corporate involvement in modern slavery, on the other hand, is often a more incidental, even if predictable, feature of established business models. Price squeeze and excessively short order timelines, for instance, are known root causes for worker vulnerability and modern slavery (Anner, 2020; Marshall, 2019; Shamir, 2012), but inter-firm communication around prices and orders will not usually contain specific considerations of such effects.

The second 'false friend' providing an undeserved legacy to corporate responsibility reporting comes from financial auditing. In recent years, both fields have moved towards convergence in their legal foundations (by extending the scope of financial reporting to non-financial aspects) and in practice (by allowing the big audit firms to establish and penetrate the market for modern slavery professionals) (Barkay and Shamir, 2025; Fransen and LeBaron, 2019; Haufler, 2018). This development is ambivalent, despite at first glance increasing the resources and the significance of various mechanisms that target modern slavery. The types and purposes of knowledge production that underlie financial auditing differ from that of modern slavery reporting. The *raison d'être* of financial auditing is distinctively institutional or systemic, namely, to ensure risk governance and thereby the order of financial markets. It draws essentially on quantitative data analysis. This is largely replicated, for instance, in the revision of the EU Corporate Sustainability Reporting Directive (2022), where comparable, quantitative, and machine-readable information is becoming the gold standard of Environmental, Social, and Governance (ESG) disclosure (Steuer and Tröger, 2022; Harper Ho, 2022; Johnston and Sjåfjell, 2020). This is not the most suitable type of data when it comes to detecting and mitigating practices of modern slavery, which requires qualitative analysis to identify informal dynamics (Chilton and Sarfaty, 2017; Sarfaty, 2017; LeBaron and Lister, 2015). Even if the 'S' in ESG can and should be understood so as to include modern slavery, the difficulty to map it in quantitative indicators has made it an underweighted dimension of the social pillar of ESG. When such measurements are attempted, they can hardly escape the reductionist rationale of quantification (Engle Merry, 2011).

Even if financial auditing is, in this regard, an unfitting antetype for corporate responsibility reporting, insights from auditing scholarship can be fruitfully transposed. Ever since the 1970s and further intensified after the financial crisis of 2008 (Pasquale, 2015), the legitimizing nature of auditing as expert knowledge practice has been put in the spotlight. Especially from a constructivist perspective, the claim has been made that auditing never delivers an accurate account of its subject matter but operates as a mystified and ritualized practice (Flint, 1988; Miller and Power, 2013).[11] Just as Power (1999) and others have established for financial auditing, corporate responsibility reports result in visual, numerical, or verbal representations of reality; they filter reality rather than providing unmediated access to it (Christensen and Schoeneborn, 2017). In this perspective, the well-documented gaps between corporate reporting and the reality of corporate practice are hardly surprising and not solely due to an unwillingness to report accurately but rooted in epistemological barriers and organizational intricacies. This gap can form a point of departure for a critique of 'transparency' as a regulatory mode, exposing its deeper fundaments and practical operations, rather than taking the gap as such already as the core of the critique.

In such a perspective interested in the processes transmission and presentation of information triggered by reporting rules, the social function of auditing then is no longer to provide accurate information but to uphold the illusion that it can do so, by concealing its foundational paradox in an 'inflationary spiral of escalating trust in nth order guardians' (Power, 1999: 135). When considering the recent 'managerialization of modern slavery law' (Monciardini et al., 2021) with an exploding number of intermediaries that compile, assess, and meta-evaluate modern slavery reports, this, too, seems to have become a self-referential practice (Valentinov et al., 2019). One explanation for this escalating logic of reporting is provided by the sociology of professions. In the field of accounting regulation, the professional organizations of accountants have played a crucial role in sophisticating accounting rules, advocating for additional layers of verification, and shielding the field from outsiders (Botzem, 2011). Similarly, financial auditors are perceived as independent experts when it comes to the *substance* of their assessments, but they remain interested parties when the objectivity of the procedures themselves is questioned – and react by suggesting ever more nuanced, complex procedures. Reporting then does not necessarily reduce complexity or secrecy but reformulates it at a higher order, since many professions are dependent on trust in the practices of reporting. Power (1999) laconically concludes that the 'history of auditing reads, like the history of regulation more generally, as a history of failure. Efforts at social control, it seems, always fail, and failure is always the condition for further attempts at control' (Power 1999: 26). In fact, the higher the degree of uncertainty in a given context, the higher the appeal of and the expectations towards transparency (Ponte and Gibbon, 2005). Yet, despite transparency falling considerably short of its promises, the accuracy of reports is often overestimated – a phenomenon which in a perspective of behavioural economics could be called a 'behavioural market failure', arising out of the attempt to remedy an informational market failure, namely the lack of information on sustainable production conditions (Hacker, 2016). This forms part of the unintended effects of reporting obligations.

Against this backdrop, the dominant critique of transparency regulation in the literature needs to be refined. While many authors see as a weakness that such rules require 'nothing but transparency' and impose no new substantive standards (what could be called a 'stringency critique'), here we have argued that corporate reporting rules are problematic not because they aim only at transparency but due to what 'transparency' in this domain means – the inner logic of transparency as regulatory mode (what could be called an 'epistemological critique'), and its uncritical transplantation to the field of corporate responsibility. In the next section, we will situate this epistemological critique within debates around governance of GVCs.

Governance of GVCs and Strategies of 'Dissociation'

As the playbook of regulatory strategies against modern slavery and other corporate wrongs along value chains is becoming more and more wide-ranging, a common challenge is how to confront the opacity, informality, and complexity of global production. Take, for instance, the example of the semiconductor chip manufacturer Intel that uses no less than 19,000 suppliers in over 100 countries to provide direct material, tools, machines, logistics, and packaging (Crawford and Joler, 2018). GVCs are not merely designed or assembled as a result of repeated 'make or buy' decisions, the distinction that in neo-classical economics favours either 'market' or 'firms' as economic organization. This view treats the market as a 'natural order' (Harcourt, 2012), a perspective that obscured how value chains are shaped by and impact upon the interplay between legal entitlements, economic opportunities, and regulatory frames. Rather, in addition to promising efficiency gains from specialization, practices like outsourcing and offshoring are enabled by a strategic play with legal niches and the blind spots of legal institutions (Sobel-Read, 2014). Consider corporate arrangements of profit-shifting for tax evasion, liability exemptions in commercial contracts, and involvement of middlemen to shield the lead firm from direct claims. Companies are engaged in practices of 'association' and 'dissociation' (Bair, 2019), understood as relational work to insulate the lead firm, its brand, and reputation from rights violations down the chain. Such practices take many forms, some of which are legal (for example, through the use of intermediaries and by reference to privity of contract), while others may be factual (remote sourcing or no proactive inquiry about local production circumstances) or arising from corporate communication (for example, in CSR statements). Lead firms' strategies of regulatory arbitrage to dissociate themselves from their production facilities – legally, economically, geographically, environmentally, culturally, and so on – are central to the current institutional structure and geography of global production. As Anna Tsing (2012) puts it, 'supply-chain capitalism makes use of the waste spaces of capitalism and modernity' (p. 62). In this perspective, GVCs appear as an emanation of constructed ambiguity, deliberate obfuscation, or 'agnotology' (Proctor, 2008), rather than merely filling a 'governance gap' (Ruggie, 2008) or being geared towards rationality and efficiency. Corporations generate organizational complexity with the aim of undermining classical ascriptions of legality, value creation, and governance. Value chains form a largely invisible connection between sites, actors, and economic processes that need to be actively 'mapped' in order to become tangible from a regulatory perspective (Eller, 2017). As a result of these practices, even lead firms would not necessarily have active knowledge of their entire chain until the factory level. For many mass consumer goods, big intermediary platforms such as the Hong Kong-based supply chain management company Li and Fung[12] connect Western buyers to a dynamic network of tens of thousands of suppliers in Asia, effectively eliminating the need to know one's own value chain until the factory-level (Nguyen, 2023).

Law in the Information Architecture of GVCs

The significance of reporting rules for the internal flow of knowledge within GVCs becomes clear when understanding the interplay between knowledge and deliberate ignorance, between governance and the search for 'ungovernance' (Desai and Lang, 2020) as driving forces behind GVCs. The level of control and the degree of knowledge of lead firms do not coincidentally result from a certain degree of complexity of GVCs, but the degree of complexity is at least partly designed to allow a desired level of control and knowledge. Hence, lead firms are sought to report instances that do not occur in their vicinity – they are not, as in most reporting regimes, 'insiders' who report to 'outsiders', but to a certain extent 'outsiders' themselves. Lead firms' lack of information is both a strategic choice and a product of legal arrangements that allow for the compartmentalization of GVCs.

This has important implications for the analysis and the design of corporate responsibility reporting rules. We can distinguish two types of information setups which such rules affect. The first 'information cycle' is *outbound* and captures the reactions of market participants and other stakeholders to the publication of a report by the lead firm. Commonly the focus of analysis, this outbound circle describes where transparency rules are expected to take effect, that is, by influencing purchasing decisions or other actions by recipients. A second relevant 'information cycle' can be labelled *inbound*, namely referring to the internal organizational communication and knowledge-building *among chain actors*, that is, those processes that gather data input as the basis of a corporate report. This second information cycle is much less studied, but it is possibly the context in which reporting rules can be more transformative than in the 'outbound' cycle. Studying the 'inbound' circle entails asking how the flow of information among chain actors and across sites is organized, whose input and whose challenges matter, and what means exist for a lead firm to remain deliberately ignorant. We have seen earlier that for multiple reasons, the output of corporate reports is of low quality – that is, unspecific and fails to capture its intended recipients' attention – and, even if such reports are being read, they rarely trigger relevant changes of behaviour. In this sense, reporting rules in practice seem to fail all elements of the abstract information model they are based upon. This suggests reversing the perspective by asking to what extent such rules can alter the regime of information circulation between myriads of chain actors. The regime of information circulation is a central part of the strategies of dissociation and the epistemic authority of a lead firm over its value chain, both upstream between suppliers (for example, regarding the selective circulation of factory-level information) and downstream towards consumers (for example, regarding the leeway in framing products as 'sustainable' or the like towards consumers). Revising and contesting this epistemic authority might be an effective step towards increasing lead firm responsibility. Constructivist scholarship that is interested in how information is 'made', rather than 'given', has been vocal in emphasizing how knowledge generation and presentation can alter power dynamics and social orders (Jasanoff, 2004). In particular, this allows an inroad to address informality in value chains – the 'loose ends' of many GVCs involving working people without contractual connections, mini-entrepreneurs, and other workforce that is deprived of legal or actual protection of fundamental labour rights. While both reporting regulation and due diligence suppose a degree of oversight on the basis of information (for example, on labour conditions, working hours, and employment terms) that is collected on the ground and processed for use at the level of corporate policies, many, if not most, labour rights violations occur in the shadow of such data-sets, on the informal side of value chains (Hsin, 2020). The more the 'formal' side of value chains is regulated, the bigger the gap to its 'informal' counterpart becomes. Strengthening the impact of many existing value chain regulations requires addressing this disconnect, rather than simply tightening the requirements on the 'formal' value chain.

Until now, legal debates have largely ignored the way law structures the flow of information on non-product-related aspects along the chain, such as by mandating actors to obtain certain information, setting up suitable institutions, and the like. For instance, current reporting regulations mostly focus on the presentation of information while giving little detail on their collection and generation. Examples for legal regimes that do take such a perspective are most notably product safety law with high obligations of traceability and documentation, and other regimes that require tracing of commodities, like under the Convention on International Trade in Endangered Species of Wild Fauna and Flora (CITES), the Kimberley Process Certification Scheme (KPCS), the EU Deforestation Regulation (Durán and Scott, 2022),[13] or the EU Forced Labour Regulation.[14] Under the EU Green Deal and its aspirations towards a circular economy, furthermore, the planned 'Digital Product Passport'[15] envisions a new generation of standardized exchange of product-related information along the value chain, both upstream and downstream.

The role of information and cognition is a common theme in contract law scholarship, however mostly in a bilateral setup, especially with a focus on the informational basis for the negotiation and conclusion of contracts (Grundmann, 2017). In the aftermath of neo-classical approaches, contract theories have reflected the costs of gathering and processing information, and discussed the mechanisms through which parties deal with contingencies, provide for adjustments in specific circumstances, and leave their contracts deliberately incomplete for others (Eisenberg, 1995). Approaches from law and economics have devoted great attention to the effects that reporting rules have on designing parties' search for information and to alleviate information asymmetry. Far less attention has gone to the question of how contracts themselves steer (or interrupt) flows of information. To be sure, contracts can have a series of explicit provisions on this matter, such as in contracts that are geared towards a transfer of knowledge as in research and development (R&D) contracts or by means of confidentiality clauses, which restrict the use of knowledge beyond the contractual relation. Lead firms use novel standardized procedures and information technology (IT) to negotiate, monitor, implement, and review their contracts – such 'contract management' generates new meta-data about the hundreds or thousands of contractual supplier relations (Kähler, 2013). Although such management devices have become a crucial infrastructure for GVCs, their use has for long been limited to coordinating a seamless flow of commodities and product-related information (especially product safety and quality). In other words, the information architecture of GVCs has long been biased towards efficiency and has thereby sustained corporate strategies of 'dissociation' from labour rights violations resulting from sourcing decisions and price squeeze. One firm-level path to contesting such 'dissociation' is to redress this bias and enhance the flow of non-product-related information from the capillaries of a GVC to the lead firm. The following section will outline possible paths towards this.

Taking on the Technicalities: Legal Coding Techniques of GVCs

What can be the role of law in such a shift? Looking at corporate responsibility reporting rules as altering the information architecture of GVCs invites us to broaden the scope of the current legal analysis of GVCs. A clearer understanding of the way law affects information circulation within GVCs will offer a new and important lens for discussions around the degree and spheres of leverage and governability within GVCs. The question of how far down the chain a lead firm can be expected to govern or to know is at the heart of all current regulatory attempts, be it on the reach of due diligence or a duty of care, the understanding of 'directly linked' entities under the UN Guiding Principles on Business and Human Rights or the degree of information expected under reporting duties. Legal and organizational literature has responded to the complexity of GVCs by trying to identify patterns of governance between firms (Gereffi et al., 2005; Salminen, 2020). Such patterns may be formalized in contractual terms, or they may draw on more informal institutions, such as business practices, trust, or reputation. Contract governance scholarship, however, often assumes a concentration of power at the lead firm level (Cutler, 2017) without unpacking the mechanisms that exercise power and circulate information. Legal and other scholarship has treated these governance mechanisms largely as 'black-box' for now and has not yet identified them as a source of deflection or watering down of value chain regulation.

Taking inspiration from Riles (2011), a preliminary toolkit to conceptualize the inner governance dynamics of value chains can be what might be termed 'value chain coding techniques', a set of mundane practices used by value chain insiders that animate the complexity of global production. In essence, these techniques comprise (*a*) legal doctrines (for example, privity of contract), (*b*) material documents (for example, CSR reports, order sheets, audits), (*c*) physical and digital infrastructure (for example, containers, supply chain management IT), and (*d*) professional routines of involved specialists (for example, supply chain managers, auditors). Recent scholarship in Law and Political Economy (Pistor, 2019), as well as ethnographic studies of investment banking (Riles, 2011), commercial arbitration (Dezalay and Garth, 1996), and trade (Turner, 2016; Griesel, 2021) have pointed to one or several of these elements to show how legal rules and practices work together to 'code' economic activities. These 'coding techniques' are responsible for the distorted translation between well-meaning rules and ongoing rights violations. In conventional regulatory theory, such techniques remain largely unnoticed, being portrayed as neutral devices that must 'comply with' the law. Many value chain regulations are, however, deliberately vague and leave a vacuum to be filled exactly by such practices (IGLP, 2016; Catá Backer, 2018; Sarfaty, 2021; Knop et al., 2012). Accordingly, companies and auditors are not mere passive 'rule-takers', but they shape norms and implementation. The technical allure of these 'coding techniques' conceals that those expert practices are crucial for enabling corporate actors to shield themselves (Kennedy, 2016).

The communication processes which reporting rules trigger among chain actors and within the lead firm's corporate structure can be understood as legally 'coded' bureaucratic practices around the collection, transmission, and processing of information. Studies on bureaucratic practices (Gitelman, 2014; Blau, 1955) have brought attention to the mundane patterns of formatting administrative knowledge through forms, spreadsheets, and other standardized documents and recording practices. Latour (2002) has emphasized the 'passage of law', characteristic of law's mode of existence, which takes place between the text of the legal provisions and the documents (that is, statements and case briefs) produced by parties in pursuance of and in reference to this. In this understanding, any form of documentation or audits that are requested along the chain in response to reporting obligations contribute to a legal ('coding') practice that has a recursive effect at the level of legal rules. In the GVC context, this role is played by supply chain management IT that ultimately operationalizes compliance, refers (or omits reference to) managers to compliance deficits, and provides the general steering tool for far-flung production networks (Sarfaty, 2020; Eller, 2020). Such technological infrastructures, often developed by digital start-ups and spurred by big data, form the basis of compliance practices with all major types of value chain regulations of recent years – ranging from reporting[16] to due diligence[17] and market access rules.[18] This highlights the centrality and need for accountability of such IT.

In short, the well-documented shortcomings of reporting rules in the field of corporate responsibility suggest a reading of such rules that no longer sees their foremost objective in overcoming information deficits of consumers, investors, and other stakeholders. Rather, reporting rules may be understood (and ultimately *redesigned*) as primarily affecting the information architecture necessary to prevent, identify, and mitigate rights violations, such as modern slavery along the chain. The current reporting practice follows a culture of 'showing', that is, upholding the impression of complete lawfulness of value chain structures, and should be 'recoded' into a culture of 'knowing', that is, by adopting an inquisitive perspective that limits strategies of corporate dissociation from local incidents. Such a shift can highlight the intrinsic connection that exists in value chain capitalism between the information architecture within GVCs and material conditions for workers and tie in with broader aspirations of democratizing global production. Among the multiple possible building blocks is a more bottom-up and inclusive drafting of corporate reports that gives voice to both formal and informal workers and their representatives (remedying the current lack of worker voice[19]), a shift from reporting about 'compliance' narrowly understood to a culture of capability building of suppliers, the implementation of whistleblowing and other forms of denouncing corporate wrongs, an expanded yet prudent use of IT and traceability tools, especially those that amplify worker voice, a better connection with knowledge on local and industry-specific parameters through NGOs, embassies, Chambers of Commerce, transnational indicators, and generally a less routinized requirement for reassessment.

Conclusion

This chapter has attempted to shed light on the rapid proliferation of reporting regulations geared towards 'transparency' in the realm of corporate responsibility and especially in the field of modern slavery. Taking the widely shared disillusionment with the practical effects of such regulations as a starting point, I have argued that reporting rules draw on a combination of highly schematic models of information economics, a certain regulatory merit acquired in other domains, and a specialized set of 'transparency professionals' in order to evade criticism of their internal contradictions as a regulatory mode for corporate responsibility. Adding to existing literature that sees the 'softness' of reporting rules as their main deficit, I have suggested that such regulations draw on self-sustaining logic and the deeply rooted appeal of transparency as societal virtue.

Against this backdrop, I have proposed to shift the understanding of corporate responsibility reporting rules from informing 'outsiders', such as consumers, investors, and other stakeholders, to the 'inside' of GVCs, by altering their information architecture. The current design of these rules is little attuned to and rarely acknowledges this dimension. Yet, it is in this direction that lead firms' strategies of 'dissociation' from rights violations down the chain can be affected most lastingly. One reason for the current absence of such a perspective in the legal literature stems from the lack of engagement with the micro- and firm-level dynamics of corporate and value chain governance, and, in particular, the role of law in the information architecture of GVCs. A reform of reporting rules needs to go hand-in-hand with a renewed focus on legal analysis of GVCs, turning 'from norms to practices' in order to expose the detailed 'legal coding techniques of GVCs', and tracing the role that information and deliberate ignorance play in the construction of corporate power. Such an analysis of the performative dimension of GVC regulation would similarly benefit modes of regulation other than reporting, in particular due diligence, that rely on and seek to impact the same information architecture to improve material conditions of production. As the debate around corporate responsibility is welcoming a veritable 'GVC turn' in recent legislations with new rules on due diligence and market access (Salminen et al., 2024), it is important to remember that those, too, will face familiar challenges of regulating GVCs and their political economy.

Notes

1. *Loi Relative au Devoir de Vigilance des Sociétés Mères et des Entreprises Donneuses d'Ordre* (Law on the Duty of Vigilance of Parent and Instructing Companies) of 21 February 2017.
2. *Gesetz über die unternehmerischen Sorgfaltspflichten zur Vermeidung von Menschenrechtsverletzungen in Lieferketten* (Supply Chain Due Diligence Act), Bundesgesetzblatt 2021 I Nr. 46 of 22 July 2021.

3. Directive (EU) 2022/2464 of the European Parliament and of the Council of 14 December 2022 amending Regulation (EU) No 537/2014, Directive 2004/109/EC, Directive 2006/43/EC and Directive 2013/34/EU as regards corporate sustainability reporting (text with EEA relevance).
4. Benkler (2013: 236–41) states that the Obama Administration's project on 'Open Data' 'suggests how the rhetoric of openness and voluntarism interacts with the rhetoric of innovation, entrepreneurship, and markets, and how both can lead to obscuring, rather than solving, the public failures that led to the movement in the first place.'
5. See notes 1–2.
6. See Valentinov et al. (2019: 298): 'The ethical injunction to complete transparency therefore has to be analysed as what it is, a discourse representing a nonsystemic understanding of the universe. . . .'
7. Pub. L. No. 89-487, 80 Stat. 250 (1966) (codified as amended at 5 U.S.C. § 522 (2018)).
8. Pub. L. No. 90-321, 82 Stat. 146 (1968) (codified as amended at 15 U.S.C. §§ 1601–1667f (2018)).
9. Pub. L. No. 91-100, 83 Stat. 852 (1969) (codified as amended in scattered sections of 42 U.S.C.).
10. See Art. 15 Treaty on the Functioning of the European Union.
11. Miller and Power (2013: 556) see auditing as the 'most powerful system of representation for social and economic life today in many national settings'.
12. See the corporate website under http://www.lifung.com/.
13. For deforestation risks in supply chains, see, for example, the online platform 'Trase', developed by the Stockholm Environment Institute, https://trase.earth/.
14. Regulation (EU) 2024/3015 of the European Parliament and of the Council of 27 November 2024 on prohibiting products made with forced labour on the Union market and amending Directive (EU) 2019/1937.
15. Regulation (EU) 2024/1781 of the European Parliament and of the Council of 13 June 2024 establishing a framework for the setting of ecodesign requirements for sustainable products, amending Directive (EU) 2020/1828 and Regulation (EU) 2023/1542 and repealing Directive 2009/125/EC.
16. Some examples of private technology solutions include Prewave (www.prewave.com), IntegrityNext (www.integritynext.com), EcoVadis (https://ecovadis.com), Altana AI (https://altana.ai), SupplyShift (www.supplyshift.net), or Osapiens (www.osapiens.com).
17. To facilitate compliance with the EU Conflict Minerals Regulation (2017/821), one of the first legislations to implement a due diligence requirement, the EU

Commission has released a document listing 'IT Solutions for Due Diligence' (1 April 2024), available at: https://single-market-economy.ec.europa.eu/system/files/2020-05/it_solutions_for_due_diligence_0.pdf.

18. The EU Forced Labour Regulation shall establish a 'Forced Labour Single Portal' operated by the EU Commission and which includes guidelines, information on bans, a database of risk areas and sectors, as well as publicly available evidence.
19. See for a detailed reconstruction of the position of workers in current paradigms of GVC regulation Marshall et al., 2023.

References

Aaken, A. van (2010). 'Regulierung durch transparenz: Verhaltensregeln für Parlamentarier und ihre realfolgen' ('Regulation through transparency: rules of conduct for members of Parliament and their real effects'). *Der Staat* 49(3): 369–403.

Akerlof, G. (1970). 'The Market for "Lemons": Quality Uncertainty and the Market Mechanism'. *The Quarterly Journal of Economics* 84(3): 488–500.

Albu, O. B. and M. Flyverbom (2016). 'Organizational Transparency: Conceptualizations, Conditions, and Consequences'. *Business and Society* 58(2): 268–97.

Amstutz, M. (2015). 'The Evolution of Corporate Social Responsibility: Reflections on the Constitution of a Global Law for Multinational Enterprises'. *Schweizerische Zeitschrift für Wirtschafts- und Finanzmarktrecht* 87(3): 189–98.

Anner, M. (2020). 'Squeezing Workers' Rights in Global Supply Chains: Purchasing Practices in the Bangladesh Garment Export Sector in Comparative Perspective'. *Review of International Political Economy* 27(2): 320–47.

Auld, G. and L. H. Gulbrandsen (2010). 'Transparency in Nonstate Certification: Consequences for Accountability and Legitimacy'. *Global Environmental Politics* 10(3): 97–119.

Bair, J. (2019). 'Dialectics of Dissociation'. *Dialogues in Human Geography* 9(1): 68–72.

Barkay, T. and H. Shamir (2025). 'Anti-Trafficking Chains in GVCs: Corporate Transparency Legislation and Worker Driven Social Responsibility'. In *Modern Slavery and the Governance of Global Value Chains*, edited by H. Shamir, B. Arora, S. Banerjee, and T. Barkay. Cambridge, UK: Cambridge University Press.

Bartley, T. (2018). 'Transnational Corporations and Global Governance'. *Annual Review of Sociology* 44: 145–65.

Ben-Shahar, O. and C. Schneider (2014). *More than You Wanted to Know: The Failure of Mandated Disclosure*. Princeton, NJ: Princeton University Press.

Benkler, Y. (2013). 'Practical Anarchism: Peer Mutualism, Market Power, and the Fallible State'. *Politics and Society* 41(2): 213–51.

Berliner, D. (2014). 'The Political Origins of Transparency'. *The Journal of Politics* 76(2): 479–91.

Blau, P. (1955). *Dynamics of Bureaucracy*. Chicago, IL: University of Chicago Press.

Botzem, S. (2011). *The Politics of Accounting Regulation: Organizing Transnational Standard Setting in Financial Reporting*. Cheltenham, UK: Edward Elgar.

Brandeis, L. (1913). 'What Publicity Can Do'. *Harper's Weekly*, 20 December, p. 10.

Bruns, A. (2023). 'From "the" Public Sphere to a Network of Publics: Towards an Empirically Founded Model of Contemporary Public Communication Spaces'. *Communication Theory* 33(2–3): 70–81.

Cafaggi, F. (2016). 'Regulation through Contracts: Supply-chain Contracting and Sustainability Standard'. *European Review of Contract Law* 12(3): 218–58.

Catá Backer, L. (2018). 'Theorizing Regulatory Governance within Its Ecology: The Structure of Management in an Age of Globalization'. *Contemporary Politics* 24(5): 607–30.

Chilton, A. and G. Sarfaty (2017). 'The Limitations of Supply Chain Disclosure Regimes. *Stanford Journal of International Law* 53(1): 1–54.

Christensen, L. T. and D. Schoeneborn (2017). 'The Corporate Construction of Transparency and (In)transparency'. In *Corporate Social Responsibility: Strategy, Communication, Governance*, edited by A. Rasche, M. Morsing, and J. Moon, 307–27. Cambridge, UK: Cambridge University Press.

Coffee, J. C. (1984). 'Market Failure and the Economic Case for a Mandatory Disclosure System'. *Virginia Law Review* 70(4): 717–53.

Crane, A. (2013). 'Modern Slavery as a Management Practice: Exploring the Conditions and Capabilities for Human Exploitation'. *Academy of Management Review* 38(1): 49–69.

Crane, A. and D. Matten (2010). *Business Ethics. Managing Corporate Citizenship and Sustainability in the Age of Globalization*, 3rd edn. Oxford, UK: Oxford University Press.

Crawford, K. and V. Joler (2018). 'Anatomy of an AI System'. Available at: https://anatomyof.ai.

Curtin, D. and A. Meijer (2006). 'Does Transparency Strengthen Legitimacy?' *Information Polity* 11(2): 109–22.

Cutler, A. (2017). ‘Private Transnational Governance in Global Value Chains’. In *The Politics of Private Transnational Governance by Contract*, edited by C. Cutler and T. Dietz, 79–98. Abingdon, UK: Routledge.

Desai, D. and A. Lang (2020). ‘Introduction: Global Un-governance’. *Transnational Legal Theory* 11(3): 219–43.

Dezalay, Y. and B. G. Garth (1996). *Dealing in Virtue: International Commercial Arbitration and the Construction of a Transnational Legal Order*. Chicago, IL: University of Chicago Press.

Durán, G. M. and J. Scott (2022). ‘Regulating Trade in Forest-Risk Commodities: Two Cheers for the European Union’. *Journal of Environmental Law* 34(2): 245–67.

Eisenberg, M. A. (1995). ‘The Limits of Cognition and the Limits of Contract’. *Stanford Law Review* 47(2): 211–59.

Eller, K. H. (2017). ‘Private Governance of Global Value Chains from Within. Lessons from and for Transnational Law’. *Transnational Legal Theory* 8(3): 296–329.

——— (2020). ‘Is “Global Value Chain” a Legal Concept? Situating Contract Law in Discourses around Global Production’. *European Review of Contract Law* 16(1): 3–24.

Engle Merry, S. (2011). Measuring the World: Indicators, Human Rights, and Global Governance. *Current Anthropology* 51(3): S83–S95.

Fenster, M. (2017). *The Transparency Fix: Secrets, Leaks, and Uncontrollable Government Information*. Stanford, CA: Stanford University Press.

Flint, D. (1988). *Philosophy and Principles of Auditing*. New York: Palgrave Macmillan.

Flyverbom, M. (2015). ‘Sunlight in Cyberspace? On Transparency as a Form of Ordering’. *European Journal of Social Theory* 18(2): 168–84.

Fransen, L. and G. LeBaron (2019). ‘Big Audit Firms as Regulatory Intermediaries in Transnational Labor Governance’. *Regulation and Governance* 13(2): 260–79.

Fraser, N. (1990). ‘Rethinking the Public Sphere: A Contribution to the Critique of Actually Existing Democracy’. *Social Text* 25/26: 56–80.

Fung, A., M. Graham, and D. Weil (2007). *Full Disclosure: The Perils and Promise of Transparency*. Cambridge, UK: Cambridge University Press.

Garsten, C. and K. Jacobsson (2011). ‘Transparency and Legibility in International Institutions: The UN Global Compact and Post-political Global Ethics’. *Social Anthropology* 19(4): 378–93.

Gereffi, G., J. Humphrey, and T. Sturgeon (2005). ‘The Governance of Global Value Chains’. *Review of International Political Economy* 12(1): 78–104.

Gitelman, L. (ed.) (2014). *Paper Knowledge: Towards a Media History of Documents.* Durham, NC: Duke University Press.

Goldbach, T. (2019). 'Why Legal Transplants?' *Annual Review of Law and Social Sciences* 15: 583–601.

Graeber, D. (2016). *The Utopia of Rules: On Technology, Stupidity, and the Secret Joys of Bureaucracy.* Brooklyn, NY: Melville House.

Griesel, F. (2021). *The Limits of Private Governance: Norms and Rules in a Mediterranean Fishery.* Oxford, UK: Hart Publishing.

Groddeck, V. von (2011). 'Rethinking the Role of Value Communication in Business Corporations from a Sociological Perspective'. *Journal of Business Ethics* 100: 69–84.

Grundmann, S. (2017). 'Information – Eine Skizze zu Theorie, Funktionalität und Kritik' (Information – A Sketch on Theory, Functionality, and Critique). In *Festschrift for Ioannis Karakostas*, 1–23. Athens: Nomiki Bibliothiki.

Habermas, J. (1987). *Theory of Communicative Action, Volume 2. Lifeworld and System: A Critique of Functionalist Reason.* Translated by T. McCarthy. Boston, MA: Beacon.

——— (1989). *The Structural Transformation of the Public Sphere: An Inquiry into a Category of Bourgeois Society.* Cambridge, MA: MIT Press.

Hacker, P. (2016). *Versicherung und Verbriefung – Der Irrweg der Kommission auf der Suche nach einer Regulierung von derivativen Finanzprodukten* (Insurance and Securitization – The Commission's Misguided Search for Regulation of Derivative Financial Products). In *Versicherungsmechanismen im Recht*, edited by C. Brehme, M. Fries, and J. Stark, 15–44. Tübingen: Mohr Siebeck.

Hale, T. N. (2008). Transparency, accountability, and global governance. *Global Governance: A Review of Multilateralism and International Organizations* 14(1): 73–94.

Han, B.-C. (2015). *The Transparency Society.* Stanford, CA: Stanford University Press.

Hansen, H. K., L. Christensen, and M. Flyverbom (2015). 'Introduction: Logics of Transparency in Late Modernity: Paradoxes, Mediation and Governance'. *European Journal of Social Theory* 18(2): 117–31.

Harcourt, B. (2012). *The Illusion of Free Markets: Punishment and the Need of Natural Order.* Cambridge, MA: Harvard University Press.

Harper Ho, V. (2017). '"Comply or Explain" and the Future of Nonfinancial Reporting'. *Lewis and Clark Law Review* 21(2): 317–55.

——— (2022). 'Modernizing ESG Disclosure'. *University of Illinois Law Review*, 277–356.

Haufler, V. (2018). 'Producing Global Governance in the Global Factory: Markets, Politics, and Regulation'. *Global Policy* 9(1): 114–20.

Hayek, F. A. von (1945). 'The Use of Knowledge in Society'. *The American Economic Review* 35(4): 519–30.

Hsin, L. (2020). 'Modern Slavery in Law: Towards Continuums of Exploitation'. *Australian Journal of Human Rights* 26(1): 165–75.

IGLP Law and Global Production Working Group (2016). 'The Role Of Law in Global Value Chains: A Research Manifesto'. *London Review of International Law* 4(1): 57–79.

Jasanoff, S. (ed.) (2004). *States of Knowledge: The Co-Production of Sciences and Social Order*. Abingdon, UK: Routledge.

Jeßberger, F. (2016). 'Corporate Involvement In Slavery And Criminal Responsibility Under International Law'. *Journal of International Criminal Justice* 14(2): 327–41.

Johns, F. (2013). *Non-Legality in International Law: Unruly Law*. Cambridge, UK: Cambridge University Press.

Johnston, A. and B. Sjåfjell (2020). 'The EU's Approach to Environmentally Sustainable Business: Can Disclosure Overcome the Failings of Shareholder Primacy?' In *Research Handbook on EU Environmental Law*, edited by M. Peeters and M. Eliantonio, 396–410. Cheltenham, UK: Edward Elgar.

Kähler, L. (2013). 'Contract-management Duties as a New Regulatory Device'. *Law and Contemporary Problems* 76(2): 89–110.

Kennedy, D. (2016). *A World of Struggle: How Power, Law, and Expertise Shape Global Political Economy*. Princeton, NJ: Princeton University Press.

Knop, K., R. Michaels, and A. Riles (2012). 'From Multiculturalism to Technique: Feminism, Culture, and the Conflict of Laws Style'. *Stanford Law Review* 64(3): 589–656.

Koivisto, I. (2016). 'The Anatomy of Transparency: The Concept and Its Multifarious Implications'. Working Paper, EUI MWP, 2016/09.

——— (2022). *The Transparency Paradox: Questioning an Ideal*. Oxford, UK: Oxford University Press.

Ladeur, K. H. (2015). 'The Social Epistemology of Risk Observation and Management. Modern Law and the Transformation of Its Cognitive Infrastructure'. In *Risk and EU Law*, edited by H. W. Micklitz, and T. Tridimas, 49–68. Cheltenham, UK: Edward Elgar.

Latour, B. (2002). *La Fabrique du Droit: Une Ethnographie du Conseil d'État* (The Factory of Law. An Ethnography of the Conseil d'État). Paris: La Découverte.

LeBaron, G. (2021). 'The Role of Supply Chains in the Global Business of Forced Labour'. *Journal of Supply Chain Management* 57(2): 29–42.

LeBaron, G. and A. Rühmkorf (2017). 'Steering CSR through Home State Regulation: A Comparison of the Impact of the UK Bribery Act and Modern Slavery Act on Global Supply Chain Governance'. *Global Policy* 8(3): 15–28.

——— (2019). 'The Domestic Politics of Corporate Accountability Legislation: Struggles over the 2015 UK Modern Slavery Act'. *Socio-Economic Review* 17(3): 709–43.

LeBaron, G. and J. Lister (2015). 'Benchmarking Global Supply Chains: The Power of the "Ethical Audit" Regime'. *Review of International Studies* 41(5): 905–24.

Luhmann, N. (2012). *Theory of Society*, Vol. I. Stanford, CA: Stanford University Press.

Mantouvalou, V. (2018). 'The UK Modern Slavery Act 2015 Three Years On'. *Modern Law Review* 81(6): 1017–45.

Mares, R. (2018). 'Corporate Transparency Laws: A Hollow Victory?' *Netherlands Quarterly of Human Rights* 36(3): 189–213.

Marshall, S. (2019). *Living Wage: Regulatory Solutions to Informal and Precarious Work in Global Supply Chains*. Oxford, UK: Oxford University Press.

Marshall, S., I. Landau, H. Shamir, T. Barkay, J. Fudge, and A. van Heerden (2023). *Mandatory Human Rights Due Diligence: Risks and Opportunities for Workers and Unions*. RMIT University Business and Human Rights Centre; TraffLab ERC; and Labour, Equality and Human Rights (LEAH) research group, Monash Business School. Available at: https://www.trafflab.org/_files/ugd/11e1f0_e1db27f1ec7f41459ac357d021f6011c.pdf.

Michaels, R. and A. Riles (2020). 'Law as Technique'. In *Oxford Handbook of Law and Anthropology*, edited by M. C. Foblets, M. Goodale, M. Sapignoli, and O. Zenker, 860–78. Oxford, UK: Oxford University Press.

Miller, P. and M. Power (2013). 'Accounting, Organizing, and Economizing'. *The Academy of Management Annals* 7: 555–605.

Monciardini, D., N. Bernaz, and A. Andhov (2021). 'The Organizational Dynamics of Compliance with the UK Modern Slavery Act in the Food and Tobacco Sector'. *Business and Society* 60(2): 288–340.

Nguyen, T. (2023). 'Hidden Power in Global Supply Chains'. *Harvard International Law Journal* 64(1): 35–84.

Nolan, J. and G. Bott (2018). 'Global Supply Chains and Human Rights: Spotlight on Forced Labour and Modern Slavery Practices'. *Australian Journal of Human Rights* 24(1): 44–69.

Pasquale, F. (2015). *The Black Box Society*. Cambridge, MA: Harvard University Press.

Phillips, N., G. LeBaron, and S. Wallin (2018). 'Mapping and Measuring the Effectiveness of Labour-related Disclosure Requirements for Global Supply Chains'. International Labour Office Research Department Working Paper, No. 32.

Pistor, K. (2019). *Code of Capital: How the Law Creates Wealth and Inequality*. Princeton, NJ: Princeton University Press.

Ponte, S. and P. Gibbon (2005). 'Quality Standards, Conventions and the Governance of Global Value Chains'. *Economy and Society* 34(1): 1–31.

Power, M. (1999). *The Audit Society: Rituals of Verification*. Oxford, UK: Oxford University Press.

Pozen, D. (2018). 'Transparency's Ideological Drift'. *The Yale Law Journal* 128(1): 100–65.

Proctor, R. N. (2008). 'Agnotology: The Missing Term to Describe the Cultural Production of Ignorance (and Its Study)'. In *Agnotology. The Making and Unmaking of Ignorance*, edited by R. Proctor and L. Schiebinger, 1–36. Stanford, CA: Stanford University Press.

Riles, A. (2005). 'A New Agenda for the Cultural Study of Law: Taking on the Technicalities'. *Buffalo Law Review* 53(3): 973–1033.

——— (2011). *Collateral Knowledge: Legal Reasoning in the Global Financial Markets*. Chicago, IL: University of Chicago Press.

Ruggie, J. (2008). *Protect, Respect and Remedy: A Framework for Business and Human Rights, Report of the Special Representative of the Secretary-General on the Issue of Human Rights and Transnational Corporations and Other Business Enterprises*. Human Rights Council, UN Doc A/HRC/8/5 (7 April 2008).

Rühmkorf, A. (2018). 'Global Supply Chain Governance: The Search for "What Works"'. *Deakin Law Review* 23(1): 63–82.

Salminen, J. (2020). 'Towards a Genealogy and Typology of Governance through Contract beyond Privity'. *European Review of Contract Law* 16(1): 25–43.

Salminen, J. and M. Rajavuori (2019). 'Transnational Sustainability Laws and the Regulation of Global Value Chains: Comparison and a Framework for Analysis'. *Maastricht Journal of European and Comparative Law* 26(5): 602–27.

Salminen, J., M. Rajavuori, and K. H. Eller (2024). 'Global Value Chains as Regulatory Proxy: Transnationalizing the Internal Market through EU Law'. In *Foundations of European Transnational Private Law*, edited by A. Beckers, H. W. Micklitz, R. Vallejo, and R. Letto-Vanamo, 367–98. Oxford, UK: Hart.

Sarfaty, G. (2017). 'Can Big Data Revolutionize International Human Rights Law'. *University of Pennsylvania Journal of International Law* 39(1): 73–101.

——— (2020). 'Translating Modern Slavery into Management Practice'. *Law and Social Inquiry* 45(4): 1027–51.

——— (2021). 'Global Supply Chain Auditing'. In *Cambridge Handbook of Compliance*, edited by D. Sokol and B. van Rooij, 977–88. Cambridge, UK: Cambridge University Press.

Schleifer, P., M. Fiorini, and G. Auld (2019). 'Transparency in Transnational Governance: The Determinants of Information Disclosure of Voluntary Sustainability Programs'. *Regulation and Governance* 13(4): 488–506.

Shamir, H. (2012). 'A Labor Paradigm for Human Trafficking'. *UCLA Law Review* 60(1): 76–136.

Sobel-Read, K. (2014). 'Global Value Chains: A Framework for Analysis'. *Transnational Legal Theory* 5(3): 364–407.

Steuer, S. and T. Tröger (2022). 'The Role of Disclosure in Green Finance'. *Journal of Financial Regulation* 8(1): 1–50.

Tsing, A. (2012). 'Ordinary Catastrophe: Outsourcing Risk in Supply-Chain Capitalism'. In *Futures of Modernity*, edited by M. Heinlein et al., 51–64. Bielefeld: transcript Verlag.

Turner, B. (2016). 'Supply-chain Legal Pluralism: Normativity as Constitutive of Chain Infrastructure in the Moroccan Argan Oil Supply Chain'. *Journal of Legal Pluralism and Unofficial Law* 38(3): 378–414.

Valentinov, V., G. Verschraegen, and K. Van Assche (2019). 'The Limits of Transparency: A Systems Theory View'. *Systems Research and Behavioral Science* 36(3): 289–300.

Valverde, M. (2009). 'Jurisdiction and Scale: Legal "Technicalities" as Resources for Theory'. *Socio-Legal Studies* 18(2): 139–57.

Watson, A. (1993). *Legal Transplants: An Approach to Comparative Law*, 2nd edn. Athens, GA: University of Georgia Press.

Weber, M. (2013). *Economy and Society (1921/1922)*. Berkeley, CA: University of California Press.

White, Harrison H. C. (1981). 'Where Do Markets Come From?' *American Journal of Sociology* 87(3): 517–47.

Zeben, J. van (2020). 'The European Green Deal: The Future of a Polycentric Europe?' *European Law Journal* 26(5/6): 300–18.

2

Transparency Legislation in Global Value Chains

Decentralization, Market Power, and Global Hierarchies

Ioannis Kampourakis*

The Law of Global Value Chains

Global value chain (GVC) analysis captures how firms become the dominant organizational form in the coordination of global social relations of production (Baglioni et al., 2017: 315), breaking with state-centric approaches to understanding economic development. Changing patterns of global production and the prevalence of outsourcing mean that industrial capacity is owned by producers in developing countries but controlled to a significant extent by lead firms located in developed economies (Gereffi, 2018: 255). From this starting point, GVC analysis focuses on how global lead firms 'drive' the actions of other firms in the chain (Gereffi et al., 2005; Gibbon et al., 2008). These dynamics of 'drivenness' are undergirded by a legal infrastructure, which plays a crucial role for the governance and coordination of the chain and for the generation and distribution of economic value (The IGLP Law and Global Production Working Group, 2016; Danielsen, 2005). A key part of this legal infrastructure are mechanisms of contractual governance, which both ensure control over value chains and formalize power asymmetries among the different actors. For instance, suppliers might be pushed to assume disproportionate financial risk, while lead firms can disengage from their contractual relationships at their

* I am thankful to Klaas H. Eller, Jade Kosché, and Hila Shamir for their most helpful comments on earlier drafts.

discretion (Anner, 2020; Hering, 2021). Yet implicit in the capacity of lead firms to control and drive the chain through mechanisms of contractual governance is also their potential to act as regulators of the production process, possibly guaranteeing labour, social, and environmental standards by pressuring suppliers. Lead firms export legal frameworks that eventually shape the law on the ground, functioning as proxies of legal homogenization and isolating economic activities from the contingent exercise of national public authority (Ferrando, 2014). This opens a door for a possible re-internalization of 'externalities' of production – of aspects of the production process that have nothing to do with product quality standards, such as labour rights and environmental standards. In other words, while the fragmentation of global production initially enables divorcing value accumulation from liability for wrongdoing, the 'drivenness' of value chains by lead firms entails at least the theoretical possibility that such firms assume broader forms of regulatory capacity with regard to distanced stakeholders – workers along the supply chains and various local communities. The possibility that lead firms internalize 'externalities' of production in supply chains reflects the conceptual premise of private governance as a response to 'governance gaps' in the regulation of the global economy (Gereffi, 2018: 253).

As the social power held by lead firms and transnational corporations becomes more and more palpable, legislative attempts to regulate transnational corporate conduct proliferate. This includes attempts to impose external limitations through, for example, market regulations against unfair trading practices or the imposition of human rights due diligence obligations. It also includes attempts to trigger internal forces of self-limitation in the private governance of GVCs. This is part of the ambition of transparency legislation, which is the focus of this chapter.[1] By 'transparency legislation', I mean the various national and supranational laws imposing non-financial reporting requirements on corporations with regard to their social and environmental impact. In theory, transparency legislation has the potential to reinforce accountability in GVCs, facilitate reputational sanctions and social enforcement, and strengthen the involvement of civil society and stakeholders in the regulation of corporate conduct. Transparency legislation has been especially framed as a key instrument in addressing modern slavery in supply chains. A well-known example is the UK Modern Slavery Act (MSA) of 2015, but other examples include the California Transparency in Supply Chains Act of 2010, which was explicitly motivated by the goal of eradicating slavery and human trafficking from supply chains, the Australian Modern Slavery Act of 2018, and the recent Fighting Against Forced Labour and Child Labour in Supply Chains Act of 2023 in Canada. However, transparency legislation has been increasingly received with scepticism in academic and policy circles. Its shortcomings are primarily associated with the content of reporting, which, in most cases, remains limited to vague commitments, as well as with the lack of mechanisms for enforcement and oversight, and with a design of market-led accountability. As a result, suggestions for reform have included improving the content of disclosures – for example, by specifying and homogenizing reporting requirements and by prioritizing more contextual and comparable information – the integration of non-financial information with companies' understanding and reporting on value creation, publishing a list of companies that are covered under the legislation, or the introduction of an oversight body with the power to review corporate disclosures (see Secretary of State for the Home Dept., 2019: 2.5; Mantouvalou, 2018; Tsagas and Villiers, 2020; Alliance for Corporate Transparency, 2018; Chambers and Vastardis, 2021).

Yet, besides criticizing the effectiveness of this legislative trend, it is worth pondering on its underpinning logic. A question that emerges is why the quest to combat modern slavery has also assumed the form of disclosure obligations as an aspect of broader regulatory packages, what this form of legal obligations signifies, and whether it is a form that, in itself, has potential to deliver in its broader aspirations for social (and environmental) sustainability. In this direction, the aspiration of this chapter is to propose a critique of the conceptual core of transparency legislation and its decentralizing, reflexive logic. Indeed, while the account presented in this chapter is informed by the debates about transparency's effectiveness, my goal is neither to analyse the current technical features of transparency legislation, nor to discuss what transparency requirements can deliver and under what conditions. My argument is that transparency legislation constitutes an aspiration of decentralized regulation through the workings of private actors, resting on an epistemology that is defined by social complexity and the inability of centralized social action to control the centrifugal dynamics of different actors and systems. While this invitation of regulatory pluralism may open new possibilities of governance in GVCs by theoretically forcing firms to discard their deliberate ignorance about the workings of supply chains, it also constitutes an institutional form that avoids 'governing'. Its aspirations of sustainability and of 'eradicating' modern slavery hardly matched by its prescription of mandatory disclosures, transparency legislation is not designed to achieve specific outcomes but rather to offer a promise of accountability and of 're-embedding' markets into social relations as a remedy to liability deficits in fragmented global production. As a regulatory mode that encourages social enforcement and relies on pressures by the market and civil society, transparency legislation seeks to question the rigidity of classic dichotomies of hard law versus soft law, or mandatory versus voluntary forms of regulation, and challenges an exclusively statist understanding of bindingness. However, the reliance on social pressures reifies existing market power asymmetries, as is most evident from a global standpoint. The market oversight that is the condition for the success of transparency legislation is more likely to originate in the Global North, the end markets of which represent the largest share of added value in value chains. This means that social and environmental sustainability in the Global South, including the eradication of modern slavery, becomes dependent on consumer and investor activity in the Global North. As I will discuss in the final section, the reliance on social pressures and market oversight showcases the shortcomings of private governance with regard to democratic participation of those who are supposed to benefit from it, while it also limits the authority of developing states to negotiate the limits of corporate conduct and define the content of 'sustainability'.

In the next section, I discuss the scope and the rationale of transparency legislation, focusing in particular on transparency legislation that targets modern slavery. In the subsequent section, I unpack the key elements of the epistemology of transparency legislation as those of decentralization, lack of 'closure', and prioritization of accountability – as opposed to exercise – of power, while also highlighting the promise this entails for changing the internal dynamics of GVC governance. I also discuss how transparency legislation implicitly suggests a reconceptualization of legal bindingness. In the following section IV, I lay out the critique of how the logic of transparency legislation contributes to the entrenchment of global hierarchies. In the Conclusion, I warn against treating corporate power as an insurmountable reality and private ordering as the only option for regulating the global economy, calling instead for a reconstitution of public power. Recognizing that GVCs are not only permeated by law but also constituted by national and international legal ordering, I highlight the need for an institutional imagination that goes beyond decentralization and private ordering driven by lead firms, to encompass new designs of centralized social action in the global economy that may contribute to goals such as the eradication of modern slavery.

The Scope and Rationale of Transparency Legislation

The last decade saw non-financial reporting for corporate activity within GVCs shift from a voluntary business practice and a relatively marginal, outlandish regulatory requirement to a diffused and mainstream institutional arrangement.[2] Making a breakthrough in the US with Section 1502 of the Dodd–Frank Act of 2010 (relating to use of conflict minerals) and the California Transparency in Supply Chains Act of 2010, transparency legislation rose to prominence as a potential solution to instances of transnational corporate irresponsibility, especially with regard to modern slavery. Notable examples of general disclosures laws that target social and environmental sustainability are the EU Corporate Sustainability Reporting Directive of 2022 – expanding the scope of the earlier 2014/95/EU Directive on Non-Financial Reporting, the German Corporate Social Responsibility Directive Implementation Act of 2017, the Canadian Extractive Sector Transparency Measures Act of 2014, the Indian Companies Act of 2013, or the Danish Financial Statements Act of 2008. Transparency requirements are also subsidiary to recent human rights due diligence legislation, including the EU Corporate Sustainability Due Diligence Directive of 2023, the EU Regulation 2017/821 on conflict minerals, the German Supply Chain Due Diligence Act of 2021 (entered into force in January 2023), the French Duty of Vigilance Law of 2017, and the Dutch Child Labour Due Diligence Law of 2019. Yet human rights due diligence legislation goes beyond transparency legislation to mandate that companies conduct human rights due diligence in their supply chains – an obligation that could possibly trigger civil liability for negligence. While the analysis presented in this chapter is to a certain extent relevant for such legislation, which also operates within the paradigm of 'publicizing private actors',[3] my focus will be on transparency legislation and its disclosure requirements.

Disclosure requirements have been especially framed as a means to address modern slavery in supply chains. A paradigmatic example is the 2015 MSA, which requires companies that supply goods or services in the UK (even if not registered as UK entities) with an annual turnover above GBP 36 million to prepare an annual statement outlining the steps they have taken to ensure slavery and human trafficking are not taking place in any part of their business or supply chains (Section 54). Transparency legislation that does not target slavery explicitly has similar scope and requirements. The recent EU Corporate Sustainability Reporting Directive (CSRD) expands the scope of companies set by the 2014 Non-Financial Reporting Directive and mandates reporting annually on 'sustainability matters', that is, 'environmental, social and human rights, and governance factors' (rec. 28). On the basis of the 'double materiality' principle, companies must report about their influence on sustainability issues and about how these issues affect the company's growth, performance, and position.

A key aspect of Section 54 of the MSA, and one that has been the target of critiques, is its light-touch approach to compliance. In describing the content of the statement, Section 54 suggests that it '*may* include information about' different categories (§ 5, emphasis added), while, most importantly, allowing companies to issue a statement that simply confirms that the organization has taken no steps to eradicate slavery and trafficking from its supply chains (§ 4b). Similarly, the Australian Modern Slavery Act of 2018 subjects companies failing to comply with the requirement for a modern slavery statement to 'naming and shaming' sanctions (§ 11) only, and the California Transparency in Supply Chains Act of 2010 allows companies to 'disclose to what extent, *if any*' it engages in particular activity or conduct (§ 3c, emphasis added). This provision in the California Act makes the Act's provision for injunctive relief (§ 3d) substantially inconsequential, as companies may be in compliance by simply reporting that they have taken no steps to eradicate slavery from their supply chains and thus be subject only to any reputational sanctions. Beyond slavery and human trafficking, but along similar lines, in the Dodd–Frank Act of 2010, compliance enforcement is dependent on private action: if a company denies use of conflict minerals, shareholders injured in the sale or purchase of a security by false or misleading statements by corporate insiders could incite compliance through a private right of action under the Securities Laws; however, the Securities and Exchange Commission lacks capacity to validate the company's report (Woody, 2012: 1338). Certain other transparency laws beyond modern slavery have a more enforceable character. For example, the German CSR Implementation Act is more invasive, prescribing heavy fines in the case of non-compliance with disclosure requirements. However, even in this case, there is no regulatory oversight to ensure the quality of the disclosures – a task which is implicitly in all cases entrusted to civil society actors (Chambers and Vastardis, 2021: 327). Such differences in enforcement aside, the key feature of transparency legislation for modern slavery, and more broadly for sustainability, is that it does not impose any obligations beyond disclosures.

The seemingly limited material scope of transparency legislation hardly matches the larger vision that inspires it. Whether explicitly, such as in the case of the UK and the Australian Modern Slavery Acts designed to address slavery and human trafficking, or in the case of Section 1502 of the Dodd–Frank Act designed to address use of conflict minerals emanating from the Congo region and the relevant humanitarian crisis, or more implicitly, such as in the case of the CSRD Directive, which seeks to contribute to the EU Green Deal goals of decoupling economic growth from resource use – transparency legislation takes transnational corporate power seriously. In other words, the increasing capacity of transnational corporations to coordinate and control crucial aspects of global production, not least through their mechanisms of supply chain contractual governance, brings to the foreground their responsibility for aspects conventionally understood as 'externalities' of production, such as labour conditions, social welfare, and environmental protection. The rationale behind the adoption of transparency legislation is partly to frame lead firms as the *regulators* of globalized production (Salminen and Rajavuori, 2019: 604), prompting them to address slavery in their supply chains and to steer such production towards goals of sustainability more broadly. The aspiration to see lead firms incorporate social values is not expressed through direct, top-down prescription and legal sanctions. Indeed, substantive compliance is voluntary, with laws like the MSA facilitating primarily reputational sanctions. Rather, transparency obligations are meant to trigger more subtle forms of stakeholder and shareholder stewardship (see Katelouzou, 2019), while also involving civil society and consumers (Reimer and Leslie, 2006) in a process of exerting learning pressures on corporate policies. Ethical consumerism, socially responsible investors, and procurement contracts tied to sustainability factors, civil society movements, and media pressures are the envisioned catalysts of a change of corporate culture towards incorporating social values. In an ideal scenario, this form of public regulation could function as a trigger for self-reflexivity and corporate self-change. This means that, under the pressures of civil society and increasingly socially responsible markets, transnational corporations would introduce binding internal norms and systems of monitoring of their societal responsibilities across their supply chain networks. As such, their transnational private ordering would in theory be permeated by social considerations, binding suppliers and creating ripple effects of social welfare protection, especially in the fields of labour rights and environmental protection.

A widespread critique against non-financial transparency is that it does not deliver on its promises (LeBaron and Rühmkorf, 2017). Disclosures are too selective and superficial (Rao and Bernaz, 2020; Birkey et al., 2018), while the information that most companies provide – often focussing solely on general commitments – does not allow readers to understand their impacts (Alliance for Corporate Transparency, 2018: 7). Reporting schemes might even allow companies to camouflage unsustainable practices with only symbolic compliance, while they could also be used as a pretext to displace more intrusive forms of regulation. Not unlike functionalist critiques of CSR (see the discussion in Bartley, 2005), or of transparency regulation in general (Fung et al., 2007), this perspective focuses on how transparency legislation in supply chains is a means to an end: transparency is employed as a regulatory tool to achieve the goal of enhancing corporate responsibility and sustainability along value chains, and it has to be evaluated based on whether it achieves said goals. Beyond critiques of mandatory disclosures in terms of their effectiveness, I focus this chapter and critique on the internal logic of transparency requirements as a mode of regulation. This logic needs to be unpacked and criticized not solely on the basis of the concrete outcomes it produces but also for how it addresses the issue of knowledge and information in the global economy and for how it reconceives and uses the legal form. I will now delve into how transparency legislation is imbued by an epistemology of decentralization and reflexivity, before moving on to how this reinforces market power asymmetries and global hierarchies.

Transparency Regulation and Global (Un)Governance

The Epistemology of Transparency Legislation

Transparency legislation is meant to be effective in a setting of a hyper-complex, 'sublime' (Slobodian, 2018: 47) world economy. Transparency obligations could be understood as the type of regulatory intervention that takes as its starting point the 'knowledge problem' in the construction of a social and economic order: How can any form of regulation – much less planning – be effective when there is no central authority or institution that can have a functional overview over the dispersed knowledge of the market economy (Hayek ,1945)? For Hayek, societal progress unfolds in parallel with the division and fragmentation of knowledge (Hayek, 1960: 24). As it becomes clear that increasing social complexity makes it impossible for any central agent, such as the state, to utilize the sum of the dispersed human knowledge, aspirations of centralized economic coordination must necessarily cede their place to solutions of decentralization. For Hayek, the most successful societies are those in which each individual is able to put their own local knowledge to its best uses (Hayek, 1945: 520). Economic coordination should be left up to the decentralized price mechanism, which is meant to convey the necessary information that enables individuals to make the best use of the resources available to them (Hayek, 1945: 528).

From a Hayekian perspective, then, awareness of the knowledge deficit of planners and regulators needs to be transposed to the institutional level and guide institutional practice. Could a similar methodology of decentralization guide legal institutions invested in social coordination? Just like Hayek's epistemology stems from a demarcation of the limits of reason to deliberately steer and transform society (Caldwell, 1997: 1872; Slobodian, 2018: 224), I suggest that transparency legislation reflects a similar 'humility' – and, in fact, distrust – about the potential of centralized social engineering. With transparency legislation, the design of a sustainable economy is entrusted to the decentralized coordination of a plurality of actors, with the state simply adjusting the incentives for the circulation of the necessary information. Behind this epistemology of decentralization lies the vision of the spontaneous order of the market economy readjusting itself to incorporate social concerns. Indeed, for Hayek, spontaneously organized complex phenomena carry significantly more potential than deliberately designed orders for the preservation and utilization of past knowledge because they are the products of genuine social evolution and not of artificial design (Hayek, 1960: 62). Following a similar logic, if transparency legislation could build social and environmental concerns into the DNA of markets – as opposed to the state imposing obligations transnational corporations can evade or only nominally follow – then this would supposedly have more beneficial consequences for everyone who partakes in these spontaneous orders.

Transparency legislation is different from classic outcome-oriented regulation, in the sense that it is deliberately designed as a never-ending process. While there is a sketch of an aspirational end-state of a sustainable and fair global economy without slavery and human trafficking, there is no concrete set of adjustments or institutional arrangements that will lead there, other than the vague aspiration to trigger internal forces of corporate self-limitation and reflexivity. Transparency legislation abandons the search for 'closure', for actually achieving a proclaimed goal, as it endorses the premise of an ever-increasing social complexity, according to which it is impossible to decisively match specific institutional structures with desired outcomes (see Desai and Lang, 2020). From this perspective, transparency requirements form part of what Desai and Lang call 'global ungovernance', which denotes transnational institution-building projects which 'at once pursue big visions with claims to universality and at the same time offer no adequate prescriptions' (Desai and Lang, 2020: 220). Yet, crucially, through this process, corporate actors are framed as rule-makers and enforcers. Transparency legislation is not only built on explicitly limited knowledge of 'what works' (Rühmkorf, 2018) – hence the reliance on corporate actors directing production – but it is also deliberately vague on what it is that it would work *for* – what the desired outcome is. This is particularly the case with transparency legislation that has broad goals, such as the CSRD. Even though it is clear that sustainability is a value worth preserving, its very content remains indeterminate (Tsagas and Villiers, 2020; Gray, 2010). Even the more precise targeting of modern slavery entails a degree of indeterminacy, as the term itself is not specifically defined in the MSA or in other relevant acts and may still be understood as lacking legal clarity, currently encompassing various forms of coercion that are prohibited by international legal instruments (Nolan and Bott, 2018: 47). The obscurity about an end goal that is only schematically outlined also precludes the possibility of failure. Rather than a map to a particular destination, transparency obligations should be understood as an experimental form, possibly providing the impetus for new legal innovations that might, in their turn, also approach an ideal of social and environmental sustainability without properly concretizing it (see Johns, 2015).

Furthermore, transparency reforms in GVCs can be better dissected when placed in the context of the broader institutional and social move towards transparency. From national and international governmental institutions to private actors and to social movements, transparency has emerged as both a regulatory mode associated with accountability, legitimacy, and a political ideal. According to Pierre Rosanvallon (2008), the origins of the persistence on transparency as a supra-ideological form of governance can be traced to a 'de-ideologization' of politics and to a disenchantment with the promise of mass politics and centralized political transformations (2008: 46). Transparency signifies the passage to a new form of democratic governance where the goal is not to conquer and exercise power but rather to make it transparent and accountable (Rosanvallon, 2008: 256). Similarly, transparency legislation in GVCs seeks to make the exercise of power within GVCs more accountable without questioning the otherwise expanding authority of private actors in directing global production.

Nevertheless, its resistance to 'closure' notwithstanding, transparency legislation creates new dynamics and opportunities for GVC regulation and governance that should not be immediately dismissed. The notion that lead firms can and must acquire information about the conduct of actors beyond their immediate vicinity frames lead firms as potential regulators of vast networks of supply chains. Yet understanding 'knowledge' as something achievable by lead firms is a *legal fiction*. Contrary to lead firms' usual claims of ignorance of events in the distant corners of their supply chain networks, in this case the legal structure itself creates the preconditions for 'knowledge': knowledge not in the sense of direct awareness of all facts but in the sense of governability – of burdening lead firms with the assumption that their overarching position implies that access to information is at least possible.[4] The governability of GVCs by means of transparency regulations would be facilitated, as Klaas Eller suggests in this volume, if transparency rules in GVCs targeted the collection and generation of information, as opposed to the presentation of information, as they currently do (Eller, 2025). By forcing lead firms to abandon their deliberate ignorance, transparency legislation could pave the way for new forms of supply chain liability. In that direction, corporate sustainability reports have been used by plaintiffs in recent cases of human rights violations to make the case for the existence of a prima facie duty of care of lead firms towards the workers and communities harmed by the activities of subsidiaries or suppliers (Chambers and Vastardis, 2021: 345; see *Jabir v. Kik*, 7 O 95/15; *Lungowe v. Vedanta Resources plc*, [2017] EWCA Civ 1528). However, so far, this has not been successful in cases of supply chain liability, while cases of parent company liability for harm committed by subsidiaries have recently had some success (see *Four Nigerian Farmers and Milieudefensie v. Shell*).

Transparency requirements might also play a role in shaping future patterns of firm boundaries, as they increase the importance of knowledge networks that transcend current boundaries (Foss 2002: 14). The rise to prominence of social auditing, in different configurations (including internal auditors and third-party auditors), is an indication of how lead firms have extended control over externalities of the production process without exercising ownership (see Jenkins, 2001; Locke et al., 2007: 61). Beyond social auditing, by recognizing the driving role of lead firms in GVCs, transparency legislation could possibly lead to 'new organisational forms' (Daft and Lewin, 1993), that is, to new ways of structuring the boundaries of the firm and its relations to the market, conceivably by prioritizing stable, long-term contracts with suppliers (Andersen and Skjoett-Larsen, 2009) or by 'rationalising' supply chains, reducing the number of suppliers to make oversight possible (Gereffi, 2014: 15). As such, certain effects of transparency regulation on the political economy of transnational firms could be palpable.

Reconceptualizing Legal Bindingness

I argued that the epistemology of transparency is one of decentralization, resistance to closure, and prioritization of accountability – as opposed to exercise – of power. I also suggested that this epistemology has the capacity to change the internal dynamics of GVCs, including the possibility of formalizing the driving role of lead firms with beneficial effects for suppliers, and presumably for workers and communities. Based on this reading, transparency legislation does not, at first, appear in line with a neoliberal perspective that accepts the economy as an 'internal limit to government' and only promotes the laws seen as necessary to protect the competitive order (Slobodian, 2018: 270).

Instead, transparency legislation has a reformist angle, drawing from theories of *reflexivity* and *responsiveness*. From this perspective, regulation can be most effective by becoming internalized by the multiplicity of social actors. In other words, the ultimate goal of regulation is to function as a learning instrument, reinterpreted and incorporated by the private actors subjected to it. In legal theory, the concept of reflexive law (Teubner, 1983) captures how regulation could avoid the pitfalls of substantive regulation without devolving into deregulation by promoting the institutionalization of reflexive structures within private actors. Such structures would eventually enhance the self-regulatory and self-limiting capacities of private actors. This is both functionally necessary, as central agents lack the necessary knowledge to inhibit the expansion of destructive rationalities that private actors may develop (Teubner, 2011a: 36–37), and normatively desirable, as it advances the agenda of democratization and constitutionalization of the economy (Teubner, 2012). Regulatory theories of 'responsive regulation', 'decentred regulation', 'new governance', or the 'post-regulatory state' (Ayres and Braithwaite, 1992; Black, 2008; Lobel, 2004; Scott, 2004) have similarly attempted to capture such regulatory transformations, stressing the importance of flexibility, negotiation, guidance, and internalization, as opposed to coercion and sanctions. In their most aspirational form, obligations of transparency could constitute the kind of reflexive structure that starts a process of self-constitutionalization of transnational companies. This is because public regulation, especially if coupled with further forms of external contestation – such as public campaigns, ethical consumerism and investing, processes of monitoring and certification, and so on – can in theory trigger the adoption of internal corporate norms that the company itself understands as binding. Significantly, such codes can then 'travel' transnationally and bind suppliers through mechanisms of contractual governance (Reinke and Zumbansen, 2019).

This reflexive logic of transparency legislation questions the rigidity of classic dichotomies of hard law versus soft law, or mandatory versus voluntary forms of regulation. Before normatively assessing the blurring of such distinctions, it is worth examining the narrative that supports it in its own terms. According to Eller (2025), questioning established dichotomies is not only part of transparency's conceptual appeal, but it also means that it should not be dismissed by sole reference to the very categories that it challenges (that it is too 'soft' or too 'voluntary'). To understand how transparency requirements, ingrained within broader CSR corporate policies, might challenge an exclusively statist understanding of bindingness, it is important to appreciate how the securement of market power in GVCs involves both business strategy and political manoeuvring (Levy and Palpacuer, 2017). Indeed, as firms negotiate their external environments and engage in multi-layered alliances and struggles with various stakeholders and other firms, civil society actors may use the leverage provided by norms, the status of which is officially non-binding, to achieve their own goals. Bartley and Egels-Zandén (2016) discuss an example where they draw attention to how union activists in Indonesia have used CSR commitments to achieve their goals, including through appeals to brands' compliance staff to resolve grievances with factory managers. In addition, transnational activist networks, such as the Clean Clothes Campaign, have lobbied for both legally binding and voluntary standards, recognizing that the latter could also provide leverage for workers (Palpacuer, 2017). In complex settings of GVC governance, where considerations of concrete reputational harm or downgrading of market position might be more significant than the distant possibility of sanctions imposed by national law, the social reality of 'bindingess' might well be different than that of the law in the books. The transformation of bindingness can be captured by pluralist, non-essentialist theories of law. According to Tamanaha (2000: 313), 'law is whatever people identify and treat through their social practices as "law"'. Rather than clinging on some form of 'publicness' and legal centralism as the key to (transnational) social transformation, transparency legislation seeks to reconfigure private governance by prompting internal corporate change, reinforcing the notion that private actors can and should become loci of both norm-production and norm-enforcement.

This narrative seeks to question the extent to which 'voluntarism' only describes a purely 'voluntary' reliance on market incentives (Sabel et al., 2000: 2), suggesting that it instead constitutes a backdoor to legal hardening, at least in specific contexts (Ruggie, 2017: 329). Courts may 'pierce the corporate veil', recognizing parent firm liability for subsidiaries' or even suppliers' conduct, inviting parent firms to take the monitoring and enforcement of codes of conduct more seriously. Codes of conduct themselves may, in certain situations, be interpreted as enforceable based on national law (Beckers, 2015), while public corporate commitments may give rise to a duty of care (see *Choc v. Hudbay Minerals Inc.* [2013] ONSC 1414). From this perspective, the kind of voluntary self-regulation that might be stirred by transparency legislation makes part of a material, patchwork quilt-like 'global constitution' (Teubner, 2011b: 197), which comprises both public and private regulation and harnesses the diverse societal forces of contestation to achieve the limitation of corporate rationalities.

However, it is questionable how pervasive the erosion of the soft law/hard law dichotomy in GVC governance is, while it is also debatable whether such an erosion always favours the limitation of powerful corporate actors. The pervasiveness of the erosion of classic dichotomies and the transcendence of 'voluntarism' depends on a series of material conditions. First, differences in firms' purpose, size, industry, and exposure to consumer pressures could result in varying degrees of existence or importance of reputational sanctions. Arguably, transparency legislation and its goal to facilitate public scrutiny and social pressures in order to trigger internal norms of self-limitation are less likely to be effective in settings where exposure to reputational damage is less probable due to the nature of goods or services produced (Berman, 2018; Baglioni et al., 2017: 320; Gereffi, 2018: 261). Second, for 'voluntary' schemes to be synergetic with public regulation or pave the way for 'legal hardening', there needs to be a substratum of public regulation or case law, along the lines of the examples mentioned above. While recent developments in a number of jurisdictions show potential for the generalization of such fruitful couplings, they remain so far inconsistent.[5] As LeBaron and Rümkorf (2017) show in their work, and contrary to the hypothesis of mutual reinforcement of public regulation and private governance (Locke, 2013: 177), the integration of private governance into public legislation can in fact undermine effectiveness (LeBaron and Rühmkorf, 2017: 26). Third, transparency legislation and the voluntary private schemes it seeks to instigate depend on the magnitude and quality of civil society's and the market's reactions. Regulation becomes meaningful through harnessing the dynamics of the social sphere (Lange and Haines, 2015). Yet the social sphere has already been shaped and determined by patterns of social hierarchy and distributional inequality. Elevating 'the Social' to a quasi-institutionalized actor for the limitation of transnational corporate activity reifies the asymmetries of social and market power into concrete legal arrangements (Kampourakis, 2021).

Embedding Global Hierarchies

It is not sufficient to suggest that reliance of transparency requirements on social pressures and reputational sanctions to become meaningful reifies market power asymmetries. Rather, it is necessary to perceive such market asymmetries in their global dimension. Despite changing patterns in end markets (Gereffi, 2014: 22), reputational sanctions and social pressures associated with ethical consumerism and the risk of disinvestment are more likely to originate in the consumer and capital markets of the Global North, which still lead world trade in merchandise and commercial services (WTO, 2019) and, most importantly, in share of added value through branding and design (UNCTAD, 2015).[6] This creates a situation in which transnational corporate actors based in the Global North are meant to use their internal and contractual systems of governance to implement reforms of environmental sustainability and social justice in the Global South as a result of market activity in the Global North (see Gereffi, 2018: 270). As such, facilitating the scrutiny of corporate conduct is not devoid of spatial and geographical connotations akin to those of core-periphery. This has an effect both on framing the limits of participation of individuals and communities in the production of norms that are to better their lives and on shaping the role of developing states in a global arena of power asymmetries.

From the perspective of individuals and communities subjected to private power, this means that they do not partake, at least indirectly, in the co-authorship of the laws that govern them. Critical and TWAIL scholarship has been attentive to how the emergence of a transnational law without state deprives even the ones who are supposed to benefit from it of a 'public voice' (Chimni, 2006: 13; Shamir, 2009: 113; Lichuma, 2021: 532), while ethnographic research also points to how local communities may lack effective participation mechanisms and yet be conceptualized as consenting contractual parties to corporate operations and providers of a 'Social License' to operate through empirical manifestations of a legally fabricated reciprocity (Knöpfel, 2020: 135). One powerful answer to the challenge of inadequate democratic legitimacy and 'voice' in private governance schemes that effective internalization of transparency rules might lead to is Teubner's suggestion that the democratic principle may be recontextualized (Teubner, 2018). The democratic principle needs not be confined within a traditional understanding of political representation but can instead take multiple forms, depending on the different epistemes of the diverse social systems in which it seeks to materialize. In that direction, the principle of *self-contestation*, that is, the responsiveness to external stimuli and pressures, and the institutionalization of sites of internal dissent, may be crucial in recontextualizing the democratic principle in transnational regimes. For example, this theoretical direction could translate into the demand for increased participation of workers and affected communities in corporate decision-making bodies. While this account entails a promise for transnational private governance, it is still susceptible to the same critique of relying on a social sphere that is permeated by structural inequalities, most glaringly on a global level, and to a further critique of reducing the demand for co-authorship to the possibility to dissent and contest decisions made by others.

From the perspective of power differentials among states, transparency legislation reinforces the authority of lead firms as regulators of GVCs, based on standards and obligations set by national legal frameworks as established in the firms' home jurisdictions. As such, not only companies but also states export their order through the legal bubbles of global networks of production. As Sundhya Pahuja (2019: 79–80) underlines, this is not in itself a novelty in the history of corporations in international law, as transnational corporations' authority can be seen on a continuum with that of colonial companies. At the same time, however, the demand of the Third World as a political and a juridical project was to subject the conduct of transnational corporations to an international legal framework, and leave the question of property, including limitations to foreign investment, to the national authority of host states (Pahuja, 2019: 82).[7] While the prospects of the latter part of that equation have been severely squeezed – even if not without contestation – by international investment law, aspects of the former part are actively debated in the discussions on an international legally binding treaty on business and human rights (see A/HRC/RES/26/9, 2014). Transparency legislation, however, points to a different path, a path in which the limits to corporate conduct are not decided in a centric fashion through international negotiations among formally equal sovereign states but instead – not unlike the regulatory model of the United Nations Guiding Principles on Business and Human Rights – remain flexible, to be determined by 'the courts of public opinion' (Ruggie, 2008: para. 54). Yet, as the driving motor of self-regulation is coded in economic terms, in market incentives and sanctions, 'public opinion' denotes the populations that have the market power to deliver such incentives or sanctions. This entails a risk of the sustainability-through-transparency discourse degenerating into another version of the 'moral responsibility' of the 'developed West' towards 'the global poor' (Pahuja, 2019: 86). The distancing from legal centralism and international law means that developing states cannot impose their rationality on corporations, which instead become accountable to the vagaries of market ethics of the Global North.

Finally, a broader critique of transparency legislation as a potential contributor to global inequalities comes from the very understanding of sustainability that underpins it. As stressed above, 'sustainability', 'sustainable development', and 'social responsibility' are open signifiers, indeterminate until filled with concrete content. All these concepts remain open to critiques that 'sustainable development is overtly directed towards sustaining growth-based development' (Pahuja, 2017: 32) and more broadly to 'greenwashing' (Cock, 2011). As Gray (2010) highlights, not only is there often a clear divergence between planetary or social sustainability and corporate sustainability, but already the core of sustainability necessarily reflects value judgements about politics, nature, and morality. If the determining factor is then 'who decides' on the desirable characteristics, metrics, qualities, and indicators of sustainability that non-financial reporting should cover, then the more that disclosure requirements set by law become specific, the more the national law of states where transnational corporations are registered extends its influence in the determination of worldwide political, social, and ecological priorities. In that sense, even promising reforms of the reporting landscape, such as Tsagas and Villiers's (2020) call to simplify reporting or Chambers and Vastardis's (2021) suggestion for formal oversight and enforcement, are bound to flesh out a concept of sustainability that is determinant for states, communities, and individuals that have not participated in its making.

Conclusion: Whither Public Power?

GVCs are not only permeated with law in the form of contractual governance but also constituted by national and international law in the first place. While it is recognized that changes in the global economy, such as the shift to offshore outsourcing, have profound implications for public governance, it is often forgotten how such changes were originally a product of institutional arrangements, in particular reforms of trade and market liberalization, as well as labour under-regulation associated with export-led growth. As GVC analysis focuses on inter-firm linkages and the role of lead firms as drivers of the chain and gatekeepers to market integration and upgrading, the importance of the state seemingly recedes in the background (Bair, 2005: 174). While shifting the attention to the power and potential of private ordering is analytically justified (see Danielsen, 2005), regulatory reforms that take corporate power as both their starting point and an unsurpassable reality cannot fully detach from the paradigm of private governance and thus share its promises and shortcomings. This is the case of transparency legislation. However, while taking corporate power and the norm-setting capacity of transnational private actors seriously is necessary in the context of the globalized economy, it does not follow that designs of centralized social action, public enforcement, and international coordination are obsolete. As GVCs have been constituted by legal ordering, legal ordering could also dismantle, reform, or repurpose them. There is no conceptual reason why private ordering should set the horizon of possibility for addressing modern slavery – or sustainability more broadly – in supply chains. In addition, not only does the state remain an important actor in GVCs as regulator, producer, and buyer (Horner, 2017), but there is also growing evidence of a trend towards stronger public regulation in the large emerging economies (Gereffi, 2018: 267). Furthermore, revived scholarly interest in the New International Economic Order proposals of the 1970s (see Slobodian, 2018) draws attention to how international cooperation for the regulation of the global economy based on principles of fairness remains a feasible – even if currently politically distant – aspiration and a guiding vision for legal transformation.

Transparency legislation constitutes a regulatory mode that is the antipode of such centralized designs, relying on market oversight and social enforcement as opposed to public authority in decision-making and enforcement. Beyond existing, practical shortcomings in being effective, the logic of transparency legislation could open an avenue for the responsibilization of lead firms as regulators of transnational networks of production, with possible beneficial repercussions for inter-firm relations, and the prospects of joint liability for human rights violations or environmental damage. At the same time, however, it is a logic that doubles down on the diffusion and prevalence of transnational private ordering instead of attempting to reassert public power – either through state institutions and public regulation or through the constitution of public power in transnational regimes, for example through more active participation of stakeholders in corporate decision-making. Yet, the recognition that GVCs are constituted by law serves as a reminder that more ambitious projects of redesign of the global economy are not by default beyond reach. It is through such a reconstitution of public power that aspirations of tackling modern slavery in supply chains may more likely be fulfilled.

Notes

1. For example, according to the EU Non-Financial Reporting Directive 2014/95/EU, 'disclosure of non-financial information is vital for managing change towards a sustainable global economy by combining long-term profitability with social justice and environmental protection' (rec. 3). However, this does

not mean that the 'ambition' of non-financial disclosures is one-dimensional: The openness of references such as 'sustainable global economy' indicates that transparency legislation is not designed in an outcome-oriented fashion.

2. Prior to the emergence and proliferation of transparency legislation discussed in this chapter, voluntary reporting initiatives, such as the Global Reporting Initiative Sustainability Reporting, had already been widespread (see KPMG, 2017).
3. Human rights due diligence legislation not only includes provisions of transparency (for example, making public a 'vigilance plan'), but it also often invites corporations to set the standards of conduct themselves (for example, in the French Duty of Vigilance Law). This exemplifies a reflexive logic that relies on reputational sanctions and social pressures, which is similar to the logic of transparency legislation I criticize in this chapter.
4. For instance, the recent Norwegian Draft Act of 2019 prescribes the 'duty to know' of 'salient risks that may have an adverse impact on fundamental human rights and decent work, both within the enterprise itself and in its supply chains' (Norwegian Draft Act, § 5[2]).
5. With regard to public regulation, Beckers (2015) brings up the example of Article 2(d) of the EU Consumer Sales Directive, which makes possible enforcement of public declarations used by traders in marketing, insofar as these characterize the product. With regard to case law that might create the synergies for 'legal hardening' of private governance, see, for example, the recent case *Four Nigerian Farmers and Milieudefensie v. Shell* [2021], Gerechtshof Den Haag ECLI:NL:GHDHA:2015:3588 on the duty of care, even if limited, of parent companies for the actions of their subsidiaries, as well as the similarly recent *Okpabi and others v. Royal Dutch Shell Plc and another* [2021] UKSC 3, in which the English Supreme Court recognized that the parent company could owe a duty of care to those harmed by the acts of a foreign subsidiary.
6. Developing countries usually participate in GVCs as providers of relatively unskilled labour and services, and do not hold the strategic control over the whole GVC machine. Thus, the 'true' value of their manufacturing exports is grossly overstated by traditional trade statistics (see UNCTAD, 2015).
7. In this direction, see also the proposals for a New International Economic Order in 1974, which acknowledged that the existing international economic order made it impossible to achieve even and balanced development and, among other things, called for effective sovereign control over natural resources and economic activities and for the regulation of transnational corporations (UN General Assembly, 1974).

References

Alliance for Corporate Transparency (2018). *2018 Research Report: The State of Corporate Sustainability Disclosure under the EU Non-Financial Reporting Directive.* https://corporatejusticecoalition.org/wp-content/uploads/2019/02/2018_Research_Report_Alliance_Corporate_Transparency-66d0af6a05f153119e7cffe6df2f11b094affe9aaf4b13ae14db04e395c54a84.pdf.

Andersen, M. and T. Skjoett-Larsen (2009). 'Corporate Social Responsibility in Global Supply Chains'. *Supply Chain Management: An International Journal* 14(2): 75–86.

Anner, M. (2020). *Abandoned? The Impact of Covid-19 on Workers and Businesses at the Bottom of Global Garment Supply Chains.* Research Report for the Center for Global Workers' Rights (CGWR).

Ayres, I. and J. Braithwaite (1992). *Responsive Regulation: Transcending the Deregulation Debate.* Oxford, UK: Oxford University Press.

Baglioni, E., L. Campling, and E. Havice (2017). 'The Nature of the Firm in Global Value Chains'. In *The Corporation. A Critical, Multi-disciplinary Handbook*, edited by G. Baars and A. Spicer, 314–25. Cambridge, UK: Cambridge University Press.

Bair, J. (2005). 'Global Capitalism and Commodity Chains: Looking Back, Going Forward'. *Competition and Change* 9(2): 153–80.

Bartley, T. (2005). 'Corporate Accountability and the Privatization of Labor Standards: Struggles over Codes of Conduct in the Apparel Industry'. *Research in Political Sociology* 14: 211–44.

Bartley, T. and N. Egels-Zandén. (2016). 'Beyond Decoupling: Unions and the Leveraging of Corporate Social Responsibility in Indonesia'. *Socio-Economic Review* 14(2): 231–55.

Beckers, A. (2015) *Enforcing Corporate Social Responsibility Codes: On Global Self-regulation and National Private Law.* Oxford, UK: Hart.

Berman, C., (2018). *Written Evidence from the Ethical Trading Initiative.* Available at https://perma.cc/75GR-GQKJ.

Birkey, R. N., R. P. Guidry, M. A, Islam, and D. M. Patten (2018). 'Mandated Social Disclosure: An Analysis of the Response to the California Transparency in Supply Chains Act of 2010'. *Journal of Business Ethics* 152(3): 827–41.

Black, J. (2008). 'Constructing and Contesting Legitimacy and Accountability in Polycentric Regulatory Regimes'. *Regulation and Governance* 2(2): 137–64.

Caldwell, B. (1997). 'Hayek and Socialism'. *Journal of Economic Literature* 35(4): 1856–90.

Chambers, R. and A. Y. Vastardis (2021). 'Human Rights Disclosure and Due Diligence Laws: The Role of Regulatory Oversight in Ensuring Corporate Accountability'. *Chicago Journal of International Law* 21(2): 323–66.

Chimni, B. S. (2006). 'Third World Approaches to International Law: A Manifesto'. *International Community Law Review* 8(1): 3–27.

Cock, J. (2011). '"Green Capitalism" or Environmental Justice? A Critique of the Sustainability Discourse'. *Focus* 63: 45–51.

Daft, R. L. and A. Y. Lewin (1993). 'Where Are the Theories for the "New" Organizational Forms? An Editorial Essay'. *Organization Science* 4(4): i–iv.

Danielsen, D. (2005). 'How Corporations Govern: Taking Corporate Power Seriously in Transnational Regulation and Governance'. *Harvard International Law Journal* 46(2): 411–25.

Desai, D. and A. Lang (2020). 'Introduction: Global Un-governance'. *Transnational Legal Theory* 11(3): 219–43.

Eller, K. H. (2025). 'The Information Architecture of Corporate Accountability: Inside Corporate Reporting Regimes in Global Value Chains'. In *Modern Slavery and the Governance of Global Value Chains*, edited by H. Shamir, B. Arora, S. Banerjee, and T. Barkay. Cambridge, UK: Cambridge University Press.

Ferrando, T. (2014). 'Private Legal Transplant: Multinational Enterprises as Proxies of Legal Homogenisation'. *Transnational Legal Theory* 5(1): 20–59.

Foss, N. J. (2002). '"Coase vs Hayek": Economic Organization and the Knowledge Economy'. *International Journal of the Economics of Business* 9(1): 9–35.

Fung, A., M. Graham, and D. Weil (2007). *Full Disclosure: The Perils and Promise of Transparency*. Cambridge, UK: Cambridge University Press.

Gereffi, G. (2014). 'Global Value Chains in a Post-Washington Consensus World'. *Review of International Political Economy* 21(1): 9–37.

——— (2018). *Global Value chains and Development: Redefining the Contours of 21st Century Capitalism*. Cambridge, UK: Cambridge University Press.

Gereffi, G., J. Humphrey, and T. Sturgeon (2005). 'The Governance of Global Value Chains'. *Review of International Political Economy* 1(1): 78–104.

Gibbon, P., J. Bair, and S. Ponte (2008). 'Governing Global Value Chains: An Introduction'. *Economy and Society* 37(3): 315–38.

Gray, R. (2010). 'Is Accounting for Sustainability Actually Accounting for Sustainability … and How Would We Know? An Exploration of Narratives of Organisations and the Planet'. *Accounting, Organizations, and Society* 35(1): 47–62.

Hayek, F. A. (1945). 'The Use of Knowledge in Society'. *American Economic Review* 35(4): 519–30.

——— (1960). *The Constitution of Liberty*. Chicago, IL: University of Chicago Press.

Hering, M. (2021). 'The Unequal Impact of COVID-19 in the Global Apparel Industry'. Available at: www.asser.nl/DoingBusinessRight/Blog/post/the-unequal-impact-of-covid-19-in-the-global-apparel-industry-part-i-the-contractual-roots-by-merec.

Horner, R. (2017). 'Beyond Facilitator? State Roles in Global Value Chains and Global Production Networks'. *Geography Compass* 11(2): e12307.

Jenkins, R. (2001). 'Corporate Codes of Conduct: Self-regulation in a Global Economy'. United Nations Research Institute for Social Development.

Johns, F. (2015). 'On Failing Forward: Neoliberal Legality in the Mekong River Basin'. *Cornell International Law Journal* 48(2): 347–83.

Kampourakis, I. (2021). 'The Postmodern Legal Ordering of the Economy'. *Indiana Journal of Global Legal Studies* 28(1): 101–52.

Katelouzou, D. (2019). 'Shareholder Stewardship: A Case of (Re)-Embedding the Institutional Investors and the Corporation?' In *The Cambridge Handbook of Corporate Law, Corporate Governance and Sustainability* (Cambridge Law Handbooks), edited by B. Sjåfjell and C. M. Bruner, 581–95. Cambridge, UK: Cambridge University Press.

Knöpfel, L. (2020). 'An Anthropological Reimagining of Contract in Global Value Chains: The Governance of Corporate–Community Relations in the Colombian Mining Sector'. *European Review of Contract Law* 16(1): 118–38.

KPMG (2017). 'The KPMG Survey of Corporate Responsibility Reporting'. https://assets.kpmg.com/content/dam/kpmg/xx/pdf/2017/10/kpmg-survey-of-corporate-responsibility-reporting-2017.pdf.

Lange, B. and F. Haines (2015). 'Regulatory Transformations: An Introduction'. In *Regulatory Transformations. Rethinking Economy-Society Interactions*, edited by B. Lange, F. Haines, and D. Thomas, 1–28. London: Bloomsbury Publishing.

LeBaron, G. and A. Rühmkorf (2017). 'Steering CSR through Home State Regulation: A Comparison of the Impact of the UK Bribery Act and Modern Slavery Act on Global Supply Chain Governance'. *Global Policy* 8(3): 15–28.

Levy, D. and F. Palpacuer (2017). 'Global Production Networks and the Changing Corporation'. In *The Corporation. A Critical, Multi-Disciplinary Handbook*, edited by G. Baars and A. Spicer, 336–45. Cambridge, UK: Cambridge University Press.

Lichuma, C. O. (2021). '(Laws) Made in the "First World": A TWAIL Critique of the Use of Domestic Legislation to Extraterritorially Regulate Global Value Chains'. *Heidelberg Journal of International Law* 81: 497–532.

Lobel, O. (2004). 'The Renew Deal: The Fall of Regulation and the Rise of Governance in Contemporary Legal Thought'. *Minnesota Law Review* 89: 342–470.

Locke, R. M. (2013). *The Promise and Limits of Private Power. Promoting Labor Standards in a Global Economy*. Cambridge, UK: Cambridge University Press.

Locke, R. M., F. Qin, and A. Brause (2007). 'Does Monitoring Improve Labor Standards? Lessons from Nike'. *Industrial and Labor Relations Review* 61(1): 3–31.

Mantouvalou, V. (2018). 'The UK Modern Slavery Act 2015 Three Years On'. *Modern Law Review* 81(6): 1017–45.

Nolan, J. and G. Bott (2018). 'Global Supply Chains and Human Rights: Spotlight on Forced Labour and Modern Slavery Practices'. *Australian Journal of Human Rights* 24(1): 44–69.

Pahuja, S. (2017). 'Changing the World: The Ethical Impulse and International Law'. In *Who's Afraid of International Law?* edited by R. Gaita and G. J. Simpson, 21–42. Clayton, Victoria, Australia: Monash University Publishing.

——— (2019). 'Corporations, Universalism, and the Domestication of Race in International Law'. In *Empire, Race and Global Justice*, edited by D. Bell, 74–93. Cambridge, UK: Cambridge University Press.

Palpacuer, F. (2017). 'Voluntary versus Binding Forms of Regulation in Global Production Networks: Exploring the "Paradoxes of Partnership" in the European Anti-Sweatshop Movement'. In *Unmaking the Global Sweatshop: Health and Safety of the World's Garment Workers*, edited by R. Prentice and G. de Neve, 57–86. Philadelphia: University of Pennsylvania Press.

Rao, M. and N. Bernaz (2020). 'Corporate Responsibility for Human Rights in Assam Tea Plantations: A Business and Human Rights Approach'. *Sustainability* 12(18): 7409.

Reimer, S. and D. Leslie (2006). 'Knowledge, Ethics and Power in the Home Furnishings Commodity Chain'. In *Geographies of Commodity Chains* (Routledge Studies in Human Geography), edited by A. Hughes and S. Reimer, 250–69. London: Routledge.

Reinke, B. and P. Zumbansen (2019). 'Transnational Liability Regimes in Contract, Tort and Corporate Law: Comparative Observations on "Global Supply Chain Liability"'. Available at: https://ssrn.com/abstract=3312916.

Rosanvallon, P. (2008). *Counter-democracy: Politics in an Age of Distrust*. Translated by A. Goldhammer. John Robert Seeley Lectures, 7. Cambridge, UK: Cambridge University Press.

Ruggie, J. (2008). *Protect, Respect and Remedy: A Framework for Business and Human Rights – Report of the Special Representative of the Secretary-General on the Issue of Human Rights and Transnational Corporations and Other Business Enterprises.* UN Human Rights Council (A/HRC/8/5).

——— (2017). 'Multinationals as Global Institution: Power, Authority and Relative Autonomy'. *Regulation and Governance* 12(3): 317–33.

Rühmkorf, A. (2018). 'Global Supply Chain Governance: The Search for "What Works"'. *Deakin Law Review* 23: 63–82.

Sabel, C., D. O'Rourke, and A. Fung (2000). 'Ratcheting Labor Standards: Regulation for Continuous Improvement in the Global Workplace'. Available at https://ssrn.com/abstract=262178.

Salminen, J. and M. Rajavuori (2019). 'Transnational Sustainability Laws and the Regulation of Global Value Chains: Comparison and a Framework for Analysis'. *Maastricht Journal of European and Comparative Law* 26(5): 602–27.

Secretary of State for the Home Department (2019). *Independent Review of the Modern Slavery Act 2015: Final Report.* Presented to Parliament by the Secretary of State for the Home Department by Command of Her Majesty. May, London.

Scott, C. (2004). 'Regulation in the Age of Governance. The Rise of the Post-Regulatory State'. In *The Politics of Regulation. Institutions and Regulatory Reforms for the Age of Governance*, edited by J. Jordana and D. Levi-Faur, 145–76. Cheltenham, UK: Edward Elgar.

Shamir, R. (2009). 'Corporate Social Responsibility: A Case of Hegemony and Counter-Hegemony'. In *Law and Globalization from Below*, edited by B. de Sousa Santos and C. A. Rodríguez-Garavito, 92–117. Cambridge, UK: Cambridge University Press.

Slobodian, Q. (2018). *Globalists: The End of Empire and the Birth of Neoliberalism.* Cambridge, MA: Harvard University Press.

Tamanaha, B. Z. (2000). 'A Non-essentialist Version of Legal Pluralism'. *Journal of Law and Society* 27(2): 296–321.

Teubner, G. (1983). 'Substantive and Reflexive Elements in Modern Law'. *Law and Society Review* 17(2): 239–86.

——— (2011a). 'A Constitutional Moment? The Logics of "Hitting the Bottom"'. In *The Financial Crisis in Constitutional Perspective: The Dark Side of Functional Differentiation*, edited by P. F. Kjaer, G. Teubner, and A. Febbrajo, 3–42. Oxford, UK: Hart.

——— (2011b). 'Transnational Fundamental Rights: Horizontal Effect?' *Netherlands Journal of Legal Philosophy* 40(3): 191–215.

——— (2012). *Constitutional Fragments: Societal Constitutionalism and Globalization*, Oxford, UK: Oxford University Press.

——— (2018). 'Quod Omnes Tangit: Transnational Constitutions without Democracy?' *Journal of Law and Society* 45(1): S5–S29.

The IGLP Law and Global Production Working Group (2016). 'The Role of Law in Global Value Chains: A Research Manifesto'. *London Review of International Law* 4(1): 57–79.

Tsagas, G. and C. Villiers (2020). 'Why "Less Is More" in Non-financial Reporting Initiatives: Concrete Steps towards Supporting Sustainability'. *Accounting, Economics, and Law: A Convivium* 10(2): 1–42.

UN General Assembly (1974). 'Declaration on the Establishment of a New International Economic Order'. 2218th plenary meeting, 17 April, New York. A/RES/3201(S-VI).

UN Human Rights Council (2014). 'Elaboration of an International Legally Binding Instrument on Transnational Corporations and Other Business Enterprises with Respect to Human Rights'. 26th session of the Human Rights Council (10–27 June), Geneva. A/HRC/RES/26/9.

United Nations Conference on Trade and Development (UNCTAD) (2015). *Tracing the Value Added in Global Value Chains: Product-Level Case Studies in China*. Available at: https://unctad.org/system/files/official-document/ditctncd2015d1_en.pdf.

Woody, K. E. (2012). 'Conflict Minerals Legislation: The SEC's New Role as Diplomatic and Humanitarian Watchdog'. *Fordham Law Review* 81(3): 1315–51.

World Trade Organization (WTO) (2019). *Trade in Merchandise and Commercial Services*. Available at: https://www.wto.org/english/res_e/statis_e/wts2019_e/wts2019chapter04_e.pdf.

3

Tackling Forced Labour in Global Value Chains

What Role for Trade Instruments?

Franz Christian Ebert, Francesca Francavilla, and Lorenzo Guarcello*

Introduction

The question of how trade governance is – and should be – linked to labour standards has long been debated among academics, policymakers, and activists (Servais, 1989; McCrudden and Davies, 2000; Barry and Reddy, 2006). Especially the insertion of labour-related requirements into the relevant trade instruments as a means to improve workers' rights in the global economy has been the subject of controversy (Alston, 1993; Bhagwati, 1995; Tsogas, 1999).[1] While largely absent from the multilateral trading framework,[2] such requirements have been included in numerous bilateral and regional trade agreements (ILO, 2013, 2016, 2019a; Corley-Coulibaly et al., 2023b) as well as unilateral trade instruments, such as trade preference schemes and import ban legislation (Tsogas, 2000; Addo, 2015; Velluti, 2020). Forced labour,[3] a form of

* This chapter is based on and partly reproduces findings previously published in Ebert, Francavilla, and Guarcello (2023). The authors are grateful to the editors of this volume as well as to Elvis Beytullayev, Weng Yin Chau, Marva Corley-Coulibaly, Michaelle De Cock, Ben Dupre, Jennifer Gordon, Hamidulla Hamdamov, Desiree LeClercq, Lisa Mardikian, Fabiola Mieres, Siu Ming Lee, Jodelen Mitra, Jude Pravin Peters, Pelin Sekerler Richiardi, Hila Shamir, Emily Sims, Kari Tapiola, Mei Trueba, and Kassiyet Tulegenova for comments and suggestions on earlier versions of this chapter. Any remaining errors are of course our own. Initial findings were presented at the 2023 Labour Law Research Network Conference in Warsaw and the 2023 Regulating for Decent Work Conference in Geneva.

modern slavery,[4] has been a key issue addressed by these instruments (Compa, 1993; Ehrenberg, 1995; Plouffe-Malette and Bisson, 2019) and, until recently, together with prison labour the only labour-related subject matter for which dedicated import ban legislation has been enacted (Bade, 2000; Fanou, 2023; Lopez and Alghazali, 2023).

This raises the question of which implications such forced labour-related clauses in trade instruments entail for addressing forced labour issues in contexts related to global value chains (GVCs). With trade in GVCs constituting 70 per cent of overall trade in 2020 (OECD, 2020), the regulation of trade can have important implications for GVC governance (Corley-Coulibaly et al., 2023). Trade instruments typically involve policy levers, including economic incentives and disincentives, that can impact actors involved in GVC governance, such as states, companies, and civil society actors (Aissi et al., 2018). However, little is known about the extent to which, and the conditions under which, they have contributed to tackling forced labour in GVCs in an effective manner,[5] that is, in a way that tackles the underlying causes of forced labour and has enduring impact.

To help address this question, this chapter proceeds in four steps. The next section analyses how forced labour considerations have been integrated into the different types of trade instruments, emphasizing the policy levers they provide to address forced labour issues. The subsequent section then turns to the practical implications of trade instruments in terms of addressing forced labour issues in global value chains. It draws on the trade and supply chain governance literatures to better understand the conditions under which trade instruments can foster long-term improvements regarding forced labour on the ground. On this basis, the following section presents a case study of the rubber glove industry in Malaysia, which was subject to a series of company-specific import bans imposed by the customs authorities of the United States between 2019 and 2022. The final section concludes by offering some broader reflections about the prospects of trade instruments as a device for tackling forced labour in a GVC context.

Forced Labour-Related Provisions in Trade Instruments

Over recent decades, clauses that address forced labour have made inroads into numerous trade instruments. These instruments involve a variety of policy levers, which range from economic incentives and disincentives to monitoring and technical cooperation.[6] Depending on their specific design, they can affect the governance of GVCs in different ways, including by incentivizing compliance or by building the capacity of the actors concerned to abide by or enforce relevant standards. This section maps the different regulatory approaches of trade instruments – bilateral and regional trade agreements and unilateral trade arrangements – and analyses the policy levers through which they can contribute to addressing forced labour in GVC contexts.

Bilateral and Regional Trade Agreements

Over the last three decades, there has been a significant increase in the number of bilateral and regional trade agreements that address issues related to forced labour (ILO, 2013, 2016; Ebert et al., 2023). As of December 2024, more than 90 of the about 370 trade agreements that were in force and had been notified to the WTO contained references to forced labour.[7] The specific ways in which forced labour concerns are addressed in trade agreements differ. A number of these agreements require state parties to implement the principle of 'the elimination of all forms of forced or compulsory labour', as embodied in the ILO's 1998 Declaration on Fundamental Principles and Rights at Work (see, for example, Agustí-Panareda et al., 2015). Some trade agreements, especially those concluded by the European Union (EU) and the European Free Trade Association (EFTA), also contain commitments regarding the implementation of the ILO's Fundamental Conventions (Velut et al., 2022; Marceau et al., 2023), including those addressing forced labour.[8] In addition, numerous labour provisions in trade agreements require state parties to enforce protective domestic labour laws, including those dealing with forced labour (Häberli et al., 2012).

Some recent trade agreements also contain trade-specific provisions on forced labour. Notably, the United States–Mexico–Canada Agreement (USMCA), which came into force in 2020, requires state parties to 'prohibit the importation of goods into its territory from other sources produced in whole or in part by forced or compulsory labor, including forced or compulsory child labor' (Article 23.6(1)).[9] A different approach involves sectoral forced labour clauses. This can be found, for example, in the EFTA-Indonesia Comprehensive Economic Partnership Agreement. The relevant clause requires state parties 'to exclude products stemming from IUU fishing, fisheries crime, forced labour or human trafficking from trade flows, including from third parties into their market' (Article 8.9(2(a)).

Depending on their specific design, labour provisions in trade agreements can provide a number of implementation mechanisms for addressing forced labour that include but transcend economic incentives and disincentives (Aissi et al., 2018). Many labour provisions provide for mechanisms to conduct government-to-government dialogue and cooperation, which can provide a forum to address a particular labour issue or help to increase a government's institutional capacity to deal with a given issue (Oehri, 2015; Ebert, 2016). Labour provisions in the EU's and EFTA's trade agreements additionally place an emphasis on stakeholder dialogue, which can provide a framework for holding countries accountable for labour standards violations (Bartels, 2013; Corley-Coulibaly et al., 2023a).

Many trade agreements furthermore provide for a framework to settle labour-related disputes between the parties. Such mechanisms range from mere consultations to a fully fledged arbitration procedure that can involve a prior complaint procedure and culminate in the adoption of a binding or non-binding panel report (Marx et al., 2017; Corley-Coulibaly et al., 2023a). In addition, a number of labour provisions, especially those contained in trade agreements and labour side agreements concluded by the United States and Canada, also provide for the possibility, as a last resort, to impose sanctions if the panel's recommendations on how to remediate a violation are not implemented (Moore and Scherrer, 2017; Velut et al., 2022). Such sanctions can consist of fines or the suspension of trade preferences (ILO, 2013, 2016).

So far, forced labour concerns have not given rise to the activation of the relevant dispute settlement mechanisms. That being said, forced labour concerns were, among other labour rights issues, the subject of a complaint filed against the Dominican Republic under the Dominican Republic–Central America Free Trade Agreement,[10] which led to prolonged government-to-government dialogue.[11] In addition, in a case pertaining to the US–Oman Trade Agreement, the establishment of pre-ratification requirements by the United States reportedly induced the legislature of Oman to improve the labour-related legislative framework. Specifically, the ratification phase of this trade agreement involved requirements to strengthen the legal prohibition of and penalties for forced labour, as well as a prohibition preventing employers from withholding workers' passports, which were partly or fully implemented (ILO, 2013).

Unilateral Trade Instruments

Trade Preference Programmes

Since the 1980s, forced labour considerations have also been included in the unilateral trade preference programmes that some trading partners have adopted. Granting trade preferences to products emanating from a given country, these programmes and any conditionality they may involve are addressed at states rather than specific companies. The United States started this trend by integrating a labour provision into its Generalized System of Preferences (GSP) (Alston, 1993),[12] as well as into several regional preference schemes, such as the Caribbean Basin Initiative and the African Growth and Opportunity Act (AGOA). These programmes allow the withdrawal of tariff preferences of a beneficiary country if the latter is found to have not taken appropriate action to protect labour rights, including with regard to forced labour (Perez-Lopez, 1988; Siroën, 2013).[13] Cases in which trade preferences were withdrawn for forced labour-related reasons include Mauretania in 2018, under AGOA, and Thailand in 2019, under the US GSP (USTR, 2018, 2019).

Furthermore, since 1994, the EU has included forced labour considerations in the withdrawal clauses of its trade preference programmes (Ebert, 2009). Forced labour considerations have also been featured, since 2001, in the EU GSP 'Special Incentive Arrangement' (GSP+) (Stolzenberg, 2019). This arrangement provides additional tariff preferences to countries that have ratified a list of international conventions, including the ILO Forced Labour Convention, 1930 (No. 29) and the ILO Abolition of Forced Labour Convention, 1957 (No. 105), and are taking steps towards their implementation (Lopez-Jurado, 2005).[14] Unlike its US counterpart, the EU GSP refers systematically to ILO Conventions when defining the term 'forced labour' and relevant state obligations (Orbie and Tortell, 2009). The clause was activated in relation to forced labour for the first – and so far only – time in a case concerning Myanmar.[15]

Import Ban Legislation

Forced labour concerns were among the first labour issues addressed by trade instruments,[16] starting with the US Tariff Act of 1930.[17] Section 307 of this Act prohibits the importation of '[a]ll goods, wares, articles, and merchandise mined, produced, or manufactured wholly or in part in any foreign country by convict labor or/and forced labor or/and indentured labor under penal sanctions'.[18] The provision's broad scope (Bhala, 1998) means that it covers the entire GVC and exercises economic leverage directly at the firm level. To date, this provision has continued to be implemented by the US customs authorities, which since 2003 have been embodied by the Customs and Border Protection (CBP) agency. Acting on its own initiative or in response to petitions from third parties, CBP can issue a 'Withhold Release Order' to bar imported goods from entry into the United States if relevant information 'reasonably but not conclusively indicates' that the good in question was made with forced labour.[19] If the suspicion is confirmed through a so-called 'Finding', CBP can seize and initiate forfeiture proceedings for the goods in question (Syam and Roggensack, 2020).

In recent years, import bans have gained increasing traction as instruments for combatting forced labour. In 2021, new US legislation established a special import ban regime for the Xinjiang Uyghur Autonomous Region of China by subjecting all goods exported from that region to an import prohibition unless the company could show that its goods had *not* been made with forced labour (Alon, 2022).[20] Furthermore, several other states and the EU have adopted import bans on goods made with forced labour. Further to a specific legal requirement to that effect contained in the United States–Mexico–Canada Agreement (USMCA), Canada amended its domestic customs legislation in 2020 to ban the importation of 'goods mined, manufactured or produced wholly or in part by forced labour' (Pellerin et al., 2021).[21] A similar import ban was enacted by Mexico in 2023 (Morales, 2023).[22] In 2024, the European Union adopted legislation to prohibit products made with forced labour in the EU market, which covers imported goods as well as goods produced in the EU for exports or domestic consumption and will apply as of 2027 (EC, 2022; Eustace, 2023; Grado, 2025).[23]

Furthermore, the US forced labour import ban legislation has evolved from a law that remained mainly in the books into an instrument of significant practical relevance. Until 2016, Section 307 of the US Tariff Act was infrequently used. From the entry into force of the provision in 1930 until the mid-1980s, only ten cases were reported where the import ban provision was actually enforced (Casey and Cimino-Isaacs, 2022).[24] Especially in the second half of the 2010s, the application of the forced labour clause in the US Tariff Act gained increasing traction. A key factor in this regard was the lifting of the so-called 'consumptive demand' clause by the US Congress in 2015,[25] which facilitated the adoption of import bans (Bell, 2016). In addition, the CBP authorities have increased their institutional capacity for the enforcement of import bans, including by creating a dedicated forced labour division (Higgins, 2023). Between 2016 and 2022, 43 enforcement actions were taken, as compared to six such actions in the 20 years prior.[26] While most import bans imposed have been company-specific, CBP has occasionally directed them at all products of a certain type or sector from a given country or region.[27]

On the whole, the above analysis shows that unilateral trade instruments, in particular the US import ban legislation, have been used more frequently as an enforcement device to address forced labour issues than the relevant clauses in bilateral and regional trade agreements. This renders them particularly relevant as an element in broader strategies to address modern slavery issues in GVCs.

The Potential of Trade Instruments to Address Forced Labour Issues in GVC Contexts: General Considerations

Section II has illustrated the policy levers provided by trade instruments that can be used to address forced labour issues in GVC contexts. Even where these clauses are activated though, it is not clear that they will necessarily lead to positive effects regarding forced labour. While a recent study concludes that forced labour import bans imposed under the US Tariff Act 'have often been a catalyst to prompt rapid changes in industries that have been resistant to reform' (Remedy Project, 2023: 14), civil society organizations have argued that import ban laws are, on their own, unable to address the structural factors underlying forced labour (Anti-Slavery International and European Center for Constitutional and Human Rights, 2021). Meanwhile, the withdrawal of trade benefits under unilateral trade preferences schemes has entailed rather limited effects in terms of addressing forced labour (see, for example, Kryvoi, 2008; Elliott and Freeman, 2003). Moreover, related economic sanctions may in some cases lead to negative effects for the workers concerned, for example by driving workers out of employment and into even more precarious conditions (see, for example, Maupain, 2005). This raises the question as to the conditions under which trade instruments can contribute to addressing forced labour in an effective manner.[28]

In-depth empirical studies on the US and EU GSPs suggest that the effectiveness of trade sanctions in tackling labour standards issues is highly context specific and hinges on several factors (Elliott, 1998; Zhou and Cuyvers, 2011). These include the economic dependence of the recipient country on the market of the sanctioning country (Elliott and Freeman, 2003). The rather minor importance of the EU common market for Myanmar's economy has, for example, been identified as a significant explanatory factor for the limited effects of the EU's withdrawal of GSP preferences in the case of Myanmar on the forced labour issues at stake (Zhou and Cuyvers, 2011; Horsey, 2023). Furthermore, some scholars have identified the political openness of the recipient country as a relevant factor. Drawing on the Freedom House Index, Elliott and Freeman (2003) find that petitions under the US GSP tend to be more successful regarding countries with a higher degree of democratic standards and participation than in cases concerning countries that were considered autocratic.[29]

In addition, the effectiveness of trade sanctions to address labour standards-related compliance deficits has been found to vary depending on the nature of the issue concerned. In particular, forced labour issues have been found to be more difficult to address than certain more 'technical' labour rights issues, such as occupational safety and health, working time, and wage issues, as they are typically more deeply linked to structural issues regarding the country's political and socioeconomic conditions (Elliott and Freeman, 2003).[30]

A particular challenge relates to addressing the root causes of forced labour problems in GVCs. LeBaron et al. (2019) discuss the root causes of forced labour within the conventional framework of factors influencing labour demand and supply. Regarding labour demand, some common features of GVCs, and supply chains in general, such as pressure on the price, cost, and speed of production, can play a role in the use of forced labour in firms' GVCs, even if they do not inevitably lead to it (LeBaron, 2021; see also Anner, 2020).[31] Outsourcing of production and labour subcontracting can create greater complexity and a lack of traceability, and they may make oversight and accountability for labour standards difficult (LeBaron et al., 2019). Furthermore, transnational labour recruitment can increase the risk of forced labour, especially debt bondage, particularly when labour market intermediaries charge workers fees for their services (Gordon, 2015; ILO et al., 2019). Meanwhile, on the supply side, poverty, low levels of education and illiteracy, and migration are important risk factors that determine people's vulnerability to forced labour (ILO, 2014).[32] In addition to these demand-side and supply-side factors, institutional factors also help to explain the prevalence and persistence of forced labour. These include policy and governance issues, such as deficient and insufficiently enforced domestic labour laws and policy frameworks, as well as lack of awareness among state institutions about how to address forced labour and lack of coordination among relevant institutions. Addressing these issues thus plays an important role in combatting forced labour, including human trafficking (Shamir, 2012), in an effective manner (ILO et al., 2019).

Scholars have emphasized that the effectiveness of transnational governance mechanisms in bringing change on the ground depends not only on their institutional design but also on how they engage with the local regulatory context in which they are applied (Bartley, 2011). Against this backdrop, an argument can be made that labour provisions in transnational governance mechanisms are likely to be most effective in the long term when they both harness and strengthen the regulatory capacity of other relevant actors – especially the state (see along these lines, Kolben, 2015). This underscores the importance of understanding the interactions between trade instruments and other regulatory layers, which may range from conflict and rivalry to substitution and complementariness (Trubek and Trubek, 2007; see also Locke et al., 2013).

In this light, the following section carries out an in-depth assessment of how these dynamics have played out in a concrete case, namely the rubber glove sector in Malaysia. This case has been chosen because it involved palpable remedial action (Remedy Project, 2023) and is often considered an 'example of the positive impact of the U.S. import ban' (Fanou, 2023: 2).[33] The section analyses how trade instruments were activated to address forced labour issues and traces the pathways through which these instruments contributed to change on the ground. In doing so, this case study aims to assess the interactions of these instruments with other mechanisms of GVC governance and inquires into the complementarities of different instruments that may have helped to tackle the relevant forced labour issues in a durable manner.

Trade Instruments as Part of Broader GVC Governance Efforts Regarding Forced Labour: The Case of the Malaysian Rubber Glove Sector

The Domestic Context

Driven by factors such as technological innovations by local firms and targeted industrial policies, Malaysia has transformed itself from a raw rubber producer into the global leader in rubber glove production (Kawano, 2019; Lebdioui, 2022). With a 53 per cent share of the world supply of rubber gloves in 2021,[34] Malaysia's rubber glove industry constitutes one of the country's most successful resource-based manufacturing sectors. In 2019, this industry generated employment for about 72,000 workers (Hutchinson and Bhattacharya, 2020). As a result of the COVID-19 pandemic, exports of Malaysian rubber gloves fluctuated significantly, first dramatically increasing in 2020 and 2021 (by 100.4 per cent and 57.5 per cent, respectively), and then contracting at the end of the pandemic (by 66.9 per cent in 2022) (ILO, 2023).[35]

Malaysia has ratified several international treaties outlawing forced labour,[36] and forced labour is prohibited by several domestic laws, including Article 6 of the Federal Constitution and Section 90b of the 2022 Employment Act.[37]

That being said, forced labour has been an issue of concern for some time in the Malaysian rubber glove industry (Coffey, 2015), as it has been in certain other Malaysian key industries, such as palm oil and electronics (Wahab, 2019; Raj-Reichert, 2020). A shared characteristic of these industries is their strong reliance on migrant workers (Buckley et al., 2022), with estimates suggesting that migrants accounted for up to 60 per cent of the workforce in Malaysia's rubber glove production in 2019 (Hutchinson and Bhattacharya, 2020). Various factors, including a highly exploitative transnational recruitment industry, legislative gaps in migrant workers' protection, and lax enforcement of labour laws, combined with entrenched corruption, have led to a situation where migrant workers in Malaysia are structurally vulnerable to forced labour (Ness, 2021; Hwok Aun and Pereira, 2023; for context, see also Hoffstaedter and Missbach, 2021). Documented cases in the rubber glove sector have involved phenomena such as debt bondage (often related to high recruitment fees), restricted freedom of movement (notably due to the retention of passports and other identity documents), substandard living conditions (in particular, with respect to accommodation), and threats and other forms of intimidation (Ellis-Petersen, 2018; Bengtsen, 2019; Hughes et al., 2022). In part, these issues were exacerbated by the COVID-19 pandemic, which, among other factors, led to increased pressure on workers due to the heightened global demand for rubber gloves (Bhutta et al., 2021).

Import Bans under the US Tariff Act and Remedial Actions at the Company Level

Following reports of forced labour issues in the Malaysian rubber glove industry, the US CBP agency issued six Withhold Release Orders (WROs) and one Finding[38] against Malaysian producers between 2019 and 2022 (ILO, 2023).[39] The first WRO against a Malaysian rubber glove supplier, issued in 2019 (Lim, 2019), triggered only limited concern at the domestic level. Initially, many industry leaders and analysts did not anticipate the WRO would have significant effects, expecting instead that other Malaysian companies would fill any market gap that might result from the WRO (Aziz, 2019).

The situation changed, however, when additional WROs were issued that affected a broader range of companies (see, for example, CBP, 2021b, 2021d, 2021e). Furthermore, in one case, after an investigation of several months into a key industry leader, CBP issued a definitive Finding that provided for the seizure of relevant goods and the commencement of forfeiture proceedings (CBP, 2021a). Moreover, the seizure authorized by the Finding went beyond the scope of the original WRO and also covered the products of a subsidiary of the company concerned that had previously not been within the scope of the import ban (Sitkowski and Kinsman, 2021). This – together with the fact that this enforcement measure was imposed in the midst of the COVID-19 pandemic – was understood as a strong message to the business community that enforcement action against forced labour in the rubber glove sector was a priority for CBP (Lee, 2020; Sitkowski and Kinsman, 2021). The Malaysian Rubber Gloves Manufacturers Association estimated the cumulative loss in revenue to the industry from rubber glove exports to the US resulting from the import bans at MYR (Malaysian ringgit) 3.6 billion (about USD 800 million) (*Malay Mail*, 2022).

These actions came on top of certain similarly aligned responses by other actors to concerns of forced labour in the Malaysian rubber glove sector. For example, the Government of Canada ended its public procurement contract with some of the Malaysian companies in question due to forced labour issues, and the management of Norway's Government Pension Fund Global put one company under a two-year period of observation (McGregor, 2022; Salim, 2022). Some of the companies also faced legal proceedings initiated by domestic authorities in relation to the aforesaid forced labour issues (see, for example, Kamel, 2020). These factors, together with the prospective loss in US market share due to the import bans (Brudney, 2020), arguably created a strong incentive for change for the companies concerned.

Indeed, the relevant Malaysian rubber glove companies have taken substantial remedial action to achieve revocation of CPB's measures. Notably, several companies affected by a CBP enforcement action have taken steps to reimburse the recruitment fees that workers had been required to pay (Remedy Project, 2023; Thomas, 2020). In order to have the Finding against it revoked, one company disbursed remediation payments of more than USD 30 million to the workers affected (CBP, 2021c) and created a fund with a volume of about USD 5 million to settle any pending forced labour allegations (Remedy Project, 2023). The company in question also changed recruitment agencies, put in place new due diligence measures to prevent abuses during the recruitment process, and improved the housing situation of migrant workers (Remedy Project, 2023). Other measures, taken by several of the companies affected by CBP enforcement action, involved revising or adopting new human resources policies. In one case, this included a new grievance mechanism, an equal pay policy for migrant and Malaysian workers, and forced labour-related capacity building for the company's human resources staff (Ong, 2022).

By the end of 2023, the improvements achieved had led CBP to modify its enforcement actions in all of the six cases (CBP, 2020a, 2021c, 2023a, 2023b, 2023c, 2024). Furthermore, research suggests that some Malaysian rubber glove companies that were not subject to import bans also reimbursed recruitment fees (Trueba and Staniland, 2023), possibly in order to prevent the imposition of a WRO.

So far, in most cases no evidence of systematic adverse effects on the workers of the companies subject to the bans has been reported (see also the case study in Remedy Project, 2023). This may partly be due to the exceptional profit margins of the rubber glove sector during the pandemic (Hutchinson and Bhattacharya, 2021), which arguably facilitated off-setting the economic costs for the remedial actions taken (Hughes et al., 2022). That being said, the US Government Accountability Office, citing other US Government sources, reported that 'as an unintended consequence of the September 2019 WRO for disposable rubber gloves produced in Malaysia, many workers' employment was terminated, which had a negative effect on workers facing exploitation' (United States GAO, 2021: 31).

Implications for Broader Policy Efforts to Tackle Forced Labour at the National Level

Taking a broader perspective, CBP's enforcement actions appear to have helped to generate momentum for tackling forced labour at the domestic level. Key in this regard was the growing perception by the Malaysian Government, among others, that the forced labour problems in the Malaysian economy could decrease the trust of foreign business partners (Chu and Latiff, 2021).

Importantly, the aforementioned enforcement actions concerning the Malaysian rubber glove sector coincided with similar developments in other industries in the country. Notably, CBP issued two WROs and one Finding on Malaysian palm oil companies (CBP 2020b, 2020c, 2022).[40] Before that, Malaysian rubber gloves had already been placed on the US List of Goods Produced by Child Labor or Forced Labor (United States Department of Labor, 2020). Similarly, Malaysia had been included on the Tier 3 list of the US Trafficking in Person Report for States 'whose governments do not fully meet the TVPA [Trafficking Victims Protection Act]'s minimum standards and are not making significant efforts to do so' (United States Department of State, 2021: 53), thus putting Malaysia at risk for withdrawal of non-humanitarian US aid.

In light of this situation, the Malaysian Ministry of Human Resources actively sought to establish a dialogue with the companies that faced forced labour import bans (Reuters, 2022). Early on, in 2020, the Ministry had already created a taskforce on labour law and compliance for the rubber-related industry (*Malay Mail*, 2020). Other national initiatives to combat forced labour appear to have evolved more or less independently of the import bans, but they may have benefited indirectly from the political momentum the bans created. This is notably the case with the National Action Plan on Forced Labour (2021–2025), adopted by the Malaysian Government in 2021,[41] the ratification of the Protocol of 2014 to the ILO Forced Labour Convention in 2022 (Buang, 2022), and several technical cooperation projects undertaken by the ILO.[42]

Furthermore, the import bans adopted under the US Tariff Act also appear to have spurred on private regulatory efforts to tackle forced labour in the rubber glove industry (Remedy Project, 2023). These include the creation of the Responsible Glove Alliance in 2022, an initiative by Malaysian rubber glove producers, which commits its members to specific due diligence and transparency requirements, among other things (Bengtsen, 2022).[43]

Implications for GVC Governance

As illustrated by the above analysis, the US import bans can be considered a driver of change in the Malaysian rubber glove sector. In addition to the economic leverage resulting from the import bans, a factor in bringing about change in the individual cases in question may have been that CBP had been working actively and early on with the companies concerned to improve the situation (Brudney, 2020). Furthermore, several contextual factors may have accounted for the remedial actions undertaken, including the importance of the United States as an importer of Malaysian rubber gloves (Rahman et al., 2021). Among others, the fact that the rubber glove industry is highly concentrated, with 'a small number of key companies' (Hughes et al., 2022: 139), may have assisted in addressing labour standards deficits in the sector.

Importantly, the import bans imposed by CBP engaged with several other governance mechanisms. Notably, in line with its recurrent practice, CBP referred to the ILO Indicators of Forced Labour as a benchmark against which to assess the situation in the factories concerned and mentioned them expressly in several of its public communications (see, for example, CBP, 2021b, 2021d). Furthermore, CBP's decisions on whether to lift an import ban relied on private auditors. These were contracted by the companies subject to import bans in order to ascertain whether they had sufficiently addressed the forced labour issues detected and should therefore have their import bans lifted (Khalid, 2022). This strong reliance on private auditors has been subject to criticism, however, because – among other factors – auditing companies had in several cases failed to determine the forced labour issues that would eventually lead to the import bans (Remedy Project, 2023).

Moreover, the reported unintentional adverse effects of an import ban on workers in a pre-pandemic case highlight the need to contemplate protective arrangements for vulnerable workers that may be affected (see also United States GAO, 2021). While the cessation of forced labour situations can be seen as a benefit in itself, if import bans are not implemented thoughtfully, they could potentially sustain or even worsen the susceptibility of the involved workers to exploitation. This could inadvertently lead to the emergence of new instances of forced labour. The latter can especially be the case if these workers find themselves unemployed, with a precarious migration status, and/or in a continued situation of debt (David et al., 2019).

To strengthen the effectiveness of import bans in tackling forced labour, some avenues could be explored to better link them with other relevant governance mechanisms and actors. In this regard, it has been suggested that CBP could more systematically request the views of civil society organizations, including local trade unions, on the situation (Remedy Project, 2023). Furthermore, CBP could also require the companies concerned to allow other actors, including those from civil society, to independently verify progress made towards addressing the forced labour issues in question. In certain cases, it may also be possible to use forced labour import bans as a device for broader workers' empowerment (Gordon, 2024; see also Fudge and LeBaron, 2024).

Furthermore, it is worth asking how the momentum created by the import bans can be more comprehensively harnessed to address some of the root causes underlying the forced labour issues in question. While some remedial actions taken by the companies concerned have addressed issues related to those root causes, notably with regard to the companies' recruitment processes, several structural issues remain, for example concerning the regulation of private recruitment agencies (ILO, 2023). Studies have also pointed to a number of additional root causes that could be addressed in this context. These include restrictions on migrant workers changing employers and unionizing and capacity issues in labour inspectorates (Hwok Aun and Pereira, 2023; ILO, 2023; Wahab et al., 2023). In some cases, linking import bans with targeted capacity-building measures for labour inspectorates, companies, or relevant trade unions might also help to address such root causes and facilitate the lifting of the import bans.[44]

Conclusion

This chapter has aimed to shed light on the potential of trade governance to effectively address forced labour issues in GVCs. Trade instruments with forced labour-related provisions have proliferated in recent decades and involve several policy levers that can contribute to tackling forced labour. The degree to which trade instruments have entailed concrete practical effects varies significantly. While for many bilateral and regional trade agreements there is no evidence that their forced labour-related provisions have been applied in practice, the situation is different for the relevant unilateral trade instruments. In particular, the application of the US forced labour import ban legislation has given rise to substantial practical implications. As evinced by the case study on the Malaysian rubber glove sector, this can contribute to specific improvements at the company level and have a wider sectoral impact. Furthermore, it can help to generate momentum for broader policy change at the national level. In doing so, the import bans at hand did not operate in an institutional vacuum but interacted with a variety of other governance mechanisms.

Notwithstanding, this case study also illustrates that trade instruments are, on their own, unlikely to be able to tackle the root causes of forced labour in a given case. This highlights the importance of utilizing these instruments to enhance relevant legal and institutional frameworks, create the conditions for meaningful social dialogue, and empower local actors for change. The case study also highlights the importance of addressing forced labour in conjunction with other labour rights issues that may render workers more prone to abuse, such as deficits in migrant worker protection and freedom of association.

The spread of forced labour clauses in trade instruments gives rise to some broader questions. One relates to the coordination between instruments that may be applicable to a given situation. In light of the difficulty of obtaining reliable information about incidences of forced labour, institutionalized information-sharing across different instruments and actors could help to increase the effectiveness of trade instruments (see, in a similar vein, EU–US Trade and Technology Council, 2023). Furthermore, providing sufficient guidance for companies will be important to enable them to properly comply with relevant requirements (see also Schwarz et al., 2022), which could also help to mitigate potential negative business impacts.

Another challenge is to determine how best to avoid unintended adverse effects of forced labour clauses in trade instruments, especially in the case of instruments with significant economic leverage, such as import bans. One aspect of this relates to making sure that these instruments do not accidentally affect workers in a harmful manner, which may require close consultations with petitioners and other relevant stakeholders (Pietropaoli et al., 2021). Forced labour clauses in trade instruments still constitute a field of regulatory experimentation, and further research will be necessary to understand more fully the effects of these instruments on workers and companies on the ground.

Notes

1. While some view them as necessary or desirable to protect workers' rights in a global economy and avoid socially adverse effects of trade (Blackett, 1999; Trebilcock and Howse, 2005), others have considered them an emanation of 'false humanitarianism' (Scheuerman, 2001) or protectionism in disguise (Dasgupta, 2000).
2. Forced labour concerns were meant to be covered by the 'Fair Labour Standards' provision of the Havana Charter for an International Trade Organization, which had emerged as part of the Bretton Woods Institutions (Bronz, 1949). However, this Charter, which would have committed Members to taking action to address 'unfair labour conditions' (Art. 7(1)), never entered into force (Zini, 2018)). Instead, the current multilateral trade framework only provides an explicit exception from relevant obligations under the General Agreement on Tariffs and Trade (GATT) for goods made with prison labour (Art. XX(e)), although the WTO legal framework can be interpreted to allow unilateral trade measures to combat forced labour (Morgandi, 2022). Proposals to tackle forced labour within the WTO trade framework have so far not been met with support (see, for example, WTO, 2021).
3. Forced Labour Convention, 1930 (No. 29), defines 'forced labour' as 'all work or service which is exacted from any person under the menace of any penalty and for which the said person has not offered himself voluntarily' (Article 2(1)). For certain exceptions from the scope of this definition, see Article 2(2) of this convention. The Protocol of 2024 to the Forced Labour Convention, 1930,

expressly encompasses measures to address the 'trafficking in persons for the purposes of forced or compulsory labour' (Article 1(3)).

4. For a conceptual reflection on these and related concepts, see Mende (2019).
5. With regard to forced labour import ban legislation, see, for example, Pietropaoli, et al. (2021).
6. This draws on Aissi et al. (2018).
7. See data available at the ILO's Labour Provisions in Trade Agreements Hub, available at: www.ilo.org/LPhub/.
8. These are Forced Labour Convention, 1930 (No. 29) and Abolition of Forced Labour Convention, 1957 (No. 105).
9. Furthermore, Article 23.6(2) USMCA requires the state parties to 'establish cooperation for the identification and movement of goods produced by forced labor'. An obligation to ban the import of goods made with forced labour has also been introduced into the Modernized Canada–Ukraine Free Trade Agreement of 2023 (Article 14.7(1)).
10. For the relevant allegations and the findings of the US National Contact Point, see Public Report of Review of U.S. Submission 2011-03 (Dominican Republic), 27 September 2013, available at: www.dol.gov/sites/dolgov/files/ILAB/legacy/files/20130926DR.pdf.
11. The related periodic reviews by the US Department of Labor are available on its website, www.dol.gov/agencies/ilab/our-work/trade/fta-submissions.
12. The legal basis for the US GSP expired at the end of 2020 and has not since been renewed by the US Congress; for this reason, it has not been in effect since January 2021 (Wong, 2025).
13. In addition, an innovative approach that involved compliance incentives at the company level and regular factory-level monitoring, including forced labour concerns, was adopted for the US trade preference programme for Haiti (Hornbeck, 2011; Blackett, 2019).
14. The current withdrawal clause and special incentive clause are contained in Art. 19(1)(a) in conjunction with Annex VIII, Part A, and Arts 9–16, Regulation (EU) No. 978/2012 of the European Parliament and of the Council of 25 October 2012 applying a scheme of generalized tariff preferences and repealing Council Regulation (EC) No. 732/2008.
15. Council Regulation (EC) No 552/97 of 24 March 1997, temporarily withdrawing access to generalized tariff preferences from the Union of Myanmar.
16. Only provisions dealing with prison labour seem to predate forced labour-related provisions; see Charnovitz (1987).

17. Soon afterwards, other countries followed suit with similar measures. Notably, in 1931 Argentina allowed increased customs duties on products made with forced labour. Three years later, Spain amended its trade legislation, extending the concept of dumping to cover 'prison or forced labour' (Charnovitz, 1987: 570).
18. 19 US Code § 1307. In this regard, the statute's definition of forced labour follows closely that of ILO Convention No. 29. On this and the related legislative history, see Armstrong (1975).
19. 19 Code of Federal Regulations § 12.42(e).
20. Section 3, Public Law No. 117–78, 117th Congress, *An Act to Ensure That Goods Made with Forced Labor in the Xinjiang Uyghur Autonomous Region of the People's Republic of China Do Not Enter the United States Market, and For Other Purposes*, adopted 23 December 2021. A similar rebuttable presumption applies furthermore to goods imported to the United States that have been made 'wholly or in part' by citizens of the Democratic People's Republic of Korea; 22 U.S.C. § 9241a(a).
21. The legal provision quoted is contained in *Customs Tariff*, S.C. 1997, c. 36, Ch. 98, Item No. 9897.00.00. As of April 2023, only one shipment had been intercepted under this provision, which was released following an appeal by the importing company (Lopez and Alghazali, 2023).
22. The relevant provisions are contained in the Acuerdo que establece las mercancías cuya importación está sujeta a regulación a cargo de la Secretaría del Trabajo y Previsión Social of 13 February 2023.
23. See Regulation (EU) 2024/3015 of the European Parliament and of the Council of 27 November 2024 on prohibiting products made with forced labour on the Union market and amending Directive (EU) 2019/1937.
24. While the early 1990s saw an increase of enforcement actions over previous years, between 2000 and 2015 only one enforcement action was adopted. See the website of the US Customs and Border Protection, www.cbp.gov/trade/forced-labor/withhold-release-orders-and-findings.
25. The clause had precluded enforcement of the forced labour clause in cases in which the goods in question were not produced in the United States 'in such quantities … as to meet the consumptive demands of the United States' (original version of Section 307 of the US Tariff Act of 1930).
26. See the website of the US Customs and Border Protection, www.cbp.gov/trade/forced-labor/withhold-release-orders-and-findings .
27. This occurred, for example, in the case of cotton products from Turkmenistan in 2018 (Natta, 2021).

28. The following two paragraphs draw on Cheong and Ebert (2016). The relevant section of that text was drafted by the first author of this chapter.
29. The analysis conducted by Schneuwly (2003) using the same dataset confirms these findings.
30. However, commentators have highlighted that other positive results may have arisen from the labour standards-related sanctions in this case: For example, sanctions can 'demonstrate the political commitment to a particular set of values and norms such as core labour standards' and 'may also deter other countries from committing violations' (Zhou and Cuyvers, 2011: 78).
31. Strong pressures regarding costs and prices can induce supplier companies to reduce labour costs in a way that augments the risk of forced labour through the abuse of workers' vulnerability, for example with the imposition of illegal wage deductions, penalties, or fines, as well as the withdrawal or non-payment of wages. Pressures on delivery time (for example, when suppliers need to complete orders in short production windows, or there are fluctuations in short-term demand) incentivize recourse to overtime, outsourcing of production, and use of informal labour contracting. All these practices increase the risk of forced labour in the GVC (ILO, 2012; ILO et al., 2019).
32. Inequality and discrimination are also factors associated with forced labour (ILO Global Business Network on Forced Labour, 2022). Poor populations have limited livelihood options, leaving them more likely to fall into debt bondage and to depend on their employers for housing, food, or the employment of their relatives – two situations considered by the ILO to be indicators of forced labour (ILO, 2012). Several studies establish a significant correlation between illiteracy and a low level of schooling, and the risk of being subjected to forced labour (ILO, 2014; LeBaron et al., 2019). Further, migrants, who are less likely to know the local language and legal frameworks, are at greater risk than the general population of becoming victims of abuse due to their vulnerability and are more frequently found in forced labour situations (ILO, 2012). Forced labour among migrant workers has been found to be more than three times higher than among non-migrant workers (ILO, Walk Free and IOM, 2022).
33. These authors and others are typically referring to the case of the rubber glove-producing company Top Glove in particular (see also Brudney, 2020; LaFianza, 2022).
34. This applies to non-surgical rubber gloves; see the relevant page at the Observatory of Economic Complexity (OEC), https://oec.world/en/profile/hs/gloves-other-than-surgical-of-rubber?yearSelector1=2021.

35. In 2022, the exported value of Malaysian rubber gloves had dropped to approximately the level of 2018 (ILO, 2023).
36. These include the ILO Forced Labour Convention, 1930 (No. 29) and the Protocol of 2014 to the Forced Labour Convention, 1930, among others (ILO, 2023). While Malaysia has also ratified the Abolition of Forced Labour Convention, 1957 (No. 105), it denounced this convention in 1990; see the ILO's Information System on International Labour Standards, available at: https://webapps.ilo.org/dyn/normlex/en/f?p=NORMLEXPUB:11200:0::NO::P11200_COUNTRY_ID:102960.
37. On the limitations of the legal framework prior to 2022, see ILO (2019b).
38. On this terminology, see the section titled 'Forced Labour-Related Provisions in Trade Instruments'.
39. For further details, see CBP's Withhold Release Orders and Findings List, available at: www.cbp.gov/trade/forced-labor/withhold-release-orders-and-findings.
40. In addition, in November 2022 a major US home appliance company cut ties with a Malaysian supplier as a result of labour rights concerns, while the latter was at the time being examined by CBP in relation to forced labour allegations (Ananthalakshmi, 2021).
41. This plan lays out strategies and related measures with a view to eliminating forced labour in Malaysia by 2030 (Hwok Aun and Pereira, 2023).
42. See, notably, the 'Supply Chains for a Sustainable Future of Work' project (GLO/22/29/EUR), which addresses, among others, the Malaysian rubber glove sector, www.ilo.org/projects-and-partnerships/projects/supply-chains-sustainable-future-work-decent-work-rubber-glove-supply-chain. Other projects aim to strengthen the rights of migrant workers in Malaysia (see the 'Protecting the Rights of Migrant Workers through Empowerment and Advocacy' project [MYS/15/01/USA and MYS/22/50/USA], https://webapps.ilo.org/DevelopmentCooperationDashboard/#b83hj3s) or the broader legal and institutional framework (see the 'Support for Labour Law and Industrial Relations Reform in Malaysia' project [MYS/16/01/USA], www.ilo.org/projects-and-partnerships/projects/support-labour-law-and-industrial-relations-reform-malaysia).
43. For further information, see www.responsibleglove.org/about/rga-overview/.
44. This might be particularly relevant in light of research suggesting that the Malaysian authorities' increased focus on companies subject to an import ban may have come at the expense of scrutiny of other companies using forced labour (Trueba and Staniland, 2023).

References

Addo, K. (2015). *Core Labour Standards and International Trade. Lessons from the Regional Context.* Heidelberg; New York; Dordrecht; London: Springer.

Agustí-Panareda, J., F. C. Ebert, and D. LeClercq (2015). 'ILO Labor Standards and Trade Agreements: A Case for Consistency'. *Comparative Labor Law and Policy Journal* 36(3): 347–80.

Aissi, J., R. Peels, and D. Samaan (2018). 'Evaluating the Effectiveness of Labour Provisions in Trade Agreements: An Analytical and Methodological Framework'. *International Labour Review* 157(4): 671–98.

Alon, S. (2022). 'Enforcing the Forced Labor Prohibition: Increasing Transparency and Mandating Supply Chain Due Diligence'. *Federal Circuit Bar Journal* 31(4): 377–406.

Alston, P. (1993). 'Labor Rights Provisions in US Trade Law: "Aggressive Unilateralism"?' *Human Rights Quarterly* 15(1): 1–35.

Ananthalakshmi, A. (2021). 'Dyson Dumps Malaysian Supplier ATA over Labour Concerns'. Reuters (Business section), 25 November.

Anner, M. (2020). 'Squeezing Workers' Rights in Global Supply Chains: Purchasing Practices in the Bangladesh Garment Export Sector in Comparative Perspective'. *Review of International Political Economy* 27(2): 320–47.

Anti-Slavery International and European Center for Constitutional and Human Rights (2021). 'Anti-Slavery International and European Center for Constitutional and Human Rights' Position on Import Controls to Address Forced Labour in Supply Chains'. Briefing Note. Available at: https://www.antislavery.org/wp-content/uploads/2021/06/Anti-Slavery-International-ECCHR-Import-Controls-Position-Paper-1.pdf.

Armstrong, C. S. (1975). 'American Import Controls and Morality in International Trade: An Analysis of Section 307 of the Tariff Act of 1930'. *New York University Journal of International Law and Politics* 8(1): 19–38.

Aziz, A. (2019). 'Glove Makers Could Benefit from US Ban on WRP Products'. *The Malaysian Reserve*, 3 October.

Bade, D. L. (2000). 'Corporate Responsibility and U.S. Import Regulations against Forced Labor'. *Tulsa Journal of Comparative and International Law* 8(1): 5–14.

Barry, C. and S. G. Reddy (2006). 'International Trade and Labor Standards: A Proposal for Linkage'. *Cornell International Law Journal* 39(3) 545–639.

Bartels, L. (2013). 'Human Rights and Sustainable Development Obligations in EU Free Trade Agreements'. *Legal Issues of Economic Integration* 40(4): 297–313.

Bartley, T. (2011). 'Transnational Governance as the Layering of Rules: Intersections of Public and Private Standards'. *Theoretical Inquiries in Law* 12(2): 517–42.

Bell, S. L. (2016). 'The US Prohibition on Imports Made with Forced Labour: The New Law Is a "Force" to Be Reckoned With'. *Global Trade and Customs Journal* 11(11/12): 580–83.

Bengtsen, P. (2019). 'Clean Gloves, Dirty Practices: Debt Bondage in Malaysia's Rubber Glove Industry'. *The Diplomat*, 22 November.

——— (2022). 'After Pressure, Growing Transparency in Malaysia's Glove Industry'. *The Diplomat*, 4 April.

Bhagwati, J. (1995). 'Trade Liberalisation and 'Fair Trade' Demands: Addressing the Environmental and Labour Standards Issues'. *World Economy* 18(6): 745–59.

Bhala, R. (1998). 'Clarifying the Trade-labor Link'. *Columbia Journal of Transnational Law* 37(1): 11–56.

Bhutta, M., B. Bostock, J. Brown, E. Day, A. Hughes, R. Hurst, A. Trautrims, and M. L. Trueba (2021). *Forced Labour in the Malaysian Medical Gloves Supply Chain Before and During the COVID-19 Pandemic: Evidence, Scale and Solutions*. ResearchGate Technical Report, July 2021.

Blackett, A. (1999). 'Whither Social Clause? Human Rights, Trade Theory and Treaty Interpretation'. *Columbia Human Rights Law Review* 31(1): 1–80.

——— (2019). 'Le Régionalisme Social Du Programme "Better Work Haiti"'. *McGill Journal of Sustainable Development Law* 14(2): 189–216.

Bronz, G. (1949). 'The International Trade Organization Charter'. *Harvard Law Review* 62(7): 1089–125.

Brudney, A. (2020). 'Using the Master's Tools to Dismantle the Master's House: 307 Petitions as a Human Rights Tool'. Corporate Accountability Lab, 31 August. Available at: https://corpaccountabilitylab.org/calblog/2020/8/28/using-the-masters-tools-to-dismantle-the-masters-house-307-petitions-as-a-human-rights-tool.

Buang, S. (2022). 'Renewing the Fight against Forced Labour in All Its Forms'. *New Straits Times*, 3 April.

Buckley, P., L. Pietropaoli, A. Rosada, B. Harguth, and J. Broom (2022). 'How Has COVID-19 Affected Migrant Workers Vulnerability to Human Trafficking for Forced Labour in Southeast Asia? A Narrative Review'. *Journal of Public Health and Emergency* 6: 1–12.

Casey, C. A. and C. D. Cimino-Isaacs (2022). *Section 307 and Imports Produced by Forced Labor*. CRS IF11360. Congressional Research Service.

CBP (US Customs and Border Protection) (2020a). 'CBP Revokes Withhold Release Order on Disposable Rubber Gloves'. 24 March.

——— (2020b). ‘CBP Issues Detention Order on Palm Oil Produced with Forced Labor in Malaysia’. 30 September.

——— (2020c). ‘CBP Issues Withhold Release Order on Palm Oil Produced by Forced Labor in Malaysia’. 30 December.

——— (2021a). ‘CBP Issues Forced Labor Finding on Top Glove Corporation Bhd’. 29 March.

——— (2021b). ‘CBP Issues Withhold Release Order on Malaysian Glove Producers’. 4 November.

——— (2021c). ‘CBP Modifies Forced Labor Finding on Top Glove Corporation Bhd’. 9 September.

——— (2021d). ‘CBP Issues Withhold Release Order on Supermax Corporation Bhd. and Its Subsidiaries’. 20 October.

——— (2021e). ‘CBP Issues Withhold Release Order on Brightway Group’. 20 December.

——— (2022). ‘Notice of Finding that Certain Palm Oil and Derivative Products Made Wholly or in Part with Palm Oil Produced by the Malaysian Company Sime Darby Plantation Berhad Its Subsidiaries, and Joint Ventures, with the Use of Convict, Forced or Indentured Labor Are Being, or Are Likely to Be, Imported into the United States in Violation of 19 U.S.C. 1307’. *Federal Register*. 28 January.

——— (2023a). ‘CBP Modifies Withhold Release Order in Response to Smart Glove’s Successful Actions to Address Forced Labor Supply Chain Issue’. 26 April.

——— (2023b). ‘CBP Modifies Withhold Release Order on YTY Industry Holdings Sdn Bhd (YTY Group) in Malaysia’. 8 February.

——— (2023c). ‘CBP Modifies Withhold Release Order against Supermax Corporation Bhd. and Its Subsidiaries’. 19 September.

——— (2024). ‘CBP Modifies Withhold Release Order on Brightway Group in Malaysia’. 11 October.

Charnovitz, S. (1987). ‘The Influence of International Labour Standards on the World Trading Regime: A Historical Overview’. *International Labour Review* 126(5): 565–84.

Cheong, D. and F. C. Ebert (2016). ‘Labour Law and Trade Policy: What Implications for Economic and Human Development?’ In *Labour Regulation and Development: Socio-Legal Perspectives*, edited by S. Marshall and C. Fenwick, 82–126. Cheltenham/Northampton: Edward Elgar.

Chu, M. M. and R. Latiff (2021). ‘Malaysia Says Forced Labour Allegations Hurting Investor Confidence’. Reuters (Business section), 1 December.

Coffey, A. B. (2015). 'Beyond Pre-reconstruction Slavery: America's Modern Day Trade Practices and Confronting Forced Labor'. *George Mason Journal of International Commercial Law* 6(2): 201–26.

Compa, L. (1993). 'International Labor Rights and the Sovereignty Question: NAFTA and Guatemala, Two Case Studies'. *American University Journal of International Law and Policy* 9(1): 117–50.

Corley-Coulibaly, M., F. C. Ebert, and P. Sekerler Richiardi (2023). 'Introduction'. In *Integrating Trade and Decent Work, Volume II: The Potential of Trade and Investment Policies to Address Labour Market Issues in Supply Chains*, edited by M. Corley-Coulibaly, F. C. Ebert, and P. Sekerler Richiardi, xviii–xxiv. Geneva: International Labour Office.

Corley-Coulibaly, M., G. Grasselli, and I. Postolachi (2023a). *Promoting and Enforcing Compliance with Labour Provisions in Trade Agreements: Comparative Analysis of Canada, European Union and United States Approaches and Practices.* Geneva: International Labour Office.

Corley-Coulibaly, M., G. Grasselli, and I. Postolachi (2023b). 'Implementation of Labour Provisions under Canadian, European Union and United States Trade Agreements'. In *Integrating Trade and Decent Work, Volume II: The Potential of Trade and Investment Policies to Address Labour Market Issues in Supply Chains*, edited by M. Corley-Coulibaly, F. C. Ebert, and P. Sekerler Richiardi, 29–66. Geneva: International Labour Office.

Dasgupta, A. (2000). 'Labour Standards and WTO: A New Form of Protectionism'. *South Asia Economic Journal* 1(2): 113–29.

David, F., K. Bryant, and J. Joudo Larsen (2019). *Migrants and Their Vulnerability to Human Trafficking, Modern Slavery and Forced Labour.* Geneva: International Organization for Migration.

Ebert, F. C. (2009). 'Between Political Goodwill and WTO-Law: Human Rights Conditionality in the Community's New Scheme of Generalised Tariff Preferences (GSP).' ZERP-Arbeitspapier 8/2009. Centre of European Law and Politics (ZERP), University of Bremen.

——— (2016). 'Labour Provisions in EU Trade Agreements: What Potential for Channelling Labour Standards-Related Capacity Building'. *International Labour Review* 155(3): 407–34.

Ebert, F. C., F. Francavilla, and L. Guarcello (2023). 'Tackling Forced Labour in Supply Chains: The Potential of Trade and Investment Governance'. In *Integrating Trade and Decent Work, Volume II: The Potential of Trade and Investment Policies to Address Labour Market Issues in Supply Chains*, edited by

M. Corley-Coulibaly, F. C. Ebert, and P. Sekerler Richiardi, 103–38. Geneva: International Labour Office.

EC (European Commission) (2022). *Proposal for a Regulation on Prohibiting Products Made with Forced Labour on the Union Market*. COM/2022/453.

Ehrenberg, D. S. (1995). 'The Labor Link: Applying the International Trading System to Enforce Violations of Forced And Child Labor'. *Yale Journal of International Law* 20(2): 361–418.

Elliott, K. A. (1998). *Preferences for Workers? Worker Rights and the U.S. Generalized System of Preferences*. Washington, DC: Institute for International Economics.

Elliott, K. A. and R. Freeman (2003). *Can Labor Standards Improve under Globalization?* Washington, DC: Institute for International Economics.

Ellis-Petersen, H. (2018). 'NHS Rubber Gloves Made in Malaysian Factories Linked with Forced Labour'. *The Guardian*, 9 December.

Eustace, A. (2023). 'The European Union's Forced Labour Regulation: Putting the "Brussels Effect" to Work for International Labour Standards'. *European Labour Law Review* 15(1): 144–65.

EU–US Trade and Technology Council (2023). *Roundtable on Due Diligence Report*. Working Group 10 – Global Trade Challenges. Trade and Technology Dialogue/Centre for European Policy Studies.

Fanou, T. (2023). *Literature Review: Forced Labour Import Bans*. GFLC, Governing Forced Labour in Supply Chains. Available at: https://gflc.ca/wp-content/uploads/2020/10/Forced-Labour-Import-Bans.pdf.

Fudge, J. and G. LeBaron (2024). 'Regulatory Design and Interactions in Worker-Driven Social Responsibility Initiatives: The Dindigul Agreement'. *International Labour Review* 163(4): 575–98.

Gordon, J. (2015). 'Global Labour Recruitment in a Supply Chain Context'. Fundamentals Working Papers, ILO.

——— (2024). 'The US Forced Labor Import Ban as a Tool to Raise Labor Standards in Supply Chain Contexts: Strategic Approaches to Advocacy'. Available at: https://ssrn.com/abstract=4756721.

Grado, V. (2025). 'Trade Prohibitions on Forced Labour Products: A First Assessment of the Forthcoming EU's Forced Labour Regulation'. *European Yearbook of International Economic Law 2024* (FirstView).

Häberli, C., M. Jansen, and J. Monteiro (2012). 'Regional Trade Agreements and Domestic Labour Market Regulation'. In *Policy Priorities for International Trade and Jobs*, edited by D. Lippoldt, 287–325. Paris: OECD.

Higgins, M. M. (2023). 'Closed Loophole, Open Ports: Section 307 of the Tariff Act and the Ongoing Importation of Goods Made Using Forced Labor'. *Stanford Law Review* 75(4): 917–77.

Hoffstaedter, G. and A. Missbach (2021). 'Facilitating Irregular Migration into Malaysia and from Indonesia: Illicit Markets, Endemic Corruption and Symbolic Attempts to Overcome Impunity'. *Public Anthropologist* 3(1): 8–31.

Hornbeck, J. F. (2011). 'The Haitian Economy and the HOPE Act'. *Current Politics and Economics of South and Central America* 4(3): 565–601.

Horsey, R. (2023). 'EU Trade Preferences and Human Rights in Myanmar'. In *Social Justice and the World of Work. Possible Global Futures*, edited by B. Langille and A. Trebilcock, 283–92. Oxford: Hart.

Hughes, A., J. A. Brown, M. Trueba, A. Trautrims, B, Bostock, E. Day, R. Hurst, and M. F. Bhutta, (2022). 'Global Value Chains for Medical Gloves during the Covid-19 Pandemic: Confronting Forced Labour through Public Procurement and Crisis'. *Global Networks* 23(1): 132–49.

Hutchinson, F. E. and P. Bhattacharya (2020). *Malaysia's Rubber Glove Industry: A Silver Lining Amidst Dark Clouds*. ISEAS Perspective 2020/138.

——— (2021). *Malaysia's Rubber Glove Industry: The Good, the Bad and the Ugly*. ISEAS Perspective 2021/35.

Hwok Aun, L. and A. Pereira (2023). *Can Malaysia Eliminate Forced Labour by 2030?* Singapore: ISEAS – Yusof Ishak Institute.

ILO (2012). *ILO Indicators of Forced Labour*. Geneva: ILO.

——— (2013). *The Social Dimensions of Free Trade Agreements*. Geneva: ILO.

——— (2014). *Profits and Poverty: The Economics of Forced Labour*. Geneva: ILO.

——— (2016). *Assessment of Labour Provisions in Trade and Investment Arrangements*. Geneva: ILO.

——— (2019a). *Labour Provisions in G7 Trade Agreements: A Comparative Perspective*. Geneva: ILO.

——— (2019b). *Situation and Gap Analysis on Malaysian Legislation, Policies and Programmes, and the ILO Forced Labour Convention and Protocol*. Geneva: ILO.

——— (2023). *Decent Work Challenges and Opportunities in Malaysia's Rubber Glove Supply Chain*. Geneva: ILO.

ILO, OECD (Organisation for Economic Co-operation and Development), IOM (International Organization for Migration), and UNICEF (United Nations Children's Fund) (2019). *Ending Child Labour, Forced Labour and Human Trafficking in Global Supply Chains*. Geneva: ILO.

ILO, Walk Free, and IOM (International Organization for Migration) (2022). *Global Estimates of Modern Slavery: Forced Labour and Forced Marriage*. Geneva: ILO.

ILO Global Business Network on Forced Labour (2022). *Eradicating Forced Labour: What Works in Practice*. 13 September.

Kamel, H. (2020). 'Top Glove to be Charged in Court for Violating Act 446'. *The Malaysian Reserve*, 1 December.

Kawano, M. (2019). 'Changing Resource-Based Manufacturing Industry: The Case of the Rubber Industry in Malaysia and Thailand'. In *Emerging States at Crossroads*, edited by K. Tsunekawa and Y. Todo, 145–62. Singapore: Springer.

Khalid, S. (2022). 'No US CBP Officers Stationed in Malaysia to Probe Forced Labour Claims'. *The Edge Malaysia*, 2 June.

Kolben, K. (2015). 'Dialogic Labor Regulation in the Global Supply Chain'. *Michigan Journal of International Law* 36(3): 425–65.

Kryvoi, Y. (2008). 'Why European Union Trade Sanctions Do Not Work'. *Minnesota Journal of International Law* 17(2): 209–46.

LaFianza, J. (2022). 'Threatening Ill-Gotten Gains: Analyzing the Effectiveness of a Forced Labor Import Ban in the European Union'. European Union Law Working Papers No. 60, Stanford-Vienna Transatlantic Technology Law Forum. Available at: https://law.stanford.edu/publications/no-60-threatening-ill-gotten-gains-analyzing-the-effectiveness-of-a-forced-labor-import-ban-in-the-european-union/.

LeBaron, G. (2021). 'The Role of Supply Chains in the Global Business of Forced Labour'. *Journal of Supply Chain Management* 57(2): 29–42.

LeBaron, G., P. Kyritsis, T. Cameron, and N. Howard (2019). *Confronting Root Causes: Forced Labour in Global Supply Chains*. London: Open Democracy.

Lebdioui, A. (2022). 'The Political Economy of Moving Up in Global Value Chains: How Malaysia Added Value to Its Natural Resource through Industrial Policy'. *Review of International Political Economy* 29(3): 870–903.

Lee, L. (2020). 'Amid Virus Crisis, U.S. Bars Imports of Malaysia's Top Glove over Labour Issues'. Reuters, 16 July.

Lim, J. (2019). 'US Bans WRP's Malaysia-made Gloves Amid Forced Labour Allegations'. *The Edge Malaysia*, 2 October.

Locke, R. M., B. A. Rissing, and P. Timea (2013). 'Complements or Substitutes? Private Codes, State Regulation and the Enforcement of Labour Standards in Global Supply Chains'. *British Journal of Industrial Relations* 51(3): 519–52.

Lopez, A. and S. Alghazali (2023). 'North American Countries Finally Align on Forced Labor Regulations'. Reuters, 28 April.

Lopez-Jurado, C. (2005). 'El Nuevo Sistema Preferencias Arancelarias Generalizadas Comunitario a la Luz de los Informes de la Organización Mundial del Comercio'. *Revista de Derecho Comunitario Europeo* 9(21): 447–84.

Malay Mail (2020). 'HR Ministry: Task Force Formed to Ensure Policy Compliance in Rubber-Based Industry'. 17 October.

——— (2022). 'Margma: RM3.6b Loss Is Cumulative Potential Loss in Export Revenue Due to WRO'. 2 March.

Marceau, G., R. Walker, and A. Oeschger (2023). 'The Evolution of Labour Provisions in Regional Trade Agreements'. *Journal of World Trade* 57(3): 1–50.

Marx, A., F. C. Ebert, and N. Hachez (2017). 'Dispute Settlement for Labour Provisions in EU Free Trade Agreements: Rethinking Current Approaches'. *Politics and Governance* 5(4): 49–59.

Maupain, F. (2005). 'Is the ILO Effective in Upholding Labour Rights? Reflections on the Myanmar Experience'. In *Labour Rights as Human Rights*, edited by P. Alston, 85–142. New York: Oxford University Press.

McCrudden, C. and A. Davies (2000). 'A Perspective on Trade and Labor Rights'. *Journal of International Economic Law* 3(1): 43–62.

McGregor, J. (2022). 'Canada Terminates $222m PPE Contract Following Forced Labour Probe'. CBC News, 19 January.

Mende, J. (2019). 'The Concept of Modern Slavery: Definition, Critique, and the Human Rights Frame'. *Human Rights Review* 20(2): 229–48.

Moore, M. and C. Scherrer (2017). *Conditional or Promotional Trade Agreements - Is Enforcement Possible? How International Labour Standards Can Be Enforced through US and EU Social Chapters.* Singapore: Friedrich-Ebert-Stiftung.

Morales, R. (2023). 'Entra en Vigor Acuerdo para Prohibir Importación de Mercancías Producidas con Trabajo Forzoso'. *El Economista*, 18 May.

Morgandi, T. (2022). *WTO Law Aspects of Import Prohibitions on Products and Services Made Using Forced Labour.* Washington, DC: International Lawyers Assisting Workers Network.

Natta, P. M. (2021). 'Anti-forced Labour Update: Stronger Legislation with an Absence of Guidance'. *Global Trade and Customs Journal* 16(5): 209–16.

Ness, I. (2021). Temporary Labour and Worker Exploitation: Southeast Asian Migration to Malaysia. In *Handbook of Migration and Global Justice*, edited by L. Weber and Claudia Tazreiter, 26–48. Cheltenham: Edward Elgar.

OECD (Organisation for Economic Co-operation and Development). (2020). 'Trade Policy Implications of Global Value Chains'. Trade Policy Brief. February.

Oehri, M. (2015). 'Comparing US and EU Labour Governance "Near and Far" – Hierarchy vs Network?' *Journal of European Public Policy* 22(5): 731–49.

Ong, S. (2022). 'Supermax Implements New Foreign Worker Management Policy Effective November 2021'. *The Edge Malaysia*, 3 January.

Orbie, J. and Tortell, L. (2009). 'The New GSP+ Beneficiaries: Ticking the Box or Truly Consistent with ILO Findings?' *European Foreign Affairs Review* 14(4): 663–81.

Pietropaoli, I., O. Johnstone, and A. Balch (2021). 'Effectiveness of Forced Labour Import Bans'. Modern Slavery PEC Policy Brief 2021-3. Modern Slavery and Human Rights Policy and Evidence Centre.

Pellerin, W., C. Scheitterlein, and T. Farrell (2021). 'Combatting Forced Labour in Supply Chains from a Canadian Customs Perspective'. McMillan, 22 December.

Perez-Lopez, J. F. (1988). 'Conditioning Trade on Foreign Labor Law: The U.S. Approach'. *Comparative Labor Law Journal* 9(2): 253–93.

Plouffe-Malette, K. and H. Bisson (2019). 'Forced Labour and Trade: A Canada–United States Comparative Analysis'. *European Review of International Studies* 6(3): 3–17.

Rahman, M. A., N. B. Shan, and A. M. Morhalim (2021). *Will Rubber Gloves Continue to Be a Key Driver of Malaysia's Exports Growth in 2021*? 18 February. MIDF Research.

Raj-Reichert, G. (2020). 'The Powers of a Social Auditor in a Global Production Network: The Case of Verité and the Exposure of Forced Labour in the Electronics Industry'. *Journal of Economic Geography* 20(3): 653–78.

Remedy Project (2023). *Putting Things Right: Remediation of Forced Labour under the Tariff Act 1930.*

Reuters (2022). 'Malaysian Firms Facing U.S. Bans over Forced Labour Summoned by Ministry'. 30 January.

Salim, S. (2022). 'World's Largest Sovereign Wealth Fund's Manager Places Supermax under Observation on Human Rights Violation Allegations'. *The Edge Malaysia*, 16 June.

Scheuerman, W. E. (2001). 'False Humanitarianism? US Advocacy of Transnational Labour Protections'. *Review of International Political Economy* 8(3): 359–88.

Schneuwly, P. (2003). 'Sind Handelssanktionen ein geeignetes Mittel zur Durchsetzung von Arbeitsnormen?: Eine Untersuchung der Wirksamkeit der Sozialklausel im US GSP'. *Aussenwirtschaft: Zeitschrift für Internationale Wirtschaftsbeziehungen* 58(1): 121–44.

Schwarz, K., E. Celiksoy, J. Smętek, E. Wolosik, K. Lubianiec, A. Makulec, and T. Landman (2022). *External Policy Tools to Address Modern Slavery and Forced Labour*. Brussels: European Parliament.

Servais, J.-M. (1989). 'The Social Clause in Trade Agreements: Wishful Thinking or an Instrument of Social Progress'. *International Labour Review* 128(4): 423–32.

Shamir, H. (2012). 'A Labor Paradigm for Human Trafficking'. *UCLA Law Review* 60(1): 76–136.

Siroën, J.-M. (2013). 'Labour Provisions in Preferential Trade Agreements: Current Practice and Outlook'. *International Labour Review* 152(1): 85–106.

Sitkowski, M. D. and M. R. Kinsman (2021). 'Forced Labor Enforcement: CBP's Latest Seizure Sends "Strong Message" to the Trade Community'. Faegre Drinker, 10 May.

Stolzenberg, H. (2019). 'Inspection of the Inspectors: Is the European Commission Sufficiently Prosecuting Violations of ILO Conventions under the GSP Regulation?' *Archiv des Völkerrechts* 57(2): 207–33.

Syam, A. and M. Roggensack (2020). *Importing Freedom: Using the U.S. Tariff Act to Combat Forced Labor in Supply Chains.* Washington, DC: Human Trafficking Legal Center.

Thomas, J. (2020). 'Glovemaker WRP to Reimburse Recruitment Fee Paid by Workers'. *Free Malaysia Today* (*FMT*), 8 July.

Trebilcock, M. J. and R. Howse (2005). 'Trade Policy and (and) Labor Standards'. *Minnesota Journal of Global Trade* 14(2): 261–300.

Trubek, D. M. and L. G. Trubek (2007). 'New Governance and Legal Regulation: Complementarity, Rivalry, and Transformation'. *Columbia Journal of European Law* 13(3): 539–64.

Trueba, M. L. and F. Staniland (2023). *Effectiveness of Forced Labour Import Bans: The Case of the U.S. Ban on Malaysia's Rubber Gloves.* 8th Conference of the Regulating for Decent Work Network, 10–12 July 2023. ILO.

Tsogas, G. (1999). 'Labour Standards in International Trade Agreements: An Assessment of the Arguments'. *International Journal of Human Resource Management* 10(2): 351–75.

——— (2000). 'Labour Standards in the Generalized Systems of Preferences of the European Union and the United States'. *European Journal of Industrial Relations* 6(3): 349–70.

United States Department of Labor (2020). '2020 List of Goods Produced by Child Labor or Forced Labor'. https://www.dol.gov/agencies/ilab/reports/child-labor/list-of-goods.

United States Department of State (2021). *2021 Trafficking in Persons Report.* Washington, DC: United States Department of State.

United States GAO (Government Accountability Office) (2021). *Forced Labor: CBP Should Improve Communication to Strengthen Trade Enforcement.* GAO-21-259.

USTR (Office of the United States Trade Representative) (2018). 'President Trump Terminates Trade Preference Program Eligibility for Mauritania'. Press Release, 2 November.

——— (2019). 'USTR Announces GSP Enforcement Actions and Successes for Seven Countries'. Press Release, 25 October.

Velut, J-B., D.B. Breinbauer, M. de Bruijne, E. Garnizova, M. Jones, K. Kolben, L. Oules, V. Rouas, F. T. Pittet, and T. Zamparutti (2022). *Comparative Analysis of Trade and Sustainable Development Provisions in Free Trade Agreements*. London: London School of Economics and Political Science.

Velluti, S. (2020). *The Role of the EU in the Promotion of Human Rights and International Labour Standards in Its External Trade Relations*. Cham: Springer.

Wahab, A. (2019). 'Human Rights Anchored in Business: Practice and Challenges in the Palm Oil Sector in Malaysia'. *Asian International Studies Review* 20(1): 1–20.

Wahab, A., A. H. Abd Murad, and R. Shamsudin (2023). 'Illuminating Causes and Barriers Underpinning Forced Labour in Nepal–Malaysia Migration Corridor'. *Journal of Strategic Studies and International Affairs* 3(1): 50–65.

Wong, L. (2025). *Generalized System of Preferences (GSP): FAQ*. IF11232. Congressional Research Service.

WTO (World Trade Organization) (2021). *The Use of Forced Labor on Fishing Vessels: Submission of the United States*. TN/RL/GEN/205.

Zhou, W. and L. Cuyvers (2011). 'Linking International Trade and Labour Standards: The Effectiveness of Sanctions under the European Union's GSP'. *Journal of World Trade* 45(1): 63–85.

Zini, S. (2018). 'Promouvoir l'ouverture commerciale et le progrès social: les normes de travail équitables dans la Charte de La Havane (1948)'. *Relations Internationales* 174(2): 53–72.

4

Will Remedy Remain Rare?

The Potential of Mandatory Human Rights Due Diligence to Redress Modern Slavery

Ingrid Landau and Shelley Marshall

Despite international instruments on trafficking and forced labour that stipulate the importance of ensuring rightsholders can access effective remedy, instances of remediation for harms including forced, bonded, and child labour, as well as trafficking, have been rare. While remedy is also a common feature of strategies to address modern slavery adopted by nation states and multinational businesses, in practice workers who have been subject to severe forms of labour exploitation in global value chains (GVCs) continue to face significant obstacles to securing redress from those who have violated, or contributed to violation, of their rights.

Obstacles to remedy are multifarious and well-documented (OHCHR, 2016; ICAR et al., 2013). GVCs are complex, involving multiple actors and crossing multiple jurisdictions, rendering it challenging to assign accountability and secure appropriate remedial measures, and most legal systems have not adapted to the reality of service and production within GVCs. Even where powerful ('lead') companies in the value chain shape the terms of supply and working conditions and are in the same jurisdiction in which the harm arising from their actions or omissions has occurred, remedial action is often stymied by labour law systems that only allow claims against direct employers. Where claims of joint employment or accessorial liability are possible under labour law, such claims are infrequent because of the stringency of tests of control or contribution, and the costs of such litigation (Marshall et al., 2023). In rare cases where litigants are successful in their legal claims, they often struggle to secure enforcement of any court order. Where the lead company that is influencing working conditions in the value chain is in another jurisdiction to where the harm has occurred, the chances of such claims succeeding are even lower (Fudge and Mundlak, 2023). Key principles underpinning private international law – such as those pertaining to jurisdiction and choice of law – largely operate to the benefit of businesses rather than those affected by their activities. Victims also face significant procedural and practical difficulties in pursuing claims transnationally through different causes of action, including torts or labour law (Fudge and Mundlak, 2023). Enforcement is also more challenging where companies are domiciled outside the country of the litigation unless there is an established reciprocal agreement or treaty in place that recognizes and enforces judgments from other jurisdictions.

In Europe, mandatory human rights due diligence (mHRDD) laws have been passed, or are being debated, which promise to do better when it comes to addressing issues of corporate responsibility for labour rights harms in transnational and cross-jurisdictional contexts. But will they deliver remedy or deepen the accountability of business? This chapter considers the extent to which they improve access to remedy for those who have been subject to forced labour and other egregious breaches of their human rights.[1] These laws are primarily directed at preventing human rights harm (including various forms of severe labour exploitation that are commonly described as 'modern slavery') in GVCs. Drawing on the concept of human rights due diligence in the UN Guiding Principles on Business and Human Rights (UNGPs) and the OECD Guidelines for Multinational Enterprises on Responsible Business Conduct (OECD Guidelines), these laws require large businesses to adopt processes to identify, prevent, mitigate, and account for how they address their actual and potential adverse human rights impacts in their own operations and value chains. They also address the issue of remedy where businesses fail to comply with mandatory requirements or to adopt inadequate due diligence measures. In this respect, they are presented as constituting an important step forward in the quest for accountability and redress for labour rights harms in value chains.

We assess the ways four existing and proposed mHRDD laws address remedy. Included in the analysis are the French Duty of Vigilance Law 2017,[2] the German Act on Corporate Due Diligence in Supply Chains 2021,[3] the Norwegian Transparency Act 2021,[4] and the European Union's Corporate Sustainability Due Diligence Directive, as approved by the European Parliament in April 2024 (CSDDD).[5] While other laws have been proposed in Europe, and modern slavery laws exist in Australia, Canada, the UK, and the USA, we focus on these four mHRDD laws as the fullest expression of the UNGPs to date. We also reflect on how these laws could be improved in relation to the provision of remedy, thereby increasing the likelihood of achieving accountability and providing remedies in cases of modern slavery. We conclude that while mHRDD in Europe can and should do more to improve access to remedy for victims of modern slavery and other human rights abuses, the policy priorities and frames that underpin these regulatory initiatives in the Economic North limit deeper forms of accountability.

This chapter is divided into four sections. We begin by discussing how we are using the term 'modern slavery' and the respective roles of states and business to provide remedy under international human rights law. We then discuss how remedy is approached and addressed in the four existing and proposed mHRDD laws. The third section of the chapter compares and contrasts how the four initiatives address key aspects of remedy and discusses ways in which these initiatives could be improved so as to afford greater prospect of accountability and remedy where labour rights harms have occurred. In the final section of the chapter, we offer some concluding observations.

Modern Slavery, Remedy, and the Role of Business

State duties and corporate responsibilities to remediate modern slavery are found in international human rights law, including conventions and soft law instruments such as the UNGPs. In this section of the chapter, we establish the foundations for the assessment conducted in the following section by revisiting the basic principles established in these instruments (see further the Introduction to this volume, Shamir et al., 2025).

Despite the term 'modern slavery' being notoriously imprecise and capacious (Shamir et al., 2025: Introduction to this volume; Kotiswaran, 2017; Chuang, 2014), there is broad global consensus that it is an unacceptable labour harm that should be prevented and remedied when prevention fails. Consistent with the treatment of modern slavery in this volume, we take the ILO's Forced Labour Convention, 1930 (No. 29), the ILO Protocol of 2014 to the Forced Labour Convention, 1930 (ILO Protocol 29), and its accompanying Forced Labour (Supplementary Measures) Recommendation, 2014 (No. 203) as our key reference points for conceptualizing what constitutes 'modern slavery' in the context of GVCs and state obligations to provide effective remedy. 'Forced labour' is defined in ILO Convention 29 as 'all work or service which is exacted from any person under the menace of any penalty and for which the said person has not offered himself voluntarily' (Art. 2(1)). This definition covers any type of situation in which a person is forced to work without his or her consent (subject to some very limited exceptions defined in Art. 2(2)). 'Menace of any penalty' is not limited to physical violence or threats thereof but also covers the threat of loss of rights and privileges, including, for example, the threat of being reported to immigration authorities (ILO, 2012: 111). Many of the types of labour exploitation covered by ILO Convention 29 are also covered by the broad definition of trafficking in the United Nations Protocol to Prevent, Suppress, and Punish Trafficking in Persons, Especially Women and Children, 2000 (the Palermo Protocol) (Shamir, 2012).

The duty of states to take effective measures to remedy modern slavery is established by several international instruments. ILO Protocol 29 requires ratifying state parties to take effective measures to ensure all victims of forced labour, irrespective of their presence or legal status in the national territory, have access to appropriate and effective remedies. ILO Recommendation 203 makes clear that remedies may include compensation for personal and material damages, such as unpaid wages and statutory social security contributions. This Recommendation elaborates on procedural rights such as access to courts and tribunals, other resolution mechanisms, and access to existing compensation schemes, the right to information in a language victims can understand, and legal assistance (preferably free of charge). International human rights instruments such as (but certainly not limited to) the International Covenant on Civil and Political Rights (UN ICCPR, 1966) and the Basic Principles and Guidelines on the Right to a Remedy and Reparation for Victims of Gross Violations of International Human Rights Law and Serious Violations of International Humanitarian Law (UNGA, 2005) also reaffirm the importance of addressing questions of remedy.

While these ILO instruments, as well as the Palermo Protocol and other international and regional trafficking laws, apply only to nation-states, others apply to businesses. Indeed, in the past 15 years, international standards have evolved to recognize that businesses also have an important role to play in preventing and remediating human rights harms (including those that constitute forms of modern slavery). Adopted by the UN Human Rights Council in 2011, the UNGPs constitute the most globally authoritative statement on the respective roles of states and businesses in preventing and remediating business-related human rights harms (including violations of workers' rights that commonly fall under the umbrella term of 'modern slavery') (OHCHR, 2011). They have been drawn upon extensively by states, intergovernmental organizations, businesses, and civil society in the design and evaluation of modern slavery-related regulatory initiatives.

The UNGPs are underpinned by three equally important and complementary pillars: (1) the state duty to protect human rights by third parties, including business; (2) the corporate responsibility to respect human rights; and (3) the need for greater access by victims to effective remedy. Like established international instruments, the UNGPs recognize that the state has the primary duty to take 'appropriate steps to prevent, investigate, punish and redress' business-related human rights abuses within their territory and/or jurisdiction (OHCHR, 2011: Guiding Principle 1). The innovation of the UNGPs was to go beyond the scope of existing instruments to establish that business also has a responsibility to avoid infringing on the human rights of others and to address human rights impacts with which they are involved (OHCHR, 2011: Guiding Principle 11). Under the UNGPs (and in the subsequently aligned OECD Guidelines), businesses can discharge this responsibility by having in place a policy commitment to respect human rights at the most senior level and remediation processes, engaging in HRDD, and having processes in place to enable remediation of harms to which they have caused or contributed.

The provision of remedies to rightsholders affected by business-related adverse human rights impacts is a core component of the UNGPs, and it is here that we focus on in our analysis. Under the UNGPs (and international human rights law more generally), remedy entails counteracting or 'making good' any harm that has occurred, and access to effective remedy includes both procedural and substantive aspects. It may take a variety of forms (depending on the context), including 'apologies, restitution, rehabilitation, financial or non-financial compensation, and punitive sanctions (whether criminal or administrative, such as fines), as well as the prevention of harm through, for example, injunctions or guarantees of non-repetition' (OHCHR, 2011: 27). The UNGPs emphasize the state's duty to ensure the effectiveness of domestic judicial mechanisms, including considering ways to reduce legal, practical, and other barriers that may lead to a denial of access to remedy (OHCHR, 2011: 28). They also make clear that states should provide effective and appropriate non-judicial mechanisms as part of a state-based system for remediating business-related human rights harms. Examples of such mechanisms include labour tribunals, national human rights institutions, and other state-supported complaint mechanisms.

The UNGPs set out two distinct but interrelated expectations for business in relation to facilitating access to effective remedy. First, businesses should establish or participate in effective operational-level grievance mechanisms. Such mechanisms are formalized and administered by businesses, alone or in collaboration with others, through which individuals and communities who may be adversely impacted by a business may directly lodge grievances and access remedy. The UNGPs set out seven criteria to ensure the effectiveness of such mechanisms and emphasize the importance of engagement and dialogue with stakeholders in design and evaluation and in resolving grievances. Second, where a business has not caused or contributed to a harm but is 'linked to' it by way of a business relationship, it should use leverage to seek to prevent future harms. This may include, for example, urging a business partner to provide remedy to affected persons (OHCHR, 2011: 24–25).

Although the UNGPs provide firm footing for remediation, they fall short of providing a framework for deeper accountability. We understand accountability as a moral or institutional relationship between different actors, in which one actor or group of actors (sometimes referred to as 'power wielders') has an obligation to explain and justify its conduct, and another actor or actors (sometimes called 'accountability holders') has the power or authority to pose questions, pass judgement, and impose consequences (Bovens, 2007: 450; Black, 2008; Macdonald, 2014). We are particularly concerned with the 'ability of these accountability holders to impose sanctions – to attach cost to the failure to meet the standards' (Buchanan and Keohane, 2006: 426). And as with many scholars who identify an 'enforcement gap' in accountability with regard to Global North–South relationships in GVCs (Landau and Hardy, 2021), a central inquiry for us is the extent that new laws and proposals will address this gap.

In the next section we apply the UNGP's framework to our assessment of existing and proposed mHRDD initiatives. In the third section, we consider in more detail these broader concerns around accountability.

Assessment of Four mHRDD Laws

Mandatory human rights due diligence (mHRDD) laws are widely regarded as the most advanced state-based instruments for holding businesses accountable for the negative human rights impacts of their transnational activities. As they are all state responses to the UNGPs, and thus heavily influenced by the principles, we assess the four initiatives against that framework regarding their effectiveness in affording access to those who have suffered harm.

Each analysis follows a similar structure. Firstly, we describe the purpose of each law, discerning whether the law is directed at preventing harms to rightsholders, protecting businesses and/or consumers, delivering remedy, or a combination of these. Subsequently, we briefly outline the coverage of the laws, identifying the scope of their applicability in terms of geographic reach, industries, and types of businesses. We then describe the broad obligations imposed by each law, dissecting the specific requirements placed on companies to undertake due diligence. Exploration next turns to the causes of action, the legal bases (civil, administrative, and so on), the actors involved, the nature of harms addressed, and the entities against whom actions can be brought. We describe the array of remedies available under each law, exploring the outcomes that victims and survivors can anticipate. We examine access to justice provisions, evaluating the mechanisms that facilitate or impede individuals or groups seeking redress. Finally, we assess the outcomes of cases thus far, if any, shedding light on the practical implications and efficacy of these laws in achieving their intended objectives.

French Duty of Vigilance Law 2017

Adopted in 2017, the French Duty of Vigilance Law seeks to 'encourage multinational companies to act responsibly with the aim of preventing tragic events' in France or abroad that would violate human rights and harm the environment, and to 'obtain remediation for the victims' where damage is sustained (Brabant and Savourey, 2017: 2). It has been described as the 'first ever duty established by a law of general application requiring multinational enterprises to monitor human rights abuses in their supply chains' and has been held up as a model for other mHRDD campaigns in Europe and beyond (Palombo, 2019: 275).

The law applies to all companies headquartered in France that employ over 5,000 employees in France or over 10,000 employees globally (including through direct and indirect subsidiaries) or foreign companies headquartered outside France, with French subsidiaries with at least 5,000 employees in France. These companies are required to establish a vigilance plan setting out:

> [r]easonable vigilance measures adequate to identify risks and to prevent severe impacts on human rights and fundamental freedoms, on the health and safety of persons and on the environment, resulting from the activities of the company and of those companies it controls … directly or indirectly, as well as the activities of subcontractors or suppliers with whom it has an established commercial relationship, when these activities are related to this relationship. (Commercial Code, Art. L.225-102-4-1)

As this provision indicates, the corporate 'duty of vigilance' established under the French law extends to cover human rights risks (including forced labour and other forms of severe labour exploitation) within subcontractors or suppliers with whom the company has an 'established business relationship', but not to other subcontractors and suppliers in its value chains.[6] Due diligence plans established under the law must include five 'vigilance measures': (*a*) a risk mapping meant for their identification, analysis, and prioritization; (*b*) regular evaluation processes regarding the situation of subsidiaries, subcontractors, or suppliers with whom there is an established commercial relationship, in line with the risk mapping; (*c*) adapted actions to mitigate risks or prevent severe impacts; (*d*) an alert and complaint mechanism relating to the existence or realization of risks, established in consultation with the representative trade union organizations within the company; and (*e*) a system monitoring implementation measures and evaluating their effectiveness.

The French law does not explicitly identify remediation of harm as an element of the corporate duty of vigilance, nor does it impose it as a clear additional obligation. However, it provides several avenues for compliance that may indirectly contribute to efforts to obtain remedy, as well as a right of civil action for victims of damage caused by the failure of a company to meet its duty of vigilance under the Act. Compliance with the French law is secured through three mechanisms: a formal notice to comply; an injunction with periodic penalty payments; and a civil liability action in tort. Any interested party may issue a formal notice to a non-complying company requesting compliance with its obligations to publish a vigilance plan. Where the company continues to fail to comply, the interested party may seek an injunction from the relevant court to order compliance, with periodic penalty payments in case of failure to comply. Finally, where a company fails to adopt and implement a vigilance plan and a risk materializes that could have been prevented by the execution of the due diligence obligations under the law, the company may be liable under French tort law for the harm incurred.

As of March 2023, 13 cases had been filed under the French law since 2017 (BHRRC, 2023). Most have been pursued in the context of NGO efforts to compel companies to take adequate or more effective action to address climate change. In the context of labour rights violations only two lawsuits have been lodged. One legal action was taken against French cosmetics company Yves Rocher in 2022 in relation to its Turkish subsidiary's dismissal of more than 130 of its employees in alleged violation of rights to freedom of association. Most relevant to the contexts of forced labour in GVCs, early in 2023, Brazilian

NGO Comissão Pastoral da Terra (CPT) and French association Notre Affaire à Tous filed a claim against BNP Paribas for providing financial services without adequate due diligence to companies in Brazil that have engaged in, inter alia, forced labour on cattle farms (Comissão Pastoral da Terra and Notre Affaire à Tous, 2023). The claimants argue that BNP's duty of vigilance plan does not adequately prevent deforestation and human rights violations. At the time of writing this complaint has yet to be resolved. It is unknown why so few cases concern labour harms beyond the normal challenges of identifying sufficient links between companies domiciled in France and labour harms occurring in different countries.

German Act on Corporate Due Diligence Obligations in Supply Chains 2021

The German Act on Corporate Due Diligence Obligations in Supply Chains came into force on 1 January 2023, after Germany shifted from hard-line opposition to such legislation to promoting it (Weihrauch et al., 2023). The law seeks to balance the improvement of access to justice for individuals affected by corporate activities in supply chains with the legitimate interests of companies in ensuring legal certainty and fair competitive conditions with 'the legitimate interests of companies in legal certainty and fair competitive conditions'.[7]

The German Act imposes due diligence obligations on companies with a registered office in Germany with at least 1,000 employees (§ 1). The law requires companies that fall within its scope to conduct due diligence, and report annually, for risks on a diverse array of human rights, including child labour, forced labour, all forms of slavery, occupational health and safety obligations, freedom of association, and unequal treatment in employment. While the Act includes a broad definition of 'supply chain' (§ 2(5)), companies are only obliged to include direct contractual partners in their risk analysis. However, an enterprise must extend its analysis further down the supply chain where it has 'substantiated knowledge' of a human rights-related violation by an indirect supplier (§ 9(3)).

Companies covered by the German law must fulfil nine due diligence obligations (§ 3). These include taking remedial action and establishing complaints procedures. Elaborating on the obligation to take remedial action, section 7 makes clear that an enterprise that discovers that a rights violation has already occurred or is imminent in its own business area or at a direct supplier must take appropriate remedial action to prevent, end, or minimize the violation without delay. This remedial action may include: the joint development and implementation of a plan to end or minimize the violation with the enterprise causing the violation; collaboration with other enterprises in sector initiatives and sector standards to increase the ability of influencing the entity that causes or may cause a harm; temporary suspension of the business relationship while efforts are made to minimize the risk; and (only in exceptional circumstances) termination of the relationship with the enterprise causing the violation. It is notable that all these remedial actions are directed at ensuring the company addresses its role in the human rights violation. None are directed at compensating the workers or restoring them to the position they would be in had the violation not occurred.

The German law requires enterprises that fall within its scope to ensure that an appropriate internal complaints procedure is in place (§ 8). This procedure should be capable of receiving complaints in relation to the enterprise, or its direct or indirect suppliers, and enabling persons to report human rights or environmental risks, as well as violations of human rights obligations resulting from the enterprise's actions in its own business area or those of its direct or indirect suppliers (§§ 8–9) (Koos, 2022). Such a complaints mechanism 'may offer a procedure for amicable settlement' of complaints and must meet certain criteria (for example, publicly available procedures, impartiality, confidentiality, and protection against retaliation). Enterprises may participate in an appropriate external complaints procedure rather than implementing their own, provided the external procedure also meets the statutory criteria.

The law does not establish any new bases for civil liability and excludes the possibility of civil liability claims by affected persons who have suffered harm as a result of a company's failure to meet its due diligence obligations under the Act (§ 3(3)) (Ruhl, 2024: 5–6). The removal of a civil liability clause from an earlier draft of the law is one of the main points of criticism of the law (Koos, 2022; Ruhl, 2024). However, the Act does not preclude other forms of liability that may arise under German private law (§ 3(3)). It also includes provisions directed at overcoming some of the recognized barriers to victims in accessing a civil remedy in German courts for human rights violations committed by companies abroad. Section 11 provides that persons affected by human rights violations may authorize a German trade union or non-governmental organization to bring proceedings in a German court on their behalf. This procedural feature will likely increase the number of lawsuits for alleged human rights violations in German courts (Schappert, 2023).

Administrative enforcement of the Act is undertaken by the Federal Office of Economics and Export Control (BAFA). As the competent authority, BAFA is responsible for monitoring compliance with the Act and is given broad powers to take appropriate and necessary measures to detect, end, and prevent violations by enterprises of their due diligence obligations (§§ 15–18). These powers include ordering an enterprise to submit a corrective action plan and/or take specific action to fulfil its obligations. BAFA can also impose fines for non-compliance (§ 23). Intentional or negligent violations of the due diligence obligations can be punished with a fine of up to EUR 8 million. If the company has an average annual turnover of more than EUR 400 million, the fine can be up to 2 per cent of the company's average annual turnover (§ 24(3)). BAFA may act on its own initiative or in response to a person with a 'substantiated claim' of an actual or imminent violation of a due diligence obligation (§ 14(1)). There is no suggestion within the Act that BAFA is empowered to take action against non-compliant enterprises on behalf of victims or to secure compensation or remediation for affected persons.

Three complaints had been submitted under the German Act by March 2024, though no decisions have been issued, so little is known as to how seriously BAFA will treat instances of non-compliance or what types of orders it will be willing to make. In contrast to the French Duty of Vigilance law, all the complaints thus far submitted concern labour harms. The first case under the German Supply Chain Due Diligence Act was filed on behalf of Bangladeshi workers in April 2023 against Tom Tailor, Amazon, and IKEA for an alleged failure to meet due diligence obligations, primarily for occupational health and safety, for 'adequately monitoring' the conditions in their factories and for 'endangering the workplace safety for employees' (Annat, 2023). On 21 June 2023, a second case was filed by the non-profit organization European Center for Constitutional and Human Rights (ECCHR) against Volkswagen, BMW, and Mercedes-Benz. The companies have been accused of failing to take appropriate measures to identify, prevent, or remediate alleged human rights violations in their supply chains in the Xinjiang Autonomous Uyghur Region. The complaint is supported by the World Uyghur Congress and the Association of Ethical Shareholders Germany. A third case, submitted in November 2023 by Oxfam together with the Ecuadorian union of agricultural workers and three other organizations against German supermarkets Rewe and Edeka, concerns human rights abuses on Latin American banana and pineapple plantations. The supermarkets are accused of not sufficiently engaging with these issues, relying instead on certifications that the complainants argue do not effectively protect workers' rights or ensure safe working conditions (European Center for Constitutional and Human Rights, 2023).

Norwegian Transparency Act 2021

The Norwegian Act relating to enterprises' transparency and actions regarding fundamental human rights and decent working conditions (Transparency Act) came into force in July 2022. The dual purpose of the law is to promote corporate respect for fundamental human rights and decent working conditions in connection with the production of goods and the provision of services, and to ensure public access to information regarding how enterprises address their adverse impacts on these rights (§ 1). The Act's emphasis on consumer rights to information reflects its origins in an NGO campaign following the collapse of Rana Plaza in Bangladesh in 2013 that mobilized more than 20,000 consumers calling for a right to information on working conditions in the apparel sector (Krajewski et al., 2021: 551–52). The material scope of the law is broad, covering fundamental human rights and decent working conditions. Fundamental rights are defined with reference to the UNGPs and the OECD Guidelines (§ 3(b)). The law's scope concerning the types of businesses affected is also comparatively expansive. It imposes due diligence obligations on all enterprises that exceed the threshold for two of the following three conditions: (*a*) sales revenues of NOK 70 million; (*b*) balance sheets total of NOK 35 million; and (*c*) average number of employees in the financial year of 50 full-time equivalent. The law also applies to larger foreign enterprises that offer goods and services in Norway and are subject to taxation in Norway.

The legislation places a duty on entities to carry out due diligence in accordance with the OECD Guidelines (§ 4). These Guidelines (and the Norwegian Act) identify six due diligence obligations, with the sixth constituting provision for or cooperation in remediation and compensation where this is required (§ 4(f)). The Act includes a novel 'right to information', by which any person may request information from an enterprise regarding how it addresses its actual and potential human rights risks (§ 6). The entirety of the upstream supply chain is covered, defined as 'any party in the chain of suppliers and sub-contractors that supplies or produces goods, services or other input factors included in an enterprise's delivery of services or production of goods from the raw material stage to a finished product' (§ 3(d)).

Supervision and enforcement of the Transparency Act fall exclusively to the Norwegian Consumer Protection Authority. The Authority began monitoring company compliance with the Act in September 2023. On the basis of a complaint lodged by any person, or on its own initiative, the Consumer Authority 'shall seek to influence enterprises to comply with the Act, including by conducting negotiations with the enterprises or their organisations' (§ 9). Where the Consumer Authority finds non-compliance, it will either obtain a written agreement from the enterprise concerned to cease the unlawful conduct or issue a decision (§ 9). This decision may take the form of a prohibition, order, enforcement penalty, or infringement penalty (§§ 11–14). Decisions may also be directed at abettors. The legislation does not expressly provide for orders to remediate harm caused, however, nor does it exclude such orders. Given that remediation is a key aspect of due diligence as defined in the Act (and the OECD Guidelines), it would be reasonable to expect that orders for remediation may be issued where requested by a complainant.

Seventeen complaints have been submitted to the Consumer Authority as of March 2024 (Bucknell, 2023). All but three of these cases have been dismissed without publicly released reasons for dismissal. Of the cases not dismissed, one was submitted against Posten by Klassekampen and concerns working conditions in the transportation industry. After receiving information from Posten on how it addresses known risks of poor working conditions associated with its transportation service providers, Klassekampen sought to obtain the names and organization numbers of all Posten's suppliers of transport with vehicles under 3.5 tons, in Norway and abroad, to verify the information provided by Posten. In July 2023, the Authority reached the conclusion that Posten had not breached the Act and that it was not necessary to require Postan to disclose the names of the suppliers to adequately respond to the information request in this case. It stated that there is no general obligation under the Transparency Act to disclose supplier lists but that it may still be necessary to name suppliers in specific cases (Norwegian Consumer Protection Authority, 2023). The second accepted complaint concerned IKEA. Framtiden i våre hender complained that IKEA had not responded adequately to an information request concerning how the company manages certain negative consequences for human rights at specified factories in Bangladesh and Pakistan. The decision by the Authority was procedural, stating that because the request of IKEA was made on the day the Transparency Act came into force, it could not reasonably be expected that IKEA would have the information requested. A third complaint is still under investigation, but we have been unable to find information about this case.

EU Corporate Sustainability Due Diligence Directive

In April 2024, the European Parliament approved the Corporate Sustainability Due Diligence Directive (CSDDD). This final text is the culmination of a protracted and fiercely contested legislative process which began in 2020 (BHRRC, 2024). The recitals to the Directive explain that the purpose of the law is to ensure that companies contribute to sustainable development through the adoption of human rights due diligence, as well as to ensure those affected by a company's failure to adopt due diligence have access to justice and legal remedies. Once the Directive has entered into force, Member States will have two years to transpose it into national law, with obligations to be phased in over a number of years.

The corporate human rights and environmental due diligence duty established in the CSDDD will apply to EU companies with more than 1,000 employees and a net global turnover of more than EUR 450 million and non-EU companies that generate turnover in the EU exceeding the above-mentioned thresholds (Art. 2). A last-minute political compromise significantly narrowed the personal scope of the law by raising the employee and turnover thresholds. The CSDDD is now estimated to apply only to around 5000 companies, or 0.05 per cent of companies in the EU (Brunetti, 2024). Unlike earlier iterations of the proposed Directive, there is no lowering of the general thresholds for companies in high-risk sectors. However, the Directive contains a review clause which expressly identifies questions around employee and net-turnover thresholds and sector-specific approaches as matters that should be revisited in the future (Art. 36).

Companies that fall within the Directive's scope will be required to undertake 'risk-based due diligence' on potential and actual adverse human rights and environmental impacts (Art. 5). The Directive defines an 'adverse human rights impact' as an impact on persons resulting from an abuse of one of the human rights enshrined in the international instruments listed in Part I, Section 1, of the Annex to the Directive (Art. 3(c)(i)). An abuse of a human right not specifically listed in Part I, Section 1 of the Annex but enshrined in the human rights instruments listed in Part I, Section 2, of the Annex will also be considered to form an 'adverse human rights impact', provided that: the human right can be abused by a company or legal entity; the human rights abuse directly impairs a legal interest protected in the human rights instrument listed; and the company could have reasonably foreseen the risk that such human right may be affected, taking into account the circumstances of the specific case, including the nature and extent of the company's business operations and its chain of activities, the characteristics of the economic sector, and the geographical and operational context (Art. 3(c)(ii)). The material scope of the due diligence obligation is thus broad and includes violation of the prohibition on forced labour in the ILO's

Forced Labour Convention, 1930 (No. 29) and in the International Covenant on Civil and Political Rights (ICCPR); violation of the prohibition of all forms of slavery in the Universal Declaration of Human Rights and the ICCPR; and violation of the prohibition of human trafficking in the Palermo Protocol. The Annex also covers violations of prohibitions related to other human rights of workers, such as rights to decent working conditions, child labour, freedom of association, non-discrimination, and an adequate living wage.

The CSDDD sets out eight due diligence obligations, which broadly align with the stages of due diligence elaborated upon in the OECD Guidelines (Art. 5(1)). Companies are to integrate due diligence into company policies and risk management systems (Art. 7); identify and assess actual or potential adverse impacts (Art. 8); prevent and mitigate potential adverse impacts and bring adverse impacts to an end and minimize their extent (Arts. 10 and 11); provide remediation for actual adverse impacts (Art. 12); carry out meaningful engagement with stakeholders (Art. 13); maintain a notification and complaints procedure (Art. 14); monitor the effectiveness of due diligence policies and actions (Art. 15); and communicate on their due diligence (Art. 16). A company is required to undertake due diligence with respect to its own operations or those of its subsidiaries; and where related to their chains of activities, those of their business partners' (Art. 8(1)). The term 'chain of activities' encompasses both activities of a company's upstream business partners related to the production of goods or the provision of services by that company, as well as activities of a company's downstream business partners related to the distribution, transport, and storage of a product of that company, where the business partners carry out those activities for the company or on behalf of the company (Art. 3(g)).

Member States are required to designate one or more national supervisory authorities to oversee compliance with due diligence obligations (Art. 24(1)). These authorities should be independent and have appropriate powers to request information and investigate; order the cessation of infringements and remedial action; and sanction companies for non-compliance with their due diligence obligations (Arts. 24–25). Member States should also ensure the availability of judicial review of decisions taken by the relevant supervisory authority (Art. 25(7)). The Directive calls on Member States to establish sanctions that are 'effective, proportionate and dissuasive' and lists factors that should be considered when determining whether to impose penalties and their nature and appropriate level. It also provides that sanctions should include pecuniary penalties that are commensurate to the company's worldwide net turnover (Art. 27).

The CSDDD addresses remedy in at least five ways. First, remediation is a component of the duty to undertake due diligence (Art. 5(d)). Member States are required to ensure that companies that have caused or jointly caused actual adverse impacts provide for remediation. Where the actual adverse impact is caused only by a company's business partner, the company 'may' voluntarily remediate the adverse impact and/or use its leverage to incentivize the business partner to remediate the harm (Art. 12). 'Remediation' is defined in the law to mean restitution of the affected persons or communities to a situation as close as possible to that they would be in had the impact not occurred, proportionate to the company's involvement (Art. 3(1)(t)). Companies are required to consult with stakeholders when adopting appropriate remedial measures (Art. 13(3)(d)). In addition, Member States are to ensure that the competent supervisory authority has the power, on its own initiative or as a result of substantiated concerns communicated to it in accordance with the Directive, to order the company to provide appropriate remediation (Art. 25).

Second, companies are required as part of their due diligence to adopt a complaints procedure through which persons and entities can submit complaints where they have 'legitimate concerns regarding actual or potential adverse impacts with respect to the companies' own operations, the operations of their subsidiaries or the operations of their business partners in the chains of activities of the companies' (Art. 5(1)(d), Art. 14(1)). Complaints should be able to be submitted by natural or legal persons who are affected or have reasonable grounds to believe that they might be affected by an adverse impact, and 'the legitimate representatives of such persons on behalf of them, such as civil society organisations and human rights defenders'; as well as trade unions and other workers' representatives representing natural persons working in the chain of activities concerned (Art. 14(2)). Member States are to require that these company-level complaints procedures are fair, publicly available, accessible, predictable, and transparent, and that companies put in place measures to prevent retaliation against any person who submits a complaint (Art. 14(3)). Where the complaint is 'well-founded', 'the adverse impact that is the subject-matter of the complaint is deemed to be identified' for the purposes of the company's due diligence. Pursuant to Article 8, the company is then obligated to undertake the measures detailed in Article 8(3)(a), including remediation where appropriate. Complainants are entitled to request appropriate follow-up on the complaint from the relevant company, to 'meet with the company's representatives at an appropriate level to discuss actual or potential ***severe*** adverse impacts that are the subject matter of the complaint, and potential remediation' and to be provided by the company with reasons why a complaint has been considered founded or unfounded and, if founded, with information on actions to be taken (Art. 14(4), emphasis added). Companies may discharge the obligations in the Directive concerning the establishment and maintenance of appropriate complaints procedures through participation in collaborative complaints procedures such as multi-stakeholder agreements or global framework agreements, providing these meet certain criteria (Art. 14(6)).

Third, the CSDDD provides for Member States to ensure that national supervisory authorities may initiate an investigation into potential non-compliance by a company of the obligations provided pursuant to the Directive on its own motion or in response to 'substantiated concerns' submitted to it (Art. 25(2)). The process by which natural and legal persons may submit such concerns is outlined in Article 26. Persons should be able to submit substantiated concerns 'through easily accessible channels' where 'they have reason to believe, on the basis of objective circumstances, that a company is failing to comply with the provisions of national law adopted pursuant to this Directive (Art. 26(1)). Supervisory authorities shall assess the substantiated concern 'in an appropriate period of time' and, where appropriate, exercise enforcement powers pursuant to Article 25 (including where appropriate by way of an order for the company to provide remediation).

Fourth, Member States are required to establish rules to ensure that a company can be held liable for damages where it has 'intentionally or negligently' failed to comply with the obligations laid down in Articles 10 and 11 and, as a result of this failure, has caused damage to a natural or legal person. (Art. 29). The Directive makes clear that a company cannot be liable where damage has been caused only by its business partners in its chain of activities. The Directive specifically provides that where a company has caused damage jointly with its subsidiary or business partner, it should be jointly and severally liable, in accordance with national law (Art. 29(5)).

Finally, the CSDDD contains provisions directed at addressing certain practical and procedural barriers to accessing judicial remedy for business-related human rights harms (Art. 29(3)). This includes reasonable costs for claimants, minimum limitation periods, the possibility of legal representation of victims by trade unions or civil society organizations, and easier access to evidence held by a defendant.

Comparison

The four instruments examined in this chapter adopt different approaches to remedy. In this section, we draw out some of the similarities and differences among them. We begin this with a brief overview, followed by a comparison of the scope of the initiatives and their impact on access to remedy. Then, we discuss the divergent approaches to company grievance mechanisms; the role of competent authorities in providing remedy; and civil liability. We also suggest potential improvements to strengthen access to remedy.

While there is a perception that mHRDD laws have been designed with the purpose of providing remedy to affected individuals, the overview of the four laws above demonstrates that there is, in fact, great disparity between these mHRDD laws with respect to their approach to remedy and the extent to which remedy is likely to be delivered. Under the French Duty of Vigilance law, civil liability appears to be the sole route through which victims may access remedy. The German law establishes a system of company-level grievance handling and administrative remedy, and the Norwegian law provides only for administrative remedy. Outcomes from civil and administrative complaints are eagerly anticipated for an indication of how rigorously the laws will be applied by courts and implemented by competent authorities. The CSDDD adopts a stronger and more comprehensive approach to remedy than the other laws examined here. However, the law's narrow personal scope may significantly limit its effectiveness as a mechanism to facilitate access to remedy for many victims of business-related human rights harms.

Scope and Inclusion of Remediation as a Due Diligence Obligation

The personal and material scope of each mHRDD initiative examined in this chapter, along with the extent to which any obligations to remediate harm provided under the law extend throughout a company's value chain, all have a direct bearing on the capacity of victims of modern slavery to access effective remedy. The material scope of the French law is broad and undefined, requiring companies to consider risks and severe impacts on, inter alia, 'human rights and fundamental freedoms'. As such, it can be determined by reference to international obligations assumed by France (Brabant et al., 2017: 6). The Norwegian transparency law and the CSDDD adopt an expansive approach, covering human rights conventions and ILO standards. The German law, in contrast, covers only child labour, forced labour, all forms of slavery, occupational health and safety obligations, freedom of association, and unequal treatment in employment, allowing for complaints on a narrower range of labour issues. While all the laws target large companies, they vary significantly with respect to thresholds imposed to determine coverage. Comparing the laws just by employment criteria, the French law is the narrowest, focusing on companies with over 5,000 employees in France or 10,000 employees globally; the German law applies to companies with over 3,000 employees in Germany or over 1,000 employees abroad; and the CSDDD will eventually apply to companies with more than 1000 employees. In contrast, the Norwegian law covers a much larger proportion of companies operating in Norway, with its small threshold of 50 full-time equivalents, thus providing rights to a larger proportion of Norwegian business.

The extent to which due diligence obligations extend throughout the value chain and whether due diligence is seen as incorporating obligations to remediate harms are key factors in determining how effectively the various mHRDD laws enable remedy. The corporate 'duty of vigilance' imposed on large companies under the French law only extends to subcontractors or suppliers with whom the company has an 'established business relationship'. However, this duty does not appear to extend to remediating harms. Civil society groups are urging companies to consider remediation as an integral part of due diligence requirements, advocating for the adoption of 'appropriate actions to mitigate risks or prevent serious impacts'. In its guidance to companies on this provision, for example, the French NGO Sherpa explains, 'The company must set up preventive, mitigation and *remediation* measures with stakeholders based on the prioritization of risks and the company's human, technical and financial resources' (Sherpa, 2019: 18, emphasis in original). Whether such expansive interpretations will prevail remains to be seen.

At first glance, the German law appears to require companies to remediate harm in their own operations and in those of their direct suppliers. The obligation also applies to indirect suppliers in relation to the complaints procedure and where the buyer has reliable information indicating a risk of violations. However, as noted above, the use of the term 'remedial action' in the German law appears to refer solely to action taken by the company to address its role in the rights violation(s). It does not entail compensation or other forms of remediation for workers affected by a company's actions or omissions.

The Norwegian Act is significantly stronger than its French or German predecessors with respect to scope. Directly incorporating the six due diligence stages in the OECD Guidelines, the Norwegian law also clearly imposes an obligation on companies to provide for or cooperate in remediation and compensation where required. However, enforcement of this obligation can only be carried out by the relevant competent authority.

The CSDDD makes clear that remediation is a separate and distinct due diligence obligation and offers a definition of remediation that broadly aligns with international human rights law. Obligations to remediate extend to harms that the company has caused or jointly caused in the company's upstream and downstream 'chain of activities'. This latter concept is novel, and the extent to which the concept will in practice depart from the broader value chain approach taken in the UNGPs remains to be seen.

In sum, the limitations on the scope of rights, types of companies covered by due diligence obligations, and the extent to which these obligations apply throughout the value chain are inconsistent with the expansive approach taken in the UNGPs. From the perspective of remediation, these limitations greatly reduce the types of harms that can be addressed, as well as the range of victim-survivors who can seek remedy. The restrictions placed on a company's obligation to conduct due diligence (and to remediate harm) are particularly problematic, given that forced labour is often most prevalent lower down the value chain, such as at the raw material and material processing stages. The French and German laws' omission of any clear obligation to remediate harms is also problematic. It is our view that a better approach would be to cover all human rights and all companies, but to have different expectations based on the company's capacity to provide remedy, considering both its size and the closeness of the breach to its operations and activities.

Grievance Mechanisms

As explained briefly in the second section, operational-level grievance mechanisms are an increasingly common feature of remedy ecosystems in GVCs. According to the UNGPs, such mechanisms can perform two important functions. First, they can act as sources of information to support the identification of adverse human rights impacts as a part of an enterprise's ongoing human rights due diligence. Second, they can act as sources of remedy, making it possible for grievances to be addressed and for impacts to be remediated early and directly, to prevent harms from compounding and grievances from escalating (UNGPs, 2011: 32).

Under the French law, 'an alert and complaint mechanism' is one of the five measures companies are required to include in their vigilance plans. This mechanism is clearly directed at achieving a monitoring function, which is the first of the two functions of a grievance mechanism identified in the UNGPs. However, the extent to which it is intended to – and will in practice– achieve the second (remedial) function is unclear. On one hand, such mechanisms must be drawn up in consultation with representative trade union organizations within companies, which are likely to advocate for robust complaints mechanisms. In its *Vigilance Plans Reference Guide*, the French NGO Sherpa is also advocating for an expansive understanding of this requirement (Sherpa, 2019: 64–69). On the other hand, the law is rather unclear as to the extent to which companies are obliged (if at all) to remediate grievances brought to their attention through such mechanisms. The law is also silent as to criteria that grievance mechanisms must meet.

Only the German law and the CSDDD elaborate on expectations surrounding company-level grievance mechanisms. The German law is exemplary in addressing issues of confidentiality and non-retribution for complainants. However, the practical accessibility of company-level grievance mechanisms for potential complainants may be limited, as settlements are subject to the discretion of the company (Dehbi and Martin-Ortega, 2023: 939). Moreover, the German law is unclear as to what extent a company is *obliged* to provide remedy to victims and to consult with them regarding the nature of this remedy, as well as the criteria against which the adequacy of any remedy provided will be assessed. Because the Norwegian Act makes explicit reference to the OECD Guidelines, guidance can be found there regarding company-level complaints handling.

The CSDDD requires companies to establish both a 'notification procedure' for when persons or organizations have information or concerns regarding actual or potential adverse impacts and a 'complaints mechanism' (Art. 14). The requirement to maintain a complaints mechanism is supplemented by a set of requirements which should help ensure these mechanisms function as effective remedial mechanisms. For example, company grievance mechanisms should be 'fair, publicly available, accessible, predictable and transparent', and the recitals to the Directive make clear that these criteria should be understood in line with Principle 31 of the UNGPs requiring procedures to be legitimate, accessible, predictable, equitable, transparent, rights-compatible, and a source of continuous learning (para 59). The Directive also contains a useful provision clarifying that the submission of a notification or complaint should not be treated as a prerequisite or preclude the person submitting them from having access to the substantiated concerns procedure or to judicial or other non-judicial mechanisms, such as the OECD national contact points where they exist (Art. 14(7)). The explicit requirement for companies to respond to complaints submitted is an important one, although it could have been supplemented by a requirement for such responses to be timely. Like the German law, the CSDDD also addresses issues of confidentiality and anti-retaliation. Companies should take 'reasonably available measures to prevent to prevent any form of retaliation by ensuring the confidentiality of the identity of the person or organization submitting the complaint, in accordance with national law' and ensure, when information needs to be shared, that it is done so in a manner that does not endanger the complainant's safety (Art. 14(3). What is considered 'reasonably available' in this context remains to be seen.

While the CSDDD appears relatively strong when compared to other mHRDD laws, the Directive fails to address stakeholder engagement in the design, implementation, and evaluation of complaints mechanisms. Article 14 is omitted from the list of articles which are subject to mandatory consultation with stakeholders (Art. 13). The UN Office of the High Commissioner for Human Rights (OHCHR) has emphasized that involving affected stakeholders in the design and performance of mechanisms is vital for trust and usage (OHCHR, 2022: 11–12). The OHCHR's two-year assessment of global best practices related to grievance mechanisms found that meaningful stakeholder engagement is pivotal for ensuring trust and utilization of these mechanisms. Likewise, CHRB data from 2023 reveals a gap between the provision of grievance mechanisms and meaningful stakeholder involvement. While 91 per cent of benchmarked companies in the apparel and extractive industries provide mechanisms, only 10 per cent involve rightsholders in their design. (CHRB, 2023). In light of these findings, it is imperative that laws mandate the involvement of workers' organizations in designing and determining the accessibility, language, and procedures of company-level complaints mechanisms. Companies should also be compelled to disclose data on lodged grievances and the outcomes, enabling scrutiny and accountability regarding their complaints handling (dos Santos and Seck, 2020: 166–67; Dehbi and Martin-Ortega, 2023: 939).

Competent Authorities

Competent authorities are essential in overseeing the implementation and enforcement of the Norwegian and German supply chain laws and the CSDDD. The EU Directive proposes the most extensive role for competent authorities, followed by the German law. Administrative supervision is not a feature of the French Due Vigilance law.

While Germany's BAFA is provided with extensive powers of enforcement, its wide discretion and the emphasis on fines raise questions concerning its effectiveness. Under the German Act, BAFA is responsible for monitoring, investigating, and enforcing business compliance with the due diligence obligations in the Act. Thus, BAFA is responsible for supervising and enforcing the obligation on companies to take remedial action where they are causing harm, and to establish a grievance mechanism in accordance with the Act. BAFA can order enterprises to submit corrective action plans with specified timelines and required actions for compliance and impose fines. It also remains unclear if, and to what extent, BAFA will be willing to use these broad enforcement powers to require companies to provide remedy to victims. The emphasis on fines also raises concerns about the Act's effectiveness in ensuring comprehensive remediation for those affected by human rights breaches within supply chains, as it seemingly leads only to financial penalties without provisions for compensation or remediation. It is also unclear how actively (if at all) BAFA will attempt to monitor the implementation and effectiveness of grievance mechanisms established in accordance with the Act.

The Norwegian Act is overseen by the Consumer Authority, which suggests that the focus of the supervisory authority will be on protecting consumers rather than victims of business malfeasance. While the Consumer Authority primarily focuses on guidance and supervision, it retains the discretion to impose infringement penalties or enforcement penalties sed for repeated violations. The level of discretion enjoyed by both the German and Norwegian supervisory authorities is somewhat concerning, as neither are labour inspectorates nor have proven expertise in modern slavery and broader human rights within supply chains or independence from business.

The approach taken in the CSDDD appears very promising to the extent that it requires Member States to establish national supervisory authorities that meet certain criteria (for example, independence), are adequately resourced, and have broad functions and monitoring, investigative, and enforcement powers. These powers include receiving 'substantiated concerns' and enforcing the due diligence obligations (including the obligation to remediate harms). The CSDDD also recognizes certain UNGP effectiveness criteria applicable to these authorities as state-based non-judicial remedial mechanisms, including independence, accessibility, and transparency. However, the extent to which these authorities will meet other elements identified as crucial in the UNGPs, such as 'predictability', 'equitability', and 'rights compatibility' remains to be seen (OHCHR, 2022: 11). Furthermore, as Holly (2024: 19) observes, '[t]he CSDDD covers a very broad range of issues and areas of law and these must be reflected in the capacities and competences of a Supervisory Authority including but not limited to: corporate law, trade law, private international law, human rights law, sector and industry-specific challenges'. Much will depend on the level of expertise of these national authorities in practice and the extent to which they are willing and capable of exercising their powers.

With respect to most of the mHRDD laws considered in this chapter, there appears scope for more explicit statutory guidance to supervisory authorities with respect to exercising their powers to promote and secure remedy for victims of business-related human rights harms (Marshall et al., 2023). We propose that state-based complaints mechanisms should provide remediation encompassing both compensation for workers and agreements for further preventative action addressing the root causes of harm. The Accord on Fire and Building Safety in Bangladesh serves as a compelling model, emphasizing not only immediate safety concerns but also systemic issues contributing to unsafe working conditions. This approach to remediation goes beyond quick fixes, involving workers and their representatives in shaping comprehensive solutions, ensuring a more inclusive and effective process.

Civil Liability

Neither the German nor the Norwegian laws on supply chain due diligence provide for civil liability. Nor do they mandate specific remedies such as public apologies, guarantees of non-repetition, or reparations in the form of damages or compensation. The German Law rules out civil liability for breaches of due diligence obligations, though liability claims can be pursued under the general law, adjudicated based on the laws of the jurisdiction in which the harm occurred. The absence of any prospect of civil liability for businesses that cause harm, and associated absence of any judicial avenue for victims to seek remedy, is a significant limitation of these laws.

Both the French law and the CSDDD provide for civil actions to be brought against companies that have failed to meet their due diligence obligations and, as a consequence, have caused harm. However, both civil liability regimes have significant shortcomings. For a start, neither law enables victims to obtain judicial remedy for harm where a company has complied with its due diligence obligations (Bueno and Bright, 2020: 801–802; Methven O'Brien and

Martin-Ortega, 2022: 25–26). There also appears to be little in these provisions to safeguard against judicial deference to corporate interpretations of due diligence, at the expense of remedies for victims (Landau, 2023; Savourey and Brabant, 2021: 51; Shift, 2022: 5–7).

Those seeking remedy under these provisions will need to establish not only that there was a breach of the due diligence obligations but also that this breach caused the harm suffered (Dusepulchre et al., 2022: 7; Savourey and Brabant, 2021: 152). Many victims are unlikely to be able to establish such a causal link because of lack of evidence or knowledge of how exactly the company's omissions caused their harm (Bernaz et al., 2022: 22). Commentators have pointed out that this is a heavy burden, especially when the damage exists further down the supply chain (Bueno and Bright, 2020: 802; Methven O'Brien and Martin-Ortega, 2022: 26; Savourey and Brabant, 2021: 152). Early attempts by affected communities in the Global South to use the French law to remedy human rights violations suggest that these challenges are real and substantial (Ancheita, 2022: 20).

While neither the French law nor the CSDDD elaborate on the nature of judicial remedies available, the CSDDD provides for the availability of injunctive relief. Such measures can be a crucial tool for preventing or halting adverse impacts. Both the French and EU laws partially address longstanding legal and practical barriers faced by workers, unions, and others when seeking judicial remedy. Neither law comprehensively tackles jurisdiction or applicable law issues in GVCs claims. However, as described above, the CSDDD contains important provisions which should make it easier for workers, trade unions, and others to obtain remedy in European courts. It also provides a mandatory overriding provision accompanying its civil liability regime (Art. 29(7)).

Inclusion of civil liability within the French Duty of Vigilance law and the CSDDD is an important step in the right direction. However, these provisions do not go far enough to facilitate access to effective remedy for victims of modern slavery in global supply chains. Measures such as the establishment of a shared burden of proof, especially in instances of limited access to information or systematic violations, would significantly improve prospects of remedy. Collective redress mechanisms, like class actions, are also important.

Conclusion

mHRDD laws undoubtedly constitute an important step towards greater corporate accountability. But accountability for what? And to whom? In this chapter, we have explored these questions by querying the extent to which, and how, these laws will improve access to effective remedy for victims of modern slavery in GVCs. Our analysis confirms that mHRDD laws in Europe are primarily directed at holding companies in the Global North to account for their efforts and actions in *preventing* human harms in their own operations, as well as in their local, regional, and global supply chains, including those in the Global South. The primary 'accountability holders' in this context – those actors with the power or authority to pose questions, pass judgements, and impose consequences – are regulators, consumers, and other stakeholders, also from the Global North. It is largely to these groups that large businesses are being asked to account. In the case of most mHRDD laws, remedy for rightsholders is a feature of these laws but a 'sideshow' rather than the main act (Leite, 2023: 205). The most recent of the laws examined in this chapter – the CSDDD – promises to begin to rectify this situation. However, the extent to which this law will deliver meaningful remedies for victims of modern slavery – particularly when they are located in the Global South – remains to be seen.

The marginalization of remedy in early mHRDD laws in Europe may not seem surprising or objectionable to policymakers implementing state obligations, given that as a concept, HRDD is primarily preventative in nature. Moreover, it may be unreasonable to expect a singular law to address the myriad of legal and practical obstacles that victims of business-related human rights harms face in today's global economy. However, these laws have been advanced at least in part on their promise of improving access to justice. It is striking, then, that only one of the four instruments examined in this chapter explicitly incorporate provisions that align substantively with understandings of remedy under international human rights law, which aim to restore the affected individual to the position they were in before the harm or as close to it as possible.

It is our opinion that this lacuna in mHRDD initiatives is indicative of the underlying norms informing mHRDD. As Dehbi and Martin-Ortega (2023: 932) remind us, while mHRDD is rooted in international standards, these laws do not prioritize the concerns of Global South states and persons. They can thus be understood as further consolidation of Eurocentric legal principles and interpretations, potentially further overshadowing the voices and rights of those directly impacted by adverse corporate practices. The continued lack of sufficient provisions within mHRDD laws providing effective access to remedy reinforces this power dynamic.

To reroute the trajectory of mHRDD in this respect, we agree with De Schutter and Burrow that although 'HRDD is essential to ensure that the EU contributes to a form of economic globalization that promotes human development, it should not become a substitute for ensuring a right to remedy for victims of corporate negligence' (De Schutter and Burrow, 2020: 43). Existing mHRDD laws offer a robust foundation for preventive measures against adverse human rights impacts, emphasizing the identification and mitigation of risks. However, balancing prevention and remedy is essential to ensure the effectiveness and fairness of mHRDD laws on a global scale.

Notes

1. Political developments since writing this chapter suggest significant impending changes to the EU Corporate Sustainability Due Diligence and the German Act on Corporate Due Diligence in Supply Chains. However, as the precise nature of these changes remains unclear, they are not included within the analysis.
2. *Loi 2017-399 du 27 Mars 2017 Relative au Devoir de Vigilance des Sociétés Mères et des Enterprises Donneuses D'ordre.*
3. Act on Corporate Due Diligence Obligations in Supply Chains, BGBl I 2021, 2959. Official English translation available at: www.bmas.de/SharedDocs/Downloads/DE/Internationales/act-corporate-due-diligence-obligations-supply-chains.pdf?__blob=publicationFile&v=3.
4. Act Relating to Enterprises' Transparency and Work on Fundamental Human Rights and Decent Working Conditions (Transparency Act). English translation available at: www.regjeringen.no/contentassets/c33c3faf340441faa7388331a735f9d9/transparency-act-english-translation.pdf.
5. European Parliament legislative resolution of 24 April 2024 on the proposal for a Directive of the European Parliament and of the Council on Corporate Sustainability Due Diligence and amending Directive (EU) 2019/1937, COM(2022) -P9-TA(2024)0329 (24 April 2024). Available at: https://eur-lex.europa.eu/legal-content/EN/TXT/?uri=CELEX%3A52022PC0071.
6. An 'established commercial relationship' is defined under French law as a stable, regular commercial relationship, taking place with or without contract, with a certain volume of business, and under a reasonable expectation that the relationship will last. *Code de Commerce* [Commercial Code] (France), art L. 442-6-I-5.
7. German Bundestag, Federal Government, Explanatory Memorandum to the Due Diligence in Supply Chains Bill, 19th Electoral Period.

References

Ancheita, A. (2022). 'Promoting Climate Justice in Transnational Fora: The Case of Unión Hidalgo vs Électricité de France and the French Corporate Duty of Vigilance Law'. In *Human Rights and Environmental Due Diligence in Global Value Chains: Perspectives from the Global South*, edited by T. Wuttke, L. Smit, A. Parshotam, A. Ancheita, and A. Meridian, 18–21. Working Paper, German Institute for International and Security Affairs. Available at: https://tinyurl.com/p47ctncm.

Annat, L. (2023). 'First Case Filed under the German Supply Chain Due Diligence Act against Tom Tailor, Amazon, and IKEA by Bangladeshi Workers'. *Due Diligence Design*, 27 April. Available at: https://tinyurl.com/39kf7ayd.

Bernaz, N., M. Krajewski, K. Mohamadieh, and V. Rouas (2022). *The UN Legally Binding Instrument and the EU Proposal for a Corporate Sustainability Due Diligence Directive: Competencies, Comparison and Complementarity*. Available at: https://corporatejustice.org/wp-content/uploads/2022/11/Complementarity-study-on-EU-CSDDD-and-UN-LBI-October-2022.pdf.

Black, J. (2008). 'Constructing and Contesting Legitimacy and Accountability in Polycentric Regulatory Regimes'. *Regulation and Governance* 2(2): 137–64.

Bovens, M. (2007). 'Analysing and Assessing Accountability: A Conceptual Framework'. *European Law Journal* 13(4): 447–68.

Brabant, S. and E. Savourey (2017). 'France's Corporate Duty of Vigilance Law: A Closer Look at the Penalties Faced by Companies'. *Revue Internationale de la Compliance et de l'Éthique des Affaires – Supplément à la Semaine Juridique Enterprise et Affaires* 50: 1–5.

Brabant, S., C. Michon, and E. Savourey (2017). 'The Vigilance Plan: Cornerstone of the Law on the Corporate Duty of Vigilance'. *Revue Internationale de la Compliance et de L'éthique des Affaires – Supplément À La Semaine Juridique Entreprise et Affaires* 50: 1–8.

BHRRC (2023). 'France's Duty of Vigilance Law'. 15 May. Available at: https://tinyurl.com/yktdc434.

——— (2024). 'Breaking: EU Parliament approves Corporate Sustainability Due Diligence Directive'. 24 April. Available at: https://www.business-humanrights.org/en/latest-news/eu-csddd-political-agreement/.

Buchanan, A. and R. O. Keohane (2006). 'The Legitimacy of Global Governance Institutions'. *Ethics and International Affairs* 20(4): 405–37.

Bucknell, E. (2023). 'Alert: The Norwegian government will start monitoring compliance with the Transparency Act'. *Due Diligence Design*, 2 September.

Available at: https://duediligence.design/the-norwegian-government-will-start-monitoring-compliance-with-the-transparency-act/.

Bueno, N. and C. Bright (2020). 'Implementing Human Rights Due Diligence through Corporate Civil Liability'. *International and Comparative Law Quarterly* 69(4): 789–818.

Brunetti, A. (2024). 'Scope of EU Supply Chain Rules Cut by 70% Ahead of Key Friday Vote'. *Euroactiv*, 15 March. Available at: https://tinyurl.com/yc5sjf9a.

Comissão Pastoral da Terra and Notre Affaire à Tous (2023). 'Comissão Pastoral da Terra and Notre Affaire à Tous v. BNP Paribas'. Available at Climate Change Database, Sabin Center for Climate Change Law, Columbia Law School: https://tinyurl.com/2z4e45af.

Chuang, J. (2014). 'Exploitation Creep and the Unmaking of Human Trafficking Law'. *American Journal of International Law* 108(4): 609–49.

CHRB (2023). 2023 'Corporate Human Rights Benchmark'. 20 November. Available at: www.worldbenchmarkingalliance.org/publication/chrb/.

Dehbi, F. and O. Martin-Ortega (2023). 'An Integrated Approach to Corporate Due Diligence from a Human Rights, Environmental, and TWAIL Perspective'. *Regulation and Governance* 17(4): 927–43.

De Schutter, O. and S. Burrow (2020). 'Mandatory Human Rights Due Diligence in the EU: The Promise and the Risk'. In *Toward EU Mandatory Due Diligence Legislation: Perspectives from Business, Public Sector, Academia and Civil Society*, 41–43. BHRRC. Available at: https://tinyurl.com/mshtvdz8.

dos Santos, D. C. and S. L. Seck (2020). 'Human Rights Due Diligence and Extractive Industries'. In *Research Handbook on Business and Human Rights,* edited by S. Deva and D. Birchall, 151–74. Cheltenham, UK; Northampton, MA: Edward Elgar.

Dusepulchre, G., S. Feierabend, and M. Neglia (2022). *Europe Can Do Better. How EU Policy Makers Can Strengthen the Corporate Sustainability Due Diligence Directive.* International Federation for Human Rights. Available at: www.fidh.org/IMG/pdf/duediligence.pdf.

European Center for Constitutional and Human Rights (2023). 'Edeka and Rewe Violate Supply Chain Law: Human Rights Violations on Banana Plantations'. Available at: www.ecchr.eu/en/case/edeka-und-rewe-verstossen-gegen-lieferkettengesetz/.

Fudge, J. and G. Mundlak (2023). 'Peeling the Onion: On Choices Judges Make in Transnational Labour Litigation'. In *Social Justice and the World of Work: Possible Global Futures Essays in Honour of Francis Maupain*, edited by B. Langille and A. Trebilcock, 249–60. Oxford, UK: Hart Publishing.

Holly, G. (2024). *The EU Corporate Sustainability Due Diligence Directive: Maximising Impact through Transposition and Implementation*. Danish Institute for Human Rights. Available at https://tinyurl.com/mr49b86f.

ICAR, CORE, and ECCJ (2013). *The Third Pillar: Access to Judicial Remedies for Human Rights Violations by Transnational Business*. Available at: https://tinyurl.com/bdf2zewn.

ILO (2012). *Giving Globalisation a Human Face*. Available at: https://tinyurl.com/n9hc5z92.

Koos, S. (2022). 'The German Supply Chain Due Diligence Act 2021 and Its Impact on Globally Operating German Companies'. Proceedings of the 2nd Riau Annual Meeting on Law and Social Sciences (RAMLAS 2021). *Advances in Social Science, Education and Humanities Research* 659: 111–15.

Kotiswaran, P. (2017). *Revisiting the Law and Governance of Trafficking, Forced Labor and Modern Slavery*. Cambridge, UK: Cambridge University Press.

Krajewski, M., K. Tonstad, and F. Wohltmann (2021). 'Mandatory Human Rights Due Diligence in Germany and Norway: Stepping, or Striding, in the Same Direction?' *Business and Human Rights Journal* 6(3): 550–58.

Landau, I. (2023). *Human Rights Due Diligence and Labour Governance*. Oxford, UK: Oxford University Press.

Landau, I. and T. Hardy (2021). 'Transnational Labour Governance in Global Supply Chains: Asking Questions and Seeking Answers on Accountability'. In *Decent Work in a Globalized Economy: Lessons from Public and Private Initiatives*, edited by G. Delautre, E. Echeverría Manrique, and C. Fenwick, 43–74. Geneva: ILO.

Leite, M. (2023). 'Beyond Buzzwords: Mandatory Human Rights Due Diligence and a Rights-based Approach to Business Models'. *Business and Human Rights Journal* 8(2): 197–212.

Macdonald, K. (2014). 'The Meaning and Purposes of Transnational Accountability'. *Australian Journal of Public Administration* 73(4): 426–36.

Marshall, S., I. Landau, H. Shamir, T. Barkay, J. Fudge, and A. van Heerden (2023). *Mandatory Human Rights Due Diligence: Risks and Opportunities for Workers and Unions*. RMIT University Business and Human Rights Centre; TraffLab ERC; and Labour, Equality and Human Rights (LEAH) Research Group, Monash Business School. Available at: www.trafflab.org/_files/ugd/11e1f0_e1db27f1ec7f41459ac357d021f6011c.pdf.

Methven O'Brien, C. and O. Martin-Ortega (2022). 'Commission Proposal on Corporate Sustainability Due Diligence: Analysis from a Human Rights

Perspective'. EP/EXPO/DROI/FWC/2019-01/Lot6/1/C/16. European Parliament, Directorate-General for External Policies.

Norwegian Consumer Protection Authority (2023). 'Forbrukertilsynet, Avgjørelser i klagesaker mot Posten og IKEA'. 4 July. Available at: www.forbrukertilsynet.no/avgjorelser-i-klagesaker-mot-posten-og-ikea.

OHCHR (United Nations Office of the High Commissioner for Human Rights) (2011). *Guiding Principles on Business and Human Rights: Implementing the United Nations 'Protect, Respect and Remedy' Framework* (UNGPs). Available at: www.ohchr.org/sites/default/files/documents/publications/guidingprinciples businesshr_en.pdf.

——— (2016). *Improving Accountability and Access to Remedy for Victims of Business-Related Human Rights Abuse.* Report to the Human Rights Council. A/HRC/32/19. 10 May. Available at: www.ohchr.org/sites/default/files/Documents/Issues/Business/DomesticLawRemedies/A_HRC_32_19_AEV.pdf.

——— (2022). *OHCHR Feedback on the Proposal for a Directive of the European Parliament and of the Council on Corporate Sustainability Due Diligence.* Available at: www.ohchr.org/sites/default/files/2022-05/eu-csddd-feedback-ohchr.pdf.

Palombo, D. (2019). 'The Duty of Care of the Parent Company: A Comparison between French Law, UK Precedents and the Swiss Proposals'. *Business and Human Rights Journal* 4(2): 265–86.

Ruhl, G. (2024). 'Cross-Border Protection of Human Rights: The 2021 German Supply Chain Due Diligence Act'. In *From Theory to Practice in Private International Law: Gedächtnisschrift for Professor Jonathan Fitchen*, edited by Justin Borg-Barthet, Katarina Trimmings, Burcu Yüksel Ripley and Patricia Zivkovic. Oxford, UK: Hart Publishing.

Savourey, E. and S. Brabant (2021). 'The French Law on the Duty of Vigilance: Theoretical and Practical Challenges since Its Adoption'. *Business and Human Rights Journal* 6(1): 141–52.

Schappert, J. (2023). 'Second Case Filed under the German Supply Chain Due Diligence Act'. *Due Diligence Design*, 6 July. Available at: https://tinyurl.com/msr5t8zs.

Shamir, H. (2012). 'A Labor Paradigm for Human Trafficking'. *UCLA Law Review* 60(1): 76–136.

Shamir, H., B. Arora, S. Banerjee, and T. Barkay (2025). 'Introduction'. In *Modern Slavery and the Governance of Global Value Chains*, edited by H. Shamir, B. Arora, S. Banerjee, and T. Barkay. Cambridge, UK: Cambridge University Press.

Sherpa (2019). *Vigilance Plans Reference Guidance*. Paris. Available at: https://tinyurl.com/yc6pamvu.

Shift (2022). *The EU Commission's Proposal for a Corporate Sustainability Due Diligence Directive: Shift's Analysis*. Available at: https://tinyurl.com/ywen5nnt.

UN ICCPR (1966). *The International Covenant on Civil and Political Rights*. Available at: https://treaties.un.org/doc/treaties/1976/03/19760323%2006-17%20am/ch_iv_04.pdf.

UNGA (2005). *Basic Principles and Guidelines on the Right to a Remedy and Reparation for Victims of Gross Violations of International Human Rights Law and Serious Violations of International Humanitarian Law*. Available at: www.ohchr.org/en/instruments-mechanisms/instruments/basic-principles-and-guidelines-right-remedy-and-reparation.

Weihrauch, D., S. Carodenuto, and S. Leipold (2023). 'From Voluntary to Mandatory Corporate Accountability: The Politics of the German Supply Chain Due Diligence Act'. *Regulation and Governance* 17(4): 909–26.

Part II

Actors

5

Directors' Duties and Decision-making in Global Value Chains

Roseanne Russell

Global value chains (GVCs) are a manifestation of the contemporary global political economy. Viewing them solely as economic constructs, however, obscures the role that law and the wider regulatory environment play in their development and facilitation. The issue of modern slavery within GVCs has been the subject of careful scrutiny from a variety of legal sub-disciplines, including labour, welfare, and immigration law. In this chapter, I examine the role of company law, and particularly the fiduciary duty of directors to act in the interests of the company, in creating conditions under which modern slavery flourishes in GVCs. I suggest that the ideology of shareholder primacy that helps shape board decision-making is flawed both normatively and as a matter of legal doctrine. The central argument advanced is that *shareholders'* interests are typically treated as a proxy for a *company's* interests due to the ambiguity in defining what it means to act in the interests of the company as a legal construct. Yet this focus on prioritizing the interests of shareholders can motivate lead companies' directors to make decisions that deliver investor returns at the expense of fundamental labour rights and human dignity. The chapter concludes by exploring the potential of incorporating principles of proportionality into board decision-making. It is suggested that this approach can enhance directors' knowledge and awareness of balancing competing interests, thereby avoiding the most egregious abuses of corporate power in the pursuit of profit.

Introduction

Writing in 2016, the IGLP Law and Global Production Working Group (the IGLP Working Group) observed that residing 'at the heart of the GVC phenomenon', law serves as 'the vehicle through which value is generated, captured, and distributed within and between organizational and jurisdictional domains, and diverse and geographically disparate business operations are coordinated and governed' (IGLP, 2016: 61). Law and the wider regulatory environment, comprising a complex mix of national, transnational, hard law, and soft law norms, are concerned with GVCs in numerous ways that influence the organization of GVCs. Company law is typically considered to be implicated in GVCs insofar as it shapes the structuring of activities within a chain and the liability (or lack thereof) of investors. A company's own legal personhood, combined with the doctrine of limited liability for shareholders, provides a highly attractive business environment: a 'shareholder's paradise' (Ireland, 2010: 848). Shareholders are shielded from liability, while shareholder primacy simultaneously ensures that directors make decisions in which investor interests are privileged. Company law can, argues Ireland, be characterized as 'a body of law able to combine the ruthless pursuit of "shareholder value" without any corresponding responsibility on the part of shareholders for the losses arising out of corporate failure or the damage caused by corporate activities or malfeasance' (Ireland, 2010: 848). Despite these misgivings about how company law is presently formulated in favour of investors' interests, there exists considerable potential for company law to be harnessed for more socially beneficial ends. Indeed, the IGLP Working Group alluded to this possibility with its observation that GVCs are 'a product of legal arrangements that *could* be organised differently' (IGLP, 2016: 60, emphasis added). Turner has similarly shown how the 'latent potential of corporate law has begun to stir and take form in practice … in order to bring about changes in business practices and the philosophy of company law' (Turner, 2016: 189). Much of this 'stirring' has occurred in the area of business and human rights. The relentless pursuit of value creation across global production has meant that 'government responsibilities to protect and fulfil human rights fall victim to policies designed to attract investment not least the maintenance of low wages and flexible labour regulations through the liberalisation of labour markets' (Buhmann et al., 2019: 338). In response, a range of regulatory measures, from the UN Guiding Principles on Business and Human Rights to the proposal for a European Commission Directive on Corporate Governance – including new rules on supply chain due diligence – have been mooted (Enneking and Veldman, 2019). Furthermore, the challenge of modern slavery has prompted a range of regulatory and disclosure initiatives. Nonetheless, as noted by Caruana et al. (2021), a significant gap exists in the literature on modern slavery in businesses across sectors and regions concerning 'the organizational and supply chain dynamics' that foster it, and 'the *business actors and models'* that enable its proliferation (2021: 252, emphasis added).

Banerjee (2021: 415) has described modern slavery as 'a viable and profitable management practice for business' and argues that it is 'an enabling condition of global neoliberal capitalism' (2021: 416). He contends that 'far from being an aberration', modern slavery 'is a logical outcome of the way our political economic system is organized' (2021: 415). Banerjee's thesis resonates with the argument that the privileging of financial investors through the norm of shareholder primacy is an outcome of the neoliberal political economy (Deakin, 2005). It follows from Banerjee's thesis that only wholesale reform of shareholder primacy and the global political economy in which it is situated will sufficiently address modern slavery. Another rationale for the prominence of shareholder primacy in corporate practice is that it serves as 'a second-best solution that is good for *all* the stakeholders in the firm' (Stout, 2002: 1200). Providing directors with a single, clear focus ultimately benefits all those connected with the company. It is this second rationale for shareholder primacy – that it is a clear direction for board members to observe – with which I wish to engage.

In the absence of systemic change of the wider global political economy, this chapter considers how board decision-making might be altered to unsettle the link between shareholder primacy and the subsequent adoption of exploitative labour practices. In this discussion, I build on both company law and the provocation by the IGLP Working Group that the ordering of GVCs is not predetermined but rather reflects normative choices regarding business conduct. I argue that decisions by the boards of lead firms informed by the ideology of shareholder primacy pave the way for the adoption of business practices focused on short-term profit and a 'race to the bottom' in terms of fundamental labour and human rights protections (Buhmann et al., 2019: 338). Conversely, decisions tempered by the need to act proportionately and balance the interests of a range of stakeholders, together with appropriate accountability mechanisms for challenging those decisions, could avoid the worst forms of abuse. The central claim advanced in this chapter is that the ideology of shareholder primacy has been allowed to take hold in business practice due to the law's ambiguity about directors' obligations in fulfilling their duty to act in the interests of the company. I argue that this lack of clarity can be ameliorated by introducing the concept of proportionality as a requirement for boardroom decisions. Requiring directors to justify their decisions on the basis of proportionality may go some way to tackle the most egregious harms inflicted on those who labour within GVCs. Focusing on boardroom decision-making aims to offer a concrete, practical proposal that may influence lead-firm behaviour. However, it by no means implies that we should abandon the pursuit of more fundamental reforms to the global political economy, particularly given how GVCs have evolved in response to these dynamics.

The chapter proceeds as follows. The following section provides a summary of how shareholder primacy has shaped business practice, despite it lacking any secure doctrinal foundation in law. It is suggested that while the law clearly mandates that directors must act in the best interests of the company they are appointed to lead, it does not provide directors with guidance about how to address the interests of myriad stakeholders. Furthermore, it suggests how adopting the concept of proportionality may influence board decision-making in favour of stakeholders beyond shareholders. It develops this argument by showing how proportionality might be applied in a GVC context, where modern slavery can operate in ways that are geographically and legally distant from the lead company in question. Lastly, the chapter addresses the challenges that such a model of proportionality will need to overcome in order to be successful.

The Centrality of Shareholder Primacy in Corporate Decision-making

Banerjee's thesis maintains that modern slavery is one consequence of business practices shaped around maximizing returns to shareholders. Similarly, Ponte and Gibbon (2015) suggest that the pursuit of shareholder value maximization and adoption of 'financial market indicators' such as a 'given ratio of post-tax return on capital employed' have led companies to restructure operations, externalize non-core activities and re-engineer supply chains (2015: 16). They observe that the degree to which companies are sensitive to pressures from 'maximizing shareholder value' impacts efforts to externalize an increasing number of functions (2015: 18). Milberg (2008) has also shown a connection between what he terms the 'shareholder value revolution' (typically viewed as an issue of corporate governance) and the increasingly globalized nature of systems of production. In his view, the demands of financial investors for higher, short-term returns have 'spurred greater globalization of production … or relocated parts of the production process in order to lower costs' (Milberg, 2008: 445).

What lies behind this focus on investors? Delivering value for shareholders is typically assumed to be the legitimate concern of directors when making board decisions. However, this is not what the doctrine of company law requires. 'Shareholder value', which rose in prominence in the 1980s, has arguably become the central idea motivating corporate decision-makers despite the absence of any sound legal basis for the concept (Stout, 2012). For Stout, '[t]he widespread *perception* that corporate directors and executives have a legal duty to maximize shareholder wealth plays a large role in explaining how shareholder value thinking has become so endemic in the business world today' (Stout, 2012: 24, emphasis added). Deakin (2005) similarly argues that the turn towards 'shareholder value' is indicative of a wider privileging of shareholder interests via the social norm of 'shareholder primacy' and not mandated by law. He cites cultural and economic changes, including hostile takeovers and the closer alignment of directors' pay with shareholder interests via the payment of remuneration in the form of shares and share options (Deakin, 2005: 14).

Behind the perception that directors must act to deliver shareholder *value* is, argues Talbot (2013), the political goal of shareholder *primacy* (2013: 145). The two concepts, while related, differ slightly. According to Sjåfjell et al. (2015: 83–84), the difference between the two concepts lies in associating shareholder primacy with a social norm prioritizing investors, while shareholder value refers to the presumed legal mandate 'that the directors run the company for the collective benefit of its shareholders'. Despite their differences, shareholder value and shareholder primacy are often confused. Wedderburn (2002) attributes this confusion to the deference towards the 'requirements of transnational capital and the hegemony of the "promotion of shareholder value"' (2002: 103). The result being 'corporate irresponsibility' (Ireland, 2018: 24).

Sjåfjell et al. (2015: 145) suggest that the lack of an explicit statement regarding the societal purpose of companies and their interests has contributed to the prevalence of shareholder interests being viewed as paramount in corporate decision-making. Given the absence of a clearly formulated corporate purpose across legal jurisdictions (Sjåfjell et al., 2015: 94), they argue for EU-level reform to establish an overarching purpose for corporations (Sjåfjell et al., 2020). Specifically, they suggest 'to create sustainable value within planetary boundaries' and define 'sustainable value' as

> creating value for the undertaking, while respecting the rights of its members, investors, employees, and other contractual parties, and promoting good governance, decent work and equality, and the human rights of its workers and affected communities and peoples. (Sjåfjell et al., 2020: 59)

The European Commission has also highlighted the need for directors' duties to be reformed, in addition to prescribing a clear purpose for the company centred around objectives that are more expansive than value creation. Based on 'evidence collected over the 1992–2018 period' it found 'a trend for publicly listed companies within the EU to focus on short-term benefits of shareholders rather than on the long-term interests of the company' (European Commission, 2020: vi). Amongst a range of causal factors for this trend was found to be the narrow interpretation of directors' duties and 'company's interest' and a tendency to read the latter as meaning 'the short-term maximisation of shareholder value' (European Commission, 2020: vi). Indeed, the European Commission found that without substantial reform of corporate governance rules, 'the social norm of shareholder primacy and short-term pressures from the financial markets will likely continue to influence corporate decision-making' (European Commission, 2020: vi). One of its recommended reforms is 'strengthening the role of directors in pursuing the company's long-term interests' (European Commission, 2020: vii).

From the perspective of company law doctrine, what is extraordinary about the dominance of shareholder primacy in shaping directors' decisions is its lack of a legal foundation. As Deakin (2005: 11) has observed, 'it is surprisingly difficult to find support within company law for the notion of shareholder primacy'. It is a fundamental principle of company law that companies have separate legal personhood from the shareholders who are its members or the directors who manage its affairs. In the UK, the default or 'model' articles that apply to companies (unless members vote to alter them) give significant delegated authority to the directors. Model article 3 provides that 'subject to the articles, the directors are responsible for the management of the company's business, for which purpose they may exercise all the powers of the company' (SI 2008/3229). This broad power vested in a director to act on the company's behalf is accompanied by a range of duties that broadly serve two goals. One is to ensure the competence of directors; the second is to ensure that directors do not put their own interests first, and instead act in the interests of the legal person they are appointed to lead – namely, the company. The fact the director owes her duties to the company is beyond doubt.[1]

As argued by Sjåfjell et al. (2015), the lack of a clear statement in company law doctrine about what it means to act in the *company's* interests has allowed those interests to be shaped by the needs of powerful investors and has become wrapped up with the ideology of shareholder primacy. This phenomenon is partly founded on a misguided notion that shareholders 'own' the company such that it ought to be run in their favour (Grantham, 1998). This perspective was also contributed by the emergence of company law as a distinct discipline from the more long-standing canon of partnership law, where members truly were collective owners of partnership assets (Ireland, 1999). Case law has, however, clarified that a share represents an interest of a shareholder in a company measured by a sum of money, primarily for purposes of liability, rather than a stake in a company's assets (*Borland's Trustees v. Steel Brothers & Co Limited* [1901] 1 Ch. 279 per Farwell J at 288).

A second rationale for pursuing shareholder value is that it (mistakenly) assumes that business should maximize (not merely increase) profits (Friedman, 1970), with law's role being to facilitate or enable shareholder primacy (Hansmann and Kraakman, 2001). This view appears increasingly anachronistic (Ramanna, 2020). The prioritization of shareholder interests is also supported by economic agency theory, which maintains that privileging shareholder concerns is justified due to their relationship of residual risk with the company. In this economic model of the firm, the company is 'a legal fiction which serves as a nexus for contracting relationships' (Jensen and Meckling, 1976: 311). While other stakeholders such as employees are presumed to have complete contracts, the contract between the directors and shareholders is presumed incomplete given the lack of clarity about what the shareholder might receive in return for his capital contribution. The residual risk borne by investors is thought to place them in an optimal position to act as effective monitors of board behaviour, despite it being descriptively inaccurate to portray the shareholders as effective monitors of executive behaviour (Keay, 2007).

Balancing Interests in Board Decision-making

The dominance of shareholder primacy ideology and the pursuit of shareholder wealth maximization have implications for directors' decision-making. Pearson (2018: 44) points to the destructive effects of this policy, arguing that 'business now appears so focused on maximizing shareholder value, it avoids all other responsibilities'. He argues that 'though widely falsified as a theory, shareholder primacy remains as a belief system shaping human behaviour across the corporate landscape and beyond' (2018: 42) and endorses the view that 'there [is] no more legal support for shareholder primacy than there is valid economic theoretical support' (2018: 54). However, the claim that business 'now avoids all other responsibilities', while representative of some corporate practices, does not fit wholly with developments in the wider regulatory environment to motivate responsible business conduct. Such developments are accompanied by demands from some sectors of the business community to retreat from a commitment to delivering shareholder value. Ireland (2018), for example, has observed how the ideology of shareholder value has 'receded' somewhat in recent times, although 'without any noticeable impact on corporate behaviour' (2018: 16).

One drawback for those directors who support balancing the demands of investors with those of labour and other stakeholders is the lack of direction given in company law as to how this can be accomplished and guidance on their obligations in this regard (Boeger et al., 2020). The UK provides an illustrative example of the difficulties facing directors when making decisions that do not privilege the interests of shareholders. Pearson (2018: 54) rightly notes that 'Anglo-American law supports the primacy of company interests', with directors mediating between different interests. However, he also argues that this 'legal position has been progressively weakened with ambiguity introduced, so as to make shareholder primacy at least potentially tenable' (2018: 54).

In the UK, this ambiguity came in the form of the wholesale review of company law in 2000 (DTI, 2000) and the introduction of section 172 of the UK's Companies Act 2006. The common law roots of section 172 lie in the directors' duty of good faith towards the company and to ensure that directors do not pursue their own interests. It is, therefore, a duty of loyalty. Section 172(1) provides as follows:

> A director of a company must act in the way he considers, in good faith, would be most likely to promote the success of the company for the benefit of its members as a whole, and in doing so have regard (amongst other matters) to –
>
> (a) the likely consequences of any decision in the long term,
> (b) the interests of the company's employees,
> (c) the need to foster the company's business relationships with suppliers, customers and others,
> (d) the impact of the company's operations on the community and the environment,

(e) the desirability of the company maintaining a reputation for high standards of business conduct, and
(f) the need to act fairly as between members of the company.

Despite a suggestion that section 172 established an 'emerging third position' between serving a plurality of stakeholder interests on the one hand and, on the other, an exclusive focus on shareholders (Kiarie, 2006: 339), the reality is less ambitious. One problem with section 172 in its current formulation is that while it is expansive enough for directors to 'have regard' to a range of factors other than the interests of financial investors so that they could consider wider issues of GVC operations or concerns over modern slavery as part of their board decision-making, there is no *obligation* on them to do so. Talbot (2013) takes an even more critical view of section 172, arguing that the UK's company law regime 'enable[s] neoliberal shareholder primacy', with section 172 having 'made acting in the interests of shareholders a statutory duty for directors' (2013: 167). In this way, argues Talbot, 'section 172 [has] effectively reconceptualised the "company" to whom the directors owe a fiduciary duty as being the interests of shareholders alone' (2013: 167).

The unease around section 172 is felt not just by some company law scholars but also by board members themselves. The UK's Institute of Directors is a supporter of the Better Business Act campaign. One goal of this initiative is to 'empower directors to exercise their judgement in weighing up and advancing the interests of all stakeholders' (Better Business Act, 2024) and not just investors. The dilemma that this proposed change aims to address is the concern that section 172, as currently drafted, leaves directors uncertain as to the extent to which directors can deviate from the maximization of shareholder value. As Walsh (2004: 349) puts it, 'leading a business that is at once socially responsive and economically competitive is a daunting managerial challenge. The theoretical challenge posed by these sometimes competing and sometimes complementary demands is no less daunting'. Arguably, what would be of assistance is a clearer framework for how competing rights and interests may be balanced.

Introducing Boardroom Proportionality as a Decision-making Framework

Proportionality sets limitations on the exercise of rights. In the context of decision-making, it provides boundaries within which those decisions can be taken and allows for the balancing of often competing interests. In the EU legal tradition, proportionality is considered 'a structured approach to balancing fundamental rights with other rights and interests in the best possible way' (Rivers, 2006: 176). Its use in law is most often seen in the sub-fields of public or discrimination law. For example, in section 19 of the UK's Equality Act 2010, the disparate impact provisions provide that where a provision, criterion, or practice appears neutral but disadvantages those with a shared protected characteristic, the employer may be able to justify the practice but only if the employer can show that it was 'a *proportionate* means of achieving a legitimate aim'. Implicit in this test is the recognition that there may be a number of ways to reach a particular objective but that there must be limits when the process of achieving that goal would place a particular group at a greater disadvantage than others. A trite example may be a practice of insisting that each employee works all day, every day. Thus, a retail employer may have a legitimate goal of ensuring that the shop is appropriately staffed during the hours of 9 a.m.–5 p.m. so that customers will always be served. In contrast, such a practice would undoubtedly impact more heavily on those with caring responsibilities. A less disproportionate way of meeting that goal could be to allow flexible work patterns.

In this part, I consider how extending the principle of proportionality into corporate decision-making ('boardroom proportionality') could ameliorate a myopic focus on delivering value for shareholders, while also empowering those directors who support moving beyond the ideology of shareholder primacy.

Choudhury and Petrin (2018: 383) suggest that the correct objective of a company 'lies on an axis between purely shareholder wealth maximization, other stakeholders' interests, and public interests'. As such, they consider it 'appropriate for corporate governance policies to include public goals, as long as they do not unduly advance one constituency's interests over another's' (2018: 383). Implicit in Choudhury and Petrin's analysis of corporate purpose is the need to adjudicate between competing interests. Yet the dominance of shareholder value means that other interests, such as those of labour in the context of GVCs, are continually mediated by what will ultimately serve investors. Although a focus on profit is often believed to benefit all stakeholders – ostensibly 'trickling down' – this perspective is too simplistic and requires a robust system for reward allocation after the event. It is a naïve model, not least because the pursuit of maximum returns for shareholders, in the form of enhanced profits, necessarily entails extracting as much value as possible from other inputs into the system of production. Under this model, 'costs', such as paying living wages and rigorously observing labour rights, require reduction or eradication. This means that non-shareholder interests will always be appraised 'as a means to the best realisation of the shareholders' ends' (Bilchitz and Ausserladscheider Jonas, 2016: 835). This approach 'clashes fundamentally with the normative foundations of fundamental rights, which require the fundamental interests of individuals never to be treated purely as instruments for the achievement of the ends of others' (Bilchitz and Ausserladscheider Jonas, 2016: 835).

An alternative approach is to address the matter at source. It is here that the idea of proportionality at the level of board decision-making may offer the potential to prevent egregious human rights breaches, including the use of modern slavery. Giving directors a framework to balance different interests is an instrumental concern and not of the same normative importance as the prevention of modern slavery in GVCs. However, decision-making grounded in principles of proportionately has the potential to lead directors away from pursuing the most profit-enhancing strategies that may be reliant on ambivalence towards decent work and respect for human rights.

Bilchitz and Ausserladscheider Jonas (2016) offer a three-pronged framework for proportionality-based decision-making, which allows directors to evaluate competing considerations:

> [T]he director must consider the three sub-questions which follow the structure of the proportionality enquiry in public law: (1) Is there a rational connection between the means to be adopted (and the restriction of the right) and the goal to be achieved for shareholders? (the 'suitability' test) (2) Is there an alternative that still achieves the goal of shareholders sufficiently but has a lesser impact on the right in question? (the 'necessity' test) (3) Is the benefit to be achieved for shareholders proportional to the harm caused to the fundamental right of the stakeholder? (the 'balancing' test). (2016: 842)

They offer an example of a Ghanaian company in which shareholders are looking to reduce costs and, in so doing, to make redundant the jobs of a handful of women 'tea ladies'. Considering the matter from the perspective of the UK's enlightened shareholder value approach captured in section 172 of the Companies Act, the directors' duty is to the company, and they must act in good faith to promote its success for the benefit of its 'members as a whole'. For Bilchitz and Ausserladscheider Jonas (2016: 847), this means that the company 'would need to consider' issues such as reputational damage and the longer-term impact of its decision-making. Arguably, requiring directors to 'consider' non-shareholder interests may be putting the requirement in section 172 too strongly, depending on the interpretation given to the phrase 'have regard to'. However, even if we accept the stronger formulation of 'consider', this still leaves the tea ladies in this example at a significant disadvantage compared to investors. The board would balance the short-term reputational harm against the longer-term costs savings and could conclude in good faith that making these roles redundant is in the company's interests.

Bilchitz and Ausserladscheider Jonas (2016) show how, in their Ghana example, adopting an alternative, proportionality model of board decision-making invokes other considerations. Using their three-pronged framework, the goal of reducing costs would be achieved by cutting jobs so their first test of suitability appears satisfied. Turning to the second test of necessity, there may be other means of cost-cutting that would have a lesser impact on the tea ladies. The potential of their framework to make a difference in board decision-making is most obviously illustrated by considering the third test of balancing. Even if all other means of cost-cutting have been exhausted and the only available option is to make the tea ladies' roles redundant, is the decision to cut jobs proportional to the rights of those women? For Bilchitz and Ausserladscheider Jonas, rooting decision-making in the context of fundamental rights would begin from a start point of recognizing the women's 'intrinsic dignity' and the wider social and economic context (such as lack of welfare provision) that could compound the harm of losing their jobs. They argue that 'the company has assumed a particular responsibility for them' due to their long-standing relationship' (2016: 847). Weighing these considerations against investor benefit, it is difficult to see how the decision to cut jobs could be proportional to shareholder benefit in this context.

Building upon the framework developed by Bilchitz and Ausserladscheider Jonas, I suggest that there are two main reasons for incorporating principles of proportionality within company law. First, there are problems with relying on the 'gap-filling' capacity of regulatory protections outside company law. One problem is a 'divergence' between labour law protections and company law, with 'company law scholarship in the UK [having] become increasingly subsumed within a US-led law and economics paradigm, which – generally speaking – has served to further emphasise the relative primacy of financial capital within the notional "firm" over the countervailing demands of labour' (Moore, 2015: 426). Suggesting that labour law alone can temper the demands made by powerful financial investors without any corresponding restrictions in company law is unrealistic when the ideology of shareholder primacy is so entrenched.

A second reason for incorporating principles of proportionality in company law is that it requires directors to consider the impact on their operations at the highest organizational levels where there is the greatest potential to influence wider corporate practice. The incorporation of the principle of boardroom proportionality can fill gaps even where legal protection of labour rights would not apply. Such is the case with discrimination law. The UK's domestic legislation on indirect discrimination provides that a claimant must first establish a discriminatory 'provision, criterion or practice' (a PCP) that places her at a substantial disadvantage. However, many of the subtle norms promulgated by the pursuit of shareholder value may not amount to a PCP however widely that is interpreted. In the UK Court of Appeal case of *United First Partners Research v. Carreras* ([2018] EWCA Civ 323), the court took a generous view of the meaning of a PCP in the context of a claim for disability discrimination. The claimant was an analyst for a brokerage and research firm with a long-hours culture. Following a cycling accident, the claimant was affected both physically and mentally. For some months after the accident, he worked no more than 8 hours per day but gradually began to stay later in the evenings. Over time, working longer hours came to be expected of him once more: 'By the date of his resignation … the Respondent [would ask] him which nights he would be working late rather than whether he was prepared to work at all' (per Lord Justice Underhill and paragraph 6 of the judgment). At first instance, the Employment Tribunal was not convinced that the claimant had been 'required' to work long hours, as he claimed:

> The Claimant was not coerced in that it was always his choice as to whether he worked late or not. The Tribunal accepts that in making this decision, there were various commercial or political factors which may well have led the Claimant to decide that it was in his interests financially/in terms of career progression to work late. However, this cannot be described as being forced to do so.

Despite the Tribunal judge conceding that choice may be informed by a range of factors, including commercial considerations, the conclusion is nevertheless that individual autonomy has triumphed despite the long-hours culture. For Underhill LJ in the Court of Appeal, however, 'requirement' was not to be confused with 'coercion'. Finding a PCP, he stated that 'requirement … may, depending on the context, represent no more than a strong form of "request" … it was made clear by a pattern of repeated requests that he was expected to [work late], and that that created a pressure on him to agree' (per Lord Justice Underhill and paragraph 31 of the judgment). In the context of this particular case, where the claimant was repeatedly asked what nights he would work late, a PCP had arisen.

The proposal outlined here, for 'boardroom proportionality', is intended to apply even in situations where the legal definition of a PCP could not be met. In the *Carreras* case, had there been no express requests to work late but rather a sense of disapproval that was never shared explicitly but nevertheless was felt as an employee left work on time, Underhill LJ might not so readily have found a PCP to apply. This is because something more elusive than a clear practice might not amount to a PCP for the purposes of discrimination law. In the framework suggested by Bilchitz and Ausserladscheider Jonas, there appears no need to identify formally a PCP that has a disproportionate impact on a specific group. Their analytical tool ultimately involves a considered reflection on whether an intended course of conduct for the benefit of shareholders is proportional to the harms caused to members of the impacted group.

The idea of boardroom proportionality seems feasible for directors making decisions with respect to their own corporate operations. However, can it really make a difference in the context of GVCs, where the decision-makers of a lead company are geographically and legally distant from the parts of the value chain wherein labour abuses often occur? In response, it might be argued that in much the same way as lead firms can shape the operation of value chains in negative ways (just-in-time supply, for example), so too a decision at the top of the chain to pursue profit-making activities only in ways that do not disproportionately impact the rights of others has the potential to influence operations in a positive way. Moreover, given the availability of other legal mechanisms to address harm caused by decisions disproportionately affecting specific groups, it is uncertain what would motivate directors to embrace proportionality at the strategic board decision-making level.

Certainly, exploring the feasibility of implementing the boardroom proportionality principle in company law requires further examination. Nonetheless, it is important to address three potential criticisms of this very idea. First, critics might consider that the exercise being asked of directors is similar to that already contained in section 172 of the Companies Act 2006. Section 172 requires directors to consider a number of factors when fulfilling their duty to promote the success of the company for the benefit of its members as a whole. The boardroom proportionality principle, however, differs in two ways: (*a*) section 172 ultimately privileges shareholders in board decision-making. Boardroom proportionality, requiring that any substantial disadvantage to fundamental rights must be justified as being a proportionate means of achieving a legitimate aim, removes this primary focus on shareholders, and (*b*) section 172's invitation to directors to 'have regard to' a range of stakeholder interests lacks any real compulsion to actively consider the impact of strategic decisions on various groups. Reframing the requirement as one that ensures that any disadvantage must be justified requires a greater deal of scrutiny and inquiry. Incorporating the boardroom proportionality principle in the Companies Act could therefore, at the very least, subject corporations' worst actions to some legal scrutiny. Moreover, giving directors a clear framework within which to make decisions would empower those who support balancing the demands of investors with those of labour and other stakeholders. While one may argue that this grants excessive power to directors, I suggest that it merely reinforces the necessity for inclusive and diverse boardrooms.

The second criticism revolves around the lack of transparency in the board's deliberations, making it challenging to enforce directors' compliance with the boardroom proportionality principle. Given that derivative actions are limited to shareholders and that rights-holders are not privy to board deliberations, the latter lack the means to file petitions for non-compliance with this principle (Boeger et al., 2020). This concern is relevant to transparency and disclosure legislation in general, alongside challenges such as comprehension and 'window-dressing'. This concern can be, at least partly, mitigated by requiring directors to disclose their discussions on matters significantly disadvantaging rights-holders by extending the right to petition for a derivative action to specific representative organizations, such as a recognized trade union or national human rights body. As the derivative action model is predicated on an application to the court for permission to continue with the action, those representative organizations would be held to the same procedural hurdles which members already face.[2] Workers exposed to severe forms of exploitation have minimal to no practical opportunities to file petitions in any case.

A final criticism relates to the lack of knowledge of lead firm directors about operations taking place across a highly fragmented, global GVC. This is not, however, a reason to dismiss the idea of proportionality in corporate decision-making. Prioritizing the maximization of shareholder profits as the company's sole goal is considered one of the major factors contributing to exploitation through GVCs. Balancing this goal with social and environmental goals, even with no concrete knowledge of operations in tiers further up the supply chain, may help reduce exploitation. Lack of knowledge therefore reveals the necessity of rigorous due diligence and disclosure rules, rather than being a justification for maintaining the status quo around directors' decision-making.

Conclusion

This chapter considered how company law may be implicated in the operation of GVCs, focusing particularly on the role of directors when making decisions in lead firms. I have suggested that corporate lawyers might address the ideology that drives directors to prioritize the interests of financial investors over those of labour and local communities. This ideology is captured in the social norm of shareholder primacy, which in turn informs the objective of maximizing value for investors. Despite there being no doctrinal basis for directors to put shareholders first in this way, it is argued that this focus on delivering profit *at any cost* for shareholders fuels the most egregious exploitation of workers in GVC operations.

Banerjee makes a convincing case that reform is urgently needed in the business model of GVC operation, where delivering shareholder value is a key part. While this would entail more deep-seated reform of our global political economy in which companies are situated, this chapter has considered whether a less ambitious but nonetheless impactful change in GVC operation could be achieved by giving greater clarity to directors in their decision-making and regulating these decisions against the principle of proportionality. In sum, it is suggested that providing directors with a clearer interpretation of what it means for them to act in the interests of the company – a fundamental issue in company law – along with a framework for balancing competing rights, might help reduce exploitation through GVCs.

Notes

1. See, for example, the UK's clear statement in section 170(1) of the Companies Act 2006.
2. See, for example, sections 261, 263(2) and 263(3) of the UK Companies Act 2006.

References

Banerjee, B. (2021). 'Modern Slavery Is an Enabling Condition of Global Neoliberal Capitalism: Commentary on Modern Slavery in Business'. *Business and Society* 60(2): 415–19.

Better Business Act (2024). 'About The Better Business Act'. Available at: betterbusinessact.org/about/.

Bilchitz, D. and L. Ausserladscheider Jonas (2016). 'Proportionality, Fundamental Rights and the Duties of Directors'. *Oxford Journal of Legal Studies* 36(4): 828–54.

Boeger, N., R. Russell, and C. Villiers (2020). 'Companies, Shareholders and Sustainability'. University of Bristol Research Paper Series Paper 007 2020.

Buhmann, K., M. B. Taylor, and E. Giuliani (2019). 'Editorial – Business and Human Rights in Global Value Chains'. *Competition and Change* 23(4): 337–45.

Caruana, R., A. Crane, S. Gold, and G. LeBaron (2021). 'Modern Slavery in Business: The Sad and Sorry State of a Non-field'. *Business and Society* 60(2): 251–87.

Choudhury, B. and M. Petrin (2018). 'Corporate Governance That "Works for Everyone": Promoting Public Policies through Corporate Governance Mechanisms'. *Journal of Corporate Law Studies* 18(2): 381–415.

Deakin, S. (2005). 'The Coming Transformation of Shareholder Value'. *Corporate Governance* 13(1): 11–18.

Department of Trade and Industry (DTI) (2000). *Company Law for a Competitive Economy: Developing the Framework*. London: Department of Trade and Industry.

Enneking, L. and J. Veldman (2019). 'Towards Responsible Business Conduct in Global Value Chains: Relevant Legal Developments in the Netherlands'. *Erasmus Law Review* 12(4): 1–5.

European Commission (2020). *Study on Directors' Duties and Sustainable Corporate Governance – Final Report*. Publications Office of the European Union. Available at: op.europa.eu/en/publication-detail/-/publication/e47928a2-d20b-11ea-adf7-01aa75ed71a1/language-en.

Friedman, M. (1970). 'The Social Responsibility of Business Is to Increase Its Profits'. *The New York Times*, 13 September. Available at: www.nytimes.com/1970/09/13/archives/a-friedman-doctrine-the-social-responsibility-of-business-is-to.html.

Grantham, R. (1998). 'The Doctrinal Basis of the Rights of Company Shareholders'. *Cambridge Law Journal* 57(3): 554–88.

Hansmann, H. and R. H. Kraakman (2001). 'The End of History for Corporate Law'. *Georgetown Law Journal* 89(2): 439–68.

The IGLP Law and Global Production Working Group (2016). 'The Role of Law in Global Value Chains: A Research Manifesto'. *London Review of International Law* 4(1): 57–79.

Ireland, P. (1999). 'Company Law and the Myth of Shareholder Ownership'. *Modern Law Review* 62(1): 32–57.

——— (2010). 'Limited Liability, Shareholder Rights and the Problem of Corporate Irresponsibility'. *Cambridge Journal of Economics* 34(5): 837–56.

——— (2018). 'Corporate Schizophrenia: The Institutional Origins of Corporate Social Irresponsibility'. In *Shaping the Corporate Landscape: Towards Corporate Reform and Enterprise Diversity*, edited by N. Boeger and C. Villiers, 13–39. Oxford, UK; Portland, OR: Hart Publishing.

Jensen, M. C. and W. H. Meckling, (1976). 'Theory of the Firm: Managerial Behavior, Agency Costs and Ownership Structure'. *Journal of Financial Economics* 3(4): 305–60.

Keay, A. (2007). 'Company Directors Behaving Poorly: Disciplining Options for Shareholders'. *Journal of Business Law* (September): 656–82.

Kiarie, S. (2006). 'At Crossroads: Shareholder Value, Stakeholder Value and Enlightened Shareholder Value: Which Road Should the United Kingdom Take?' *ICCLR* 17(11): 329–43.

Milberg, W. (2008). 'Shifting Sources and Uses of Profits: Sustaining US Financialization with Global Value Chains'. *Economy and Society* 37(3): 420–51.

Moore, M. T. (2015). 'Comment: Bridging the Gap between Labour Law and Company Law'. *Industrial Law Journal* 44(3): 425–29.

Pearson, G. (2018). 'Destruction by Ideological Pretence: The Case of Shareholder Primacy'. In, *Shaping the Corporate Landscape: Towards Corporate Reform and Enterprise Diversity*, edited by N. Boeger and C. Villiers, 41–59. Oxford, UK; Portland, OR: Hart Publishing.

Ponte, S. and P. Gibbon (2005). 'Quality Standards, Conventions and the Governance of Global Value Chains'. *Economy and Society* 34(1): 1–31.

Ramanna, K. (2020). 'Friedman at 50: Is It Still the Social Responsibility of Business to Increase Profits?' *California Management Review* 62(3): 28–41.

Rivers, J. (2006). 'Proportionality and Variable Intensity of Review'. *Cambridge Law Journal* 65(1): 174–207.

Sjåfjell, B., A. Johnston, L. Anker-Sørensen, and D. Millon (2015). 'Shareholder Primacy: The Main Barrier to Sustainable Companies'. In *Company Law and*

Sustainability: Legal Barriers and Opportunities, edited by B. Sjåfjell and B. J. Richardson, 79–147. Cambridge, UK: Cambridge University Press.

Sjåfjell, B., J. T. Mähönen,, T. A. Novitz, C. Gammage, and H. Ahlström (2020). 'Securing the Future of European Business: SMART Reform Proposals'. University of Oslo Faculty of Law Research Paper Series, No. 2020–11.

Stout, L. (2002). 'Bad and Not-So-Bad Arguments for Shareholder Primacy'. *Southern California Law Review* 75(5): 1189–210.

——— (2012). *The Shareholder Value Myth: How Putting Shareholders First Harms Investors, Corporations and the Public.* San Francisco, CA: Berrett-Koehler.

Talbot, L. (2013). *Progressive Corporate Governance for the 21st Century.* London: Routledge.

Turner, R. J. (2016). 'Transnational Supply Chain Regulation: Extraterritorial Regulation as Corporate Law's New Frontier'. *Melbourne Journal of International Law* 17(1): 188–209.

Walsh, J. P. (2004). 'Introduction to the "Corporate Objective Revisited" Exchange'. *Organization Science* 15(3): 350–63.

Lord Wedderburn of Charlton (2002). 'Employees, Partnership and Company Law'. *Industrial Law Journal* 31(2): 99–112.

6

Anti-trafficking Chains

Structural Comparison of Corporate Transparency Legislation and Worker-driven Social Responsibility

Tamar Barkay and Hila Shamir*

The campaign to address severe forms of labour market exploitation in markets around the world has led activists, unionists, policymakers, and legislators to explore the role of corporations in driving human trafficking and modern slavery (LeBaron, 2020). Based on the understanding that lead firms are not merely complicit actors but active contributors – through their purchasing and sourcing practices – to violations of workers' human rights and labour standards, the focus on corporations seeks to expand corporate responsibility to working conditions throughout global value chains (GVCs) (Anner, 2015). In

* We are grateful to the generous and insightful comments we received for earlier versions of this article from Ioannis Kampourakis, and Klaas H. Eller, as well as from seminar groups and conference audiences at the University of Toronto, Haifa University, Tel Aviv University, TraffLab (ERC) research group, the SASE conference (2021), and the Law and Society Association Conference (Lisbon, 2022). The research has received support from ERC StG grant agreement No. 756672, TraffLab: Labor Perspective to Human Trafficking, PI Prof. Hila Shamir/Tel Aviv University, as well as from ChainGE Lab (ERC) funded by the European Union, Horizon ERC grant ERC-2022-COG (Project No. 101088188, PI Hila Shamir). Views and opinions expressed are, however, those of the author(s) only and do not necessarily reflect those of the European Union or the European Research Council Executive Agency (ERCEA) (the 'granting authority'). Neither the European Union nor the granting authority can be held responsible for them. It received further funding from the Israel Science Foundation (ISF) grant no. 1866/20. We are deeply grateful to Debbie Siton for her rigorous and dedicated research assistance and editing.

this chapter, we compare two labour governance models that have developed in the quest to combat modern slavery.

To better comprehend the structural aspects of efforts to eradicate modern slavery within GVCs and the dynamics created around them, as well as the measures pursued and their implications, we further develop and employ our analytical concept of 'anti-trafficking chains'. This term refers to the provision of anti-trafficking services by both non-profit and for-profit entities to multinational corporations (MNCs), mirroring the logic and structure of supply chains (Barkay et al., 2024). The comparative analysis presented here focuses on two types of anti-trafficking chains: one that has proliferated following the enactment of State Anti-Trafficking laws in various countries and another that emerged from the deployment of the Worker Social Responsibility (WSR) model. This analysis seeks to discern the extent to which State Anti-Trafficking laws provide the expected hardening of soft-law anti-trafficking tools and to identify the conditions under which anti-trafficking chains may transform corporate behaviour and serve as drivers of change in human trafficking in GVCs.[1] To this end, this chapter offers a structural analysis of the governance models behind State Anti-Trafficking laws and WSR and of the power dynamics created by each.

Over the last two decades, enormous financial resources and organizational efforts have been invested, globally and nationally, in confronting human trafficking. Nevertheless, as systematically reported by the International Labour Organization (ILO), despite these efforts, the prevalence of human trafficking practices continues to pose an ever more worrying and pressing global challenge (ILO, 2017, 2018). As a result, in more recent years, scholars and policymakers have gradually come to recognize that the traditional tools used to combat human trafficking and other severe forms of harm in employment and labour exploitation – criminalization of traffickers, strict border control, and ex-post human rights assistance to identified victims – fall short (Dottridge, 2014; Chuang, 2014; Nolan and Bott, 2018). Concomitantly, scholars have developed anti-trafficking structural paradigms, such as the labour and development approaches, that identify the resistant nature of human trafficking in the power relationships and structures upon which contemporary local and global labour markets are built and operate (Shamir, 2012; Kotiswaran, 2019). These structural approaches argue that human trafficking – a major source of today's corporate revenues – is enabled and perpetuated by the intrinsic governance gaps that exist in GVCs (Raigrodski, 2016; Crane et al., 2019).[2]

This increasing emphasis on the importance of transforming the labour-market structures that enable and sustain human trafficking, and on the need to address issues of labour governance within GVCs, is reflected in the emergence of a new set of anti-trafficking tools that rely on the notion of 'corporate social responsibility' (CSR). Since the late 1990s, both the imbalance between the overwhelming influence of MNCs on labour markets, on the one hand, and the inability or unwillingness of states and transnational bodies to adequately regulate them, on the other, have led to a global spread of CSR models and practices and their integration in the corporate risk-management toolbox.

However, the recognition within the anti-trafficking field that corporations bear responsibility for their negative social and environmental impacts is a relatively recent trend. The CSR anti-trafficking tools include three main types: corporate self-regulatory (so-called soft-law) initiatives; State Anti-Trafficking legislation; and WSR schemes. This chapter focuses on the latter two, developed largely in response to mounting evidence of the ineffectiveness of corporate self-regulatory initiatives (New, 2015; Bartley, 2018).

Several countries have now adopted legislation aimed at addressing workers' rights in global supply chains (Coneybeer et al., 2023). This trend can be divided into two main legal approaches: 'transparency' and 'human rights due diligence' (HRDD). Under the transparency approach, laws require firms that meet specific threshold criteria to disclose the actions they are taking to protect workers' rights and to address issues of human trafficking in their supply chains. The goals of such laws are to increase the level of transparency in supply chain management and to expose corporations that allow severe exploitation in their supply chains to public and consumer pressures. Examples of such laws are the California Transparency in Supply Chains Act (2010), Section 54 of the United Kingdom (UK) Modern Slavery Act (2015), Australia's Modern Slavery Act (2018), and the European Union (EU) Non-Financial Reporting Directive (2014).

In contrast, under the HRDD approach, laws go beyond requiring mere disclosure. They obligate firms to undertake HRDD to identify potential human rights violations in their supply chains, to prevent them from happening, to mitigate them, and to account for how they are to be managed, including protection of workers' rights (Landau, 2023). HRDD legislation may range from a wide assessment of the working conditions of labourers down the supply chain to more specific child labour, forced labour, or modern slavery-related due diligence requirements. Examples of such laws are Section 1502 of the United States (US) Dodd-Frank Act (2010), the EU Conflict Minerals Regulation (2017), the Dutch Child Labour Due Diligence Law (2019), Germany's Supply Chain Due Diligence Act (2021), Canada's Forced Labour and Child Labour in Supply Chains Act (2023), and the European Corporate Sustainability Due

Diligence Directive (2024). The latter marks the current prevailing trend among EU countries towards HRDD legislation (McCorquodale and Nolan, 2021; Marshall et al., 2023).

The underlying premise on which current formulations of State Anti-Trafficking laws are based – be they transparency- or HRDD-driven – is that the threat of having severe worker exploitation exposed poses a real business risk that will compel firms to take corrective action. Therefore, such laws often lack stringent enforcement mechanisms and sanctions, whereas the statutory reporting duties they introduce are crafted to allow and encourage consumers and investors to monitor corporations. Many in the anti-trafficking field view State Anti-Trafficking laws as promising tools for combatting human trafficking in GVCs (Han et al., 2022). Nevertheless, critical voices raise concerns regarding the capacity of State Anti-Trafficking legislation to make the required change, especially in the form of transparency laws. They argue that the tendency of legislators and policymakers to rely on market-oriented compliance mechanisms, and their adherence to the rationale of voluntary corporate responsibility rather than liability, cast serious doubt on the potential effectiveness of State Anti-Trafficking laws (Koekkoek et al., 2017; Phillips et al., 2018; Voss et al., 2019; Ford and Nolan, 2020). In light of such criticism, we explore the reasons for the limited effectiveness of anti-trafficking chains created in response to transparency laws in transforming severely exploitative employment practices in GVCs, compared to the impact of anti-trafficking chains arising out of the WSR approach.

WSR, much like State Anti-Trafficking legislation, presents an alternative approach to the identified failures of CSR (Gordon, 2017). It has been developed alongside other instruments for social dialogue-based supply chain governance by unions and workers' civil society organizations to compensate for the absence or limited labour law protections under supply chain capitalism (Reinecke and Donaghey, 2020). By establishing enforceable, negotiated agreements among workers, employers, and lead firms, worker-led labour governance instruments offer an alternative to both state-led and corporate-led approaches. Unlike corporate voluntarism or top-down regulation, these mechanisms leverage the power of affected workers and their coalitions. The literature distinguishes worker-led instruments based on actors involved, scope, and regulation modes, focusing mainly on Transnational Industrial Relation Agreements (TIRAs)[3] and WSR Initiatives (Haipeter et al., 2021; Blasi and Bair, 2019). TIRAs are bargained-for agreements between lead firms (either single or multiple firms) and trade unions (local, global, or both). These agreements span global supply chains and result in legally binding documents with enforcement mechanisms, including dispute resolution processes such as enforceable and binding arbitration (Ashwin et al., 2020). Under WSR schemes, workers, their direct employers (suppliers), and lead firms (purchasers) negotiate agreements stipulating that lead firms will only contract with suppliers that comply with universal labour standards. Importantly, the standards are strictly monitored and enforced by rigorous inspection bodies that are independent of corporations and suppliers and overseen by workers (Blasi and Bair, 2019).[4]

Proponents of this approach believe that it expands corporate engagement and genuine commitment to labour rights issues. The leading example and most successful case of the WSR model in action is the Fair Food Program (FFP) – a partnership of farmers, farmworkers, and retail food companies that aims to ensure fair wages and humane working conditions for farmworkers. The FFP was initiated and founded by the Coalition of Immokalee Workers, a worker-led human rights organization in Immokalee, Florida. Among other examples are: the Milk with Dignity Program, led by the organization Migrant Justice in the dairy sector in Vermont (USA); the Accord on Fire and Building Safety in the Bangladeshi garment sector; and the Lesotho agreements that focus on preventing gender-based violence and harassment in the garment sector.

In some ways, WSR is almost a mirror image of State Anti-Trafficking legislation and, particularly, transparency laws. First, WSR is driven by the bottom-up, grassroots activism of workers and their communities, joined by consumers, placing workers' voices and needs at its centre (Asbed and Hitov, 2017). Second, in contrast with the soft-law approach of transparency legislation, WSR's defining feature is its effective enforcement and monitoring mechanism, backed up by market consequences. Third, WSR creates a clear set of labour rights obligations that are directly informed and designed by workers' needs, unlike transparency laws that, thus far, have failed to include specific substantive requirements regarding workers' rights. Indeed, while the literature has severely criticized transparency laws as ineffective, WSR has been celebrated by many commentators as a prime solution to the labour governance deficit in GVCs (Asbed and Hitov, 2017; Blasi and Bair, 2019; Dias-Abbey, 2019a; Gladstone, 2020; Reinecke and Donaghey, 2021; Mieres and McGrath, 2021; Angelini and Curphey, 2022).

Despite the differences in the respective approaches of State Anti-Trafficking legislation and WSR, we compare them here from the perspective of the anti-trafficking chains they generate. We argue that the limited impact of transparency laws and the relative success of WSR schemes can be better understood by examining the two models through the lens of power resources and distribution within their anti-trafficking chains. To this end, we offer a structural analysis of the anti-trafficking chain developed in the UK construction sector following the enactment of the UK Modern Slavery Act (MSA) in 2015, alongside the anti-trafficking chain that emerged from the implementation of the WSR model by the FFP. The analysis of the former draws on data from exploratory research conducted between October 2018 and October 2019, employing a multiple-method qualitative design. This included content analysis of modern slavery statements published by 93 construction companies, semi-structured interviews with key actors in the UK anti-trafficking field, and participant observation in a modern slavery training session, also in the UK. Given the extensive body of research on the FFP, our analysis of the anti-trafficking chain in this instance draws on a range of secondary resources, including academic studies and policy reports, all of which we critically reviewed and analysed.

This comparative analysis primarily focuses on the power dynamics within GVCs in response to anti-trafficking initiatives. Therefore, while there are significant dissimilarities between the operational aspects of the supply chains of the GVCs in question, our analysis does not dwell on these aspects. Instead, it examines the different logics and structural interventions of the MSA and FFP in the respective value chains – construction supply chains in the UK and the fresh-tomato supply chain in the US. The qualitative nature of this research design requires us to exercise caution when attempting to generalize insights to broader contexts. However, for the purposes of this study, we contend that both the research design and the diversity of the cases examined not only do not impede our ability to compare anti-trafficking chains but also facilitate the elucidation of the *structural* factors that influence the efficacy of anti-trafficking chains in bringing about change.

The chapter proceeds as follows: The following section introduces the notion of *anti-trafficking chains*, linking it to critical perspectives in the literature on GVCs. In the third and fourth sections, we analyse the dynamics of the anti-trafficking chains that were developed in response to the enactment of the UK MSA and the implementation of the WSR approach in Florida's FFP, respectively. Drawing on the comparison between these two types of anti-trafficking chains, the fifth section discusses the inherent shortcomings of transparency legislation versus the potential of the WSR model to significantly improve working conditions in the lower tiers of GVCs and eradicate human trafficking throughout the supply chain.

Anti-trafficking Chains

The growing emphasis of anti-trafficking efforts on the governance of GVCs in the last decade, alongside the growing public awareness of the issue of human trafficking, has led hundreds of corporations to adopt anti-trafficking codes of conduct. It has also given rise to an anti-trafficking industrial complex[5] comprising numerous civil society organizations, for-profit organizations, professional bodies, and multi-level and cross-sectoral initiatives. These organizations and entities provide the corporate sector with a range of anti-trafficking services and solutions (McGrath and Watson, 2018; Monciardini et al., 2021).

In the GVC literature, such organizations and initiatives are framed within what is termed a 'supporting environment', which is conceived by some scholars as a legal and social grid external to the value-creation process within which GVCs operate (Frederick, 2019: 31–32). We argue that this framing does not sufficiently capture the dynamics and power relations created both within the anti-trafficking industrial complex and between the organizations and entities that comprise this complex and the lead firms with which they engage (cf. Ponte et al., 2019). Instead, we introduce the term 'anti-trafficking chains' to refer to the dynamic web of anti-trafficking actors, initiatives, and activities in GVCs. Our conceptualization of a *chain* of anti-trafficking efforts in GVCs emphasizes the asymmetrical interdependence and supply-chain logic that characterize their modes of operation vis-à-vis lead firms and other entities in GVCs. Such an analysis of anti-trafficking efforts – one that focuses on the link between the structural dynamics of anti-trafficking chains and how they interact with GVCs – is instrumental to an understanding of the factors impacting their effectiveness as labour governance mechanisms.

Our conceptualization of anti-trafficking chains draws on the writings of critical GVC scholars who explore how value-creation processes generate and disguise a range of exploitative relationships and employment practices (Havice and Pickles, 2019; Nathan, 2019). We align with the neo-Gramscian perspective that, in recent decades, GVC governance is an increasingly contested terrain, where corporate, state, and national and international civil society actors vie to shape and control (Bair and Palpacuer, 2015; Palpacuer, 2019; Anner, 2023). Adopting this analytical lens, we observe that the struggle over GVC governance has evolved into a pendulum-like movement regarding the role of the state. The global spread of private CSR governance mechanisms since the 1990s marks a shift towards 'decentring the state'. Conversely, the emergence of State

Anti-Trafficking legislation in recent years heralds a countermovement towards 'recentring the state' (Bartley, 2018; Palpacuer, 2019). Nevertheless, as corporate actors have successfully managed to mitigate the impacts of both movements on their operations, positive consequences for the welfare and working conditions of workers in the lowest tiers of GVCs have been markedly limited.

These observations raise the question of the specific conditions under which labour governance in GVCs would not be simply neutralized by the power imbalance and dynamics of GVCs. Further, we aim to better understand how, and to what extent, the structural and dynamic conditions under which anti-trafficking chains operate within GVCs affect their outcomes. We suggest that, unlike the anti-trafficking chains created by transparency legislation, which primarily engage with powerful lead firms, the WSR model fosters 'bottom-up' anti-trafficking chains that empower workers and, consequently, holds richer potential to serve as an effective labour governance mechanism in GVCs.

Supply Chain Dynamics under the UK Modern Slavery Act

Background

Section 54 of the 2015 MSA was the first piece of legislation in Europe to explicitly address human trafficking in supply chains. It was introduced during the Act's amendment phase after extensive deliberations, propelled by concerted pressure from a coalition of international and national civil society organizations urging the UK Government to specifically address the issue of modern slavery and human trafficking in supply chains (Pollitt, 2014). During the legislative process, multinational and local corporations had established a business lobby that championed a diluted model of transparency legislation among both legislators and NGOs (LeBaron and Rühmkorf, 2019). Ultimately, it was this model that informed the drafting of Section 54.

Section 54 requires any commercial organization with business activities in the UK and with an annual turnover of at least £36 million to publish a 'modern slavery and human trafficking' statement, approved by its board of directors and signed by a director, each financial year. The supplemental guidance of the MSA clarifies that, while companies are not required to guarantee that their supply chains are 'slavery free', they *are* expected to describe in their published statements the measures they have taken that year to eradicate modern slavery from their business and supply chains. Similarly, companies are not mandated to implement specific measures against human trafficking in their supply chains. However, those that have not taken any measures are required to issue an annual statement to that effect.

Rather than obligating corporations to undertake concrete actions, the MSA suggests six areas that may be included in the report: the business and supply chain structure; slavery and human trafficking policies; due diligence processes; the parts of the supply chain where there are risks of slavery and human trafficking and the measures that have been taken to mitigate them; and effectiveness of anti-trafficking policies and training. Lastly, in line with the principal rationale of transparency legislation from the business perspective – that human trafficking in supply chains poses a reputational risk – to ensure compliance with these minimal disclosure requirements, Section 54 explicitly relies on 'consumers, investors and Non-Governmental Organisations (NGOs) to monitor compliance and apply pressure on businesses' (Field et al., 2019: 39), rather than on state mechanisms for monitoring and enforcement (Craig, 2017; Sarfaty, 2020; Carrington et al., 2021).[6]

In July 2019, four years after the enactment of the MSA and following the publication of an independent review commissioned by the UK Home Office (Field et al., 2019), the latter launched a public consultation. The exercise was designed to invite feedback from the public and commercial and civil society stakeholders on proposed changes regarding: the content of modern slavery statements; the introduction of an annual deadline for statement publication; civil penalties; the applicability of the Act's provisions to the public sector; and potential features for a government-run reporting service for modern slavery statements. Following the consultation process, in July 2021, the UK Government introduced the Modern Slavery (Amendment) Bill to the House of Lords, aiming to strengthen the provisions of Section 54.[7] However, due to the prorogation of Parliament, this progressed no further. Meanwhile, new immigration laws introduced in the UK – the Nationality and Borders Act (2022) and the Illegal Migration Act (2023) – have been criticized for jeopardizing vulnerable individuals and victims of human trafficking by failing to offer them adequate support and protection (Brown, 2023; Weir et al., 2024).

Anti-trafficking Chains in the UK Construction Sector

The construction industry is globally recognized as one of the sectors most prone to severe labour exploitation (Cockbain and Brayley-Morris, 2018; Trautrims et al., 2021; UNODC, 2020). The UK construction sector is no exception. While there are no exact figures for trafficking and forced labour victims in the UK by sector, it is widely agreed that several sector-specific factors place construction workers at very high risk of exploitation and abuse (Werdmuller von Elgg, 2016; CIOB, 2018; FLEX and Stride, 2018; Guilbert, 2018). In particular, the sector's extreme volatility and fragmentation drive construction companies to rely heavily on outsourcing/subcontracting and on labour intermediaries and low-wage, low-skilled, and migrant workers (CITB, 2019; Rhodes, 2019; Pickard, 2023). Often not covered by regulatory agencies, these workers are the least protected and hence the most vulnerable to exploitation (Fudge, 2018).

Enactment of the MSA in March 2015 enhanced existing anti-trafficking efforts in the UK and gave rise to numerous others initiated by advocacy groups, NGOs, multi-stakeholder, (cross-)sector initiatives, and service providers. As a result, a thriving market for anti-trafficking initiatives, professional guidance, and legal services emerged. Notably, while the Chartered Institute of Building (CIOB) had already launched an anti-trafficking campaign in 2014,[8] it was only after the enactment of the MSA that anti-trafficking efforts around construction significantly increased and gradually attracted a response from the sector.

These anti-trafficking efforts were initiated by professional bodies, industrial associations, state agencies, and civil society organizations and most often consist of alliances with construction companies. Among such efforts are non-profits, such as 'Supply Chain Sustainability School', 'Stronger Together', and 'Hope for Justice'; professional bodies and associations like the CIOB, the Building Research Establishment, and the Construction Industry Training Board; and many law and accountancy firms, which provide construction companies with assistance in preparing formal modern slavery and human resources statements to comply with the Act.

Additionally, the UK's Gangmasters and Labour Abuse Authority (GLAA), a government agency tasked with investigating labour exploitation and other illegal labour market activities, has played a key role in anti-trafficking efforts within the construction sector. Specifically, between October 2017 and November 2022, the GLAA operated a joint sector-wide agreement called the Construction Protocol.[9] The move was intended to address human trafficking in the sector by fostering private–public and inter-sector collaborations, setting standards, supporting best practices, and sharing knowledge among its signatories.[10] In November 2022, however, the GLAA withdrew from all its sector-specific protocols, including the Construction Protocol, stating that it had 'moved to putting [its] resources into developing and supporting more focused partnership activity which is business-owned, with the GLAA providing the strategic oversight and expertise'.[11]

Based on our interviews and analysis of modern slavery statements published by construction companies that were signatories to the GLAA Protocol, these anti-trafficking efforts have led to a gradual increase in the sector's compliance with the minimal legal requirements of Section 54 of the MSA, as well as to an increase in awareness of human trafficking issues among construction companies. Nevertheless, like companies in other sectors (BHRC and MSR, 2021), many of the statements published by compliant construction companies are of poor quality, providing no or minimal information on the six recommended reporting areas and undertaking no proactive or beyond-compliance measures (see also Monciardini et al., 2021). A small group of companies within the sector, aiming to mitigate human rights risks in their supply chains and thereby secure their reputation, has initiated an intra-industry alliance. This alliance developed anti-trafficking tools that extend beyond mere symbolic compliance with Section 54 provisions, Yet, it has failed to engage a significant number of construction companies (Trautrims et al., 2021). All in all, despite the vibrant anti-trafficking activity developed around the construction sector since the enactment of the MSA, actors in the field suggested to us that the Act has not succeeded in driving any substantial corporate action to combat labour exploitation in supply chains.

We argue that the gap between the booming anti-trafficking activity around the construction sector, on the one hand, and the actual impact on the ground, on the other, has been structurally sustained by anti-trafficking actors being positioned as suppliers of human trafficking solutions and services to corporations. Due to the MSA's reliance on market compliance mechanisms and the inherent imbalanced power relations between corporations and anti-trafficking actors, the latter have been forced into a supply chain dynamic that has significantly limited their leverage over corporate behaviour. Such a dynamic particularly affects anti-trafficking activities in the construction sector, which is far less susceptible to consumer demands and pressures compared to other sectors such as retail or consumer goods. Interviewees suggested that the absence of major litigation or media coverage relating to trafficking in the UK construction sector had contributed both to construction companies' perception of immunity to external criticism and pressures and to the ambiguity and uncertainty surrounding the extent of modern slavery in the sector. Hence, human trafficking in construction supply chains creates little reputational risk.[12]

While the companies have increasingly adhered to the MSA's minimum reporting requirements, they have rarely taken measures beyond standard anti-trafficking compliance, suggesting that they may have complied with the MSA only for the potential regulatory risk it poses. Our findings show that training programmes and other generic toolkits were the most-reported measures implemented by compliant construction companies.[13] This was also supported by the observations of interviewees, who noted that construction companies' reporting trends were influenced by the structure and characteristics of the sector's supply chains, and particularly by their fragmentation. Severe labour exploitation is typically expected to occur in tiers 4 and 5 of the supply chain; yet, often, lead firms have limited to no knowledge of suppliers and subcontractors beyond tier 1 or 2. Consequently, compliant construction companies tend to adopt anti-trafficking measures such as employee training sessions on modern slavery that do not require their involvement in the very tiers of their supply chains where the gravest violations may occur.

The reporting requirements introduced in the construction sector, and, more broadly, the corporate market for 'modern slavery tools and solutions' created by the MSA, have bound anti-trafficking efforts in supply chains to activities that allow corporations to comply with the minimal commitments specified in their published statements. The numerous anti-trafficking initiatives, organizations, and consultancies that offer construction companies a range of services, including training programmes, due diligence audits, and other solutions to assist them in complying with the Act mirror this reality. Under these circumstances, anti-trafficking initiatives, which often rely for their reliability and legitimacy on sector support and are constantly competing for corporate contracts and sponsorship for their funding (Hielscher et al., 2017; Mikołajczak, 2017), are forced into a weak position vis-à-vis lead firms, with little to no capacities to transform actual corporate behaviour. Furthermore, as companies may prefer, due to reputational considerations, to purchase anti-trafficking *services* rather than publicly sponsor anti-trafficking initiatives, such initiatives are pushed to offer their services just like for-profit consultancies. Their role, then, revolves primarily around aiding corporations to comply with the Act's requirements, rather than being regarded as stakeholders with the capacity to exert pressures on companies to tackle labour trafficking within their supply chains. Under such circumstances of dependency on corporate funding, far from challenging the power dynamics of the supply chain, anti-trafficking efforts become subsumed into them.

In sum, our analysis shows that the MSA has given rise to an anti-trafficking chain wherein anti-trafficking initiatives are constructed as suppliers catering to the needs of those who source them. Contrary to the explicit intention of the

MSA, which expects consumers, investors, and NGOs to monitor compliance, no meaningful market-oriented compliance mechanism has emerged, nor has an institutional environment developed with the leverage to inspire and promote significant change in corporate practices. Lastly, our findings indicate that the current arrangements encourage corporations and anti-trafficking initiatives to prioritize compliance with the MSA's minimum requirements only. This suggests that the MSA has not only failed to harden the soft edges of compliance and self-regulatory tools but, in fact, may also have weakened them altogether.

Anti-trafficking Chain Dynamics under the WSR Model

Background

The WSR model positions workers who labour at the bottom of supply chains as active agents in setting and leading the agenda for CSR and provides them with a new form of power within GVCs to protect and enforce their own rights. The model seeks to fill the governance vacuum created by the legal structures, corporate strategies, and financialization of the global economy that constitute 'supply chain capitalism' (Tsing, 2009) and contractually distance capital from the production process and labour through complex value chains and multi-tiered supplier structures. WSR creates direct contractual relations between workers or their representatives and lead firms in a process of multi-party negotiation between the firms, their suppliers, and the workers. The model was developed following the success of the Coalition of Immokalee Workers' (CIW) FFP campaign that significantly improved the working conditions of farm workers in the tomato fields of Immokalee, Florida.

CIW is a grassroots organization made up of farmworkers from Florida's tomato industry (Giagnoni, 2011). The tomato fields in this state were once notorious for their widespread exploitative working conditions, including identified cases of forced labour and modern slavery (Marquis, 2017). The CIW began its organizing effort to improve workers' rights in the early 1990s by demanding that growers – their direct employers – comply with basic rights and refrain from worker exploitation (Estabrook, 2011). When traditional methods failed to transform the harsh working conditions in the fields, CIW members redirected their efforts towards brands at the top of the supply chain. They suspected that pressure exerted on the part of the chain that generated the most profit, while the share taken by the growers – their direct employers – was, in fact, shrinking (Asbed and Hitov, 2017), might produce greater leverage. It is this insight that led them to initiate the FFP.

The FFP is a private governance scheme that, through pressure from workers and consumers, induces lead firms (mostly supermarkets and fast-food chains) and growers to sign legally binding agreements. These agreements establish an enforcement method to secure workers' rights by incorporating mechanisms such as Health and Safety committees operating on farms. This enables workers to actively participate in shaping their working environment, thereby guaranteeing worker voice and engagement in the process. The original campaign began in 2001, based on alliances and solidarity between workers and consumer groups – predominantly, student organizations and faith-based communities. Following a long and challenging campaign that included an effective consumer boycott, the first agreement was signed with Taco Bell in 2005 (Leary, 2005; Asbed and Hitov, 2017). Gradually, and not without resistance, other fast-food chains and supermarkets – such as McDonalds, Burger King, Whole Foods, Walmart, and others – joined the FFP.[14] Today, the FFP is widely regarded as a success story that transformed the once-harsh working conditions of farm labourers into a decent and safer work environment (Marquis, 2017).

The FFP programme includes two key elements. The first is a price premium – an additional 'penny per pound' increase in the cost of tomatoes, paid by the buyers (lead firms) and used to increase the wages of workers and help fund the programme and its enforcement mechanisms. The second is a human rights-based code of conduct, for buyers and growers, informed and designed by workers. Among other stipulations, it defines 'zero tolerance violations' – such as sexual violence, physical and gun violence, and forced labour. The code of conduct has proven to be impactful, leading to changes in harvesting and farm practices that have improved workers' lives, wages, and working conditions.

One issue tackled by the FFP, for example, was the long-established practice of obliging workers to overfill the buckets they used to collect the crop (known as 'cupping' or 'topping off'). As they are generally paid per bucket, this practice unjustly created a *de facto* reduction in workers' wages. The FFP eliminates cupping and, as a result, achieves a wage increase of up to 10 per cent (FFSC, 2017: 60). Additional provisions in the code provide workers with shade in the fields and allow for later start times, enabling them to see their families in the mornings and thereby accommodating a better quality of life. Importantly, the FFP's code mandates direct employment of workers by farmers, rather than through labour intermediaries who, within the power structure of supply chains, often take advantage of farmworkers' vulnerability to severe exploitation (Estabrook, 2011; Marquis, 2017; Dias-Abey, 2019a). These elements are accompanied by important complementary components: an emphasis on community-building and worker-to-worker education, Health and Safety committees, and the guarantee of worker voice in the workplace.

Crucially, the programme also developed an innovative and elaborate enforcement, monitoring, and sanction process. Given the general failure of other private (as well as public) enforcement schemes to secure vulnerable workers' rights and labour standards (Fine and Bartley, 2019), this process is particularly noteworthy (Marquis, 2023). In 2011, the FFP established a monitoring and enforcement body – the Fair Food Standards Council (FFSC). The FFSC operates as an effective, rigorous enforcement body that conducts external auditing and processes and investigates complaints from workers (Dias-Abey, 2019a). It consists of independent professional investigators who speak the workers' native languages. These investigators spend a significant amount of time in the fields alongside the workers. FFSC's investigations include conversations with at least half of the farm's workforce; system audits of the farm's management and operations; assessment of the grower's compliance with the code; and financial audits of compensation and payroll issues (Brudney, 2016; Marquis, 2017: 123–27).

The auditing system complements the worker complaints hotline, which is operated around the clock by staff who speak Spanish, Haitian Creole, and English. Complaints are processed effectively and efficiently, with over half of them resolved within two weeks (FFSC, 2021: 38–39). The complaint-resolution process prioritizes collaboration and correction. Accordingly, corrective measures, such as suspension from the programme, are collaboratively developed with farms, taking into account their specific situations (Angelini and Curphey, 2022; FFSC, 2021: 8). Overall, functioning as an independent monitoring body and fostering an extensive and efficient operation, the FFSC has created an environment in which workers feel safe to report legitimate complaints without fear of reprisal (Dias-Abey, 2019b).

Together, these different elements of the programme – grassroots organizing, foregrounding worker knowledge and voice, worker-to-worker education, a broad worker–consumer coalition, leveraging the power of lead firms (buyers) over growers, emphasizing buyers' responsibility, binding contracts, and an effective enforcement mechanism backed by economic sanctions – have transformed work for the tomato pickers of Florida. Being recognized as an exemplary programme in addressing workers' rights violations and modern slavery[15] has allowed the FFP to expand to other agricultural products as well as to additional growers and buyers in other parts of the US. Concomitantly, while the CIW continues to receive fees from buyers as well as philanthropic donations, its expansion and recognized track record have enabled it to start receiving consultancy fees (Marquis, 2023: 31).

In 2015, the CIW and FFP, alongside other workers' rights organizations, established the Worker-driven Social Responsibility Network (WSR Network). The term 'Worker-Driven Social Responsibility' was chosen to mark and promote the model as an alternative to conventional CSR-based models that centre on corporate-led codes or multi-stakeholder initiatives (MSIs) (Ben-Ozer, 2021; Humphrey et al., 2023). Furthermore, by creating the WSR Network, they explicitly sought 'to develop and implement a strategy to expand the model into other sectors and regions'.[16] To date, the WSR model has been implemented in four industrial and geographic contexts. Examples of such initiatives include, first, the Accord on Fire and Building Safety in Bangladesh, signed in 2013 in response to the Rana Plaza disaster that resulted in the death of over 1,100 workers (Mieres and McGrath, 2021). In 2018, after completing its initial five-year implementation phase, the Bangladesh Accord was extended, with important functions added in anticipation of a move to the hands of a national Ready-Made Garments Sustainability Council. Then, in 2021, it was renewed and updated as the International Accord for Health and Safety, with a national council taking over its operations. By 2023, ten years since it was first established, over 200 signatories had signed the Accord. That same year, inspired by the innovation of the Bangladesh Accord, Pakistan created its own Accord on Health and Safety in the Textile and Garment Industry[17] (Humphrey et al., 2023).

In a second example of an initiative based on the WSR model, the Milk with Dignity Program for dairy farmworkers in Vermont has been in operation since 2017, when Ben and Jerry's became its first signatory (Marquis, 2023). A third example is that of the Lesotho Agreements, signed in 2019, which present a focused adaptation of the WSR model, specifically targeting gender-based harassment and violence in five garment factories in Lesotho (Pillinger, 2022). A fourth example is the Dindigul Agreement. This was established following the murder of Jeyasre Kathiravel, a garment worker, at the hands of her supervisor at Eastman Exports' Dindigul factory. This legally binding agreement aims to end gender-based violence and harassment in the garment industry. It was signed in April 2022 by Eastman, a major clothing and textile manufacturer in Tamil Nadu, India; the Tamil Nadu Textile and Common Labour Union (TTCU); the Asia Floor Wage Alliance (AFWA); and Global Labor Justice – International

Labor Rights Forum (GLJ–ILRF), with the support of multinational fashion companies HandM, Gap, and PVH (Fudge and LeBaron, 2024).

Other active efforts to implement the WSR model include the Building Dignity and Respect Program, which aims to secure human rights, fair treatment, a safe workplace, and a voice for non-unionized construction workers in the Minneapolis–Saint Paul area of the US;[18] and the partnership between the CIW, the FFP, and the International Transport Workers' Federation. This initiative seeks 'to build and launch a pilot program to identify and combat human rights violations on commercial fishing vessels in the United Kingdom'.[19] In February 2023, FFP's efforts to expand the WSR model globally were recognized and supported by the US Department of Labor, which granted FFP USD 2.5 million for this purpose in international cut-flower farms.[20]

Anti-trafficking Chains under the WSR Model

As a governance mechanism, the WSR approach presents a unique mix of traditional labour union elements and features from more recent models of CSR. Like CSR, WSR relies on consumer and economic pressures to induce lead firms to take on voluntary codes of conduct that they are legally free to abandon at any time, on the unspoken understanding that the decision to abandon a code's requirements carries possible reputational and economic risks.[21] Similar to labour unions, WSR champions workers' voice, leadership, knowledge, and power. Both WSR and CSR also assign the responsibility for workers' rights not only to suppliers but, importantly, to lead firms.

However, some key elements of the WSR model distinguish it from CSR, including its worker-driven process, its focus on effective monitoring and enforcement, and its grounding in legally binding contracts. WSR's key innovation – in response to its primary criticism of existing CSR programmes – is its emphasis on workers' voice in the programmes designed to combat worker exploitation. Speaking to this criticism, Gordon (2017: 4) observes that, 'frequently, the parties most affected by labor codes and MSIs – the workers whose lives are affected by the standards being negotiated – have no say in any part of their design or implementation'.

Another important element that distinguishes WSR from CSR and structurally enables the WSR model to escape the power dynamics inherent to supply chains is the relationship between lead firms and their suppliers. CSR codes often impose requirements on suppliers that, due to their high costs, meet supplier resistance (Anner, 2020; Gordon, 2017). WSR's significant innovation to address this flaw is the aforementioned price premium, which places the financial burden on the lead firms instead by requiring them to cover the increase in the workers' wages and contribute to the FFP. Furthermore, in addition to this premium, the WSR model also addresses suppliers' price-squeeze by rewarding suppliers that sign up to anti-exploitation commitments with exclusive sourcing contracts (or long-term commitments) with lead firms. These additional layers of stability and mutual reliance help shift corporations' relationship with suppliers 'from confrontation to collaboration' (Marquis, 2017: 131).

Taking after labour unions, WSR centres on workers' collective voice and agency. However, WSR programmes do not enjoy the traditional protections, or trappings, of labour law. This is the case because labour law is geared towards the dyadic employer–employee relationship, and, therefore, under both individual employment law and collective bargaining law it is suppliers, rather than lead firms, that are the workers' employers and the ones contractually and legally obligated to grant their rights. As a result, neither the codes of conduct nor the contractual relations in the WSR model receive the special contractual force of stability and durability provided in many national laws for collective bargaining agreements (Shamir, 2016). Although negotiations may lead to an enforceable contract (as in the case of the FFP), other elements of the scheme still rely on the voluntary actions of lead firms and, to a large extent, depend on consumer pressures that may fluctuate. Therefore, conceiving of WSR as a form of multi-party collective bargaining within the supply chain is helpful to underscore its 'labour-like' quality while acknowledging the differences.

A key difference between WSR and labour unions is that WSR does not find its power resources and bases of authority in labour law protections – such as those mobilized when organizing collective efforts and strikes – but, rather, in the leverage of worker–consumer coalitions over lead firms. In an age of union decline, and when unions are often characterized as unresponsive to the needs of the most vulnerable workers and ill-suited to changing employment patterns in the global economy, alt-labour organizations such as WSR initiatives seem a more impactful and effective alternative (Fine, 2006; Gordon, 2007; Dias-Abey, 2018). WSR manages to be worker-led yet not bound by the limited restrictions of labour law (such as restrictions on secondary boycotts) and labour politics. The WSR's use of market power frees it from the politics and jurisdiction of any single legal–political context and enables it to thrive even in labour-repressive environments, such as Florida (Fine and Bartley, 2019).

FFP leaders stress the model's independence from state law and politics and its ability to 'address supply-chain problems around the world, largely, although not entirely, without regard to international borders or differing legal norms' (Asbed and Hitov, 2017: 526–27). Still, scholars insist on the importance of legal systems to underpin WSR campaigns and mechanisms. Specifically, the ability to enforce contractual obligations is key to providing 'teeth' to the arrangement, and the existence of transparency legislation (and the resulting prosecutions) plays a vital role in addressing severe exploitation, raising public awareness, and pressuring lead firms and growers to join the FFP programme (Dias-Abey, 2019b; Fine and Bartley, 2019). While these sets of rules are external to traditional labour politics and public debates around workers' rights and 'free' markets, they are nonetheless critical to the effective operation of WSR and render the state significant – even if not sufficient – in its design and implementation.

The WSR's most mature and successful case, the FFP, leveraged particular features of the fresh-tomato supply chain to sustain the initiative. First, the market for fresh tomatoes in the US is concentrated around a small number of powerful buyers that are reputation-sensitive (Fine and Bartley, 2019: 269). Second, the State of Florida is the country's biggest producer of tomatoes. It supplies 90 per cent of winter tomatoes in the US (Greenhouse, 2014), making its tomato supply indispensable to restaurants and supermarket supply chains. Third, the tomato supply chain is short – it consists of growers and buyers, and sometimes wholesalers – making it relatively easy to pass the wage premium down the chain, as well as to trace the relationships between buyers and growers (Dias-Abey, 2019b). It also makes it easier for each lead firm to trace labour exploitation throughout its entire chain. In contrast, in more complex supply chains, such as those in global markets, lead firms often claim that it is virtually impossible to gather information on the working conditions of labourers in the lowest tiers. This is complemented by the fourth feature: the supply chain is *domestic*. The fact that tomatoes are produced, sold, and consumed within the US makes it easier to create an 'imagined community' of workers and consumers, allowing for face-to-face meetings and interaction in the solidarity network. Fifth, the geographical concentration of many workers in one location (in this case, Immokalee) facilitated the creation of a strong grassroots mobilization that is strengthened by community meetings, shared life experiences, and direct and personal interaction. Moreover, the FFP evolved from a prolonged organizing campaign, which produced comprehensive knowledge of the chain structure and the needs of workers and other actors within it. Finally, tomatoes are a relatively cheap commodity that is consumed regularly and that some buyers and consumers are willing and able to pay more for, making the 'penny per pound' campaign feasible. It may be more difficult to gain buyer and public support in sectors that are more price-sensitive, such as the example of the construction sector discussed earlier.

The same features that enabled the FFP to thrive also make it difficult to replicate. Many of these features are missing from the intricate, multi-tiered, and multi-sited supply chains of other consumer goods (for example, apparel or electronics) (Babineau and Bair, 2020; Brudney, 2021). More geographically dispersed, multi-tiered, competitive, complex, expensive supply chains, or more symmetrical chains (where lead firms are not as well positioned to absorb the wage premium) may require significant adaptation to make the model work. Indeed, even the Bangladesh Accord may require adaptation, as its effectiveness as a governance mechanism has weakened since the transition of its functions to the national Ready-Made Garments Sustainability Council in 2020 and the shift in power from the international union federations and NGOs to national actors, more easily influenced by a lobby of local garment manufacturers (Sarkar, 2023; Champagne, 2021; Kang, 2021; see also Bair et al., 2020). Accordingly, despite the promise and potential of WSR, its success is closely dependent on each particular supply-chain structure and the anti-trafficking chains that can be created in and around it.

Analysis and Conclusion

The analysis of anti-trafficking chains under the first labour governance approach we examined – chains triggered by transparency legislation in the UK – suggests that their lack of proven impact on exploitative labour practices is arguably a result of the positioning and operation of anti-trafficking initiatives and bodies as *suppliers*. First, the minimal demands of the MSA may limit innovations in the anti-trafficking field since it focuses corporate attention on meeting formal requirements based on process rather than content. Fearing intensified liability, and inclined to stick to the minimum standards set in the MSA, corporations produce thin statements that embody few commitments to tangible outcomes. Second, transparency legislation's typical reliance on consumer-based market enforcement mechanisms leads to profoundly imbalanced power relations between anti-trafficking actors and lead firms, in which anti-trafficking efforts are dependent on corporate funding. Therefore, we argue that anti-trafficking transparency legislation might not be merely ineffective but, worse, may undermine anti-trafficking efforts.

The other labour governance approach considered in this chapter, the WSR model, does appear to create an effective anti-trafficking chain. At its best, it manages to break free of the typical supply chain dynamics, enabling deep and systemic changes in corporate practices and on-the-ground working conditions. The effectiveness of the anti-trafficking chain in the case of the WSR model is a result of the power and authority it derives from a strong and well-orchestrated coalition, led by workers, that is not forced into the position of an 'anti-trafficking service provider'.

The WSR approach creates an anti-trafficking chain that places the workers' organization leading it in a position that gains its strength from being fully internal to the product supply chain. At the same time, the anti-trafficking chain relies on well-informed external power resources, through the worker–consumer coalition that maintains pressure on lead firms and provides the economic incentive to participate in the programme. These dual bases of power and authority enable WSR anti-trafficking chains to challenge, rather than strengthen, the dynamics of the supply chain. Recognizing labour as a decisive element in production (Kumar 2020: 208), the WSR model emphasizes the importance of active worker leadership and involvement. By coupling this approach with targeted consumer pressures, WSR anti-trafficking chains have the potential to operate as effective private supply-chain labour governance mechanisms.

We therefore suggest that WSR offers a third alternative situated somewhere between labour unions and CSR that opens an avenue of institutional imagination and novel possibilities in securing labour rights in supply chains. While WSR can be seen as a form of MSI, unlike traditional MSIs, it is worker-led and includes effective enforcement and monitoring mechanisms backed by legally binding contractual commitments. While WSR can also be seen as a form of union, it does not solely address employers, nor does it necessarily require organizing workers. As such, the WSR model can employ more flexible and innovative strategies. The alternative it offers bestows anti-trafficking chains with the potential to transcend the pendulum-like movement of GVCs' labour governance between de-centring and re-centring the state and to find new power resources in private law (binding contracts), powerful workers' organizations, solidarity networks, and coalitions with workers.

However, despite the great potential effectiveness of WSR, it may prove challenging to replicate and sustain in certain environments (Kunz et al., 2023). First, as we have seen, the WSR model has been implemented in only a few specific contexts and has faced different challenges in each (challenges that are beyond the scope of this chapter). Particularly, as evidenced by the recent weakening of the Bangladesh Accord, the WSR model has not yet proven sustainable in global, long, and complex supply chains. Second, the absence of state regulators in the WSR's compliance mechanism is perceived to be an advantage in certain settings due to its potential to empower workers' organizations in hostile political environments, weak states, or transnational settings. However, as in the case of the renewed Bangladesh Accord, a lack of state involvement may prove to be a disadvantage. It may be required especially in contexts characterized by fragile or unattainable intra-organizational and transnational solidarity, lead firms that are immune to consumer and public pressures, or supply chains involving expensive and durable consumer goods (housing, household appliances, computer equipment, and so on) that are associated with high financial risk.

The comparison between anti-trafficking transparency legislation and the WSR model casts doubt on the adequacy and explanatory force of the distinction between soft and hard law in the anti-trafficking field (cf. Karlsson-Vinkhuyzen and Vihma, 2009; Choudhury, 2018). While critiques of soft law underline how it reflects and reproduces power structures and relations, the power dynamics that both facilitate hard law and are facilitated by it are often overlooked. Yet, the two are not so far apart. This is evident, as we have shown, in the power relations at play in shaping the provisions of the MSA. Further, these relations are continuously reproduced in the powerful position of corporations vis-à-vis anti-trafficking services and state agencies in the Act's implementation.

Despite this criticism, we do believe that State Anti-Trafficking legislation has made a significant step in shifting its gaze away from criminal actors as the main perpetrators of human trafficking and criminal law and border control as the main tools to address it. Based on our findings, we contend that State Anti-Trafficking law's ability to draw the attention of policymakers to *corporate* responsibility for severe forms of labour market exploitation – that is, to the structural market conditions under which such modern slavery actually occurs – constitutes positive progress.

However, such a 'soft version of hard law' in the form of the UK MSA would not suffice to counter the forceful supply-chain dynamics that undergird and enable human trafficking across supply chains. The newest European trend of HRDD legislation is admittedly seen as more promising in its potential to lead to a significant change in labour rights within GVCs. But critics note that, to date, the design and implementation of HRDD laws have fallen short in several aspects, including their inadequate corporate liability provisions and their limited scope of coverage of the companies to which they apply, the rights they protect, and the reach of the due diligence requirement (Landau and Marshall, 2025). Also of concern is the lack of mandatory requirements to establish institutional platforms for engaging with workers and trade unions, coupled with relatively weak monitoring and enforcement mechanisms (Marshall et al., 2023). We therefore argue that, to effectively address human trafficking, State Anti-Trafficking legislation should intensify the demands placed on lead firms to increase their liability while creating a broader institutional environment that involves governmental bodies, unions, and workers' organizations.

In conclusion, in terms of its proven ability to make a lasting on-the-ground impact and leverage the power structure of the supply chain to drive significant transformation in corporate behaviour, WSR's architecture makes it a promising anti-trafficking governance mechanism compared to State Anti-Trafficking legislation. State Anti-Trafficking legislation has not yet succeeded in challenging the structural dynamics that create and sustain human trafficking in supply chains. In contrast, the current success of WSR programmes in mobilizing corporate behaviour, securing workers' human rights, and improving working conditions is, first and foremost, based on putting workers' agency at the centre. By enhancing workers' capacities to articulate their demands for change in their working conditions, set standards, and monitor corporate compliance, and by backing them with legally binding contracts and enforceable market sanctions, the WSR model, as this chapter has shown, may hold promise as a template for the future of anti-exploitation endeavours. That said, it appears to be incompatible with certain sectors and supply chains. The question then arises as to which normative horizon will shape the continued development of the WSR model. It remains to be seen whether it will continue to leverage the power structure and dynamics of GVCs – specifically, the imbalanced power relations between lead firms and suppliers – to secure labour rights and improve working conditions, or whether it will challenge the fundamental logic of the supply chain model and advance just redistributive mechanisms of the value created throughout the GVC.

Notes

1. While many legislators and scholars favour the term 'modern slavery' to describe severe forms of labour market exploitation, others argue that it limits

our understanding of the exploitation spectrum and the nuances of coercion it entails (Chuang, 2014; Fudge, 2018; see also Shamir et al., 2025). In this chapter, we adopt the latter stance, and therefore use the term 'human trafficking'. Nevertheless, whenever the original phrasing to which we refer uses the term 'modern slavery', we adhere to it as well.

2. In recent years, to capture the dominance of global brands in shaping labour conditions across GVCs, some scholars have developed the concept of 'monopsony capitalism' (Kumar, 2020; Nathan, 2021; Nathan et al., 2022).
3. TIRAs are also known as global, transnational, or international framework agreements (Hammer, 2005), or transnational company agreements (Schömann, 2012).
4. Framing the WSR model as part of other developments in the field, some scholars refer to it by different terms. For example, Reinecke and Donaghey (2021) discuss WSR as part of a wider 'worker-driven supply chain governance' model. Dias-Abbey (2019b) sees it as an example of what he terms 'supply chain collective bargaining', and Blasi and Bair (2019) discuss it as part of 'multi-party bargaining models for global supply chains'.
5. The notion of the 'anti-trafficking industrial complex' was originally coined by Carol Leigh in the context of sex trafficking. Leigh used this term to refer to the social and financial opportunities opened to individuals and organizations involved in anti-trafficking and, more broadly, humanitarian networks – sometimes at the expense of the victims' best interests (Leigh, 2017).
6. It should be noted that Subsection 54(11) does provide the Secretary of State with the power to seek an injunction against non-compliant organizations.
7. For the Modern Slavery (Amendment) Bill, see https://bills.parliament.uk/publications/41860/documents/390.
8. The CIOB's campaign was launched in Qatar during a meeting of the Members' Forum. For further background, see, for example, www.ciob.org/modern-slavery-to-remain-priority.
9. GLAA website: www.gla.gov.uk/i-am-a/i-use-workers/construction-protocol/.
10. At its peak, there were over 250 signatories to the Construction Protocol, a majority of which were companies in the sector. Arguably, the large number of construction companies among the signatories could be attributed to the fact that the Protocol was initiated by a regulatory agency in the sector. At the time of our research and interviews, there were 147 signatories to the Protocol.
11. See the GLAA website: www.gla.gov.uk/i-am-a/i-use-workers/protocols-make-way-for-business-owned-prevention-activity/.

12. In contrast, several interviewees mentioned the 'John Lewis beds scandal' as an example of an explosive case that triggered a change in the retail sector. In July 2013, UK media reported that the police found that trafficked men of Hungarian nationality, who were kept in cramped and squalid conditions and paid GBP 10 a week, were employed by a UK bedmaking firm that supplied beds to the John Lewis retail chain, among other companies (BBC News, 2015).
13. On the centrality of modern slavery training programmes in the response of the UK construction sector to the MSA, see also Trautrims et al. (2021).
14. For a full list of the FFP's partners, see https://fairfoodprogram.org/partners/.
15. In 2014, the CIW received the Obama Presidential Award for Extraordinary Efforts to Combat Trafficking in Persons. See the CIW website: https://ciw-online.org/blog/2015/01/presidential-medal-combatting-slavery/ .
16. See the WSR Network website: https://wsr-network.org/about-us/mission/.
17. Pakistan Accord website: https://internationalaccord.org/new-pakistan-accord/
18. WSR/Building Dignity and Respect website: https://wsr-network.org/bdrreport/.
19. International Transport Workers' Federation website: https://www.itfglobal.org/en/news/global-union-federation-leading-labour-based-human-rights-organisation-join-forces-end.
20. US Department of Labor website: www.dol.gov/newsroom/releases/ilab/ilab20230214.
21. Buyers can opt out of the FFP, though this has not yet occurred, or choose not to join if they withstand public pressure. Wendy's is a prime example of a fast-food chain that has so far refused to join the FFP, despite an intensive coalition campaign. See the Boycott Wendy's campaign: www.boycott-wendys.org/.

References

Angelini, A. and S. Curphey (2022). 'The Overlooked Advantages of the Independent Monitoring and Complaint Investigation System in the Worker-driven Social Responsibility Model in US Agriculture'. *Business and Human Rights Journal* 7(3): 494–99.

Anner, M. (2015). 'Labor Control Regimes and Worker Resistance in Global Supply Chains'. *Labor History* 56(3): 292–307.

——— (2020). 'Squeezing Workers' Rights in Global Supply Chains: Purchasing Practices in the Bangladesh Garment Export Sector in Comparative Perspective'. *Review of International Political Economy* 27(2): 320–47.

——— (2023). 'The Contested Terrain of Global Production: Collective versus Private Labor Governance on Guatemalan Nanana Plantations'. *Review of International Political Economy* 31(1): 382–408.

Asbed, G. and S. Hitov (2017). 'Preventing Forced Labor in Corporate Supply Chains: The Fair Food Program and Worker-driven Social Responsibility'. *Wake Forest Law Review* 52(2): 497–532.

Ashwin, S., C. Oka, E. Schuessler, R. N. Alexander, and N. Lohmeyer (2020). 'Spillover Effects Across Transnational Industrial Relations Agreements: The Potential and Limits of Collective Action in Global Supply Chains'. *ILR Review* 73(4): 995–1020.

Babineau, K. and J. Bair (2020). 'The Art of Using Supply Chains to Defend Worker Rights'. *Open Democracy*, 14 December. Available at: www.opendemocracy.net/en/beyond-trafficking-and-slavery/art-using-supply-chains-defend-worker-rights.

Bair, J. and F. Palpacuer (2015). 'CSR beyond the Corporation: Contested Governance in Global Value Chains'. *Global Networks* 15(s1): S1–S19.

Bair, J., M. Anner, and J. Blasi (2020). 'The Political Economy of Private and Public Regulation in Post-Rana Plaza Bangladesh'. *ILR Review* 73(4): 969–94.

Barkay, T., J. Davies, I. Pietropaoli, and H. Shamir (2024). 'Anti-trafficking Chains: Analyzing the Impact of Transparency Legislation in the UK Construction Sector'. *Law and Social Inquiry* 49(4): 2152–83. Available at: https://doi.org/10.1017/lsi.2024.6.

Bartley, T. (2018). *Rules without Rights: Land, Labor, and Private Authority in the Global Economy*. Oxford: Oxford University Press.

BBC News (2015). 'Dewsbury Bed Factory Run on "Slave Workforce"'. 7 October. Available at: www.bbc.com/news/uk-england-leeds-34468745.

Ben-Ozer, Y. (2024). 'Worker Driven Social Responsibility: A Workable Model to Transform Exploitative Labor Markets or a Context-Specific Success?' *Geography Research Forum* 43(1): 81–104.

BHRC–Business and Human Rights Centre and MSR–Modern Slavery Registry (2021). *Modern Slavery Act: Five Years of Reporting*. Available at: https://media.business-humanrights.org/media/documents/Modern_Slavery_Act_2021.pdf.

Blasi, J. and J. Bair (2019). *An Analysis of Multiparty Bargaining Models for Global Supply Chains*. Conditions of Work and Employment Series No. 105. Geneva: ILO. Available at: www.ilo.org/publications/analysis-multiparty-bargaining-models-global-supply-chains.

Brown, G. (2023). 'Business Is Booming for Human Traffickers Because They Know They'll Get Away with It'. *The Guardian*, 6 September. Available at: www.

theguardian.com/commentisfree/2023/sep/06/business-human-traffickers-modern-slavery.

Brudney, J. (2016). 'Decent Labour Standards in Corporate Supply Chains: The Immokalee Workers Model'. In *Temporary Labour Migration in the Global Era: The Regulatory Challenges*, edited by J. Howe and R. Owens, 351–76. Oxford, UK; Portland, OR: Hart Publishing.

——— (2021). 'Reflections on Labor Standards in Global Supply Chains: Innovation and Scalability'. In *Power, Participation, and Private Regulatory Initiatives: Human Rights under Supply Chain Capitalism*, edited by D. Brinks, J. Dehm, K. Engle, and K. Taylor, 205–23. Philadelphia, PA: University of Pennsylvania Press.

Carrington, M., A. Chatzidakis, and D. Shaw (2021). 'Consuming Worker Exploitation? Accounts and Justifications for Consumer (In)action to Modern Slavery'. *Work, Employment and Society* 35(3): 432–50.

Champagne, J. (2021). 'From Public Relations to Enforceable Agreements: The Bangladesh Accord as a Model for Supply Chain Accountability'. In *Power, Participation, and Private Regulatory Initiatives: Human Rights under Supply Chain Capitalism*, edited by D. Brinks, J. Dehm, K. Engle, and K. Taylor, 154–79. Philadelphia, PA: University of Pennsylvania Press.

Choudhury, B. (2018). 'Balancing Soft and Hard Law for Business and Human Rights'. *International and Comparative Law Quarterly* 67(4): 961–86.

Chuang, J. (2014). 'Exploitation Creep and the Unmaking of Human Trafficking Law'. *American Journal of International Law* 108(4): 609–49.

CIOB (2018). *Construction and the Modern Slavery Act: Tackling Exploitation in the UK*. Bracknell: CIOB. Available at: https://tinyurl.com/3tp3jtj3.

CITB (2019). *Migration and Construction: The View from Employers, Recruiters and Non-UK Born Workers in 2019*. Peterborough: CITB. Available at: https://tinyurl.com/2jhkexfr.

Cockbain, E. and H. Brayley-Morris (2018). 'Human Trafficking and Labour Exploitation in the Casual Construction Industry: An Analysis of Three Major Investigations in the UK Involving Irish Traveller Offending Groups'. *Policing: A Journal of Policy and Practice* 12(2): 129–49.

Coneybeer, J., M. Boersma, S. Bolger, K. Kallio, R. Maguire, E. O'Brien, A. Payne, and T. Rissanen (2023). *Human Rights Regulatory Frameworks*. Narrabri: Cotton Research and Development Corporation. Available at: https://eprints.qut.edu.au/237935/1/Human_Rights_Regulatory_Frameworks.pdf.

Craig, G. (2017). 'The UK's Modern Slavery Legislation: An Early Assessment of Progress'. *Social Inclusion* 5(2): 16–27.

Crane, A., G. LeBaron, J. Allain, and L. Behbahani (2019). 'Governance Gaps in Eradicating Forced Labour: From Global to Domestic Supply Chains'. *Regulation and Governance* 13(1): 86–106.

Dias-Abey, M. (2018). 'Justice on Our Fields: Can "Alt-labor" Organizations Improve Migrant Farm Workers' Conditions?' *Harvard Civil Rights–Civil Liberties Law Review* 53(1): 167–211.

——— (2019a). 'A Socio-Legal History of the Coalition of Immokalee Workers'. In *Theorizing Labour Law in a Changing World: Towards an Inclusive Labour Law*, edited A. Blackham, M. Kullmann, and A. Zbyszewska, 125–48. Oxford, UK: Hart Publishing.

——— (2019b). 'Using Law to Support Social Movement-Led Collective Bargaining Structures in Supply Chains'. *Australian Journal of Labour Law* 32(2): 123–45.

Dottridge, M. (2014). 'How Is the Money to Combat Human Trafficking Spent?' *Anti-Trafficking Review* 3: 3–14.

Estabrook, B. (2011). *Tomatoland: How Modern Industrial Agriculture Destroyed Our Most Alluring Fruit*. Kansas City, MO: Andrew McMeel Publishing.

FFSC (2017). *Fair Food 2017 Annual Report*. Available at: https://fairfoodstandards.org/2017-annual-report.pdf.

——— (2021). *Fair Food Program 2021*. Available at: https://fairfoodprogram.org/wp-content/uploads/2022/02/Attachable-Size-SOTP-2021-Report.pdf.

Field, F., M. Maria, and B. Butler-Sloss (2019). *Independent Review of the Modern Slavery Act 2015: Final Report*. London: Home Office. Available at: www.gov.uk/government/publications/independent-review-of-the-modern-slavery-act-final-report.

Fine, J. (2006). *Worker Centers: Organizing Communities at the Edge of the Dream*. Ithaca, NY: Cornell University Press.

Fine, J. and T. Bartley (2019). 'Raising the Floor: New Directions in Public and Private Enforcement of Labor Standards in the United States'. *Journal of Industrial Relations* 61(2): 252–76.

FLEX and J. Stride (2018). *Shaky Foundations: Labour Exploitation in London's Construction Sector*. London: Focus on Labour Exploitation (FLEX). Available at: https://labourexploitation.org/app/uploads/2018/04/Shaky-Foundations.pdf.

Ford, J. and J. Nolan (2020). 'Regulating Transparency on Human Rights and Modern Slavery in Corporate Supply Chains: The Discrepancy between Human Rights Due Diligence and the Social Audit'. *Australian Journal of Human Rights* 26(1): 27–45.

Frederick, S. (2019). 'Global Value Chain Mapping'. In *Handbook on Global Value Chains*, edited by S. Ponte, G. Gereffi, and G. Raj-Reichert, 29–53. Cheltenham, UK: Edward Elgar Publishing.

Fudge, J. (2018). 'Illegal Working, Migrants and Labour Exploitation in the UK'. *Oxford Journal of Legal Studies* 38(3): 557–84.

Fudge, J. and G. LeBaron (2024). 'Regulatory Design and Interactions in Worker-driven Social Responsibility Initiatives: The Dindigul Agreement'. *International Labour Review* 163(4): 575–98.

Giagnoni, S. (2011). *Fields of Resistance: The Struggle of Florida's Farmworkers for Justice*. Chicago, IL: Haymarket Books.

Gladstone, A. (2020). 'Worker Driven Social Responsibility Agreements: A New Future in Labor Rights Protections'. *Fordham International Law Journal* 44(2): 549–604.

Gordon, J. (2007). *Suburban Sweatshops: The Fight for Immigrant Rights*, Cambridge, MA: Belknap Press (Harvard University Press).

——— (2017). 'The Problem with Corporate Social Responsibility'. An updated and expanded version of 'The Problem with MSIs', a public talk given by the author on 11 June 2014 at Open Society Foundations, New York City. Available at: https://wsr-network.org/wp-content/uploads/2017/07/Gordon-CSR-vs-WSR-FINAL-July-2017.pdf.

Greenhouse, S. (2014). 'In Florida Tomato Fields, a Penny Buys Progress', *New York Times*, 24 April. Available at: www.nytimes.com/2014/04/25/business/in-florida-tomato-fields-a-penny-buys-progress.html.

Guilbert, K. (2018). 'Migrant Workers Prey to Modern Slavery in UK Construction Industry: Charities'. Reuters, 9 April. Available at: www.reuters.com/article/britain-trafficking-construction-idUKL8N1RM1QW.

Haipeter, T., M. Helfen, A. Kirsch, S. Rosenbohm, and C. Üyük (2021). 'Industrial Relations at Centre Stage: Efficiency, Equity and Voice in the Governance of Global Labour Standards'. *Industrielle Beziehungen* 28(2): 148–71.

Han, C., F. Jia, M. Jiang, and L. Chen (2022). 'Modern Slavery in Supply Chains: A Systematic Literature Review'. *International Journal of Logistics Research and Applications* 27(7): 1206–27. Available at: https://doi.org/10.1080/13675567.2022.2118696.

Hammer, N. (2005). 'International Framework Agreements: Global Industrial Relations between Rights and Bargaining'. *Transfer: European Review of Labour and Research* 11(4): 511–30.

Havice, E. and J. Pickles (2019). 'On Value in Value Chains'. In *Handbook on Global Value Chains*, edited by S. Ponte, G. Gereffi, and G. Raj-Reichert, 169–82. Cheltenham, UK: Edward Elgar Publishing.

Hielscher, S., J. Winkin, A. Crack, and I. Pies (2017). 'Saving the Moral Capital of NGOs: Identifying One-sided and Many-sided Social Dilemmas in NGO Accountability'. *VOLUNTAS: International Journal of Voluntary and Nonprofit Organizations* 28(4): 1562–94.

Humphrey, J., T. Fanou, and J. Fudge (2023). 'Literature Review: Worker-driven Social Responsibility'. GFLC, McMaster University. Available at: https://gflc.ca/wp-content/uploads/2020/10/LitReview_WSR_May2023_Final.pdf.

ILO (2017). *Global Estimates of Modern Slavery: Forced Labour and Forced Marriage.* Geneva: ILO. Available at: https://www.ilo.org/sites/default/files/wcmsp5/groups/public/%40dgreports/%40dcomm/documents/publication/wcms_575479.pdf.

——— (2018). *Ending Forced Labour by 2030: A Review of Policies and Programmes.* Geneva: ILO. Available at: https://www.ilo.org/sites/default/files/wcmsp5/groups/public/%40ed_norm/%40ipec/documents/publication/wcms_653986.pdf.

Kang, Y. (2021). 'The Rise, Demise and Replacement of the Bangladesh Experiment in Transnational Labour Regulation'. *International Labour Review* 160(3): 407–30.

Karlsson-Vinkhuyzen, S. I. and A. Vihma (2009). 'Comparing the Legitimacy and Effectiveness of Global Hard and Soft Law: An Analytical Framework'. *Regulation and Governance* 3(4): 400–20.

Koekkoek, M., A. Marx, and J. Wouters (2017). 'Monitoring Forced Labour and Slavery in Global Supply Chains: The Case of the California Act on Transparency in Supply Chains'. *Global Policy* 8(4): 522–29.

Kotiswaran, P. (2019). 'Trafficking: A Development Approach'. *Current Legal Problems* 72(1): 375–416.

Kumar, A. (2020). *Monopsony Capitalism: Power and Production in the Twilight of the Sweatshop Age.* Cambridge, UK: Cambridge University Press.

Kunz, N., T. Chesney, A. Trautrims, and S. Gold (2023). 'Adoption and Transferability of Joint Interventions to Fight Modern Slavery in Food Supply Chains'. *International Journal of Production Economics* 258: 108809.

Landau, I. (2023). *Human Rights Due Diligence and Labour Governance.* Oxford, UK: Oxford University Press.

Landau, I. and S. Marshall (2025). 'Will Remedy Remain Rare? The Potential of Mandatory Human Rights Due Diligence to Redress Modern Slavery'. In *Modern Slavery and the Governance of Global Value Chains*, edited by H. Shamir, B. Arora, S. Banerjee, and T. Barkay. Cambridge, UK: Cambridge University Press.

Leary, E. (2005). 'Immokalee Workers Take Down Taco Bell'. *Monthly Review* 57(5), 1 October. Available at: https://monthlyreview.org/2005/10/01/immokalee-workers-take-down-taco-bell.

LeBaron, G. (2020). *Combatting Modern Slavery: Why Labour Governance Is Failing and What We Can Do About It.* Cambridge, UK: Polity Press.

LeBaron, G. and A. Rühmkorf (2019). 'The Domestic Politics of Corporate Accountability Legislation: Struggles over the 2015 UK Modern Slavery Act'. *Socio-Economic Review* 17(3): 709–43.

Leigh, C. (2017). 'The Anti-Trafficking Industrial Complex'. Talk at Brown U. Center for the Study of Slavery and Justice.

Marquis, S. L. (2017). *I Am Not a Tractor! How Florida Farmworkers Took on the Fast Food Giants and Won.* Ithaca, NY: Cornell University Press.

——— (2023). *Worker-driven Social Responsibility: A New Proven Model for Defining, Claiming and Protecting Workers' Human Rights.* Center for Labor and a Just Economy. Available at: https://clje.law.harvard.edu/app/uploads/2023/06/7.13.23_WSR_Report_Final.pdf.

Marshall, S., I. Landau, H. Shamir, T. Barkay, J. Fudge, and A. van Heerden (2023). *Mandatory Human Rights Due Diligence: Risks and Opportunities for Workers and Unions.* RMIT University Business and Human Rights Centre; TraffLab ERC; and Labour, Equality and Human Rights (LEAH) research group, Monash Business School. Available at: https://media.business-humanrights.org/media/documents/TraffLabReport_March23.pdf.

McCorquodale, R. and J. Nolan (2021). 'The Effectiveness of Human Rights Due Diligence for Preventing Business and Human Rights Abuses'. *Netherlands International Law Review* 68(3): 455–78.

McGrath, S. and S. Watson (2018). 'Anti-slavery as Development: A Global Politics of Rescue'. *Geoforum* 93: 22–31.

Mieres, F. and S. McGrath (2021). 'Ripe to Be Heard: Workers' Voice in the Fair Food Program'. *International Labour Review* 160(4): 631–47.

Mikołajczak, P. (2017). 'Importance of Funding Sources to the Scale of Activity of Social Enterprises'. *Finanse, Rynki Finansowe, Ubezpieczenia* 88(2): 135–44.

Monciardini, D., N. Bernaz, and A. Andhov (2021). 'The Organizational Dynamics of Compliance with the UK Modern Slavery Act in the Food and Tobacco Sector'. *Business and Society* 60(2): 288–340.

Nathan, D. (2019). 'Labour in GVCs: An Analytical Framework'. In *Perspectives on Neoliberalism, Labour and Globalization in India: Essays in Honour of Lalit K. Deshpande*, edited by S. Sundar and K. R. Shyam, 255–71. Singapore: Palgrave Macmillan.

——— (2021). 'From Monopoly to Monopsony Capitalism'. *The Indian Journal of Labour Economics* 64: 843–66.

Nathan, D., S. S. Bhattacharjee, S. Rahul, P. Kumar, I. Dhagani, S. Singh, and P. Swaminathan (2022). *Reverse Subsidies in Global Monopsony Capitalism: Gender, Labour, and Environmental Injustice in Garment Value Chains*. Cambridge, UK: Cambridge University Press.

New, S. J. (2015). 'Modern Slavery and the Supply Chain: The Limits of Corporate Social Responsibility?' *Supply Chain Management: An International Journal* 20(6): 697–707.

Nolan, J. and G. Bott (2018). 'Global Supply Chains and Human Rights: Spotlight on Forced Labour and Modern Slavery Practices'. *Australian Journal of Human Rights* 24(1): 44–69.

Palpacuer, F. (2019). 'Contestation and Activism in Global Value Chains'. In *Handbook on Global Value Chains*, S. Ponte, G. Gereffi and G. Raj-Reichert, 199–213. Cheltenham, UK: Edward Elgar Publishing.

Phillips, N., G. LeBaron, and S. Wallin (2018). 'Mapping and Measuring the Effectiveness of Labour-related Disclosure Requirements for Global Supply Chains'. Research Department Working Paper No. 32, ILO, Geneva. Available at: https://researchrepository.ilo.org/esploro/outputs/995264814602676.

Pickard, J. (2023). 'More Foreign Workers Will Be Let in to Fill Labour Market Gaps'. *Financial Times*, 15 March. Available at: www.ft.com/content/ff36e2f1-cfbd-4554-9853-1eebaa59a8ee.

Pillinger, J. (2022). *Risks of Gender-based Violence and Harassment: Union Responses in the Mining, Garment and Electronics Sectors*. Available at: https://tinyurl.com/mr8vrbry.

Pollitt, M. (2014). 'Unfinished Abolitionists: Britain Returns to the Frontline of the War on Slavery'. *The New Statesman*, 16 October. Available at: www.newstatesman.com/politics/2014/10/unfinished-abolitionists-britain-returns-frontline-war-slavery.

Ponte, S., T. J. Sturgeon, and M. P. Dallas (2019). 'Governance and Power in Global Value Chains'. In *Handbook on Global Value Chains*, edited by S. Ponte, G. Gereffi and G. Raj-Reichert, 120–37. Cheltenham, UK: Edward Elgar Publishing.

Raigrodski, D. (2016). 'Creative Capitalism and Human Trafficking: The Business Case for Eliminating Forced Labor and Human Trafficking from Global Supply Chains'. *William and Mary Business Law Review* 8(1): 71–134.

Reinecke, J. and J. Donaghey (2021). 'Towards Worker-driven Supply Chain Governance: Developing Decent Work through Democratic Worker Participation'. *Journal of Supply Chain Management* 57(2): 14–28.

Rhodes, C. (2019). 'Construction Industry: Statistics and Policy'. Briefing Paper Number 01432. London: House of Commons Library. Available at: https://researchbriefings.files.parliament.uk/documents/SN01432/SN01432.pdf.

Sarfaty, G. (2020). 'Translating Modern Slavery into Management Practice'. *Law and Social Inquiry* 45(4): 1027–51.

Sarkar, S. (2023). 'Ten Years after the World's Deadliest Garment Factory Disaster'. *The Progressive Magazine*, 25 April. Available at: https://progressive.org/latest/ten-years-after-worlds-deadliest-factory-disaster-sarkar-230425.

Schömann, I. (2012). 'Transnational Company Agreements: Towards an Internationalisation of Industrial Relations'. In *Transnational Collective Bargaining at Company Level: A New Component of European Industrial Relations?*, edited by I. Schömann, R. Jagodzinski, G. Boni, S. Clauwaert, V. Glassner and T. Jaspers, 197–217. Brussels: ETUI.

Shamir, H. (2012). 'A Labor Paradigm for Human Trafficking'. *UCLA Law Review* 60(1): 76–136.

——— (2016). 'Unionizing Subcontracted Labor'. *Theoretical Inquiries in Law* 17(1): 229–55.

Shamir, H., B. Arora, S. Banerjee, and T. Barkay (2025). 'Introduction'. In *Modern Slavery and the Governance of Global Value Chains*, edited by H. Shamir, B. Arora, S. Banerjee, and T. Barkay. Cambridge, UK: Cambridge University Press.

Trautrims, A., S. Gold, A. Touboulic, C. Emberson, and H. Carter. (2021). 'The UK Construction and Facilities Management Sector's Response to the Modern Slavery Act: An Intra-industry Initiative against Modern Slavery'. *Business Strategy and Development* 4(3): 279–93.

Tsing, A. (2009). Supply Chains and the Human Condition. *Rethinking Marxism* 21(2): 148–76.

UNODC–United Nations Office on Drugs and Crime (2020). *Global Report on Trafficking in Persons*. New York and Vienna: United Nations. Available at: www.unodc.org/documents/data-and-analysis/tip/2021/GLOTiP_2020_15jan_web.pdf.

Voss, H., M. Davis, M. Sumner, L. Waite, I. Ras, D. Singhal, and D. Jog (2019). 'International Supply Chains: Compliance and Engagement with the Modern Slavery Act'. *Journal of the British Academy* 7(s1): 61–76.

Weir, E., A. Trautrims, and D. Smyth (2024). *Agriculture and Modern Slavery Act Reporting*. Nottingham, UK: University of Nottingham Rights Lab. Available at: https://tinyurl.com/5ds8r64f.

Werdmuller von Elgg, J. (2016). *Hidden in Plain Site: Modern Slavery in the Construction Industry*. New York: LexisNexis. Available at: https://tinyurl.com/zr8fuuas.

7

Human Supply Chain as Global Value Chain

Employer Control in Nepal–GCC Low-wage Labour Recruitment

Sahiba Gill

For over a decade, scholars have documented forced labour among low-wage migrant workers in Gulf Cooperation Council (GCC) countries such as Qatar, the United Arab Emirates (UAE), and Saudi Arabia (Blaydes, 2023; Fernando and Lodermeier, 2022; Iskander, 2021; Parreñas, 2021).[1] A broad understanding within this literature is that among the root causes of this phenomenon in the GCC are abuses perpetrated during workers' recruitment from their home countries, such as extortionate fees, misinformation, and coercion. Recruitment is conducted by intermediary firms in workers' home countries, known as 'recruiters' or 'recruitment firms'. Eighty per cent of low-wage migrant workers in the GCC migrate through these channels (Mendoza, 2012).

Yet, despite the proliferation of this method, the scholarship on forced labour in the GCC contains few studies on recruitment and even fewer that include interviews with the recruiters themselves (Gardner, 2012; Kern and Müller-Böker, 2015). This gap in the literature is particularly notable since scholars of forced labour have renewed their focus on recruitment as a driver of forced labour of migrant workers globally (Crane et al., 2021; Crane and LeBaron, 2018), including as a structural feature of contemporary global capitalism (Crane and LeBaron, 2018; Mantouvalou, 2023; Shamir, 2012) and with colonial origins (Buckley et al., 2023; Iskander, 2021; Wright, 2021). Within this scholarship, a growing number of studies suggest that the recruitment of low-wage migrant workers should be understood as a 'human supply chain', a concept developed by Jennifer Gordon as an analogy to product global value chains (GVCs) (Gordon,

2017; Buckley et al., 2023; Farbenblum and Nolan, 2020; LeBaron, 2020; Pittman, 2018; Hernández-León, 2021; Milkman, 2020).

According to this framing, employers are seen as lead firms at the top of the human supply chain, mirroring the portrayal of lead firms at the top of product supply chains within the GVC literature (Gordon, 2017). Empirical studies have shown that many product supply chains are, in fact, lead firm- or buyer-driven – meaning that the lead firm holds the greatest bargaining power, as well as the greatest ability to influence the terms of its contracts with suppliers (Gereffi, 2018). Similarly, Gordon theorizes that, in human supply chains, the employer, as the lead firm, possesses both the greatest bargaining power and the ability to influence its contracts with suppliers (recruiters). Therefore, Gordon argues, human supply chains are 'employer-driven'. Based on this understanding, the 'human supply chain' approach holds that efforts to regulate the human supply chain to address recruitment abuses should begin with regulating employers. Yet, despite the importance of empirical studies to the GVC literature (Gereffi, 2018), there appears to be a lack of empirical studies dealing with employer control in human supply chains, and particularly so when it comes to studies employing the concept of the human supply chain as a GVC.

This chapter aims to address this gap by presenting original empirical qualitative research into the recruitment of low-wage workers migrating from Nepal to the GCC, also referred to in this chapter as the low-wage Nepal–GCC migration corridor. Based on the understanding of recruitment as a human supply chain, this chapter examines whether and how GCC employers control recruitment processes from Nepal through their contracts with Nepali recruiters, and the extent to which these employers are accountable for the recruitment abuses experienced by low-wage workers brought in from Nepal.

This inquiry centres on two questions. First, to what extent does the human supply chain within the low-wage Nepal–GCC migration corridor reflect key elements of a buyer-driven value chain, as outlined in the GVC literature – that is, can we empirically show that the human supply chain is, indeed, employer-driven? Second, what role does employer control play in abuses perpetrated during recruitment that contribute to forced labour? To address these questions, the chapter adopts the analytical approach commonly employed in GVC analyses. This approach involves several key elements, including: mapping the GVC to identify the actors, activities, and flows of goods, services, and information across countries; understanding the governance structures and power relations within the GVC by analysing contractual arrangements, buyer–supplier relationships, and the distribution of power and profits among different actors; identifying the possibilities and challenges of social upgrading, and the risk of downgrading within value chains, particularly for developing countries; and, finally, considering the elements of social upgrading for workers (Gereffi, 2018).

This chapter concludes that, in the low-wage Nepal–GCC migration corridor, there *is* a human supply chain that is employer-driven, conforming to key features of a buyer-driven value chain. Notably, the employer has greater bargaining power than recruiters and wields that power through the supply chain relationship to impose certain standards for recruitment that are favourable to its business aims – as reflected in the contract terms it sets for recruiters. In addition, within an employer-driven human supply chain, employers have significant control over recruitment processes and, therefore, may be considered to cause or contribute to recruitment abuses themselves.

This chapter provides an initial empirical analysis of one example of human-supply-chain-as-GVC. Further, it sets out empirical evidence demonstrating that, as the human supply chain understanding of recruitment suggests, the social upgrading of human supply chains requires employers to be regulated. The chapter proceeds as follows. The first section lays out an analytical framework for examining the GCC's human supply chain, explaining recruitment abuses in the GCC and the existing approaches adopted in scholarly literature and advocacy reports to understand recruitment, including as a human supply chain. This section also introduces key elements that often appear in GVC analyses and their relevance to human supply chains. The next section provides a factual background on the case study of the low-wage Nepal–GCC migration corridor and a summary of the research methodology applied in this inquiry. The following section presents the research findings, while the final section draws conclusions.

Analytical Framework: The GCC's 'Human Supply Chain'

Recruitment Abuses and Forced Labour in the GCC

The GCC states are major global destinations for low-wage migrant workers, despite the known exploitative labour conditions they maintain.[2] One in ten migrants around the world has migrated to a GCC state; and, within the GCC states, on average, seven in every ten residents are migrants, a proportion that is among the highest in the world (ILO, 2021a). Most migrant workers in the GCC are employed in low-wage jobs in sectors including construction, domestic work, landscaping, driving, sanitation, janitorial services, security, and hospitality and food services, among others.

For over a decade, forced labour among low-wage migrant workers in the GCC has been well-documented in the literature. GCC states grant low-wage migrant workers the right to work there through their tied-visa or temporary worker programmes that typically issue two-year non-renewable visas, known as *kefala* or the *kefala* system across the GCC region (EUI and GRC, 2019). Under the *kefala* system, the kind of visas available to low-wage migrant workers restricts them from freely leaving their employment – both in law and in practice – and GCC states prohibit migrant workers from exercising their rights to freedom of association and collective bargaining. These restrictions heighten the power imbalance between workers and their employers (Garrett, 2020; HRW, 2021). Because GCC states share relevant legal structures like *kefala*, as well as labour markets, political economies, and migration corridors, this chapter follows the common practice of describing labour conditions for low-wage workers in the GCC states at the regional level (Khalaf et al., 2015).

Despite recent reforms in the *kefala* system across various states, commentators still observe great commonality in the situation of low-wage migrant workers in the region who work under this system. Documented cases of labour exploitation have identified several systematic practices: extortionate recruitment fees, especially relative to workers' salaries; misinformation and coercion during recruitment; passport confiscation; unpaid wages; poor employer-provided living conditions; hazardous working conditions; a violation of the right of freedom of association; and national-origin and racial discrimination (Amnesty International, 2014, 2016, 2017; Equidem, 2020; Equidem and GLJ-ILRF, 2022; HRW, 2009, 2010, 2012, 2016).

Low-wage GCC employers typically do not travel abroad to hire low-wage migrant workers directly from their home countries and engage intermediary firms to do this for them instead. These firms are described variously in the literature as 'recruitment agencies', 'recruitment offices', or 'recruitment firms'. For simplicity, this chapter refers to such entities as 'recruiters' and the process of workers being hired by an employer in the GCC by this means as 'recruitment'. The practice of employers using recruiters to hire workers who migrate through temporary work visas is common globally (Gordon, 2017) and is reflected in the proliferation of such recruiters in labour-exporting states (Jones et al., 2015). Recruiters typically provide a package of services for employers: advertising open positions, sourcing and vetting workers to fill those positions, preparing workers' applications for temporary work visas in the GCC, preparing workers' applications for emigration clearance from their home countries, and coordinating workers' medical testing and air travel to the GCC (Jones et al., 2015). To hire migrant workers, GCC employers need only engage a recruiter and apply to their government for temporary work visas for the incoming employees they want to hire (EUI and GRC, 2019).

While recognizing that low-wage migrant workers exercise choice, agency, and personal power during migration and employment in GCC states, it is important to note that the exploitation and labour rights violations – including extortionate recruitment fees, misinformation, and coercion – that are known to be rife in the recruitment process for low-wage work in the GCC serve as significant constraints on workers' power (Iskander, 2021; O'Connell Davidson, 2013).

Recruitment fees are understood here as payments workers make for their recruitment (ILO, 2020). Such payments often cover actual costs, such as flight tickets, passports, visas, and required medical tests (International Labour Office, 2018). However, payments also cover the cost of recruiters' services, and recruiters and their agents – individuals with professional social networks that connect workers to recruiters for foreign employment – commonly engage in 'rent-seeking', meaning they are prone to charging workers additional, illegitimate, and excessive amounts (ILO, 2020). Rent-seeking practices vary widely, resulting in considerable variation in recruitment fees, even among workers migrating along the same migration corridor (ILO, 2020). These fees often amount to several times workers' monthly salaries in the GCC, and workers typically have to use their savings or borrow money in order to cover them (ILO, 2020; Martin, 2017). Thus, the fact that workers must *pay* to gain access to labour opportunities in the GCC – and that the amounts involved are so high relative to their existing capital and future earnings – heightens the power imbalance between workers and employers. Once employed, workers must divert income that would otherwise be used for consumption or savings to pay off debts incurred through handing over these fees or to recoup savings spent on them. Consequently, workers dealing with the financial burden of having paid such large sums tend to avoid leaving unacceptable employment arrangements, lodging complaints, or organizing against their employers in the GCC (ILC, 2009; Martin, 2017; UNODC, 2015).

In a further abusive practice associated with the recruitment process, recruiters and agents commonly misinform workers about the terms of their employment in the GCC, coercing them into inferior terms compared to what they would otherwise accept. Thus, there are often significant gaps between promises and reality regarding job locations, positions, wages, and working conditions (Farbenblum et al., 2013; Paoletti et al., 2014). Workers commonly rely on these misrepresentations when deciding whether to accept a position (Paoletti et al., 2014). Sometimes, recruiters correct misinformation provided by agents; but, by the time they do, workers have often already incurred debt or depleted their savings.

If a worker should balk at the now-clarified terms and conditions and communicate their wish to withdraw from the process, recruiters and agents may coerce them to migrate by keeping the recruitment fees and claiming that they are non-refundable even if the worker does not ultimately migrate. Consequently, recruiters and agents lead workers to believe that, if they choose not to migrate, it could lead to financial ruin, since any alternative job available locally would likely pay too little to allow them to recoup the amount already paid (Amnesty International, 2017; Jones et al., 2015; Paoletti et al., 2014). Thus, in addition to the coercion low-wage migrant workers in the GCC face under the tied-visa regime of the *kefala* system (Niezna, 2022) and the coercive impact of the costs of migration (O'Connell Davidson, 2013), they are also coerced by recruiters who misinform them, thereby exacerbating the power imbalance between workers and employers.

Recruitment abuses contribute in several ways to forced labour and trafficking under applicable national and international laws. According to the International Labour Organization (ILO) Forced Labour Convention, 1930 (No. 29), forced labour includes 'all work or service which is exacted from any person under the menace of any penalty and for which the said person has not offered himself voluntarily' (Art. 2). Due to recruitment abuses, many migrant workers in the GCC do not actually offer themselves 'voluntarily' for work as defined by the Convention (ILC, 2012). In addition, many employers in the GCC confiscate their migrant workers' passports, using them as leverage to threaten workers with penalties, in the form of detention and deportation – actions recognized as penalties under the Convention (Harroff-Tavel and Nasri, 2013; ILC, 2012). Furthermore, the United Nations (UN) Trafficking in Persons Protocol (2000) provides that the act of recruitment or receipt of persons by means of, *inter alia*, coercion, fraud, deception, or abuse of vulnerability – and, for the purpose of exploitation, including for the purpose of forced labour – constitutes trafficking. Therefore, under the UN Protocol, any recruiter or employer involved in the hiring or receipt of migrant workers in the GCC who are employed under conditions of forced labour is engaged in trafficking in persons (Harroff-Tavel and Nasri, 2013; Parreñas, 2021). Lastly, the domestic laws of GCC states prohibit trafficking and forced labour, although enforcement is limited (EUI and GRC, 2019).

At the time of writing, no effective legal regulations were in place in workers' home countries or in the GCC to prevent recruitment abuses, despite their role in forced labour and trafficking. Under national laws, GCC countries prohibit recruiters from taking payments from workers. However, because recruitment occurs in the migrant workers' home countries, both GCC states and workers' home countries argue that this issue primarily falls within the legal jurisdiction of the latter (International Labour Office, 2007). Yet migrant workers' home countries typically lack both the economic incentive and the capacity to regulate recruitment effectively (Farbenblum et al., 2013; Rodriguez, 2010). In addition, home countries perceive that effective domestic regulation would likely increase costs for GCC employers, potentially pushing them to source workers from alternative sending states and, consequently, reducing incoming remittances. These remittances constitute significant sources of foreign earnings for home countries (World Bank, 2020). For these reasons, several bilateral agreements between GCC states and migrant workers' home countries, including India, Nepal, Bangladesh, Indonesia, Pakistan, the Philippines, and Sri Lanka, face weak enforcement (Bhagat, 2023; Chilton and Woda, 2023; Livnat and Shamir, 2023; Wickramasekara, 2015).

In recent years, 'soft law', non-binding principles under international law, stating that employers, rather than workers, should bear recruitment costs as part of businesses' human rights obligations, have gained traction. Nevertheless, adherence to such principles remains low, in practice, across the world, including in the GCC region (IHRB, 2021; ILO, 2019; IOM, 2021). Human rights due-diligence soft law and emerging hard law in Germany and the European Union require companies to conduct due diligence regarding abuses they cause or contribute to; however, as we have seen, GCC employers generally deny having any role in recruitment abuses.

Labour Recruitment as Human Supply Chain

Academic scholarship – primarily in the fields of anthropology and geography – concerned with low-wage migrant workers in the GCC widely recognizes the role of recruitment in labour abuses. Recruitment payments result in reduced earnings and debt, leading to circular and precarious migration to the GCC for low-wage workers (Buckley, 2012; Parreñas, 2015). Additionally, as we have seen, excessive fees, misinformation, and coercion during recruitment also contribute to labour control, which is a key part of the political economy of the GCC (Hanieh, 2011; Khalaf et al., 2015). Furthermore, the recruitment of low-wage migrant workers in the GCC, especially from South Asia, has been compared to historical indenture (Buckley et al., 2023; Wright, 2021).

Yet, the recruitment process itself – including the recruiters as actors within it – remains largely unexamined in empirical academic scholarship on low-wage labour in the GCC. Anthropologist Andrew Gardner studies the recruitment of low-wage migrant workers to the GCC as a 'recruitment industry' characterized by private, profit-seeking actors, firms, and individuals (Gardner, 2012), but his research primarily relies on interviews with migrants. Migration policy scholars have conducted studies of recruitment including interviews with recruiters, examining recruitment as part of what Lindquist terms state 'migration infrastructure' including the regulation and licensing of recruiters (LeBaron and Phillips, 2019; Rodriguez, 2010; Xiang and Lindquist, 2014). However, such studies focus almost exclusively on recruiters' role in facilitating migration, rather than on the abuses recruiters conduct during the recruitment process (Kern and Müller-Böker, 2015; Shrestha, 2018), with a few notable exceptions (Alkan, 2021; Babar, 2021; Chu, 2010; Kurlander, 2019). It is worth noting that it is international and advocacy organizations that have conducted the few studies available that *are* based on interviews with recruiters and focus on recruitment abuses (Amnesty International, 2017; Breeding, 2011; Jones et al., 2015; Segall and Labowitz, 2017).

The scholarship on business in the context of forced labour has further examined the recruitment process and recruiter business models, yielding insights that international and advocacy organizations have applied to analyse the recruitment of low-wage migrant workers to the GCC. Scholars of forced labour argue that recruiters operate as firms with firm-level business models that are embedded within global economic structures such as product supply chains (Crane, 2013; Crane et al., 2021; Farbenblum and Nolan, 2017; Crane and LeBaron, 2018). Despite the absence of empirical studies dealing with recruiters in this scholarship, international and advocacy organizations have built on this insight to analyse the business model adopted by recruiters and its role in facilitating recruitment abuses, including in the GCC (Jones, 2015a; Jones, 2015b; Segall and Labowitz, 2017).

These studies conceptualize recruiters as following a basic firm model, engaging in income-generating activities that yield profit. They have found that it is not the GCC employers that pay recruiters for their recruitment services (as is customary when a company outsources a service to a subcontractor). Instead, recruiters' business model is built on charging their recruitment fees to the prospective workers. The more workers they succeed in dispatching abroad, the greater their profits. Finally, these studies collectively observe that the recruiters' business model perpetuates recruitment abuses, especially concerning recruitment fees, that migrant-sending states have failed to prevent, consistent with the aforementioned literature.

Drawing from GVC scholarship, Gordon (2017) provides a deeper structural understanding of the recruitment business model through her concept of the 'human supply chain', which refers to the recruitment of low-wage migrant labour. Specifically, Gordon makes a conceptual comparison between the roles of lead firms or buyers within product supply chains and the roles of employers within human supply chains. In this analogy, just as the former act as the buyer at the top of the supply chain of a subcontracted product such as a t-shirt, the latter serve as the buyer at the top of the supply chain of the subcontracted product that is *labour*. In other words, the product in recruitment is the migrant worker, rather than a physical product, hence the term 'human supply chain.' Similarly, according to Gordon, recruiters in human supply chains, to whom employers have delegated worker recruitment, are analogous to suppliers in product supply chains, to which the lead firm has subcontracted product production. Based on this parallel, Gordon suggests that both product and human supply chains are what is termed in GVC terminology 'buyer-driven'. This essentially means that lead firms or buyers in human supply chains, buying the product of migrant labour, enjoy significant bargaining power over suppliers, often due to low barriers to entry for suppliers into the market, resulting in numerous rival suppliers and relatively few lead firms (Kumar, 2020; Nathan et al., 2016; Weil, 2014). Moreover, as the GVC literature illustrates, in buyer-driven supply product chains, buyers coordinate and dictate standards of production down the supply chain through their contracts with suppliers, imposing profit-maximizing terms in their favour – such as low prices or short timelines – that exert downward pressure on their suppliers' labour standards (Anner, 2018, 2019, 2020; Kumar, 2020; Nathan et al., 2016; Weil, 2014).

Adding to this dynamic, GVC studies have shown that a governance gap exists in product supply chains because lead firms are generally not legally responsible for labour conditions along those chains (Weil, 2014). Furthermore, such studies suggest that addressing the governance gap in buyer-driven supply chains – by making lead firms responsible for labour conditions in the chains – would drive 'social upgrading', such as improved working conditions and labour standards and rights (Gereffi and Lee, 2016).

Following these understandings, Gordon (2017) observes a similar governance gap in buyer-driven *human* supply chains, since recruitment abuses are considered within the domain of workers' home countries' jurisdictions, and, therefore, employers are generally exempt from accountability for such abuses. Focusing on the recruitment of low-wage migrant workers through tied visas to the United States from Mexico, Gordon proposes closing such a governance gap by imposing tort liability for recruitment abuses on US lead-firm employers. She argues that incentivizing employers to pay for recruitment and use their bargaining power to regulate the human supply chain would not only prevent abuses in the recruitment process but also potentially drive social upgrading. Emphasizing that 'a structural problem requires a structural solution' (Gordon, 2017: 450), Gordon's concept of a human supply chain is an important addition to the critical anti-trafficking literature. It supports the position that the harms caused to migrant workers through recruitment abuses are not merely 'generated by anomalous bad actors but instead are structural', and, therefore, that 'criminalizing bad apples among recruiters is not likely to correct' such abuses (Gordon, 2017; see also Yea, 2021).

This chapter aims to contribute to the literature on recruitment by strengthening the empirical understanding of this structural problem and potential structural solutions as alternatives to traditional anti-trafficking approaches. A comparison of the GVC literature on product supply chains and existing literature on the recruitment of migrant workers highlights two significant questions or gaps that should be addressed in order to develop an empirical understanding of recruitment as a human supply chain and that the extant research on recruitment has not yet answered.

The first gap pertains to the contract between employers and recruiters. In the GVC product supply chain literature, an examination of the contract between lead firm and supplier is essential for understanding key features of the GVC – such as the bargaining power between the parties and how the lead firm sets profit-maximizing standards for production (Anner, 2018, 2019, 2020; Kano et al., 2020). In human supply chains, studies indicate that employers either do not pay, or pay too little to, the recruiters they hire. While these studies argue that this contributes to abuse associated with recruitment fees charged to workers, there are no empirical studies examining the actual contracts between employers and recruiters and the terms therein, including the imbalance of bargaining power between the two parties. This insight is important because, in light of similar analyses in the GVC literature, it would seem that there is employer control over the human supply chain if (*a*) employers wield bargaining power over recruiters and (*b*) the employer, as the lead firm, sets profit-maximizing standards for production (Weil, 2014).

The second gap concerns how employer control over the human supply chain translates into recruitment abuses. The empirical GVC literature has shown a connection between lead firm–supplier contracts, suppliers' production processes, and labour practices (Gereffi, 2018; Weil, 2014). Lead firms' profit-maximizing standards often have demonstrable negative impacts on workers at their subcontracted suppliers (Weil, 2014). For example, in garment supply chains, empirical studies reveal that low prices stipulated in contracts between lead firms and suppliers are directly correlated with higher production targets and lower wages for workers employed by the supplier. Indirectly, they contribute to increased risks of other labour violations, such as denial of the right to freedom of association (Anner, 2018, 2019, 2020). These studies also show that additional contract terms, such as production timelines, exacerbate labour violations. For example, when lead firms implement profit-maximizing standards that push down labour standards at their suppliers, while still demanding compliance with all relevant laws, suppliers may resort to practices such as document fraud to conceal unpaid wages (Anner, 2018; HRW, 2019).

The absence of such studies on recruitment as a GVC means there is no empirical evidence to show how contracts between employers and recruiters impact recruitment abuses. Particularly, there is insufficient research on how employers' failure to pay for recruitment or their paying too little to recruiters impacts all forms of recruitment abuses, and whether additional contract terms in human supply chains, such as contract deadlines, contribute to these abuses. However, it is reasonable to infer from similar analyses in the GVC literature that, in an employer-driven human supply chain, employers' considerable influence over recruitment processes amounts to control, meaning that they can cause or contribute to recruitment abuses and, ultimately, forced labour. This understanding suggests that addressing recruitment abuses within human supply chains requires employer regulation, as part of a shift towards social upgrading, as advocated by Gordon (2017),

Aiming to address the gaps identified in the literature thus far, this chapter focuses on the low-wage Nepal–GCC migration corridor as a case study for empirically analysing recruitment as a human supply chain. This analysis centres around two questions: (*a*) Is the human supply chain in the Nepal–GCC migration corridor employer-driven? (*b*) How do employer practices impact recruitment abuses, and to what extent do they perpetuate forced labour in employment? To explore these questions and better understand the imbalances in bargaining power between employers and recruiters and their implications for employer–recruiter contracts, the analysis makes use of concepts from the GVC literature.

Before turning to the analysis itself, the following part introduces the factual background of the case study of the Nepal–GCC labour recruitment corridor and outlines the research methodology applied in this inquiry.

Case Study Background and Methodology

Labour Recruitment from Nepal to the GCC

Many actors are involved in labour recruitment through this migration corridor: recruiters, GCC employers, GCC countries, the Nepali State, and the workers themselves. At the time of our research for this case study, in 2015, an estimated two million Nepalis, out of a total population of 28 million, worked abroad (Jones et al., 2015), and 477,690 workers had left Nepal on temporary work visas (Government of Nepal, 2020). More than 80 per cent of migrants from Nepal are male, and around 60 per cent are engaged in low-wage work (Government of Nepal, 2020). The country has periodically banned or restricted women from migrating to the GCC, and a total ban was in effect at the time of research in 2014 and 2015 (Bhagat, 2023; ILO, 2015).

Eighty-eight per cent of migrants from Nepal arrange their foreign employment via recruiters (Government of Nepal, 2020). Nepali law requires recruiters to hold a government license, for which they must put down a security deposit and undergo a background check. In 2015, there were 932 officially registered recruiters operating in Nepal (Government of Nepal, 2016), and the number appears to have remained largely stable through publication (FairSquare Projects, 2021). Recruiters are also permitted to use the services of up to ten licensed agents, who are individuals with professional social networks connecting workers to recruiters for foreign employment. Nepal primarily sends male workers to low-wage jobs in the GCC in sectors such as construction (Government of Nepal, 2020). Since at least 2008, most Nepali male migrant workers have migrated to GCC states – predominantly, Saudi Arabia, Qatar, the UAE, and Kuwait (Government of Nepal, 2020; Jones et al., 2015).

Nepal's Ministry of Labour, Employment, and Social Security (MoLESS), particularly its Department of Foreign Employment (DoFE), serves as the primary regulatory body for labour migration (Government of Nepal, 2020). The Foreign Employment Act of 2007 and its associated Foreign Employment Rules (2008) and Foreign Employment Policy (2012) together provide the legislative and administrative frameworks empowering the DoFE to regulate recruitment. Additionally, Nepal has signed bilateral labour agreements and memoranda of understanding with nine countries, including Qatar, the UAE, and Bahrain, among the GCC states (Government of Nepal, 2020). Nepal has also ratified the UN Trafficking Protocol and ILO Forced Labour Conventions.

Despite these protective measures, and even after legal reforms such as the failed 'Free Ticket, Free Visa' policy (Amnesty International, 2017; FairSquare Projects, 2021; Paoletti et al., 2014), for Nepali migrant workers recruited to the GCC, recruitment abuses are systematic. The reality is that Nepal, like many other labour-exporting countries, has neither the economic incentive nor the capacity to regulate recruitment effectively. Nepal ranks as the fifth most remittance-dependent country globally. According to Nepal's central bank, as of 2020, Saudi Arabia, Qatar, and the UAE each contributed 11–14 per cent of Nepal's remittances (Government of Nepal, 2020). Given this context, effective regulation of recruitment that increases the cost of hiring migrant workers from Nepal could jeopardize its remittance flows if GCC employers were to seek cheaper labour from other countries instead. Hence, Nepal encourages foreign employment to stimulate inward foreign capital flows (Government of Nepal, 2020). Indeed, as one study shows, despite the DoFE having the authority to handle complaints of recruitment abuses, less than 1 per cent of migrant workers from Nepal to the GCC had their cases registered and remediated. This low rate of resolution is largely attributed to barriers impeding access to justice for workers (FairSquare Projects, 2021; Paoletti et al., 2014).

The process constituting the human supply chain from Nepal to the GCC has been described as occurring over two phases: hiring and emigration (Jones et al., 2015). During the first phase, workers are hired in a process that involves the aforementioned recruitment fees and misinformation. This phase commences when a GCC employer and Nepali recruiter agree to recruit workers from Nepal (Jones et al., 2015). The recruiter must obtain approval from Nepal's DoFE for the employer's job description, known in the industry as a 'demand letter' (Jones et al., 2015). The DoFE reviews the demand letter for compliance with its requirements, including information about the employer, available positions (for example, 50 carpenters), minimum wages, and maximum recruitment fees

(Jones et al., 2015, Government of Nepal, 2020). For example, in 2015, Nepal's minimum wage for Nepali workers in the UAE was 1,200 UAE dirhams per month (USD 327 at the time), and the cap on recruitment fees for jobs in the GCC was set at NPR 70,000 (approximately USD 600 at the time), though fees regularly surpassed this amount (Jones et al., 2015). Similarly, after 2015, the cap was lowered, but studies show fees remained at the same levels and exceeded the new lower cap (Amnesty International, 2017; FairSquare Projects, 2021).

Upon DoFE approval of the demand letter, recruiters begin recruiting workers, primarily using unlicensed agents (Jones et al., 2015). The latter act as intermediaries between prospective workers, commonly from rural villages where they stay during the first phase, and recruiters, located in the capital Kathmandu or other major cities (Jones et al., 2015). Once the recruiter has filled the available positions, they ask the GCC employer to secure work visas for the hired workers (Khalaf et al., 2015). It is during this phase that workers typically pay recruitment fees to agents. For example, in 2016, Amnesty International reported that Nepali workers were paying an average of NPR 137,000 (USD 1,346) to secure jobs abroad (Amnesty International, 2017; Verité, 2012).

During the second phase, workers emigrate through a process that involves recruiter misinformation, coercion of workers, and fraud to conceal recruitment fees. Once the GCC employer secures visas for the workers, the recruiter prepares the workers for emigration (Jones et al., 2015). This involves ensuring they have transport to Kathmandu, where the country's main international airport is located, and, once there, ensuring they undergo required training, sign their contracts, and submit the required final application to the DoFE for permission to emigrate. The application must include a receipt for recruitment fees paid, which typically is falsified and does not reflect the actual amount paid, but does show an amount that complies with the aforementioned cap on fees (Jones et al., 2015). It is now, with the workers far from home and staying in hostels in Kathmandu, that recruiters often resort to threats of financial ruin to coerce them into accepting the real (unfavourable) terms of employment, about which the workers were misinformed initially (Amnesty International, 2017; Jones et al., 2015; Paoletti et al., 2014; FairSquare Projects, 2021). In addition, this process also commonly involves recruiters reporting recruitment fee amounts to the DoFE that comply with the government cap but do not accurately reflect the actual amount that workers paid (Jones et al., 2015; Amnesty International, 2017).

In sum, labour recruitment from Nepal to the GCC involves coordination among various actors, with abusive practices arising at different points in the process.

Methodology

The findings presented in this chapter are based on empirical qualitative research, which involved conducting interviews at 43 recruitment agencies in Kathmandu from January to April 2015. The interviews focused on recruitment for work in the GCC across various low-wage sectors – excluding domestic work, due to an effective ban on that activity at the time of research (International Labour Office, 2015). The sample consisted of both large and small recruiters, with the number of workers sent abroad yearly ranging from 300 to 4,000, and a mode of 1,000 workers sent abroad per year.

Recruiters were initially selected using random sampling from among all registered recruiters in Nepal whose office addresses were identifiable on Google Maps; registered recruiters are publicly listed online by the Nepal Association of Foreign Recruitment Agencies (NAFEA). Subsequently, snowball sampling was employed, using references and geographic proximity to previously interviewed recruiters. Interviews were conducted with owners, part-owners, or department heads of each recruiter, primarily in English. However, the author conversed in Nepali for certain interviews when necessary. The interviews followed a semi-structured format, covering topics such as the recruitment process and the recruiter's relationships with GCC employers. Interviewees were assured of full anonymity. No identifying data were collected, and none are included in this chapter.

Findings

The findings in this section are organized in response to the two primary research questions delineated earlier (regarding whether the human supply chain is employer-driven, and abusive recruitment practices). First, the data indicate that human supply chains from Nepal to the GCC *do* exhibit an employer-driven nature, evidencing an imbalance of bargaining power reflected in the enforceable contracts between employers and recruiters. GCC employers use their superior bargaining position to dictate profit-maximizing contract terms that are heavily skewed in their favour. Second, like the dynamics observed in product supply chains, the terms imposed by lead firms – in the case of human supply chains, the employers – were found to harm workers, both directly and indirectly. Within the human supply chain from Nepal to the GCC, employer-imposed contract terms contribute to recruitment abuses including exorbitant recruitment fees, the deliberate dissemination of misinformation, and coercive practices aimed at compelling workers to accept unfavourable terms of employment. Let us now examine each of these broad findings in more depth.

Human Supply Chains from Nepal to the GCC as Employer-driven

Nepali recruiters reported a demonstrable imbalance of bargaining power between themselves and GCC employers, in the latter's favour. This dynamic was established from the outset: they described their services being engaged via a competitive bidding process, whereby employers solicited multiple bids and selected the most profitable for them. Employers would threaten to find a lower bid if the recruiter did not agree to their terms. This situation was the product of what recruiters commonly described as 'unhealthy competition' among recruiters vying for GCC employers' business. Many interviewees attributed this competition to the low entry barriers into the recruiter market, especially after Nepal's civil war ended in 2006 and the government rapidly increased the number of available licenses – although licenses have since been capped at roughly 900 (Government of Nepal, 2020). Because of this competition, recruiters felt they had to accept employers' terms to secure enough clients to make a profit. One recruiter memorably said, '… you would go bankrupt [otherwise]'.

A small minority of recruiters reported not maximizing profits or the number of workers sent abroad. These recruiters reported that having other sources of financial stability – such as owning other profit-generating businesses or operating with low fixed costs because they owned rather than rented their office building – allowed them to operate with a different business model. These recruiters were the only ones who reported being able to uphold minimum standards for their contracts with employers. For example, they required employers to cover recruitment costs. As a result, these recruiters worked with a relatively small but loyal clientele of employers willing to meet their minimum standards.

Most of the recruiters, however, reported that their negotiations with employers often resulted in verbal or written (email) agreements that were deemed enforceable contracts. They communicated with employers primarily by phone and email to discuss recruitment matters and negotiate the contract terms. These verbal or otherwise informal agreements held legal weight under general principles of law, including those in Nepal. The interviewees emphasized that their contracts with employers were binding, and any deviation from the agreed terms on their part could result in penalties imposed by employers; however, they did not mention any mechanisms available to them to enforce contract terms against the employers.

The penalties imposed on them were cited as significant deterrents to non-compliance with contract terms and included loss of future business opportunities; loss of security deposits or only partial payment for services rendered; and the repatriation of workers to Nepal at the recruiter's expense. In these circumstances, recruiters expressed concerns that non-compliance could jeopardize potential future business with the employer, thus compelling them to comply with the contract terms. Furthermore, they reported that employers often required a security deposit at the outset of a contract, which would be refunded only upon satisfactory completion of the agreed services. Failure to comply with the contract terms to the employer's satisfaction would result in the recruiter losing all or part of that deposit. It is important to distinguish this scenario from cases where the same term, 'security deposit', was used euphemistically to describe a bribe to secure business.

Recruiters also noted that payment for recruitment services was contingent upon the successful completion of agreed services, allowing employers to penalize any breach of contract by either partial or non-payment. Finally, recruiters highlighted that the possibility of having to pay for having workers repatriated to Nepal was a significant threat, as they perceived that Nepal's Foreign Employment Act mandated them to cover the repatriation costs and that failure to do so might result in government intervention, though enforcement is, in practice, low (Paoletti et al., 2014). Interviewees further elucidated the dynamic with employers, suggesting that the latter leveraged their bargaining power to enforce profit-maximizing contract terms favourable to them around five key issues: cost; the number of workers recruited; timelines; legal compliance; and worker preparedness.

Cost: recruiters reported that employers used their bargaining power to minimize their expenditure on recruitment, sometimes paying nothing for it or even turning a profit by outsourcing labour recruitment and soliciting bribes from recruiters in exchange for their business. Few employers covered all recruitment costs, with some contributing only a portion of the expenses. Many employers opted for the lowest bid, which often meant paying nothing for recruitment while also seeking bribes for their business. Recruiters described these conditions as employer-imposed, expressing a preference for those willing to cover all or at least some of the recruitment costs, although such employers were rare.

The number of workers recruited: employers often require recruiters to deliver a large crew of workers with the same skill set all at once, such as 50 carpenters all sent to the destination on the same day. They also mentioned that employers required the hired workers to emigrate and travel together to the employer's destination country, to facilitate efficient transport from the destination airport to the employer's location. These demands for relatively large numbers of workers often entail the use of agents, who have networks capable of reaching large numbers of workers, especially when facing tight deadlines. As we will see, the involvement of agents in the process adds a further layer of factors that lend themselves to producing worker abuses.

Timelines: employers often demand that workers be delivered within short deadlines. Typically, employers asked recruitment to be completed within 10–16 days, a timeframe deemed barely feasible by recruiters, who disclosed instances of violating Nepali law to meet deadlines. Such violations included initiating hiring before the DoFE approval of the aforementioned demand letter (job description) and resorting to bribery to expedite DoFE approval for demand letters or fast-track emigration clearances. The time pressures imposed by employers, then, lead to a situation in which, in the first phase of the recruitment process, recruiters hire workers through agents – a process that can be completed as quickly as in two or three days. Workers then do not need to travel to Kathmandu to meet the recruiters directly until the second phase, by which time they are already hired and preparing to emigrate.

Timing as a contract term in this human supply chain serves as an illustrative example of how employers' greater bargaining power over recruiters enables them to establish and enforce contract terms in their favour. Recruiters reported that they had to accept employers' demands on the timeline for recruitment, fearing the loss of business to other recruiters. Only a small minority of recruiters were able to resist employer demands and push back on unreasonable timelines. Against this backdrop, consider the recruitment process without employer-imposed penalties. In such a scenario, employers would still wield bargaining power over recruiters during negotiations. However, as recruitment progresses, the bargaining power would shift. Between the hiring and emigration phases – when employers have secured work visas for hired workers, but before the workers emigrate and begin work – replacing recruiters becomes challenging for employers. The latter have already invested time and money in securing visas for specific workers hired by a particular recruiter, necessitating the delivery of these workers to avoid visa wastage.

Employers wanting to replace the hired recruiter at this stage would actually have to start the recruitment process from scratch, including asking the relevant GCC government to cancel the workers' visas – a costly procedure. In this scenario, recruiters would have greater bargaining power relative to employers because the employer depends on them to deliver the workers, which would enable recruiters to renegotiate terms in their favour. For instance, recruiters might request additional time to deliver workers beyond the employer's deadline, knowing that the employer needs the workers, even if delivered late. This scenario aligns with what the GVC literature describes as a 'hold-up problem', where one party can exploit its power to its advantage by slowing progress down (Haruvy et al., 2019). In the actual human supply chain between Nepal and the GCC, where employer-imposed penalties exist, employers mitigate the 'hold-up' scenario by enforcing contracts with recruiters through penalties exacted if services are not completed as agreed. Consequently, employers maintain an advantageous position in bargaining power over recruiters throughout the contract duration.

Legal compliance: employers demand that all paperwork required by Nepali law be meticulously prepared. Nepal's DoFE approves the demand letter in the first phase and issues workers' emigration clearances in the second phase. In addition, recruiters noted that obtaining the proper paperwork is in the employers' interest, because it provides evidence of compliance with Nepali law in the event of any future labour dispute in the GCC. However, recruiters suggested that employers do not have an interest in ensuring the *completeness and accuracy* of the information on the paperwork – for example, whether a receipt for recruitment fees and attestation that the worker did not pay more than the amount shown on the receipt are accurate. We will see later that this wilful ignorance facilitates recruitment abuses.

Worker preparedness: employers expect workers to be prepared to begin work as soon as they arrive at the employer's site. This means, at the very least, workers being familiar with their basic job description and terms of employment – for example, understanding that they are traveling to Saudi Arabia to work as a mason at USD 200 per month. For positions requiring prior experience or training, employers expect workers to be fully qualified. Recruiters reported that hiring qualified workers often presents challenges because employers may doubt that a worker considered skilled in Nepal, such as a locally trained electrician, possesses the key skills required in the GCC (Iskander, 2021). Additionally, they noted that employers sometimes repatriate workers considered unprepared or unqualified for the job back to Nepal at the recruiter's expense.

In sum, employers in human supply chains from Nepal to the GCC leverage their bargaining power to establish enforceable verbal contracts and impose abusive contract terms to favour their interests. In response to the first research question, then, contracts with recruiters can be considered employer-driven.

Employer-driven Human Supply Chains from Nepal to the GCC: Impact on Recruitment Abuses

In this employer-driven human supply chain, the employer-imposed contract terms described by recruiters benefit employers while detrimentally affecting workers, resulting in various recruitment abuses. These impacts may be direct, for example when employers not paying for recruitment results in passing on the costs to workers, or indirect, such as when short timelines encourage the kind of processes that make recruitment abuses more likely. Employers' contributions to recruitment abuses in employer-driven human supply chains parallel the role of lead firms in perpetuating worker abuses within buyer-driven product supply chains (Anner, 2018, 2019, 2020; Weil, 2014). The remainder of the findings, presented next, review how employer-imposed contract terms can culminate in different recruitment abuses in the human supply chain from Nepal to the GCC.

First, when employers use their bargaining power to minimize their recruitment costs, the direct result is that recruiters pass on costs to workers. This scenario arises when employers underpay or do not pay at all, making recruiters pay for the process instead. As recruiters alone cannot absorb the cost of recruitment *and* operate without payment for their services, they seek such payment from the workers. This dynamic within human supply chains mirrors that of product supply chains, where lead firm-imposed low prices paid to suppliers often result in lower wages for suppliers' workers (Anner, 2018; Weil, 2014).

Second, employers' use of their bargaining power to demand that recruiters deliver a large and work-ready crew (often with a specific skill-set) within a tight timeframe indirectly cultivates recruitment abuses in several ways. It encourages recruiters to use agents, leading to high recruitment fees driven by agent rent-seeking, dissemination of misinformation by agents in the first phase of recruitment, and subsequent coercion during the second phase. This parallels the dynamics observed in product supply chains, where short production timelines contribute to supplier practices that heighten the risk of worker abuse (Anner, 2019).

Third, the employers' demand to obtain, and sometimes fast-track, the paperwork required by Nepali law without ensuring its accuracy not only fails to address underlying recruitment abuses but also arguably complicates any endeavour to demonstrate employer accountability. For example, a recruitment fee receipt for an amount lower than the worker actually paid may serve as evidence in the destination country that the employer believed the recruitment fees to be both legal and minimal. Thus, the workers' home country recruiter would be accountable for any irregularity or abuse identified; however, the recruiter can also use such a receipt to disavow knowledge of recruitment fees and shift blame to the agent. Either scenario creates difficulties in any future claim by a worker regarding abusive fees. Furthermore, when a signed contract is presented as evidence of a worker's consent, it may conceal coercion to extract a signature for an unfavourable contract they would otherwise refuse to sign.

This dynamic is comparable to that of lead firms in buyer-driven product supply chains, which pressure suppliers to comply with legal requirements on paper while also imposing contract terms, such as low prices, that hinder effective compliance. This practice is illustrated in the GVC literature, showing how suppliers are encouraged to engage in document fraud, such as falsifying wage records (Anner, 2018; HRW, 2019).

Fourth, recruiters reported that employers typically expect workers to be prepared to begin work immediately upon arrival in the destination country – despite possessing only basic information about the role and, where required, relevant qualifications. This pressurizing practice effectively increases the likelihood of misinformation and coercion during recruitment because it encourages recruiters to comply with employers' requirement to produce workers who are cognizant of the conditions and job-ready, even if they are not. That is, it incentivizes recruiters and/or agents to routinely mislead workers into emigrating, as perfectly illustrated by one account given during the research, relating to the two phases of recruitment.

In this case, the agent initially misled the worker by promising a wage higher than that in the contract, which the recruiter corrected in the second phase when they met the worker in Kathmandu to sign the employment contract and prepare them for emigration. At that time, the recruiter correctly informed the worker of the actual terms of their contract – to which the worker logically did not want to consent, given the prior misinformation. To induce the worker to continue with the emigration process, the recruiter then falsely claimed that, if the worker signed the contract, the recruiter would explain the situation and convince the employer to offer a different (and better) job with a higher wage. He did this despite knowing the employer would not grant such a request.

As discussed earlier regarding the hold-up problem, for the recruiter to find a replacement for a worker in the second phase, when workers already have a visa and a flight booked, is effectively impossible – and the recruiter risks being charged a penalty by the employer if they allow the worker simply not to emigrate. Thus, under the terms of recruiters' contracts with employers, it is less costly for the former to simply mislead workers; while the misinformation happens at the level of the agent, the root cause of that wrongdoing is the employers' penalty. This example is yet another illustration of how employers cause or contribute to recruitment abuses.

Conclusion

In the Nepal–GCC migration corridor, the human supply chain is employer-driven, aligning with key elements of a buyer-driven value chain. This includes the employer's greater bargaining power over recruiters, which is wielded to impose questionable recruitment requirements that are then reflected in the contract terms between the employer and recruiter. Importantly, through the employer-driven human supply chain, employers have significant control over recruitment processes, contributing significantly to recruitment abuses but at arm's length.

This chapter shows that, like product supply chains, human supply chains can be empirically understood using the GVC framework. Through the case study of the Nepal–GCC human supply chain, the chapter offers further evidence in favour of the social upgrading of these chains through regulation (as articulated in Gordon, 2017), by regulating *employers*. As the human supply chain model suggests, changes in employer 'purchasing practices' in recruitment – that is, changes to the terms that employers impose in their contracts with recruiters – could prevent recruitment abuses. Applying the GVC framework and terminology to the context of labour recruitment, changing employer practices can be understood as a form of social upgrading in which modifications to the lead firm's practices with regard to its supply chain – here, the *human* supply chain – result in improved social outcomes, namely, recruitment abuses minimized or prevented. The findings from the Nepal–GCC case illustrate that employers hold the most power to engage in social upgrading and that the opportunities for social upgrading are substantial: employer-imposed contract terms have been shown here to cause or contribute to recruitment fees (which are ultimately borne by the worker) and indirectly contribute to recruitment abuses.

This case study offers a new approach – the empirical study of 'human supply chains' using the GVC framework – to understanding the problem of recruitment abuses among low-wage migrant workers. While the topic of upgrading falls beyond the scope of this chapter, applying the GVC framework to understand human supply chains provides a valuable lens through which to comprehend employers' use of power at different points in the recruitment process, demonstrating that exploitation is a structural problem that warrants a structural solution. The findings of the case study thus speak to the argument that recruitment abuses are not the product of individual 'bad apples' and that to criminalize individual abusive practices is to misunderstand how exploitation is actually perpetuated in these human value chains (Gordon 2017; Yea 2021). The approach adopted here provides a much-needed means of empirically understanding the role of employers as the actors in the human supply chain and their role in recruitment abuses contributing to forced labour in the GCC. In product supply chains, empirical GVC studies have been used to empirically demonstrate that lead firms cause or contribute to human rights harms and thereby provide evidence that these firms are responsible under national and international business and human rights laws and norms. This chapter suggests that future empirical study of 'human supply chains' can be used in a similar way, by demonstrating that employers cause or contribute to recruitment abuses and related human rights harms, including forced labour – and using such evidence to hold employers accountable under international and national law.

Notes

1. This chapter adopts the term 'forced labour' rather than 'modern slavery' to avoid terminology that marginalizes the role of racial capitalism including the Atlantic slave trade in contemporary injustice. *See* Blackett (2018); Gross and Thomas (2019).
2. The six GCC states are Bahrain, Kuwait, Oman, Qatar, Saudi Arabia, and the United Arab Emirates.

References

Alkan, H. (2021). 'Temporal Intersections of Mobility and Informality: Simsars as (Im)moral Agents in the Trajectories of Syrian Refugees in Turkey and Germany'. *Migration Letters* 18(2): 201–13.

Amnesty International (2014). *Exploited Dreams: Dispatches from Indian Migrant Workers in Saudi Arabia*. Available at: www.amnesty.org/en/documents/asa20/025/2014/en.

——— (2016). *The Ugly Side of the Beautiful Game: Exploitation of Migrant Workers on a Qatar 2022 World Cup Site*. Available at: www.amnesty.org/en/documents/mde22/3548/2016/en.

——— (2017). *Turning People into Profits: Abusive Recruitment, Trafficking and Forced Labour of Nepali Migrant Workers*. Available at: www.amnesty.org/en/documents/asa31/6206/2017/en.

Anner, M. (2018). 'CSR Participation Committees, Wildcat Strikes and the Sourcing Squeeze in Global Supply Chains'. *British Journal of Industrial Relations* 56(1): 75–98.

——— (2019). 'Predatory Purchasing Practices in Global Apparel Supply Chains and the Employment Relations Squeeze in the Indian Garment Export Industry'. *International Labour Review* 158(4): 705–27.

——— (2020). 'Squeezing Workers' Rights in Global Supply Chains: Purchasing Practices in the Bangladesh Garment Export Sector in Comparative Perspective'. *Review of International Political Economy* 27(2): 320–47.

Babar, Z. (2021). 'Purveyors of Dreams: Labour Recruiters in the Pakistan to Saudi Arabia Migration Corridor'. *Migration and Development* 10(1): 68–85.

Bhagat, A. (2023). 'Entrapment Processes in the Emigration Regime: The Presence of Migration Bans and the Absence of Bilateral Labor Agreements in Domestic Work in Nepal'. *Theoretical Inquiries in Law* 23(2): 222–45.

Blackett, A. (2018). 'Slavery Is Not a Metaphor'. *American Journal of Comparative Law* 66(4): 927–35.

Blaydes, L. (2023). 'Assessing the Labor Conditions of Migrant Domestic Workers in the Arab Gulf States'. *International Labour Review* 76(4): 724–47.

Breeding, M. (2011). 'India–Gulf Migration: Corruption and Capacity in Regulating Recruitment Agencies'. In *Migrant Labour in the Gulf Working Group Summary Report*, 18–19. Washington, DC: Georgetown University. Available at: https://eprints.soas.ac.uk/12410/1/eprints_osella_georgetown_qatar.pdf.

Buckley, M. (2012). 'From Kerala to Dubai and Back Again: Construction Migrants and the Global Economic Crisis'. *Geoforum* 43(2): 250–59.

Buckley, M., P. Chakravartty, and S. Gill (2023). 'From Indenture to "Good Governance": eMigrate and the Politics of Reforming Global Labour Supply Chains'. *Antipode* 55(1): 90–112.

Chilton, A. and B. Woda (2023). 'The Expanding Universe of Bilateral Labor Agreements'. *Theoretical Inquiries in Law* 23(2): 1–64.

Chu, J. (2010). *Cosmologies of Credit: Transnational Mobility and the Politics of Destination in China*, Durham, NC: Duke University Press.

Crane, A. (2013). 'Modern Slavery as Management Practice: Exploring the Conditions and Capabilities for Human Exploitation'. *Academy of Management Review* 38(1): 49–69.

Crane, A. and G. LeBaron (2018). 'Methodological Challenges in the Business of Forced Labour'. In *Researching Forced Labour in the Global Economy: Methodological Challenges and Advances*, edited by G. LeBaron, 25–43. Oxford, UK: Oxford University Press.

Crane, A., G. LeBaron, K. Phung, L. Behbahani, and J. Allain (2021). 'Confronting the Business Models of Modern Slavery'. *Journal of Management Inquiry* 31(3): 1–22.

Equidem (2020). *EXPOsed: Discrimination and Forced Labor Practices on EXPO 2020 Dubai*. Available at: www.equidem.org/assets/downloads/Equidem_EXPOsed_ART_WEB.pdf.

Equidem and GLJ-ILRF (Global Labour Justice–International Labour Rights Forum) (2022). *We Work Like Robots: Discrimination and Exploitation of Migrant Workers in FIFA World Cup Qatar Hotels*. Available at: https://laborrights.org/sites/default/files/publications/Equidem_We_Work_Like_Robots_Report.pdf.

EUI (European University Institute) and GRC (Gulf Research Center) (2019). *The Legal Framework of the Sponsorship Systems of the Gulf Cooperation Council Countries: A Comparative Examination*. Available at: https://cadmus.eui.eu/bitstream/handle/1814/37966/GLMM_ExpNote_2015_10.pdf?sequence=1andisAllowed=y.

FairSquare Projects (2021). *Nepal to Kuwait and Qatar: Fair Recruitment in Review*. Available at: https://fivecorridorsproject.org/uploads/C2_3_Nepal_Kuwait_Qatar-overview-and-pathways.pdf.

Farbenblum, B. and J. Nolan (2017). 'The Business of Migrant Worker Recruitment: Who Has the Responsibility and Leverage to Protect Rights?' *Texas International Law Journal* 53(1): 1–44.

Farbenblum, B., E. Taylor-Nicholson, and S. Paoletti (2013). *Migrant Workers' Access to Justice at Home: Indonesia*. New York: Open Society Foundations.

Fernando, A. N. and A. Lodermeier (2022). 'Understanding Adverse Outcomes in Gulf Migration: Evidence from Administrative Data from Sri Lanka'. *International Migration Review* 56(1): 155–75.

Gardner, A. (2012). 'Why Do They Keep Coming? Labour Migrants in the Gulf States'. In *Migrant Labour in the Persian Gulf*, edited by M. Kamrava and Z. Babar, 41–58. Georgetown University, Center for International and Regional Studies, School of Foreign Service in Qatar. London: C. Hurst and Co..

Garrett, A. (2020). 'The End of *Kafala*? Evaluating Recent Migrant Labor Reforms in Qatar'. *Georgetown Journal of International Affairs* 21: 201–08.

Gereffi, G. (2018). *Global Value Chains and Development: Redefining the Contours of 21st Century Capitalism*. Cambridge, UK: Cambridge University Press.

Gereffi, G. and J. Lee (2016). 'Economic and Social Upgrading in Global Value Chains and Industrial Clusters: Why Governance Matters'. *Journal of Business Ethics* 133(1): 25–38.

Gordon, J. (2017). 'Regulating the Human Supply Chain'. *Iowa Law Review* 102(2): 474–89.

Government of Nepal (2016). *Labour Migration for Employment: A Status Report for Nepal 2014/2015*. Available at: https://webapps.ilo.org/wcmsp5/groups/public/---asia/---ro-bangkok/---ilo-kathmandu/documents/publication/wcms_500311.pdf.

——— (2020). *Nepal Labour Migration Report 2020*. Available at: www.developmentaid.org/api/frontend/cms/file/2020/12/Migration-Report-2020-English.pdf.

Gross, A. J. and C. Thomas (2016). 'The New Abolitionism, International Law, and the Memory of Slavery'. *Law and History Review* 35(1): 99–118.

Hanieh, A. (2011). *Capitalism and Class in the Gulf Arab States*. New York: Palgrave Macmillan US.

Harroff-Tavel, H. and A. Nasri (2013). *Tricked and Trapped in the Middle East*. Geneva: International Labour Organization.

Haruvy, E., E. Katok, A. Ma, and S. Sethi (2019). 'Relationship-specific Investment and Hold-up Problems in Supply Chains: Theory and Experiments'. *Business Research* 12(1): 45–74.

Hernández-León, R. (2021). 'The Work That Brokers Do: The Skills, Competences and Know-how of Intermediaries in the H-2 Visa Programme'. *Journal of Ethnic and Migration Studies* 47(10): 2341–58.

HRW (Human Rights Watch) (2009). *'The Island of Happiness': Exploitation of Migrant Workers on Saadiyat Island, Abu Dhabi*. Available at: www.hrw.org/reports/uae0509webwcover.pdf.

——— (2010). *Walls at Every Turn: Abuse of Migrant Domestic Workers through Kuwait's Sponsorship System*. Available at: www.hrw.org/sites/default/files/reports/kuwait1010webwcover.pdf.

——— (2012). *For a Better Life: Migrant Worker Abuse in Bahrain and the Government Reform Agenda*. Available at: www.hrw.org/sites/default/files/reports/bahrain1012ForUpload.pdf.

——— (2016). *'I Was Sold': Abuse and Exploitation of Migrant Domestic Workers in Oman*. Available at: www.hrw.org/sites/default/files/report_pdf/oman0716web_1.pdf.

——— (2019). *'Paying for a Bus Ticket and Expecting to Fly': How Apparel Brand Purchasing Practices Drive Labor Abuses*. Available at: www.hrw.org/sites/default/files/report_pdf/wrd0419_web2.pdf.

——— (2021). 'Saudi Arabia: Labor Reforms Insufficient; Abusive Elements Remain; Changes Exclude Domestic Workers'. 25 March. Available at: www.hrw.org/news/2021/03/25/saudi-arabia-labor-reforms-insufficient.

IHRB (Institute for Human Rights and Business) (2021). *Dhaka Principles for Migration with Dignity*. Available at: https://dhakaprinciples.org.

ILC (International Labour Conference) (2012). *Giving Globalization a Human Face: General Survey on the Fundamental Conventions Concerning Rights at Work in Light of the ILO Declaration on Social Justice for a Fair Globalization, 2008*. Available at: www.ilo.org/resource/conference-paper/report-iii1b-giving-globalization-human-face-general-survey-fundamental.

ILO (International Labour Organization) (2009). *The Cost of Coercion: Global Report under the Follow-up to the ILO Declaration on Fundamental Principles and Rights at Work*. Available at: https://webapps.ilo.org/wcmsp5/groups/public/---ed_norm/---declaration/documents/publication/wcms_106268.pdf.

——— (2019). *General Principles and Operational Guidelines for Fair Recruitment and Definition of Recruitment Fees and Related Costs*. Available at: https://webapps.ilo.org/wcmsp5/groups/public/---ed_protect/---protrav/---migrant/documents/publication/wcms_703485.pdf.

——— (2020). *A Global Comparative Study on Defining Recruitment Fees and Related Costs: Interregional Research on Law, Policy and Practice*. Available at: https://webapps.ilo.org/wcmsp5/groups/public/---ed_protect/---protrav/---migrant/documents/publication/wcms_761729.pdf.

——— (2021a). *Labour Migration (Arab States)*. Available at: www.ilo.org/regions-and-countries/arab-states/ilo-arab-states/areas-work/labour-migration.

——— (2021b). *Rapid Assessment of the Impact of COVID-19 on Private Recruitment Agencies in Nepal*. Available at: www.ilo.org/publications/rapid-assessment-impact-covid-19-private-recruitment-agencies-nepal.

International Labour Office (2007). *Guide to Private Employment Agencies: Regulation, Monitoring and Enforcement*. Available at: www.ilo.org/publications/guide-private-employment-agencies-regulation-monitoring-and-enforcement.

——— (2015). *No Easy Exit: Migration Bans Affecting Women from Nepal*. Available at: www.ilo.org/publications/no-easy-exit-migration-bans-affecting-women-nepal.

——— (2018). *Findings from the Global Comparative Study on the Definition of Recruitment Fees and Related Costs*. Available at: https://www.ilo.org/media/210491/download.

IOM (International Organization for Migration) (2021). 'IRIS Ethical Recruitment'. Available at: https://iris.iom.int.

Iskander, N. (2021). *Does Skill Make Us Human? Migrant Workers in 21st-Century Qatar and Beyond*. Princeton, NJ: Princeton University Press.

Jones, K. (2015a). 'For a Fee: The Business of Recruiting Bangladeshi Women for Domestic Work in the Middle East'. Working paper No. 2/2015, ILO, Geneva. Available at: www.ilo.org/publications/fee-business-recruiting-bangladeshi-women-domestic-work-jordan-and-lebanon.

——— (2015b). *Recruitment Monitoring and Migrant Welfare Assistance: What Works?* Geneva: International Organization for Migration. Available at: www.iom.int/sites/g/files/tmzbdl486/files/migrated_files/What-We-Do/docs/Recruitment-Monitoring-Book.pdf.

Jones, K., S. Morin, P. Dobree, and W. Irimu (2015). *The Migrant Recruitment Industry: Profitability and Unethical Business Practices in Nepal, Paraguay and Kenya*. Geneva: ILO. Available at: https://www.ilo.org/sites/default/files/wcmsp5/groups/public/@ed_norm/@declaration/documents/publication/wcms_574484.pdf.

Kano, L., E. W. K. Tsang, and H. W. Yeung (2020). 'Global Value Chains: A Review of Disciplinary Literature'. *Journal of International Business Studies* 51(4): 577–622.

Kern, A. and U. Müller-Böker (2015). 'The Middle Space of Migration: A Case Study on Brokerage and Recruitment Agencies in Nepal'. *Geoforum* 65: 158–69.

Khalaf, A., O. AlShehabi, and A. Hanieh (2015). *Transit States: Labour, Migration and Citizenship in the Gulf*. London: Pluto Press.

Kumar, A. (2020). *Monopsony Capitalism: Power and Production in the Twilight of the Sweatshop Age*. Cambridge, UK: Cambridge University Press.

Kurlander, Y. (2019). 'The Marketisation of Migration: On the Emergence, Flourishment and Change of the Recruitment Industry for Agricultural Migrant Workers from Thailand to Israel'. Doctoral thesis, Haifa University, Israel.

LeBaron, G. (2020). *Combatting Modern Slavery: Why Labour Governance Is Failing and What We Can Do about It*. Cambridge, UK: Polity Press.

LeBaron, G. and N. Phillips (2019). 'States and the Political Economy of Unfree Labour'. *New Political Economy* 24(1): 1–21.

Livnat, Y. and H. Shamir (2023). 'Gaining Control? Bilateral Labor Agreements and the Shared Interest of Sending and Receiving Countries to Control Migrant Workers and the Illicit Migration Industry'. *Theoretical Inquiries in Law* 23(2): 65–94.

Mantouvalou, V. (2023). *Structural Injustice and Workers' Rights*. Oxford, UK: Oxford University Press.

Martin, P. (2017). *Merchants of Labour: Recruiters and International Labour Migration*. Oxford, UK: Oxford University Press.

Mendoza, D. R. (2012). *Regulating Private Recruitment in the Asia–Middle East Labour Migration Corridor*. Washington, DC: Migration Policy Institute.

Milkman, R. (2020). *Immigrant Labor and the New Precariat*. New York: Polity.

Nathan, D., M. Tewari, and S. Sarkar (eds.) (2016). *Labour in Global Value Chains in Asia*. Cambridge, UK: Cambridge University Press.

Niezna, M. (2022). 'Paper Chains: Tied Visas, Migration Policies, and Legal Coercion'. *Journal of Law and Society* 49(2): 362–84.

O'Connell Davidson, J. (2013). 'Troubling Freedom: Migration, Debt, and Modern Slavery'. *Migration Studies* 1(2): 176–95.

Paoletti, S., E. Taylor-Nicholson, B. Sijapati, and B. Farbenblum (2014). *Migrant Workers' Access to Justice at Home: Nepal*. New York: Open Society Foundations.

Parreñas, R. S. (2015). *Servants of Globalisation: Migration and Domestic Work*, 2nd edn. Redwood City, CA: Stanford University Press.

——— (2021). *Unfree: Migrant Domestic Work in Arab States*. Redwood City, CA: Stanford University Press.

Rodriguez, R. M. (2010). *Migrants for Export: How the Philippine State Brokers Labour to the World*. Minneapolis, MN: University of Minnesota Press.

Segall, D. and S. Labowitz (2017). *Making Workers Pay: Recruitment of the Migrant Labor Force in the Gulf Construction Industry*. New York: NYU Stern Center for Business and Human Rights. Available at: https://globalinitiative.net/wp-content/uploads/2018/01/Making-Workers-Pay.-Recruitment-of-the-Migrant-Labor-Force-in-the-Gulf-Construction-Industry.pdf.

Shamir, H. (2012). 'A Labor Paradigm for Human Trafficking'. *UCLA Law Review* 60(1): 76–136.

Shrestha, T. (2018). 'Aspirational Infrastructure: Everyday Brokerage and the Foreign-employment Recruitment Agencies in Nepal'. *Pacific Affairs* 91(4): 673–93.

UNODC (United Nations Office on Drugs and Crime) (2015). *The Role of Recruitment Fees and Abusive and Fraudulent Recruitment Practices of Recruitment Agencies in Trafficking in Persons*. Available at: www.unodc.org/documents/human-trafficking/2015/Recruitment_Fees_Report-Final-22_June_2015_AG_Final.pdf.

Verité (2012). *Labor Brokerage and Trafficking of Nepali Migrant Workers*. Available at: https://verite.org/wp-content/uploads/2023/10/Humanity-United-Nepal-Trafficking-Report-Final_1.pdf.

Weil, D. (2014). *The Fissured Workplace: Why Work Became So Bad for So Many and What Can Be Done to Improve It*. Cambridge, MA: Harvard University Press.

Wickramasekara, P. (2015). *Bilateral Agreements and Memoranda of Understanding on Migration of Low Skilled Workers: A Review*. Geneva: ILO. Available at: www.ilo.org/publications/bilateral-agreements-and-memoranda-understanding-migration-low-skilled.

World Bank (2020). 'COVID-19 Crisis through a Migration Lens'. Migration and Development Brief 33. Available at: www.knomad.org/sites/default/files/2020-11/Migration%20%26%20Development_Brief%2033.pdf.

Wright, A. (2021). 'From Slaves to Contract Workers: Genealogies of Consent and Security in Indian Labour Migration'. *Journal of World History* 32(1): 29–43.

Xiang, B. and J. Lindquist (2014). 'Migration infrastructure'. *International Migration Review* 48(1): 122–48.

Yea, S. (2021). 'Towards Critical Geographies of Anti-human Trafficking: Producing and Precluding Victimhood through Discourses, Practices, and Institutions'. *Progress in Human Geography* 45(3): 513–30.

Part III

Sectors

8

The Problem of the 'Modern Slavery' Discourse on Workers' Attempts to Centre Work

Case Studies from the Indian Context

Lorena Arocha, Bindhulakshmi Pattadath,
Meena Gopal, and Roshni Chattopadhyay

As many have warned, the expansionism or 'exploitation creep' (Chuang, 2014) that characterizes discourses around 'modern slavery' has only succeeded in clouding the issue, both legally and politically, rather than rendering it more visible (see also Miers, 2003; O'Connell-Davidson, 2015; Quirk, 2018). As Chuang (2014: 611) explains, this 'exploitation creep' has entailed the consideration of an ever-broadening range of practices as falling under the 'modern slavery' umbrella term. Chuang centres her attention on two related paradigmatic shifts that have allowed this to happen: the reframing of all forced labour as trafficking and the labelling of trafficking as, by definition, slavery (2014: 611). 'Modern slavery' has therefore become a catch-all and highly malleable term, which can include practices as disparate as selling sexual services online, generational bonded labour in India, low-level drug distribution in the UK, and forced marriage.

This 'exploitation creep' has produced two broad policy responses. On the one hand, we have seen the emergence of a hegemonic position referred to in the literature as 'modern slavery abolitionism' (Chuang, 2014; O'Connell-Davidson, 2015). This locates the source of these ostensibly exploitative labour practices in deviant/criminal entities (organized crime groups and/or rogue multinational corporations). Under the abolitionism paradigm, preventative policies have included the banning or restriction of migration for 'vulnerable' populations, often women from the Global South (Kempadoo and Doezema, 1998; Doezema, 2002; Kapur, 2005; Andrijasevic, 2007; Agustín, 2007); the 'rescue, protection and rehabilitation' of individual victims identified in contexts of destination;

and the prosecution of perpetrators. Abolitionism invests in moral crusades along an axis of evil, presenting 'modern slavery' as an exceptional problem to be driven-out (Bunting and Quirk, 2014) and characterized by methodological individualism (LeBaron and Ayers, 2013: 874). Conceptualizing 'modern slavery' as the result of evil criminals or rogue companies, abolitionist policies thus invisibilize the very conditions in which such exploitative and unfree relations thrive. This unnuanced, 'one-size-fits-all' approach fails to consider historically determined systems and relations of power that underpin exploitative and unfree labour.

On the other hand, 'exploitation creep' has also led to the introduction of a policy stance that draws attention to the unequal relations between capital and labour. This labour approach to modern slavery (Shamir, 2012; see also Shamir et al., 2025) does not do away with the identification of 'victims' and their 'rescue' from contexts of labour exploitation, but it fundamentally aims to address the structural conditions at the heart of the power differential between capital and labour (Shamir, 2012).

Accordingly, the policy toolkit available to those aiming to tackle 'modern slavery' now incorporates a range of public and private efforts to regulate labour relations (Shamir, 2012). Some of this thinking has already been incorporated into modern slavery legislation at national and international levels, such as the Modern Slavery Acts of the UK and Australia (2015 and 2018, respectively). Under such legislation, states now require large businesses to disclose the actions they are taking to address 'modern slavery' in their global value chains (GVCs) (see Shamir et al., 2025). As Taylor and Shih (2019: 133) explain, under this legislative turn, tackling 'modern slavery' became the responsibility of private sector businesses too.

The link between GVCs and 'modern slavery' is a recent development that has brought together two very different sets of actors: moral crusaders or modern slavery abolitionists invested in criminal justice solutions, and business scholars, activists, and leaders working on regulatory initiatives to address human rights violations in GVCs. This convergence of actors from different realms, as indicated by Shamir et al. (2025) in the Introduction to this volume, has produced a 'proliferation of business and human rights initiatives aimed at tackling modern slavery in GVCs' (McGaughey et al., 2021).

These initiatives can be categorized by the profiles of the actors that lead them, namely, industry-driven, state-driven, or worker-driven (Shamir and Barkay, forthcoming). To date, the results of the first kind of initiative (in the form of private corporate social responsibility [CSR] charters) and the second kind (state-driven transparency and human rights due-diligence legislation) are disappointing in terms of correcting human and labour rights violations in GVCs. But their combined failures make the few successful worker-driven social responsibility (WSR) initiatives a very promising alternative (for more detail, see Mieres and McGrath, 2021; Asbed and Hitov, 2017; Fine and Bartley, 2019; Sellers, 2021). WSR models centre workers' agency and the potential of collective bargaining to transform unequal relations between capital and labour. However, the conditions under which these become successful are context-driven, meaning that their scalability is fundamentally contingent. What is therefore clear is that the 'rescue and rehabilitation' of individual victims and the panoply of company-led risk assessments and labour inspections have struggled unsuccessfully to bring about much meaningful transformation for their intended beneficiaries.

The Context of India

India has become the paradigmatic country par excellence for modern slavery abolitionists (see Craig et al., 2019). The research that we present in this chapter is motivated by an interest in confronting the failures of the 'modern slavery' and 'trafficking' discourses to foreground the contextual and historical dynamics that lead to exploitative and unfree labour conditions in India. To this end, we take a case study approach to reflect on the trajectories of the collectivizing attempts by Indian workers in informal, precarious, and unfree labour.

More specifically, we focus on two case studies that speak to the two aforementioned shifts that led to the emergence of an expanded notion of 'modern slavery', as discussed by Chuang (2014). Both these cases are located in the state of Maharashtra, situated in the western region of the country (capital: Mumbai). For the first shift, the recasting of forced labour as trafficking, we explore the system of sugarcane harvesting in India; for the second shift, the re-labelling of trafficking itself as slavery, we focus on the collectivizing efforts of Indian migrant sex workers in a semi-rural region.

But before we introduce our methodological approach to data collection and the case studies themselves, we would like to clarify our own position with respect to the 'modern slavery' discourse. We agree with scholars who problematize the 'modern slavery' and 'trafficking' discourses within Western systems of knowledge that are organized around dualisms and shaped by colonial/imperial racialized encounters (Kempadoo and Shih, 2022). The policy solutions on offer obscure these racialized origins and their Western/Global

North epistemic centre (Kempadoo and Shih, 2022). This coloniality of 'modern slavery' is exemplified in the policies prescribed to tackle this phenomenon in relation to the economies and peoples of the Global South. Instances of 'modern slavery' are cited to portray them as some variation of underdeveloped, backward, traditional, or not-yet-modern.

Discursively, then, policy solutions often call for 'development' and are tied to the political and economic hegemony of the West, to its 'liberal notions of modernity, democracy and (un)freedom, and to "philanthrocapitalism"' (Kempadoo and Shih, 2022: 5) and market-based solutions (Dottridge, 2021, cited in Kempadoo and Shih, 2022; Shih and Chuang, 2021). Often, when 'modern slavery' is identified in countries in the Global South such as India, policymakers are quick to interpret it (and all forms of unfree labour) as a symptom of underdevelopment. Hence, they prescribe 'development' as a solution. The position we adopt here contests that interpretation. We hold that unfree labour, far from being the result of underdevelopment, is often *co-constituted* by these very development policies, for capitalist development is only possible *because of* unfree labour.

The incorporation of forced labour, modern slavery, and trafficking into the United Nations (UN) Sustainable Development Goals (SDGs) – specifically, Target 8.7 – has led to further calls for a development approach to trafficking (Kotiswaran, 2019). This approach should not offer 'development' as a solution to modern slavery but, rather, contest the very meaning of 'development' and understand its historical trajectories (and failures) as the starting point (Kotiswaran, 2019: 380). We agree with scholars such as Kotiswaran (2019) who hold that 'development' in the SDGs relies on export-oriented, industrially based growth – that is, on policies that have led to the environmental degradation most acutely felt in contexts of the Global South. Under this neoliberal system of knowledge, human rights are subservient to growth, while questions of (under)development often collude with ideas of (not-yet-modern) culture. After reaching an unspecified threshold, economic growth is meant to trickle down to the lower echelons of society – those most disadvantaged by development programmes.

We see limitations in the labour approach, not least because it is still centred on the identification and rescue of victims. In general, GVC initiatives tend to omit issues relating to labour (Mezzadri, 2017). Scholars have endeavoured to overcome these limitations by either reintegrating political economy concerns (Selwyn, 2012) or using alternative frameworks such as that of the Global Production Network (for example, McGrath, 2013). In this chapter, we apply

Mezzadri's (2017) 'sweatshop regime' concept as a more productive framework for analysing the presence of exploitation and unfreedom in our two case studies. Mezzadri's analysis employs a Marxist–feminist political economy framework to conceptualize how 'free' and 'unfree' forms of labour are both crucial to processes of surplus extraction in contemporary global economic structures. Importantly for us, she understands 'unfree' labour not as the result of yet-to-be-realized processes of industrial modernization; rather, she affirms that 'the sweatshop regime *already is* our industrial modernity' (Mezzadri, 2017: 188, emphasis in the original). Indeed, approaching the relationship between 'free' and 'unfree' labour this way, in non-binary terms, sits within a long-standing scholarship critiquing modernization theories tied to European genealogies (Bhambra, 2014: 15). Such theories promise economic growth and prosperity to the underdeveloped and developing 'world' without regard for how this Western 'peculiar modernity' was enabled and sourced. Similarly, Sanyal's (2007) discussion of the 'capital–non-capital complex' conceives capitalism as a process that creates the necessary conditions for non-capitalist processes to be brought into existence and reproduced (2007: 15). Nevertheless, his conceptualization retains the developed–developing dichotomy.

Drawing on aspects of these theories, we adopt a framework that does not view capitalism as a homogenizing force via processes of proletarianization but as a force that effectively creates the conditions for informality, precarity, and unfreedom to exist. Further, in our analysis of our two case studies, we employ Mezzadri's helpful conception of a labour structure, such as the sweatshop regime. The focus on labour structures enables us to draw attention to how preexisting social differences delineated around gender, caste, and class are mobilized, subjugating workers and externalizing the costs of social reproduction. Moreover, the centrality of the 'labouring body' in Mezzadri's work is invaluable in understanding our case studies. This idea speaks to the simultaneous commodification and exploitation of workers' distinct corporality according to a hierarchy in which, in the lower echelons, the body of the worker becomes a primary 'raw material' and, as such, becomes depleted.

Before turning to discuss our methodological approach, the final point we would like to make concerns the role of workers' efforts in collective organization in India. Both our case studies are set in the informal economy. In the case of India, this sector is significant: according to some estimates, it accounts for over 90 per cent of workers in the economy, though this varies across the sector (Murthy, 2019). Informal sector workers face more challenges to collectively organize. Generally speaking, trade unionism relates mostly to workers in the organized/formal sector; furthermore, in India, it has been in decline for decades. This decline may be explained as the result of the collusion of capitalist interests with those of the state and the close associations between political parties and the unions themselves. Therefore, a large majority of Indian workers are not only not recognized legally as 'employees' but are also 'legitimately' ineligible for individual or collective labour rights (Swaminathan and Rani, 2021: 5). This inequality disproportionally affects women, as their labour is often invisible. Here, we build on the work of those exploring how disenfranchised and informal workers in India are developing strategies to organize collectively despite the challenges, and examine the concessions, albeit still marginal, that their struggle has secured (Agarwala, 2013; Kalpana, 2021). Our case studies highlight the significance of this coming together, especially for women workers in highly precarious and stigmatized sectors.

Methodology and Data

The two case studies we present in this chapter emerged from a pilot study intended to capture the work experiences and collectivizing efforts of workers across several economic sectors in India characterized by precarity, informality, and unfreedom. Our data collection included sectors such as waste-picking, sugarcane cutting, quarrying work, sex work, construction work, garment production, and agriculture, all typified by an over-representation of women, migrants, and workers from the subaltern Dalit and Adivasi communities.

During the summer of 2019, we conducted site visits and spoke with the workers themselves, as well as with activists, trade union representatives, and non-governmental and grassroots-organization staff to learn about their mobilization and organizing efforts. When possible, individual and group interviews were recorded, with the informed consent of all participants present, and ample notes were taken in all other instances. Interviews were all anonymized, transcribed, and translated into English where necessary. Pseudonyms are used in all direct interview quotes reproduced in this chapter. The transcripts were analysed thematically by two of the authors of this chapter. All workers' experiences were shaped by patriarchal, class, and caste-based relations, and these intersectional identities were taken into consideration for inclusion when conducting the fieldwork and speaking to participants. Our project was approved by the Ethics Review Board of the Tata Institute Social Sciences and the Ethics Committee at the University of Hull Social Sciences Department.

The two case studies are representative of the paradigmatic shifts discussed earlier. Our first case study explores how the labouring bodies of migrant women on sugarcane plantations are both commodified and exploited through the joint enterprise of a labour system, mediated via contractors, that is operationalized by binding advance payments and unregulated private health clinics. Our second case study, exploring the conditions and organizing efforts of sex workers, reveals how commodification and exploitation go hand-in-hand and confirms the significant role of healthcare provision in reinforcing the stigmatization of the workers' labouring bodies. Both case studies challenge the modern slavery discourse that seeks to obliterate the historical and contemporaneous factors that contribute to the deployment of forced labour. As we discuss next, they also challenge the view that these are exceptional instances of 'modern slavery' in an otherwise 'normal' functioning of market processes (Mezzadri, 2017: 192; Bunting and Quirk, 2014).

Case Study 1: Sugarcane Cutting in Maharashtra

India is believed to be the birthplace of sugarcane, a good that merchants have carried to all corners of the world (Singh et al., 2021). The history of sugar production is irredeemably linked to colonialism and the Transatlantic slavery system. Its mass production can be traced back to the colonization of the Atlantic islands in the fifteenth century and its subsequent trajectory towards the Americas. Sugar is one of the fundamental crops at the heart of colonial expansion: it fuelled industrialization and spearheaded Western modernity projects, exploiting and depleting colonized lands and peoples.

In the Indian state of Maharashtra, the history of sugar production is enmeshed with one of the deadliest examples of British colonial policies, the Great Famine of 1876–78 that decimated the local population. At a time of drought that led to crop failure, British authorities continued to export grain to England, to the detriment of the people of India. In a bid to stem the ongoing drought–famine cycle, the British began a series of infrastructural relief projects, including the construction of the Nira Left Bank canal in western Maharashtra in 1876 (Attwood 1985 and 2005, cited in Lalvani, 2008: 1479). This irrigation potential explains the concentration of sugarcane production in the state.

Sugar is India's second-largest agri-business (Yadav and Choubey, 2021), and Maharashtra is now the second-largest sugar-producing state in the country (Kulkarni and Agarwal, 2023). Sugar mills – approximately 150 cooperatives and 100 private factories – produced about 10.5 million tonnes of sugar in the period 2022–23 (Kulkarni and Agarwal, 2023). Historically, crop planting was in the hands of wealthy farming families, often Marathas, the dominant caste group in the state (Lalvani, 2008). The first sugar cooperative was established in Maharashtra after India gained independence from Britain in 1947, and its success led to the establishment of a system that granted industrial licenses to sugar cooperatives alone (Lalvani, 2008: 1475). Conversely, private factories were in decline, and it was not until the liberalization of the Indian economy in 1991 that the trend changed (Lalvani, 2008).

Since then, the growth of privately held sugar factories has outpaced that of cooperatives (Lalvani, 2008). Farmers' stake in the industry extends beyond crop cultivation, as they are often shareholders in private factories or involved in cooperatives. Private factories now lead the production of sugar, which conforms to Western business models favoured by major industrial buyers. Multinational corporations such as Coca-Cola, PepsiCo, Nestlé, and Cadbury are all known to buy sugar from private factories in Maharashtra.

One peculiar characteristic of sugar production in the state is that the harvesting and transportation of sugarcane to the mills are usually arranged by the factories themselves. The business rationale for this is that it is believed to be a more efficient system for coordinating the sugarcane-crushing process, thus providing economies of scale (Pisal et al., 2022). For recruitment purposes, factories contact contractors (middlemen, or *mukadams*) and inform them about their labour requirements for the coming harvest season (Kulkarni and Agarwal, 2023: 7). The *mukadams* then go out into nearby towns and villages to recruit and hire workers directly or bring in sub-contractors to hire them. Factories borrow from state or private banks with different interest rates to provide contractors with an advance to cover the costs of hiring. These advances are then given to the hired workers to keep them bound to the contractor (Lalvani, 2008). Factories also compete with each other to announce higher cane prices to attract sugarcane farmers to their mills, indicating the profitability of the sector (Lalvani, 2008).

Historically, agricultural activities such as crop harvesting were carried out by attached labourers (Breman, 1996, 2010). Entire families thus entered into generational bondage relations with big landowners in the Indian feudal system, where lower-caste groups were offered certain limited protections in exchange for their permanent labour (Breman, 2010). Though this type of bondage *per se* has disappeared, capitalist economic development, particularly since the 1990s, has led to increased worker circulation or an army of 'footloose labour' (Breman, 1996) detached from the land. For employers, this meant that a new system was needed to ensure a continued supply of labour – a system that Breman (2010) refers to as 'neo-bondage'. Employers also use the aforementioned contractors to secure the labour of internal migrant workers via the payment of advances as a mechanism to bind workers to a certain economic activity for a season. This practice prevails despite bonded labour legislation and case law having outlawed such labour arrangements.

Every season, which lasts about six months from October to March each year, between 1.2 and 1.6 million migrant workers are involved in sugarcane cutting (harvesting) in Maharashtra (Kulkarni and Agarwal, 2023). This arduous process has not been mechanized and is conducted entirely manually by migrant workers belonging to lower-caste (Dalit) and tribal (Adivasi) groups. Seasonal migrant workers come from the districts of Beed, Jalgaon, Nashik, Jalna, and Ahmednagar in Maharashtra or from the adjacent states of Madhya Pradesh and Karnataka.

These migrant workers engaged for the duration of the harvest are not directly employed by the sugarcane factories but by the aforementioned network of contractors and sub-contractors. The amount of the advance payment given to the male head of household by the contractor is usually impossible to earn in one season (Kulkarni and Agarwal, 2023). This creates a debt, which compels migrant households to have to return the following season. Being socially and economically marginal, they are unable to resist the power of contractors by refusing work under these conditions. Under this arrangement, the work of women and children is subordinated to that of men, as we will see later in this chapter. The cutters are contracted in pairs, almost always a married couple, known as a *koyta* (Marathi for sickle). Each *koyta* is paid INR 250 per tonne of sugarcane cut. A group of approximately 20 people forms a *toli* (9–12 *koytas*), with each *toli* working under a contractor, who is often also a truck owner.

Migrant workers are constantly on the move, staying in any one location for a period of just 15–20 days during the season. Sometimes they stay in the purview of sugarcane mills, where facilities might be available. More often, they have no option but to stay by the roads close to the cultivated land. Women workers are always at a disadvantage under these labour arrangements. They live, and manage all work and care tasks, in very harsh conditions. Migrant workers often live in makeshift tents with no access to toilet or cooking facilities. Their working day starts at 3–4 a.m., when they wash and relieve themselves in the wild to avoid any unwanted attention. They then cook the family's main meal of the day before travelling to the farm to cut sugar for 12–16 hours. Managing menstruation is not only difficult due to the lack of hygiene facilities but also because slowing down or taking any days off translates into less sugarcane cut and a financial penalty. Adding to their burden, women often work throughout their pregnancies and have to resume work soon after delivery.

Koytas, formed when a couple marries, become independent economic units, and this creates an incentive for early marriages among migrant sugarcane-cutting families. After the cutting season is over, some (male) sugarcane cutters migrate to work as construction labourers, while the women, children, and elderly family members remain in the home villages. Hence, not only do sugarcane factories fail to take responsibility for the cutters as employees, but they also avoid bearing any of the costs in the reproduction of this labour. The 'invisible economies of care' (Shah and Lerche, 2020) are borne squarely by the women sugarcane cutters.

In 2019, journalists highlighted the plight of these women in the Marathwada region of Maharashtra, uncovering a deeply worrying phenomenon: an unusually high number of women involved in sugarcane harvesting in the Beed district had undergone hysterectomies. Alarmingly, news emerged that *mukadams* were financing these (medically unnecessary) operations via advances that were tying women and their families to sugarcane cutting (Jadhav, 2019; Shelar, 2019). The National Commission for Women in India called on the Maharashtra State Chief Secretary to prevent this practice from continuing. A committee headed by the Maharashtra Health Department's Principal Secretary was mandated to conduct a fact-finding investigation into the matter. Our research began in July 2019 just after this fact-finding mission had left.

The early sensationalized reporting around the strikingly high incidence of hysterectomies in this district led to the impression that this was an exceptional case. However, evidence gathered through research on women's access to reproductive health services shows that these practices are more widespread than this one case might indicate (Desai et al., 2011; Boseley, 2013; Luksaite, 2016). Studies also show that a great number of these procedures are being performed by private health providers, especially on women in rural areas, working in different sectors (Srivastava, 2018; Padhee, 2019).

The explosion of interest from researchers, journalists, and social activists following the media storm created a momentum that potentially constituted a genuinely transformative opportunity. An informal platform of women sugarcane workers, local social activists, and feminist researchers collaborating with national non-governmental organization (NGO) platforms emerged organically, and this collectivization offered a route towards re-centring some of the concerns of women sugarcane cutters.

These women workers wanted to draw attention to their living and working conditions, especially while working away from home, where a lack of access to adequate food, hygiene, healthcare, and childcare overburdened them. Hygiene was of particular concern because the very poor and unsanitary conditions at these sites augmented the incidence of infections and reproductive health issues. Furthermore, the working rhythms and the advance payment system with its financial penalties discouraged women from taking any breaks at all, even during late-stage pregnancy and shortly after giving birth. Indeed, the lack of basic infrastructure at the sugar plantations not only contributes to the highly exploitative conditions under which these migrant women work but also evidences how the sugar industry in Maharashtra externalizes all social reproductive costs.

We can observe, then, how the sugarcane-cutting labour regime submits the female labouring body to its directives. Starting from an advance-payment system that creates debt to tie the labour of men, women, and children, the regime moulds the 'ideal' female labouring body for sugarcane cutting. Disincentives ensure that she does not take breaks in her excessively long working day. An unnecessary hysterectomy may be performed on her while simultaneously addressing gynaecological issues that she may develop due to the lack of hygienic facilities while at work. This ensures that she also avoids inconveniencing the system by getting pregnant, thereby minimizing disruptions to her working patterns and productivity due to childbirth and childcare. This commodification of the woman worker's body is also made possible by a private healthcare sector that profits from procedures that these women do not need and that push them into further debt.

This scenario sheds light on the extent to which migrant workers are exploited by a labour regime in the sugar industry colluding with a buoyant private healthcare sector. This was clearly visible during our field visit to Beed City, where private clinics dotted the main road. Perpetuating this dynamic is the fact that the Indian government knowingly capitalizes on the booming private healthcare sector (Sengupta and Nundy, 2005). Together, these forces literally and symbolically wear down and deplete the labouring bodies of these migrant women.

Unpacking the System of Exploitation

'Modern slavery' abolitionists would call for all victims to be identified, rescued, and rehabilitated and for perpetrators to be brought to justice. However – at best – this approach is impractical, given that there are estimated to be 1.6

million workers under this seasonal 'tied' scheme in any given year. Worse, the women sugarcane cutters we spoke to were vehemently against such an approach that criminalizes their exploitation and 'rescues' them, leaving them without any other livelihood option. Given the lack of labour opportunities in their villages, these workers *rely* on this seasonal harvesting work in the sugarcane fields. What they do call for is a solution to their poor working conditions, which they blame for the high incidence of hysterectomies. They demand better housing during the harvesting season, access to hygienic sanitary conditions, access to food and cooking facilities, and support with childcare and their children's schooling.

India's Bonded Labour (System) Abolition Act of 1976 legislated against all types of traditional attached labour, including the use of advance payments to tie workers to an activity over more than one season. Case law, too, such as the Supreme Court's decision in *PUDR vs Union of India* (1982) SC 1473 and *Sanjit Roy vs State of Rajasthan* (AIR 1983 SC 328), 'has specifically held that non-payment of minimum wages amounts to forced labour in terms of Article 23 of the Constitution of India' (Kulkarni and Agarwal, 2023: 50). In the case of Maharashtra, since the 1976 Act was passed, official statistics on the incidence of bonded labour indicate that the identification of bonded labourers has not been consistent. In the course of our fieldwork, we were shown documentary evidence (certificates), dated to 1997, indicating that some of the sugarcane cutters were in bonded labour. However, beyond that year, our research uncovered not one certificate or other formal document showing that sugarcane cutters have been identified and rehabilitated as bonded labourers. Maharashtra state authorities consistently claim that no bonded labour is present in the region's agricultural sector, despite the parallel increase in the reliance on family labour in sugarcane harvesting since the late 1990s (Sharma and Prakash, 2011), and despite the reality of labourers trapped in cycles of debt to contractors that we witnessed.

For this identification and rehabilitation of bonded labourers to take place, there would need to be willingness on the part of not only the national government but also the state government – for example, by constituting vigilance committees to operationalize the 1976 Act. The evident *unwillingness* might be best explained by how powerful the sugar lobby is in Maharashtra. It is well known that sugar 'barons', as they are often referred to, have historically constituted an important power structure in the state (Lalvani, 2008: 1475). Many Members of the Legislative Assembly had connections within the sugar industry, and the industry has been a significant contributor to election funds (Lalvani, 2008: 1477).

This case study also serves to demonstrate how industry-driven voluntary CSR models and state-driven efforts to eradicate malpractice have delivered very little in terms of addressing the material living and working conditions of migrant workers such as these sugarcane cutters. Since this case of the hysterectomies came to light (Jadhav, 2019), numerous investigations by local-state and national government bodies and ministries have explored the ongoing conditions of migrant workers in the industry. Even in cases where multinational corporations (such as Coca-Cola, PepsiCo, and Cadbury) are found to be buyers of sugar produced in state-operated mills, as a recent *New York Times* investigation by Megha Rajagopalan and Qadri Inzamam (2024) proved, these companies claim they have no knowledge of unfree work practices in the sugar production in their GVCs and, at most, promise to conduct their own investigations.

The aforementioned informal platform of sugarcane cutters, social activists, and feminist researchers that formed in 2019 began to use public testimonies in an effort to fundamentally shift the public gaze away from the sensationalized reporting that (incorrectly) identified the high incidence of hysterectomies among women in the region as an exception. Instead, they demanded that more attention be paid to the structural socioeconomic conditions that kept women tied to precarious and unfree work. Their activism efforts focused on articulating petitions to the state for measures of social protection and workers' welfare (Menon, 2019), primarily to address the externalization of all social reproductive costs in a sugar-production labour regime where no one is legally responsible for the cutters' well-being.

These emergent collectivizing efforts have prompted several governmental responses, although early signs are that these responses lack active commitment to change. For instance, the Government Resolution of September 2021 (Kulkarni and Agarwal, 2023: 14) ordered that all sugarcane workers be registered and identity cards issued to them. The government also established the Gopinath Munde Sugarcane Welfare Corporation Limited in 2019 to formulate and implement social and welfare schemes for sugarcane workers. In addition, funds were raised via a levy charged to sugar mills per tonne of sugar processed (Kulkarni and Agarwal, 2023: 15). However, in the 2023 Factual Report on the Working Conditions of the Sugarcane Cutters in Maharashtra to the High Court in Mumbai, authors Kulkarni and Agarwal (2023) demonstrate that this registration is still not taking place. This is the way sugarcane factories – whether cooperatives or private companies – and their multinational corporate clients avoid responsibility as employers. The Factual Report also showed that none of the funds raised via the Gopinath Munde Sugarcane Welfare Corporation had been disbursed. A 2019 state government investigation also recommended the passing of the Maharashtra Clinical Establishment Act to enforce minimum standards and regulate and audit private hospitals, but the strength of the medical lobby has so far prevented this from happening (Kulkarni and Agarwal, 2023). Therefore, as Kulkarni and Agarwal (2023) concur, viewing sugarcane labourers as social welfare beneficiaries/victims rather than as workers duly entitled to labour rights has thus far not delivered any real transformation in their reality.

As we have seen, none of the approaches aimed at eradicating 'modern slavery' has provided the much-needed tools to visibilize the joint mechanisms through which women's labouring bodies, in sugar production and other sectors, are commodified, exploited, and depleted. Nor do they help illuminate how this production-labour regime colludes with – indeed, relies upon – a burgeoning private healthcare sector to reproduce preexisting social relations based on gender, caste, and class. These approaches towards eradicating 'modern slavery' frame the presence of these unfree practices in the sugar industry in India as the result of underdevelopment, when, in fact, it is the very result of late-capitalist development processes vigorously pursued since the 1990s. For half a decade now, we have known of the material conditions of women sugarcane cutters; yet, despite numerous initiatives, both grassroots and state-driven, no real material change has come to fruition.

Case Study 2: Migrant Sex Workers in Rural Maharashtra

Sex work in India has always been practiced in diverse forms, both historically and in the contemporary context (Gangoli, 2006: 115). The commercialization of sexual services only took place under British rule, where the first 'red-light areas' were established to concentrate commercial sex work in designated zones, as a 'necessary evil' to meet the sexual needs of single men living away from their families in British India (Ballhatchet, 1980: 70, cited in Gangoli, 2006: 115).

Today's Indian laws 'tolerate' the presence of sex workers, whose work is criminalized but who can often be perceived as victims (Ballhatchet, 1980: 117). The most important pieces of national legislation are the 1956 Suppression of Immoral Traffic Act (SITA) and its amendment, the 1986 Immoral Traffic in Women and Girls (Prevention) Act (ITPA) (Ballhatchet, 1980: 118). Both Acts penalize prostitution, meaning the activities related to commercial sex work such as brothel-keeping, procuring, and detaining for prostitution, and even living off the earnings of commercial sex work. These Acts also clearly conflate prostitution with trafficking. The only shifts that the 1986 Act introduced were a change of focus from suppression to prevention and the introduction of gender-neutral language (Goyal and Ramanujam, 2015). At the national level, there were various attempts at introducing new legislation to further curb prostitution in response to the onset of the HIV/AIDS global epidemic in the 1990s, but all failed. This was partly the result of the success of sex workers' mobilizations.

In Maharashtra, efforts to have sex work legalized were intimately connected to the control of HIV/AIDS (Gangoli, 2006: 123). Two bills dealing with issues relating to the formalization of prostitution were introduced between 1989 and 1994 in a bid to prevent the spread of HIV/AIDS (Gangoli, 2006). They both provided for the compulsory registration of all 'prostitutes' and for every woman in prostitution to be subjected to compulsory medical examinations (Gangoli, 2006: 124). Rather than offering protection to the women in question, the bills only served to further stigmatize them and render them vulnerable to harassment by police officers. The 1994 Bill, which ultimately did not pass into law, even called for any women infected with a sexually transmitted disease to be branded (Gangoli, 2006: 125).

It was in this context that, in the early 1990s, a journalist arrived at a town in western Maharashtra to report on alleged police harassment of women involved in prostitution. Our study participants recalled that the arrival of this journalist and the subsequent reports instigated a sex workers' rights movement by, and for, sex workers in the area. The women sex workers were initially quite reluctant to get together, talk, and share their experiences, as they did not see, at the time, what benefits this could bring. Aside from police harassment, another crucial challenge that affected their day-to-day lives was the inability to access healthcare facilities and, in the case of HIV/AIDS infection, adequate treatment.

Sex work in this particular town was organized as sex work was usually done, be it in brothels, in hotels, or home-based. Most of the workers had migrated, leaving their original places of residence for various reasons such as domestic violence at home, lack of livelihood, migrating to seek other means of living, and so on. They had to develop different strategies to be able to bring together their disparate experiences of sex work and form a common cause to organize themselves. Often, the delivery of health-related information and resources became the most effective way for them to reach out to all workers in the sector.

Drawing parallels between sex work and other equally precarious forms of work in the informal sector was another strategy the sex workers deployed. With the assistance of this journalist, they developed a socio-political strategy aimed at bringing sex workers together as a collective to overcome the stigmatized nature of their work, which was denying them access to crucial healthcare and other kinds of social security. Sex workers in India have historically been treated as vectors of contagion and labelled as immoral and 'bad women'. Furthermore, their criminalization renders them and their children particularly vulnerable.

These women used the initial negative public attention of news reports in the local press to then broaden the terms of the discussion. They sought to challenge the 'bad women' stereotype and demanded the recognition of their humanity on their own terms. Only with this recognition could they begin to raise awareness and mobilize to address the violence, harassment, and exploitative conditions under which they had always worked – realities that were compounded by caste, gender, migration, and sexuality. The formalization of their collective mobilization into the establishment of the first sex-worker organization in the country – which the workers themselves call a union, albeit without external validation of this status – provided them with a formal structure under which several programmes were initiated. These covered crucial issues such as HIV/AIDS prevention, rights education, and the empowerment of sex workers as a community (Pillai et al., 2008).

Despite the commodification (and exploitation) of sex workers' bodies, the dominant discourse about sex work persistently de-couples it from the market, with prostitution considered to be the very antithesis of work (Kotiswaran, 2011: 54). It is precisely the inability to equate sex work with 'real' work that enables it to be considered an exception, as modern-slavery and prostitution abolitionists claim. What this does is leave the body of the sex worker open to the violence, stigmatization, and discrimination it has always been met with, forcing 'sex workers into a "waged work-relation" at the lowest possible wage' (Kotiswaran, 2011: 60, referencing Fortunati, 1995: 122). The sex workers in our study challenged this exceptionality. In one revealing exchange, they compared their situation to that of domestic workers:

> … but, you see, other scenarios where money is involved, it is seen as work. For example, if I go to Maira's house of my own accord and I do her dishes and come back, it is fine but if I go again and do the same work and ask Maira for money, then it is work. So why are you … calling sex work a crime; when there is a monetary transaction, you call it work, don't you?

The embodiment of sex work is at the heart of abolitionists' insistence on equating it with slavery. Under slavery, human beings are reduced to *nothing but* their bodies (O'Connell-Davidson, 2014: 516, referencing Brace, 2004), and it is this indivisibility between the body and the person that emerged as problematic in our field interviews. The sex workers highlighted instead the similarities between their claims and those of other wage workers, contending that their conditions are not peculiar. In sex work, the body matters, but this feature is not unique to this sector. The particularities of workers' bodies are also relevant to employment in all sectors, for instance in contexts as diverse as domestic work, waste management, and the civil service (or even, as the sex workers pointed out to us, the work of a Prime Minister). The sex workers we spoke to suggested that their realities are better understood by taking a longer view and exploring the histories of struggle against the commodification of all labour power (O'Connell-Davidson, 2014), to render visible the similarities between their claims and those of other wage workers.

The importance of labouring bodies' differences and divisions has been fundamental to accumulation processes at the heart of capitalism, including late-capitalist processes (Federici, 2004; Bhattacharyya, 2018). While liberal theory imagines labour as a property that can be sold separately from the self, Marx argued that labour power could not be separated from the person selling it (Marx, 1954, referenced in O'Connell-Davidson, 2014: 522). Labour movements, both old and new, use this very claim to frame their political struggles, emphasizing that workers are not commodities. Yet Indian sex workers' efforts continue to be disregarded by the mainstream trade union movement. Their attempts to register their organization as a national trade union have, so far, failed. At first, their claim was rejected by the Labour Office on the grounds that their occupation was not considered 'work'. By the time of our interviews, in 2019, their second attempt had been stalled for the preceding four years. The sex workers told us that trade union representatives agree with their cause, informally, but are unable to provide that recognition officially due to the legal landscape in India.

In the last couple of decades, international developments have provided some limited grounds to support these efforts in India. The International Labour Office, for instance, acknowledged sex work as informal labour, albeit it did so only in an official Report of the Committee on HIV/AIDS, accompanying the publication of its standard entitled 'Recommendation Concerning HIV and AIDS and the World of Work, 2010 (No. 200)'. Despite this partial acknowledgement by an international body, sex workers in rural Maharashtra complained of the persistent silencing of their position in policymaking processes. They are either effectively shut out of conversations due to the complex and legalistic jargon used in meetings they can attend, or they are denied invitation and entirely kept out of policy-drafting forums by (non-sex-worker and privileged) women who write policies behind closed doors, contravening the motto adopted by sex workers' organizations of 'nothing about us without us'.

Thus prevented from having their voices heard in policymaking, the sex workers we spoke to during our 2019 field visit identified anti-trafficking efforts and interventions emergent since the 1990s – and the more recent 2018 national Trafficking Bill in particular – as major threats to their social standing and livelihoods. The 'raid, rescue, and rehabilitation' measures of anti-trafficking interventions instigated under the 1986 ITPA Act gravely undermine their ability to exercise their rights and often have the opposite effect to that claimed by abolitionists.

Seen as victims rather than workers, sex workers are often sent to 'rehabilitation' centres from which they exit with increased debts unpayable via the socially acceptable feminized activities in which they are trained in these centres (such as sewing). As a result, sex workers not only face harassment and violence by a whole host of local stakeholders, including clients, landlords, criminals, and shopkeepers but, importantly, are also often harassed and abused by those who claim to protect them. Sex workers referred to the entire network of rehabilitation centres as a parallel industry. Indeed, in discussions around the passing of the Trafficking Bill, one of the arguments these stakeholders made against sex workers' demands was the impact they would have in terms of potential rehabilitation-centre closures (Pai et al., 2018). Abolitionist feminists, social reformers, and state and law-enforcement interests have all joined in preventing the recognition of sex work *as work*, relegating the very people involved in the sector to the fringes of policymaking processes.

Sex workers want sex work to be considered work, but with limitations. They do not call for it to be legalized and regimented in the same way as other sectors, as this would be impractical in light of how sex work operates and the vulnerability of those involved in it (O'Connell-Davidson, 2014: 528). The application of a global CSR-type model to sex work would be, at best, challenging, given the tenuous and complex links with capital across diverse sex work arrangements and sites (Kotiswaran, 2011: 237). At worst, it would be impossible, due to the widespread insistence on seeing sex work as anything *but* work. In India, as elsewhere, sex workers' collectives favour decriminalization and oppose legalization (Gangoli, 2006). Under legalization, as we saw in earlier efforts in Maharashtra, women in prostitution would be forced to identify themselves and register, meaning that labour inspectors, who are so central to the social responsibility model, would be entitled to check the women's work and living conditions. Sex workers see labour inspectors as representatives of a repressive, violent, and extracting state (Kotiswaran, 2011: 222) and, hence, as unable to offer them the protection promised under social responsibility interventions.

The case of sex workers in Maharashtra demonstrates how localized dynamics in terms of gender, caste, class, and sexuality are co-constituted in sex work. This renders these migrant women vulnerable to exploitation and expropriation, not only by a host of local actors but also even by modern slavery abolitionists and social reformers who insist on the exceptionality of sex work. However, while women's collectivization is yet to achieve the recognition of sex work as work, it has served its members to know themselves, first as humans and then as workers, by engaging in what has been termed 'epistemic disobedience' (Mignolo, 2009). As with the sensationalist reporting in the case of sugarcane cutters, in this semi-rural part of Maharashtra, sensationalist public accounts – this time, around the spread of HIV/AIDS – drew attention to sex workers in the 1990s. They used this negative reporting to broaden the discussion and articulate demands in terms of work. As one of these sex workers explained to us:

> ... if you have sex for free, then it is not a crime, but if you take money, then it is a crime. A situation where there is monetary transaction is considered as work, while it is not work when there is no monetary transaction. Thus, we say that, because there is a monetary transaction in sex work, it should be recognised as work.

Against abolitionist and conservative Hindutva ideals of femininity, sex workers' articulations run counter to capitalist processes that rely on difference and division. Sex workers urge us to create the possibility for a common political subjectivity embracing all whose work is not valued. They do not want to be brought into the fold of formal (productive) work arrangements but to create an alternative cosmology of value and meaning, in which, in light of the increasing relevance of the service sector, sex work is situated as valuable work.

Re-centring Work and Workers' Demands

The introduction of 'modern slavery' into the UN SDGs fuels the idea that unfree and exploitative labour arrangements are an indicator of underdevelopment in Global South contexts. Under this rubric, scenarios involving informalized, precarious, unfree, and exploitative work are considered evidence of pre-modern, pre-capitalist relations, and the best course of action for states under such circumstances is to press on with policies that encourage industrialization. This mindset holds that development will eventually trickle down and reach those who toil in the shadows of the formal economy. Proletarianization is conceptualized here as a homogenization process that eventually brings everyone into the fold of waged, 'free' labour.

However, the persistence and greater significance of the informal sector in much of the Global South after more than seven decades of structural development policies and interventions, as well as the recognition of its significance in economies once considered 'developed', tell a very different story. Challenges to this narrative are not new. In the 1980s, underdevelopment and dependency theories called for alternatives to liberal capitalism. Theories that recognize multiple modernities point to the intimate relational connections between industrialization and colonial extractive processes, free and unfree labour relations. And, yet, the aforementioned SDG 8.7 – which, among other goals, seeks to rid the world of forced labour and put an end to modern slavery and human trafficking – is situated within the parameters of this emancipating modernist project. 'Modern slavery' abolitionists and those developing initiatives to clean up GVCs have all leaned into this 'modernisation fetish' (Mezzadri, 2017: 189), offering an ahistorical and decontextualized 'flattening' of the world narrative. From controlling cross-border migration, especially of women and children, to CSR models designed to address extreme cases of in-country labour exploitation in industrial settings and increased criminalization of prostitution (as sex can never be 'true work'), the list of interventions and policy prescriptions is both long and often counter-productive.

Since the 1990s, when India liberalized its economy, not only has the informal sector (in which women account for a large proportion of the labour force) burgeoned but informality is also even encroaching into the formal labour sector. 'Unfree' labour formations have proven resilient in this context and go hand-in-hand with these developments. A historical overview of the trajectory of capitalist development demonstrates its continuous demand for the violent and forceful dispossession, exploitation, and expropriation of new sources of wealth in land and people, a process that was not linear and often co-existed with (and relied upon) pre-capitalist social and political formations (Federici, 2004: 215–16). But this process also requires the transformation of the human body into a work-machine and the subjugation of women to the reproduction of the workforce, with a resulting accumulation of differences and divisions within the working class in terms of gender, race, and other intersections that have helped to make invisible and intensify labour exploitation (Federici, 2004: 220–21). Our case studies are illustrative of these very phenomena.

We have looked at how migrant labour in the sugarcane industry and in sex work in Maharashtra are 'unfree'. Their experience and struggles point to a conceptualization that moves beyond the focus on productive work and shatters the illusion of primitive accumulation without social reproduction (Federici, 2004). In the case of the sugar plantations, we saw how this industry externalizes all social reproductive costs, exploiting migrant women's work and bodies. Women's work is only partially remunerated within the *koyta*, and their bodies are depleted and converted into work-machines. Nowhere is this clearer than in the reliance of the sugar industry on a liberalized (privatized) healthcare sector that manufactures the ideal female labouring body through the provision of unnecessary medical interventions. In the case of the sex workers, it is the inability of the discourse to recognize the transactional nature of sex work within a market of sexual services that lies at the heart of its lack of recognition as work. This contributes to the relegation and expulsion of all sex workers to the fringes of society, further embedding their continued violent exploitation.

As sex workers explained to us, soon after Narendra Modi, leader of the *Hindutva* Bharatiya Janata Party (BJP) became Prime Minister of India, the 2016 demonetization policy was introduced, which took INR 500 and 1,000 bank notes out of circulation. The national government heralded this as a measure to reduce the size of the shadow economy, but it gravely reduced the earning capacities of informal workers, including sex workers. This has been compounded by the moralizing framework adopted in much of the governance of the BJP government, especially with respect to women and chastity. It is the *sex* in sex work that makes it exceptional, even if that *sex* is not what the workers themselves consider to matter in explaining their conditions.

To date, some of the literature exploring the possibilities of collective action in sectors where production is characterized by low levels of knowledge (Nathan, 2020) has been quite pessimistic about the powers of collective organization to produce significant and positive changes in the lives of these workers. Though this is true in the situations portrayed in our two case studies, as workers are yet to realize the structural transformations they have been demanding, the value of this collectivization is nonetheless important. It provides workers with space to explore and better understand their conditions, to compare their working lives to those of others in different economic sectors, and to build solidarity networks with other organizations and collectives that provide them with resources they lack. This dynamism often delivers vital relief in the day-to-day crises these workers face, which allows them to ride the tide of very challenging and often life-threatening situations, such as during and after the COVID-19 pandemic. What the migrant workers of our case studies (and India) know is that they have always only had themselves to rely on.

References

Agarwala, R. (2013). *Informal Labor, Formal Politics, and Dignified Discontent in India*. Cambridge, UK; New York: Cambridge University Press.

Agustín, L. (2007). *Sex Work at the Margins: Migration, Labour Markets and the Rescue Industry*. London: Zed Books.

Andrijasevic, R. (2007). 'Beautiful Dead Bodies: Gender, Migration and Representation in Anti-Trafficking Campaigns'. *Feminist Review* 86(1): 24–44.

Bhambra, G. K. (2014). *Connected Sociologies*, 1st edn. London; New York: Bloomsbury Academic.

Bhattacharyya, G. (2018). *Rethinking Racial Capitalism: Questions of Reproduction and Survival*. London; Lanham, MD: Rowman and Littlefield International, Ltd.

Boseley, S. (2013). 'Women's Lives Put at Risk in India by Private Healthcare Providers'. *The Guardian*, 7 February. Available at: www.theguardian.com/society/sarah-boseley-global-health/2013/feb/07/india-healthcare.

Breman, J. (1996). *Footloose Labour: Working in India's Informal Economy*. Cambridge, UK: Cambridge University Press.

——— (2010). 'Neo-bondage: A Fieldwork-based Account'. *International Labor and Working-Class History* 78(1): 48–62.

Bunting, A. and J. Quirk (2014). 'The Politics of Exception: The Bipartisan Appeal of Human Trafficking'. *Open Democracy*, 6 October. Available at: www.opendemocracy.net/en/beyond-trafficking-and-slavery/politics-of-exception-bipartisan-appeal-of-human-trafficking.

Chuang, J. A. (2014). 'Exploitation Creep and the Unmaking of Human Trafficking Law'. *American Journal of International Law* 108(4): 609–49.

Craig, G., A. Balch, H. Lewis, and L. Waite (2019). *The Modern Slavery Agenda: Policy, Politics and Practice*. London: Policy Press.

Cruz, K. (2018). 'Beyond Liberalism: Marxist Feminism, Migrant Sex Work, and Labour Unfreedom'. *Feminist Legal Studies* 26(1): 65–92.

Desai, S., T. Sinha, and A. Mahal (2011). 'Prevalence of Hysterectomy among Rural and Urban Women with and Without Health Insurance in Gujarat, India'. *Reproductive Health Matters* 19(37): 42–51.

Doezema, J. (2002). 'Who Gets to Choose? Coercion, Consent, and the UN Trafficking Protocol'. *Gender and Development* 10(1): 20–27.

Federici, S. (2004). *Caliban and the Witch: Women, the Body and Primitive Accumulation*, 3rd edn. Brooklyn, NY: Autonomedia.

GAATW (Global Alliance Against Traffic in Women) (2007). *Collateral Damage: The Impact of Anti-Trafficking Measures on Human Rights around the World*. Bangkok: GAATW. Available at: https://tinyurl.com/4xnmh6ew.

Gangoli, G. (2006). 'Prostitution in India: Laws, Debates and Responses'. In *International Approaches to Prostitution: Law and Policy in Europe and Asia*, edited by G. Gangoli and N. Westmarland, 115–40. Bristol, UK: Policy Press.

Gereffi, G. (2018). *Global Value Chains and Development: Redefining the Contours of 21st Century Capitalism*. Cambridge, UK: Cambridge University Press.

Jadhav, R. (2019). 'Why Many Women in Maharashtra's Beed District Have No Wombs.' *The Hindu Business Line*, 11 April. Available at: www.thehindubusinessline.com/economy/agri-business/why-half-the-women-in-maharashtras-beed-district-have-no-wombs/article26773974.ece.

Kapur, R. (2005). *Erotic Justice: Law and the New Politics of Postcolonialism*. London: Glass House Press.

Kempadoo, K. (2011). 'Introduction'. In *Trafficking and Prostitution Reconsidered: New Perspectives on Migration, Sex Work, and Human Rights*, edited by J. Sanghera and B. Pattanaik, vii–xxxiv. London; New York: Routledge.

Kempadoo, K. and E. Shih (2022). *White Supremacy, Racism and the Coloniality of Anti-Trafficking*. London; New York: Routledge.

Kempadoo, K. and J. Doezema (1998). *Global Sex Workers: Rights, Resistance, and Redefinition*. London; New York: Routledge.

Kotiswaran, P. (2011). *Dangerous Sex, Invisible Labor: Sex Work and the Law in India*. Princeton, NJ: Princeton University Press.

——— (2019). 'Trafficking: A Development Approach'. *Current Legal Problems* 72(1): 375–416.

Kalpana, K. (2021). 'Fixing Responsibility: Informal Workers' Struggles in Tamil Nadu'. *Anveshi Broadsheet on Contemporary Politics* 15 (Tenth Anniversary Edition – State–Capital Nexus: Implications for Labor): 55–56. Available at: www.anveshi.org.in/wp-content/uploads/2021/03/Anveshi-Labour-broadsheet-English.pdf.

Kulkarni, D. and R. Agarwal (2023). 'Factual Report on the Working Conditions of the Sugarcane Cutters in Maharashtra'. In the High Court of Judicature at Bombay Civil Appellate Jurisdiction Suo Moto Writ Petition No. 1 of 2023.

Lalvani, M. (2008). 'Sugar Co-operatives in Maharashtra: A Political Economy Perspective'. *The Journal of Development Studies* 44(10): 1474–505.

LeBaron, G. and A. J. Ayers (2013). 'The Rise of a "New Slavery"? Understanding African Unfree Labour through Neoliberalism'. *Third World Quarterly* 34(5): 873–92.

Lerche, J. and A. Shah (2018). 'Conjugated Oppression within Contemporary Capitalism: Class, Caste, Tribe and Agrarian Change in India'. *The Journal of Peasant Studies* 45(5–6) (Special Issue on Agrarian Marxism): 927–49. Available at: www.tandfonline.com/doi/epdf/10.1080/03066150.2018.1463217?needAccess=true.

Luksaite, E. (2016). 'The Intimate State: Female Sterilisation, Reproductive Agency and Operable Bodies in Rural North India'. Thesis submitted for the degree of Doctor of Philosophy at the Division of Anthropology, Department of Social Sciences, Media and Communications, Brunel University London. Available at: brunel.ac.uk.

McGrath, S. (2013). 'Fuelling Global Production Networks with Slave Labour? Migrant Sugar Cane Workers in the Brazilian Ethanol GPN'. *Geoforum* 44: 32–43.

Menon, M. (2019). 'Beed: High Hysterectomy Rate among Sugarcane Cutters Signals Unethical Medical Practices, Poor Work Conditions'. *FirstPost*, 16 June. Available at: www.firstpost.com/india/beed-high-hysterectomy-rate-among-sugarcane-cutters-signals-unethical-medical-practices-poor-work-conditions-6807101.html.

Mezzadri, A. (2017). *The Sweatshop Regime: Labouring Bodies, Exploitation, and Garments Made in India*. Cambridge, UK: Cambridge University Press.

Miers, S. (2003). *Slavery in the Twentieth Century: The Evolution of a Global Problem*. Walnut Creek, CA; London; New York; Oxford: Altamira Press.

Mignolo, W. D. (2009). 'Epistemic Disobedience, Independent Thought and Decolonial Freedom'. *Theory, Culture and Society* 26(7–8): 159–81.

Murthy, R. (2019). 'Measuring Informal Economy in India, Indian Experience'. Paper presented at the 7th IMF Statistical Forum: Measuring the Informal Economy (14–15 November, Washington, DC). Available at: www.imf.org/en.

Nathan, D. (2020). 'Digitization and the Reorganization of GVCs'. *The Indian Journal of Labour Economics* 63(S1): 173–79.

O'Connell Davidson, J. (2014). 'Let's Go Outside: Bodies, Prostitutes, Slaves and Worker Citizens'. *Citizenship Studies* 18(5): 516–32.

——— (2015). *Modern Slavery: The Margins of Freedom*. Houndmills (Basingstoke) and New York: Palgrave Macmillan.

Padhee, M. (2019). 'Private Doctors Are Pushing Women in India to Undergo Dangerous Hysterectomies They Don't Really Need'. *FirstPost*, 9 August. Available at: www.firstpost.com/health/private-doctors-are-pushing-women-in-india-to-undergo-dangerous-hysterectomies-they-dont-really-need-7015171.html.

Pai, A., M. Seshu, and L. Murthy (2018). 'In Its Haste to Rescue Sex Workers, "Anti-Trafficking" Is Increasing Their Vulnerability'. *Economic and Political Weekly (Engage)* 53(28), 14 July. Available at: www.epw.in/sites/default/files/engage_pdf/2018/07/18/3460-1531898935.pdf.

Pillai, S., M. Seshu, and M. Shivdas (2008). 'Embracing the Rights of People in Prostitution and Sex Workers, to Address HIV and AIDS Effectively'. *Gender and Development* 16(2): 313–26.

Pisal, M. S., A. V. Gavali, R. B. Hile, and R. R. Nirgude (2022). 'To Study the Growth and Development of Sugar Industry in Maharashtra'. *The Pharma Innovation Journal* SP-11(8): 1766–69. Available at: www.thepharmajournal.com/archives/2022/vol11issue8S/PartW/S-11-8-185-767.pdf.

Quirk, J. (2018). 'When Human Trafficking Means Everything and Nothing'. In *Contemporary Slavery: The Rhetoric of Global Human Rights Campaigns*, edited by A. Bunting and J. Quirk, 67–96. Ithaca, NY; London: Cornell University Press.

Rajagopalan, M. and Q. Inzamam (2024). 'The Brutality of Sugar: Debt, Child Marriage and Hysterectomies'. *New York Times*, 24 March. Available at: www.nytimes.com/2024/03/24/world/asia/india-sugar-cane-fields-child-labor-hysterectomies.html.

Sanyal, K. (2007). *Rethinking Capitalist Development: Primitive Accumulation, Governmentality and Post-Colonial Capitalism*. New Delhi: Routledge.

Selwyn, B. (2012). 'Beyond Firm-centrism: Re-integrating Labour and Capitalism into Global Commodity Chain Analysis'. *Journal of Economic Geography* 12(1): 205–26.

Sengupta, A. and S. Nundy (2005). 'The Private Health Sector in India Is Burgeoning, but at the Cost of Public Health Care'. *British Medical Journal* 331(7526): 1157–58.

Shah, A. and J. Lerche (2020). 'Migration and the Invisible Economies of Care: Production, Social Reproduction and Seasonal Migrant Labour in India'. *Transactions of the Institute of British Geographers* 45(4): 719–34.

Shamir, H. (2012). 'A Labor Paradigm for Human Trafficking'. *UCLA Law Review* 60(1): 76–136.

Shamir, H. and T. Barkay (forthcoming). *Labor Governance Chains: A Comparative Structural Analysis*.

Sharma, A. K. and B. Prakash (2011). 'Causes and Consequences of Supply–Demand Gap for Labour in Sugarcane in India'. *Agricultural Economics Research Review* 24: 401–07.

Shelar, J. (2019). 'A Harvest of Crushed Hopes: Why Number of Hysterectomies Are High in Maharashtra's Beed District'. *The Hindu*, 10 August. Available at: www.thehindu.com/news/national/other-states/in-beed-a-harvest-of-crushed-hopes/article28969404.ece.

Shih, E. and J. Chuang (2021). 'How Has Philanthrocapitalism Helped or Hurt the Anti-Trafficking Movement?' *Open Democracy*, 1 February. Available at: www.opendemocracy.net/en/beyond-trafficking-and-slavery/how-has-philanthrocapitalism-helped-or-hurt-anti-trafficking-movement.

Singh, S., S. K. Srivastava, and S. Jangirala (2021). 'System Dynamics Analysis of Sugarcane Supply Chain in Indian Sugar Industry'. *Global Business Review* 26(2): 468–80. https://doi.org/10.1177/0972150921999521.

Srivastava, R. (2018). 'Private Doctors Perform Most Hysterectomies in India: Survey'. Thomson Reuters Foundation, 11 January. Available at: www.reuters.com/article/us-india-women-health-idUSKBN1F02GJ.

Swaminathan, P. and U. Rani (2021). 'Editorial: Re-visiting the Labour Question'. *Anveshi Broadsheet on Contemporary Politics* 15 (Tenth Anniversary Edition – State–Capital Nexus: Implications for Labor): 2–5. Available at: www.anveshi.org.in/wp-content/uploads/2021/03/Anveshi-Labour-broadsheet-English.pdf.

Taylor, L. R. and E. Shih (2019). 'Worker Feedback Technologies and Combatting Modern Slavery in Global Supply Chains: Examining the Effectiveness of Remediation-Oriented and Due-Diligence-Oriented Technologies in Identifying and Addressing Forced Labour and Human Trafficking'. *Journal of the British Academy* 7(s1): 131–65.

Yadav, G. and R. Choubey (2021). 'Growth and Development of Sugar Industry in India'. *International Research Journal of Modernization in Engineering Technology and Science* 3(7), July: 1278–82. Available at: www.irjmets.com/uploadedfiles/paper/volume3/issue_7_july_2021/14894/1628083579.pdf.

9

The Complexities of Construction Labour in India and the Invisibility of Labourers from the Global Value Chain

Saie Shetye and Divya Priyadarshini

The construction sector holds great economic importance worldwide. It is recognized as the 'biggest non-agricultural industry in the capitalist world' (Srivastava and Sutradhar, 2016: 2). It stands as the foremost consumer of raw materials globally, and it was forecast to achieve growth of 4.2 per cent annually from 2018 to 2023 in terms of market value (Carbon Pricing Leadership Coalition and International Finance Corporation, 2018). Furthermore, its interdependence with various sub-sectors – such as cement, iron, steel, and brick production, and service sectors such as education, finance, or health – makes it an important part of numerous global value chains (GVCs). Indeed, major construction companies often serve as lead firms in both product value chains and human supply chains (Gordon, 2017; Crane et al., 2019; Barkay et al., 2024).

This interdependence between the construction sector and numerous sub-sectors involves both vertical and horizontal intersections within diverse value chains. The scale of the processes, phases, and stakeholders involved in the construction process within these diverse value chains – such as design, production, conversion of raw materials into manufactured products, and on-site construction – highlights the sector's economic significance (Carbon Pricing Leadership Coalition and International Finance Corporation, 2018: 2). Nevertheless, the sheer number of processes, combined with 'the fixed-term, project-based nature of relationships along the supply chain' contributes to a highly fragmented and multi-tiered structure in the sector (Carbon Pricing Leadership Coalition and International Finance Corporation, 2018: 2). Construction projects are not only characterized by significant variability in type and scale, ranging from buildings to major civil engineering projects and large-scale infrastructures, but are also at the mercy of 'local conditions, purpose, regulations, codes, and resources that evolve with time' (Carbon Pricing Leadership Coalition and International Finance Corporation, 2018: 6). Therefore, to understand the complexities of labour exploitation within construction projects, a highly nuanced analysis of GVCs is required.

While GVC frameworks are useful for understanding exploitative practices such as trafficking or modern slavery in various industries, in the case of construction they have largely been applied to global markets or large-scale projects. To address exploitation within national boundaries or at local levels, a shift from the GVC framework to a domestic value chain (DVC) framework is imperative. Crane et al. (2019: 87) rightly argue that 'the focus on GVCs instead of domestic supply chains has made it unclear whether and to what extent forced labour is actually associated with production for export rather than local consumption'. As noted, the GVC framework emphasizes the product and the various stages of production flowing mainly from the 'input-output structure' (Crane et al., 2019). The product value chain in the construction sector is diverse and easily traceable from its beginning (raw materials) to the finished product (the built structure). However, the human/labour supply chain that is intricately interwoven here is much less readily identified, and certainly less discussed in the literature (Crane et al., 2019). This chapter addresses this gap by focusing on the human supply chain in the final stage of the broader construction-product value chain: on-site construction. More specifically, it examines the recruitment and working conditions of construction workers in India.

The construction sector in India serves as a crucial economic driver. According to a recent report, the Indian construction sector's 2018 output expanded by 8.8 per cent in real terms – up from 1.9 per cent the previous year, indicating an increased influx of workers into the sector (GlobalData, 2019). Labourers are primarily contracted to work informally (Ethiraj, 2020; Srivastava and Jha, 2016), making it particularly challenging to scope and study the labour supply chain in India. In a recent collaborative publication, the International Labour Organization (ILO) and the research-policy network WIEGO estimated that two billion people (61 per cent of the global employed population) work in the informal sector (Bonnet et al., 2019). This informality renders the workers particularly vulnerable to exploitation.

The construction sector workforce in India, primarily composed of internal migrants, is usually subcontracted through a multi-tier human supply chain. Worker contracts vary considerably depending on factors such as the magnitude and nature of the project in question, the special design requirements of the buildings, annual investments by the construction company, and the complexities of the work that the labour force is required to perform on the construction site. Many construction projects are thus materialized through smaller, short-term contracts. Exacerbating this precariousness, many labourers are also brought in on verbal contracts and through kinship networks. Furthermore, variations in the scale of the workforce and its composition across different stages of the on-site construction process add to the invisibility of these workers' contributions to the larger value chain, particularly on smaller construction sites. Consequently, they often remain outside the scope of legal frameworks governing the value chains.

The sector is also characterized by pervasive informality: many labourers are hired by subcontractors who, themselves, have been brought in on mere verbal contracts and through kinship networks. In spatio-temporal terms, these workers may be on-site for limited periods only, frequently moving to new sites upon project completion or the conclusion of their own tasks. This movement can span single construction sites, cities, or across states and countries, rendering the nature of informal work in the construction sector ephemeral and mobile. Scholars studying the sector describe workers as experiencing a sense of spatial discontinuity, though the type of work remains largely the same (Srivastava and Sutradhar, 2016; Shivakumar et al., 1991). This form of circular migration is a distinctive characteristic of the construction sector in India that also increases workers' vulnerabilities and ephemerality.

This chapter focuses in particular on recruitment practices in the construction sector, the movement of workers, and bargaining in the shadow of existing legislation. Drawing on Hila Shamir's labour approach to human trafficking (2012), complemented by Prabha Kotiswaran's development approach (2019), we suggest that, to address exploitative recruitment practices and working conditions in the sector, the root causes of workers' vulnerability – which lie in structural and socio-cultural factors – need to be re-thought and transformed. Following Shamir's analysis, we argue that severe forms of labour exploitation in the construction sector should not be understood as exceptions but rather as logical manifestations of the underlying conditions and structural characteristics of the Indian construction sector. We contend that these exploitative recruitment practices can be best understood by adopting the labour approach framework and focusing on market conditions such as partial regulatory frameworks and inadequate application of workers' protections. Moreover, we seek to go beyond this analysis by exploring workers' movement and informality through Kotiswaran's development approach, which considers the larger context of agricultural distress, forced migration, and socio-cultural hierarchies. Drawing from the frameworks already developed, we seek here to lay the groundwork for developing a 'worker-centric approach' to understanding the dynamics of the value chain in the construction sector in India.

In the next part, we introduce our research methodology. We then proceed to a detailed study of the factors that contribute to construction workers' vulnerability in the Indian construction sector, including regulation, exclusions, and lack of enforcement of protections within the predominantly informal workforce of construction sites. This is followed by an analysis of labour market dynamics and characteristics within the context of the developmental state. Additionally, we explore the movement – internal migration – of Indian construction workers into urban areas, interpreting it as a consequence of increasing distress migration reflecting the growing insecurities among the less privileged. Finally, we overlay this understanding with Kotiswaran's development approach to offer a more holistic analysis of the employment of labourers in the sector within the context of social hierarchies, reflected in hiring practices, working culture, and informality within the construction sector. By combining the labour and development approaches, our aim is to address lacunae in the existing legislation and literature in this field, providing us with better tools to understand the potential role of the state in protecting workers' rights.

Methodology

The inquiry presented in this chapter relies on both primary and secondary data sources. Academic studies, including journal articles dealing with the construction sector, trafficking, supply chains, and GVCs have been reviewed for the purpose of analysis. Other secondary sources consulted here include books; Indian labour laws; census data; government, non-governmental, and stakeholder reports; and landmark judgments and court orders relating to construction workers in India. Analysis of secondary literature revealed that the Indian construction sector is highly fragmented but that most studies focus on large projects such as real estate and infrastructure development. Fewer studies focus on small and short-term construction projects whose labour force includes both skilled and unskilled workers.

To complete the picture, primary data were gathered through semi-structured interviews with construction workers and a sample of organizations in Delhi advocating for their rights. The study employed mixed methods in the field. The fieldwork was conducted from September to November 2019, in the National Capital Territory of Delhi. To highlight the nuances of construction work, we selected two residential building sites in the Vasant Kunj locality, where houses were actively under construction. Proximity to the home of one of the authors enabled non-participant observation of the workers' daily lives at the sites. All the workers who were interviewed stayed in temporary shelters at the sites, and this allowed us to observe their work and after-work routines and the conditions they were staying in. Additionally, we conducted interviews with 10 construction workers present at the sites outside of working hours. Interviews with advocacy organizations – such as the National Campaign of Construction Workers spearheaded by NIRMANA – that actively work to secure construction workers' rights provided insight into existing gaps in sectoral laws. Attempts to interview subcontractors, however, proved unsuccessful. All references to interviewees have been anonymized (using fictitious names, where necessary, to ensure privacy).

Worker Vulnerability in the Indian Construction Sector

This part covers the numerical presence of construction workers in this ever-growing sector and attempts to trace their movement patterns. It is widely recognized that many workers employed in the Indian construction sector are circular migrants or seasonal labourers (Srivastava, 2011; 2020a), often eluding official counts and census data. The uncertainty surrounding the actual number of workers employed in the construction sector impedes the proper implementation of the law, thereby exposing workers to vulnerabilities and exploitation. Furthermore, the movement of workers from their place of origin to the destination sites is not always linear, in the sense that the workers undertake circular and seasonal migration while also moving from one site to the other. These complexities prompt an examination of the position of workers and the structure of the DVC in the Indian construction sector and how the dynamics of the human supply chain work. The causes of worker mobility are numerous, and since the presence of informal workers is extremely difficult to systematically trace, their contribution to the DVC remains obscure. A brief analysis of worker numbers and migration patterns can enhance our understanding of their vulnerabilities and emphasize the lack of recognition of their presence in the Indian DVC.

Numerical Overview of the Construction Sector

Here, we attempt to understand the structure of the Indian construction sector and the reasons behind its circular migration phenomenon,[1] which often results in a significant number of migrants being excluded from the census count. A *migrant*, as defined by the Census of India, is 'a person enumerated in the census at a different place than his/her place of birth' (Registrar General of India, 2011b: 1). Consequently, the Census fails to adequately account for short-term or circular migrants. The Government of India's National Sample Survey Office (NSSO) published a report on internal migration covering the period 2007–08, in which it defined *short-term migrants* as 'persons who had stayed away from the village/town for 1 month or more but less than 6 months during the last 365 days *for employment or in search of employment*' (NSSO, cited in Ministry of Statistics and Programme Implementation, 2010: H-iii). However, according to Ravi Srivastava (2020b), most circular migration lasts between seven and nine months. The definitional ambiguity thus potentially leaves a substantial number of circular migrants from being considered in any official statistics.

Most short-term migration in India ultimately serves the construction sector (see Table 9.1), and estimates suggest that there are more short-term migrants than long-term migrants (Ministry of Housing and Urban Poverty Alleviation, Government of India, 2017). According to Srivastava (2011), the number of short-term migrants was estimated to be 40–50 million, while long-term migrants numbered 30–35 million. No further figures have been released since then, but it is reasonable to assume that they have risen tremendously.

Table 9.1 Occupational structure of short- and long-term male migrant worker population in India

	Rural Origin		Urban Origin	
	Short Term	**Long Term**	**Short Term**	**Long Term**
Primary	24.9%	59.5%	13.2%	14.7%
Manufacturing	16.8%	13.1%	26.0%	19.9%
Construction	**41.6%**	**5.3%**	**25.2%**	**5.3%**
Traditional Services	13.0%	11.3%	23.0%	25.0%
Others	3.7%	10.7%	12.6%	35.1%
Total	100%	100%	100%	100%

Source: NSSO (2007–08), quoted in Ministry of Housing and Urban Poverty Alleviation, Government of India, *Report of the Working Group on Migration* (2017: 13).

Construction is the second-largest employment sector after agriculture in India, with the latter employing 60 per cent of the country's workers. In recent years, the agricultural sector has experienced distress, while the manufacturing sector has faced stagnation. The ensuing decline in employment opportunities has led to increased seasonal/circular migration from rural areas to urban centres. According to the Government of India's *Periodic Labour Force Survey 2017–18* (Ministry of Statistics and Programme Implementation, Government of India, 2019), 11.7 per cent of male workers and 4.1 per cent of female workers were engaged in construction work in urban areas. The sector's contribution to employment has significantly increased, even in rural India, where the proportion of male and female workers engaged in construction has risen considerably over the years, from just 1.7 per cent in 1977–78 to 14.5 per cent in 2017–18 for males and from 0.6 per cent in 1977–78 to 5.3 per cent in 2017–18 for females. In urban areas during the same period, the percentage for males increased from 4.2 per cent in 1977–78 to 11.7 per cent in 2017–18; and, for females, it rose from 2.2 to 4.1 per cent (Ministry of Statistics and Programme Implementation, Government of India, 2019).

A report by the NSSO (2016–17) puts the number of construction workers in India at around 74 million (NSSO, cited in Saha et. al., 2021). This implies that the construction sector, being one of the major employers of migrant workers (or workers in general), needs more robust legal safeguards and a worker-centric framework to reduce exploitation and inequalities.

However, existing frameworks and legislation are not only faced with implementational constraints but must also contend with data insufficiencies. If the aforementioned numbers and estimates are taken into account, it appears there is an underestimation of the number of circular migrants in the construction sector. Furthermore, since no specific survey is undertaken to ascertain the number of migrant workers in the construction sector, a section of migrant workers remains unaccounted for in the official data. Even the (unofficial) data reported independently by different organizations or advocacy networks are not pulled together to gauge the extent of the problem. A lack of coherence in the data pertaining to the internal migrants in the construction sector makes for difficulty in implementing the law as well.

Mobility and Construction Work

Besides the natural human impulse to search for a dignified way of living and a way to fend for oneself and care for one's family, several specific factors – indebtedness, agricultural distress, poverty – contribute to internal migration towards the construction sector in India. Deshingkar and Akter (2009: 5) report that 'circular migration is the main form of mobility for work and that such migration is higher among the poor and especially SCs and STs [Scheduled Castes and Scheduled Tribes]'. As one of the major absorbers of the migrant population, the construction sector attracts both skilled craftspeople and tradespeople (masons, carpenters, electricians, plumbers, and so on) and unskilled workers. Although there is some room for upward mobility, poorer, lower-caste, and tribal migrants tend to remain in low-paid, unskilled jobs (Bowers, 2019; Roy, 2019). Roy (2019: 78) has suggested that the 'highly fragmented nature of India's construction industry contributes to the vulnerabilities of circular labour migrants'. The working and living conditions and wages are questionable, drawing the attention of many scholars, activists, and human rights organizations. Respondents from the field corroborated that men are paid more than women and that there is further discrimination among men on-site, based on skill and seniority. Determining seniority among migrant labourers in the construction sector is problematic since one worker who is new to one particular site may have worked for some time on another site and acquired different skills there, yet may not be accorded any seniority on the new site. The ephemerality of workers in the construction sector makes for fluid hierarchies. Despite these vulnerabilities and hardships, one study estimated that a quarter of short-term inter-state circular migrants are active in this sector (Srivastava, 2020b); and, if we include the intra-state circular migrants, then 50–60 per cent of workers employed in the construction sector are circular migrants (Srivastava, 2020b).

Srivastava et al. (2014: 7) note that 'contractors, along with family members or kinfolk of the labourers, are the ones who influence the decision of the worker to migrate'.[2] Similarly, Roy (2019: 83), in his analysis of circular migration in Bihar, points to the fact that mobility outside rural boundaries is the result of the 'dynamic interaction between political inclusion and spatial mobility'. He suggests that the decision to migrate is greatly influenced by villagers seeking opportunities beyond the traditional boundaries of caste occupation, driven by 'growing subaltern confidence' (Roy 2019: 82). Other scholars, too, argue that, apart from the push-and-pull factors of economic growth, the quest to break free of hierarchical social and caste structures in rural communities may also drive migration. Roy's case study from Bihar illustrates how the decline in power of the upper-caste landlords, the growing land ownership of lower-caste peasants, and the untouchable workers caught in-between this conflict lead the latter groups to migrate. Migration occurs mostly among those lower down the caste hierarchy who were previously agricultural labourers on the landholdings of upper-caste landlords. Similarly, Danailova-Trainor and Laczko (2010) found that development initiatives aimed at alleviating poverty may contribute to migration, since people move out of abject poverty and migrate in search of a better life with their newfound confidence and knowledge.

These factors can be understood as social consequences of economic conditions. Most migrant workers possess extremely scant assets in terms of landholdings and lack reliable sources of income in their native villages. Bowers (2019: 21) argues that 'the increasing number of landless and land-poor families in rural India' has led to limited options for sustaining their livelihood. In these circumstances, circular or seasonal migration serves as a crucial subsistence strategy (Srivastava and Sutradhar, 2016). Bowers (2019) also highlights that the growing construction sector acts as a major alternative to agricultural work when it comes to absorbing migrants, owing to its demand for unskilled labour.

However, scholars posit that individuals migrate to cities not to establish new homes but, rather, to support their households back in their villages. According to Picherit (2009) and Pattenden (2012), the construction sector offers the best compensation and sustainability for such scenarios since it allows workers to return home intermittently. Circular migration thus enables construction workers to fulfil 'aspirations and objectives which largely remain rurally rooted – the paying off of agricultural loans; the marking of lifecycle events; … and in their most basic form, the sustenance of one's family' (Bowers, 2019: 32).

Applying the Labour and Development Approaches to the Indian Construction Sector

On the one hand, the legal discourse on modern slavery has focused on a criminal justice response that attempts to prosecute traffickers and perpetrators such as employers and buyers – alas, with little success. On the other hand, the human rights approach to trafficking depends primarily on the 'two central expressions of international willingness to address trafficking', namely the United Nations Protocol to Prevent, Suppress and Punish Trafficking in Persons, Especially Women and Children, 2000 (Trafficking Protocol) and the US Trafficking Victims Protection Act of 2000 (TVPA) (Shamir, 2012: 78). In the paper entitled 'A Labor Paradigm for Human Trafficking', Shamir (2012) argues that the human rights approach and the criminal justice response to the issue of the unprecedented increase in modern slavery are inadequate.

Following the ratification of the two aforementioned legal instruments, many states formed their own anti-trafficking legislation and policies that can be characterized as victim-oriented and deeply rooted within the larger principles of 'prevention, prosecution and protection'. However, as Shamir (2012: 79) further emphasizes, 'the implementation of these international and national legal instruments has focused on sex trafficking – the trafficking of women and girls into the sex industry for prostitution – while tending to ignore labor trafficking – the trafficking of persons for the purpose of labor exploitation into other labor sectors'.

Shamir's paper poses the problem that the human rights approach to trafficking may leave employers' exploitation of employees in some major labour sectors around the globe unaddressed. She contends that 'human trafficking is better understood as predominantly an issue of economic labor market exploitation, and therefore a labor approach to trafficking is required to deal with the phenomenon's underlying causes' (Shamir, 2012: 80).

The findings and recommendations of Shamir (2012) thus draw our attention to the overlooked exploitative practices prevalent in the construction sector, leading us to advocate a more holistic theoretical framework to focus on labour exploitation practices. We share Shamir's view that the human rights approach to trafficking has, to some extent, become part of the problem, as today's anti-trafficking efforts concentrate mostly on criminalization of the exploiter. Less attention is given to the supply chain, employment conditions at the source of movement, and destination sectors and geographical areas. Furthermore, criminalization overlooks the willingness of the trafficked person to return to the place of employment, thus affording them less opportunity to break the cycle of exploitation or acquire more negotiating powers. In the construction sector, then, most of the exploitative activities of the employers are overlooked by legal intervention; and, since the workers are mostly migrants, they suffer social and political exclusion (Roy, 2019: 93).

In presenting the labour paradigm, Shamir's focus remains on the structural aspects of the labour market that she frames as the primary cause of workers' vulnerability and exploitation. This paradigm then addresses the workers' weak bargaining positions, substandard working conditions, and lack of rights. Shamir believes that the trafficked person can exert agency in changing their own situation. She also – like Chuang (2010) and other critics of the anti-trafficking framework – argues that more attention should be paid to the movement/migration of labour and to the working conditions attached, some of which the migrants might agree to and some of which they might not.

However, this is where we would like to depart from Shamir's argument in favour of largely expanding on the definitional and categorical understanding of trafficking. She argues for human trafficking to be seen as labour market exploitation as the issue at the root of the human trafficking problem. She does not go as far as dismissing the terminology of 'trafficking' altogether. Trafficking, for Shamir, is 'severe labor exploitation that shares characteristics with other forms of worker commodification, which is, to some extent, typical of all employment contracts' (Shamir, 2012: 82). According to this understanding, the distinction between worker exploitation and trafficking is thus a matter of degree and not kind, with trafficking being at one extreme of the continuum of commodification.

The arguments presented in the study by Shamir (2012) are written in the context of cross-border migration, which tends to be permanent, suggesting that unionization could be a possible policy response that improves the bargaining power of workers. However, motifs of exploitation are also discernible even in the national informal sectors, construction being one such arena. As we have seen, a large proportion of migrant workers in India find employment in the construction sector, which is characterized by its discrete and fragmented nature and the high incidence of informal employment that relies on a circular-migrant workforce (Roy, 2019). Nevertheless, for short-term local migrations, where destinations vary, as seen in India, there need to be other solutions. Informal employment in the construction sector typically involves circular migrants, whose vulnerabilities are well documented (Connell et al., 1976; Roy, 2019: 78). Concomitantly, exploitative practices in the Indian construction sector often go unnoticed, due to the social and political exclusion faced by migrant workers (Roy, 2019: 93).

In light of these observations and oversights, we argue for a more holistic and comprehensive framework to examine labour exploitation practices. Kotiswaran's (2019) development framework calls for a more holistic and micro approach. This framework moves away from the carceral criminal justice model, seeking instead to address the root causes of trafficking and exploitation within the global economic order. Taking the example of India, Kotiswaran argues against a single universal development approach. Like Shamir, she also criticizes the transnational legal order for its focus on trafficking as an organized crime that calls for a criminal justice response. A crucial insight from her work, diverging from Shamir's framework, is the significant proportion of unorganized workers in India. She contends that even as the state liberalizes, it continues to implement welfarist measures to secure its vote bank. Kotiswaran emphasizes the need for labour reforms and improved implementation of labour laws to tackle the root causes of labour trafficking, arguing that Indian laws have been grounded in Indian realities while also being quite progressive in terms of workers' rights and social security.

In this regard, Kotiswaran references the National Rural Employment Guarantee Scheme (NREGS), which promises work to potential labourers for 100 days. She also mentions labour law reforms – via the Contract Labour (Regulation and Abolition) Act, 1970 (CLRAA);[3] the Bonded Labour System (Abolition) Act, 1976 (BLSAA);[4] and the Inter-state Migrant Workmen Act, 1979 (IMWA)[5] – as indicative of the state's progressiveness in terms of workers' rights and social security. According to Kotiswaran, these legal reforms reflect Indian realities and account for the diversity of informal labour and other social factors in India by providing definitions and solutions to employer–contractor–employee relationships without labelling them as 'trafficking'. She notes that the global trafficking debate, along with the laws derived from it, often distinguishes between 'traffickers'/'exploiters' and the 'trafficked'. However, she argues, these labels are inadequate and restrictive when applied to the Indian construction sector because, in many informal labour sectors in India, supply chains are built on kinship networks, blurring the lines between employer–employee and trafficker–trafficked relationships.

Kotiswaran (2019: 415) concludes by advocating for a development approach to trafficking that 'focuses on addressing root causes rather than an ex post facto approach based on prosecutions, raids, rescues and paternalist models of institutionalised rehabilitation'.

Nevertheless, her inclusive welfarist approach does not address the full spectrum of reasons influencing migrant construction workers to leave their native villages and seek work elsewhere. For example, Roy (2019) identifies social structures, dignity, and the desire for a respectable lifestyle as factors driving migration. Bowers (2019) also highlights that, in addition to financial vulnerabilities in their native villages, the aspiration for an urban lifestyle influences the decision of some migrants to leave. Shetye (2020), one of the authors of this chapter, found that the breakdown of social relations and the rejection of non-normative lifestyles compel women to undertake unsafe migration, a pattern not fully explained by Kotiswaran's theorization. In such cases, the development framework may fail to consider the subjective realities of migrants, especially in the cyclical and fluid construction sector.

While we acknowledge that each of the two frameworks helpfully endeavours to encompass larger areas of influence pertinent to the issue of trafficking and exploitation, neither can be applied to *all* sectors – and certainly not to the Indian construction sector. To distinguish our work from these frameworks, we present the legal perspective in the next part, followed by an analysis of our field experiences to incorporate the subjective realities of workers and contractors in the construction sector, often overlooked in the discourse on modern slavery.

The DVC of the Indian Construction Sector and Worker Vulnerability: The Need for a New Framework

The Legislative and Regulatory Framework: Insufficient Protection of Construction Workers

Article 39 of India's Constitution mandates the state to direct its policies towards securing the right to an adequate means of livelihood, ensuring equal pay for equal work for men and women, safeguarding the health and strength of workers, and ensuring that citizens are not forced by economic necessity to undertake work unsuited to their age or strength. Article 41 guarantees the right to work, and Article 42 concerns just and humane conditions of work and maternity benefits. Together, these constitutional rights establish basic minimum standards for workers, irrespective of their status.

As noted earlier, the construction sector is regulated by the BOCWA. This Act sets out the conditions of work for establishments that employ 10 or more workers in a year (cumulatively) (Section 1(4)).[6] It covers skilled, semi-skilled, and unskilled construction workers between the ages of 18 and 60 who have been employed for at least 90 days in the preceding 12 months. Given the requirement for a minimum of 10 workers, in practice, it tends to be only larger projects, including residential and commercial ones, that fall under the jurisdiction of this Act, as smaller building projects commissioned by individual homeowners are effectively excluded unless they employ a greater number of workers. The Act includes social security provisions for pension contributions, maternity benefits, the education of children through Social Welfare Boards, and provisions regulating hours of work, wages, access to drinking water, housing facilities, crèches, first aid, canteens, and safety measures for workers on larger sites.

Importantly, this Act provides for social security for all building and construction workers (pertaining to establishments employing at least 10 workers) through the establishment of Social Welfare Boards in Indian states. These Boards provide social security by collecting a *cess* (tax) under a sister law, the Building and Other Construction Workers Welfare Cess Act,[7] which was enacted in 1996. Under the Cess Act, the tax is levied according to Section 3, which mandates that it must be between 1 and 2 per cent of the construction cost. The proceeds of the cess are to be paid by the local authority or by the collecting state government to the respective board, after deducting the cost of collection, which may not exceed 1 per cent of the amount collected. Additionally, the Act includes a provision for obligatory interest charged on the cess collected in cases of delayed payment. However, the implementation of the BOCWA faces two main problems. First, there is poor registration of workers due to lack of awareness, circular migration, and unorganized hiring practices and, second, there are bureaucratic delays on the part of the national and state governments and a lack of intent to fulfil the commitment to provide welfare benefits.

In a landmark case concerning the welfare of construction workers (Writ Petition (Civil) 318 of 2006), the orders of the Honourable Supreme Court illuminated the under-utilization of cess and the poor registration of workers. In one significant order, dated 19 March 2018, the Court addressed the implementation of BOCWA and the Cess Act. Given the highly unorganized nature of the construction sector, the Court stressed the importance of implementing the social welfare measures outlined in the Acts and the need for proper constitution and auditing of the Social Welfare Boards collecting cess. The Court also highlighted the fact that only 28 million out of 45 million construction workers were registered with these Boards, meaning that far too many workers were not receiving the social security benefits provided for in the Cess Act. These Social Welfare Boards were tasked with providing assistance in a range of areas, including accident insurance, pension disbursements, loan approval, and financial support to fund children's education. Initially, the Court observed that, while cess was being collected by state governments, the benefits were not reaching the workers, and significant amounts of unutilized cess were reported across the country.

In a meeting with a trade unionist, the authors of this chapter learned that low registration was due to the unorganized nature of the work and the difficulty of providing the required proof of 90 days of work in a given 12-month period. Demonstrating these 90 days was challenging because workers moved frequently from one site to another, because of the nature of contracting, and because there was a general lack of awareness about maintaining proper documentation (such as timesheets) among both workers and employers. Moreover, the workers had neither stable employers nor stable contractors, often finding work through informal channels such as word of mouth and kinship networks. Furthermore, the requisite knowledge of laws and even the understanding of the need to register under the Act were limited and patchy, the trade unionist explained.

Issues with registration persist despite the issuance of identity cards. During our fieldwork, we encountered two types of cards. The first type (Figure 9.1) is facilitated by a trade union and provides job and family details, along with the signature of the inspecting officer. In contrast, the second (more informal) type (Figure 9.2) (in this case, maintained by a contractor at a construction site we visited) lacks any relevant details from a social security or identification perspective.

In addition to the BOCWA and the Cess Act, other regulations, too, influence working conditions and hiring practices. The CLRAA (1970) and the IMWA (1979) regulate the terms and conditions of work and labour migration. The CLRAA regulates working conditions in establishments employing a

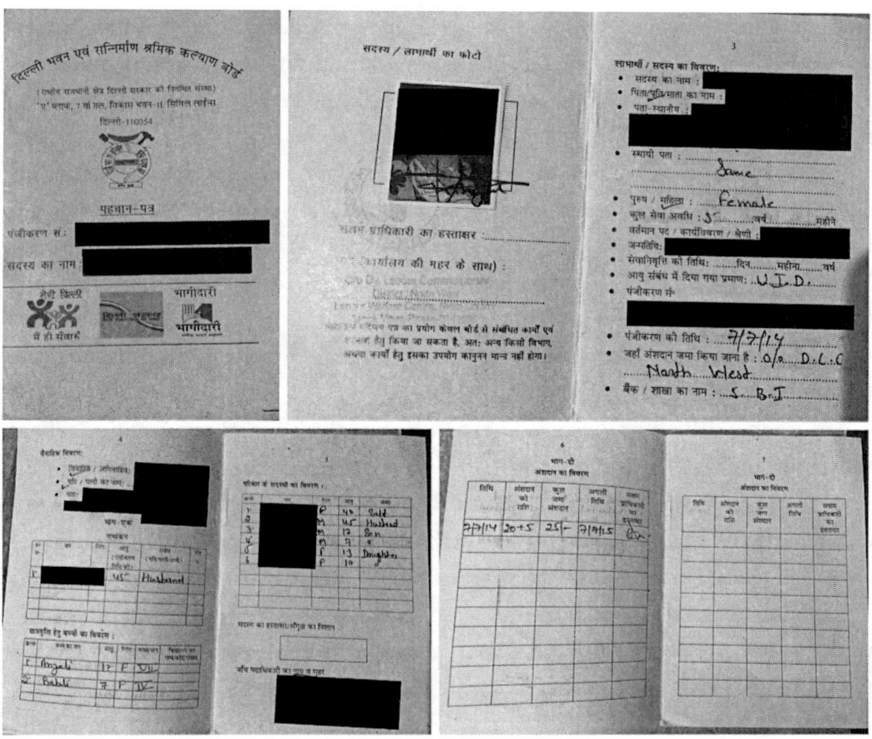

Figure 9.1 Identity card issued by Delhi Building and Construction Workers' Welfare Board

Source: The authors.

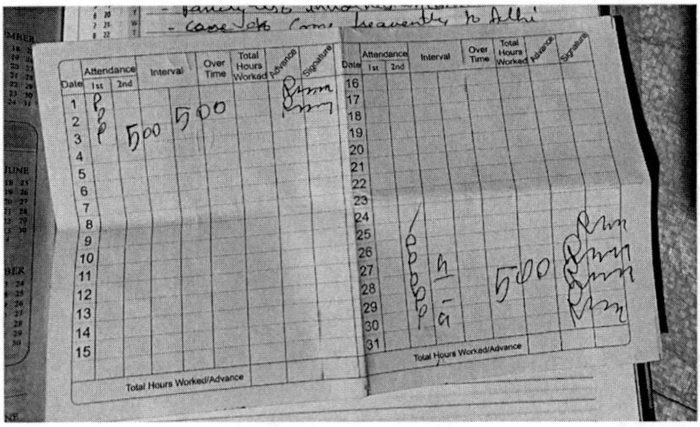

Figure 9.2 Identity card issued by a local contractor in Delhi

Source: The authors.

minimum of 20 workers: for example, the principal employer is obligated to provide specific facilities in the workplace. Under certain circumstances of employment, however, employers are exempt from CLRAA obligations. The IMWA regulates the hiring of inter-state migrant workers and mandates establishments and contractors to provide various facilities and social security to these workers, including provision for transport expenses.

More recently, the Indian government introduced new labour codes to consolidate some older (general and sector-specific) labour laws. These codes cover: (*a*) Wages (passed in 2019); (*b*) Industrial Relations (2020); (*c*) Social Security (2020); and (*d*) Occupational Safety, Health, and Working Conditions (2020). While these laws did not come into force until April 2021, after the data-collection period for our inquiry, the following offers a brief analysis of the clauses therein.

A notable difference lies in the expanded applicability of these codes, where the threshold for the number of workers was increased across the spectrum. The codes on social security and occupational safety continue to apply to establishments that employ 10 or 20 workers. However, the Occupational Safety, Health, and Working Conditions Code makes some distinctions for establishments where hazardous activities are carried out, leaving many workers out of these regulatory protections. Formerly, the CLRAA applied to establishments/contractors hiring at least 20 workers. This threshold was amended by the Occupational Safety, Health, and Working Conditions Code, increasing it to 50 workers. This Code also subsumed the IMWA, with the threshold from 5 to 10 workers.

Unions and activists have advocated for the application of these laws to *all* establishments where workers are hired. Scholars, too, have time and again pointed to how the older labour laws were not effectively implemented due to low worker registration, circular migration, and the temporary nature of the work, making legal entitlements inaccessible. These new Codes do nothing to address these issues, and they further weaken collective organization. We further believe the increase in the threshold for their application will likely leave even more workers outside the protective scope of social security and labour laws. However, implementation of these Codes has been postponed due to delays in the drafting of Rules under the Act.

Additionally, an analysis of trafficking laws shows that these do not address exploitation in the construction sector explicitly but, rather, in other more generalized contexts. For instance, the Trafficking in Persons (Prevention, Care and Rehabilitation) Bill, 2021, defines exploitation as

> at a minimum, the exploitation of the prostitution of others or other forms of sexual exploitation including pornography, any act of physical exploitation, forced labour or services, slavery or practices similar to slavery, servitude or forced removal of organs, illegal clinical drug trials or illegal bio-medical research or the like.

Such laws therefore overlook sector-specific realities or the DVC of construction and other sectors.

Migration as a Driver of Unregulated Recruitment and Exploitative Working Conditions in the Construction Sector: Tracing the DVC in India

There is a growing body of literature dealing with the exploitative nature of the construction sector in India (Roy, 2019; Bowers, 2019). Bowers (2019) addresses the precarious working conditions at construction sites in terms of the payments of wages and other financial obligations, accommodation standards, employer conduct, and on-site safety. However, the extant scholarship often overlooks narratives surrounding the mobility of construction workers from one site to another and the nature of that movement. This part attempts to explore this aspect.

It is well known that construction site work, whether on large or small projects, is time-bound. Roy (2019) and Srivastava and Jha (2016), for instance, have discussed the temporary nature of this work, which creates scenarios where workers are constantly having to seek new sites and employment opportunities. The movement of Indian construction workers often gravitates towards districts with higher levels of urbanization, such as Delhi-NCR, Gujarat, Maharashtra, Western Madhya Pradesh, Telangana, Tamil Nadu, Karnataka, and West Bengal. Furthermore, rural-to-rural mobility is common for migrant construction workers, leading to clusters in eastern and southern Uttar Pradesh, Chhattisgarh, and Odisha as well, where urbanization rates are low (Roy et al., 2017). According to those authors, major receiving cities for construction workers include Mumbai, Ahmedabad, Delhi, Chandigarh, and Kolkata, where most of the work is related to domestic projects.

Middlemen, including contractors or subcontractors, play an important role in mediating employment, reducing transaction costs for both employers and workers and determining working conditions. Studies have observed substantial variations in recruitment patterns across different types of projects. The construction sector, both globally and in India, presents disjunctures in capital production processes as well as in hierarchies of contracting and subcontracting, thus making negotiations difficult for workers (Srivastava and Jha, 2016; Clark and Herrman, 2004, cited in Srivastava and Jha, 2016).

Rama,[8] a respondent in the present study, worked at the construction site (field site) along with her husband, performing tasks related to cement-mixing and carrying building materials. This type of work was considered unskilled, which is typical for the entire construction sector. In contrast, a male respondent, Chaman Lal,[9] was more experienced and skilled in cementing techniques, enjoying a higher position and wage. Women often start and continue as helpers to their male counterparts, resulting in employers favouring lower pay for women. Female workers have limited opportunities for skill enhancement while balancing their unpaid household and care work, while men progress to skilled positions. This pattern was evident in the case of Rama and Chaman Lal, illustrating the sector's lack of regulation, albeit while offering opportunities to both skilled and unskilled workers.

As discussed earlier, most of the population in the construction sector in India consists of circular migrants (Roy, 2019; Srivastava, 2011). Circular migrants continuously move from one site to another, either following existing contractors or seeking work with new ones. In a study on the Bengaluru construction sector, Bowers (2019) describes how different projects provide various arenas of interaction and negotiations for workers. Drawing on the concept of 'ethnographies of mobility' (Roy, 2019: 78), unless a construction project is long-term, there is arguably a continuous movement of workers among various sites within any given destination city (Bowers, 2019). The factors that lead to migration, as Roy (2019) suggests, are linked to the social structural conflicts of the village, the quest for dignified lives, and a growing confidence among subalterns. Adding to these factors driving worker migration, Bowers (2019) also suggests agricultural distress, landlessness, and hopes of creating a better future as contributing to these circular migrations. The construction workers anticipate the completion of their current projects and start looking for their next opportunities at different sites. Sometimes, they move with the same contractor from one site to another, while at other times they rely on a network of kinship ties from their village to find work.

Instances of dependency on kinship were evident in our conversations with another interviewee, Churan Singh,[10] at a local construction site in Delhi. He informed us that, since his wife was from Delhi, he was in continuous contact with her family members in that area. His wife's brothers worked in shops, and they sometimes found renovation/refurbishment work for him. His mother-in-law was also proactive in helping him find work in Delhi, often coordinating with local contractors in the Munirka area. He explained:

> I am not bound by any contractor. I go wherever I find some work. Working at the construction site is our temporary engagement every year. My wife and I work in the brick kilns in Punjab. We work there for six to seven months before the monsoon starts. During our off months, we look for any employment. Mostly it is at construction sites where we find unskilled labour opportunities.

He also mentioned that he had moved to several locations to work but mostly tried to stay close to Punjab, where he was working at the brick kiln. The ephemerality of construction sites and his lack of expertise limit employment opportunities for him and his wife. These factors also require him to constantly move from one place to another when he is not working at the kiln, with construction work being a fall-back source of employment.

The site-to-site movement of construction workers may also be linked to their relationship with the contractor or the construction company. Bowers (2019) notes that small companies working on multiple small projects tend to maintain relations with their workers by either withholding payment or providing advances beforehand, ensuring that the same workers move to the new site with the company. In some instances, construction workers remain on one site for long periods due to the continuous nature of the project, relying on the contractor for the next project when the first one finishes. Another aspect is the role of multiple contractors and kin in securing the next assignment for work, as observed at our fieldwork site. The workers we interviewed mentioned their networking skills and said they were in touch with several contractors and kin from their native villages; and they also referred to the practical kinship relationships (Bourdieu, 1977) they had developed while working at the sites. Keeping in touch with multiple contractors provided the workers with a sense of security that they would be able to find work somewhere. As Bhanwar Singh explained:[11]

> … finding work isn't difficult. We already know our next two subsequent locations for work. It is due to working for a long time in the sector that we have developed our connections. When we were new from our village, it was a completely different scenario….

Other interviewees also highlighted the role that practical kinship plays in finding work. Workers prefer these associations with people they already know rather than relying on the contractors or people at the sites where they work. Mamta,[12] for instance, spoke about the importance of such relationships:

> I was able to work as a domestic help when my husband was working at a site in the Western part of Delhi. A friend of my husband asked him to tell me to get in touch with his wife, who was also working as [a] domestic help. This way, I found a different job [from] working at the site. It was more convenient then. But since my husband has to move for work from one site to the next, I too have to do [so], as per his convenience. Moving from one place to another has taken away my sense of belonging.

Furthermore, due to the temporary, intermittent nature of migrant workers' presence at any given site, they are unable to 'draw upon the same means of collective organisation as settled workers' (Bowers, 2019: 20). Site-to-site movement, in one sense, *perpetuates* migrant precarity and dependency on employers and other forms of social relations. It also became clear from our field study that the power to control recruitment in the construction sector DVCs lies with the main contractor of the project. Even subcontractors rely heavily on these major contractors to get work. The power is diluted as we move further down the hierarchy. This is also true in the case of profit margins, as the main contractor claims the lion's share. In this pecking order, as construction workers are merely temporary employees hired without any written contract, they lack any say in the negotiations over the split in profits of the project secured by the contractor. All these factors collectively make migrant lives precarious.

The labour market is one of the most important channels through which migration affects the well-being of informal construction workers. How migrants secure jobs in destination areas, their working conditions, wages, availability of social security, and their associational and bargaining power are all largely interwoven with each other in the available labour market. The uncertainties that construction workers face in the potential job market stem from their low skills profile, their lack of knowledge of remedies, and their status as internal migrants.

Despite the presence of forced labour, the cases discussed here do not resemble typical, straightforward examples of trafficking. Nevertheless, the nature of the work and the hiring practices surrounding them create situations of severe exploitation. Figure 9.3 illustrates the hierarchy of employers and hiring practices. The emphasis is mainly on individual residential projects (IRPs) where direct hiring occurs or where work is awarded to a builder who acts as the main contractor.

Subcontracting occurs at various levels and involves the hiring of skilled, semi-skilled, and unskilled labour, often facilitated through kinship networks or via known labourers. There are typically no written contracts with the labourers for present or subsequent hirings. In Figure 9.3, we can observe that, for a given building project/IRP, recruitment may be managed through a subcontractor or through other labourers. In many instances, a given labourer (see L1, upper left-hand portion of Figure 9.3) can transition into a subcontractor (SC) role with experience and may then recruit new migrant workers (L1, L2, L3, and so on) through his own contacts. There can be other instances in which a labourer (see L1, upper right-hand portion of Figure 9.3) might recruit another labourer through personal networks from their village (hence, we see multiple L1s in Figure 9.3), and one of these will further recruit another labourer (L2), and so the chain continues through kinship networks. Notably, power and profits within such supply chains mainly remain at the product supply chain level, although power dynamics may vary at different subcontracting levels, often becoming diluted.

In our description of the labour supply chain, the fluidity of intermediaries (for example, a more experienced worker may transition into a small contractor or may bring their relatives to construction sites) often blurs the worker–contractor

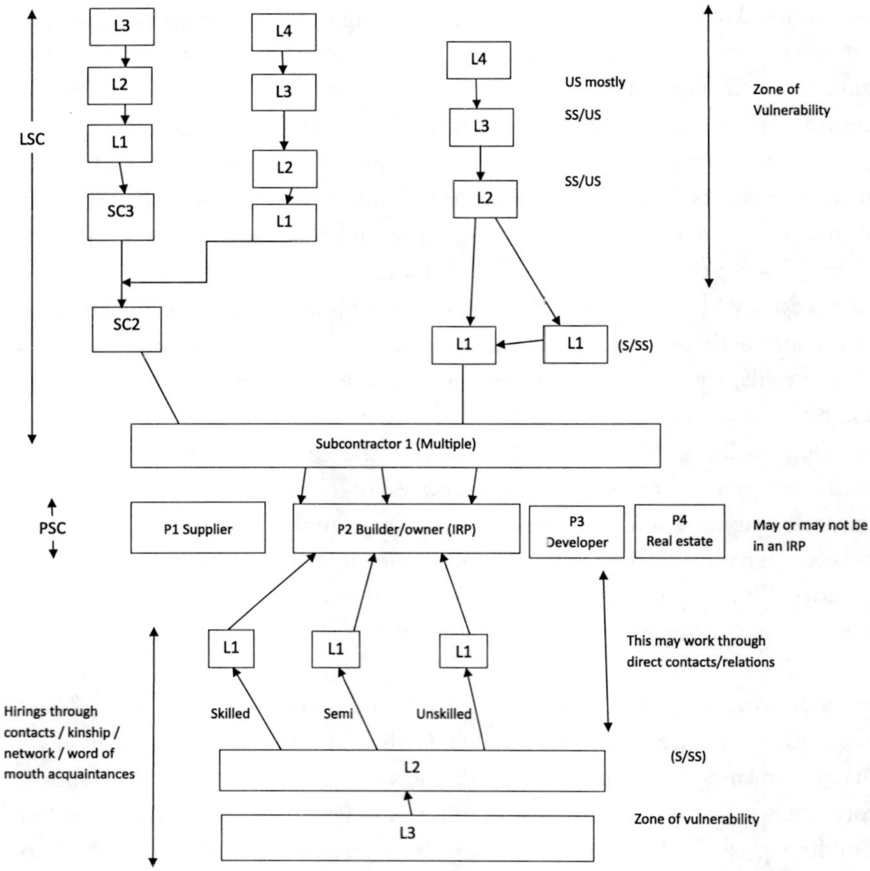

Figure 9.3 Illustration of supply chains in the construction sector in India giving rise to forced labour/modern slavery.

Source: Adapted to the Indian context from Crane et al.'s (2019) framework, based on the data collected in the present study.

Note: Key: US – Unskilled; SS – Semi-Skilled; S – Skilled; L – Labourer; SC – Subcontractor (1 – main contractor); P – Product; PSC – Product Supply Chain; LSC – Labour Supply Chain; P2 – Employer.

relationship, making it difficult to establish accountability along the chain. Licensing of contractors, as practised in other countries, may not effectively ensure proper wages and contracts because of the fluidity of roles. The labourers we interviewed were subcontracted at various levels and had no contact with the builders or premises' owners. In many instances, kinship networks played a crucial role in their recruitment for work at the sites. It was evident at the sites we studied that the entire labour force was segregated into different categories based on their skill sets and hierarchies. Thus, we argue that traditional policy responses by the state and the stakeholders to labour exploitation remain inadequate in this context.

Towards a New Framework

Both Shamir and Kotiswaran, on whose work we heavily draw, have made important contributions to the discourse on trafficking and modern slavery. However, as we have observed in this chapter, their work stops short of providing a culturally and industry-tailored approach. To address the realities specific to circular migrants and fragmented workspaces – such as those that characterize the Indian construction sector – one needs to go beyond the development approach and the labour approach to human trafficking. The highly unregulated recruitment practices in the construction sector and the circular nature of workers' employment patterns render it difficult for either of these two frameworks to address the sector's nuances. In this final part, therefore, we attempt to develop a new framework that adopts a bottom-up perspective – one that takes into consideration workers' lived realities. We focus on the seasonal nature of construction work, the resources the workers leave behind (such as the houses and land in the rural areas from which they migrate), and the various policy linkages that remain in the rural areas where they are registered for various social security benefits.

While addressing the issue of trafficking and/or modern slavery, we keep in mind the diverse conditions prevalent at both the source and the destination for those migrating. Conditions at the origin, for instance, including the omnipresent caste system and its hierarchies, rigid social norms, (lack of) access to education, and the quest for dignified employment, all affect migration and employment outcomes at the destination. The increasing incidence of distress migration to construction labour also points to the growing insecurity among economically vulnerable sections of the population.

There is a need to understand construction work within the context of agricultural distress, job insecurity, and social hierarchies that are reflected in the hiring practices and working culture, some of which, like caste, are highly resistant to change. Another crucial aspect that our proposed framework must take account of is the fluidity of roles in the labour supply chain. A contractor/trafficker in one instance might well have been an employee/trafficked individual in the past. While there are aspects of wage-advances and debt that bear a resemblance to those found in forced labour and trafficking situations, effective responses in such cases might not be through the criminal justice system, following the popular rescue–rehabilitation model often used in counter-trafficking efforts.

Employee–employer relations need not be seen from the anti-trafficking perspective at all, and the language of trafficking and modern slavery needs to evolve to accommodate the fluidity of value chains. Additionally, when discussing the larger GVC of the construction sector, academia and the industry recognize production-related and labour-related value chains. Both Shamir's and Kotiswaran's frameworks are insufficient when it comes to recognizing the contributions of migrant workers who silently support the DVCs.

This significant omission – by which Indian construction workers do not readily fall under the concept of the GVC, and particularly the DVC – can be traced back to the foundational ideas that define it. According to Nathan (2020), the GVC can be understood within the dichotomies of a lead firm and a supplier firm, each of which has further vertical and horizontal relations. However, when the Indian construction sector is placed within the analytical framework of value chains, it appears to have a highly fragmented structure with separate, unaligned sectors including design, production, raw materials for manufacturing, and the construction process itself. Construction workers, following Nathan's logic (2020), should come under the *supplier firm*. However, the highly fragmented structure of supplier firms fails to take into account the contribution of such workers to the value chain. This can be attributed to the constant movement of these workers, the fluidity of their roles at different construction sites, and their dependency on several networks/contractors to find work. It is only through a more diversified and expanded understanding of the GVC, in addition to acknowledging the presence of the DVC, that all contributors can be identified. Furthermore, our discussion in this chapter of GVCs suggests that DVCs and sector-specific approaches need to be included in policymaking.

Concerning the contractors, Deshingkar and Akter (2009) have highlighted those small contractors (*mukadams* and *mistris*)[13] who do not fall under labour law as they work informally to recruit migrant construction workers. Consequently, their workers also go unnoticed by the law and are absent from the value chains, while the common informality of their relations with workers – coupled with the corresponding lack of accountability and also the fluidity of their roles – only compounds the lack of transparency in the DVC.

The sense of exploitation within the value chain resembles Shamir's (2012) pointed analysis suggesting that the labour framework should examine a *continuum* of exploitation along the value chain, rather than viewing exploitation as an exceptional event, as traditionally understood in the case of modern slavery. We further suggest that the causes or push factors of distress migration are better understood beyond the economic benefits for migrants. As we saw earlier, Roy (2019) and Shetye (2020) suggest that the search for dignity and the breakdown of social support systems are significant causes of migration too. These lived experiences do not find space in the present discourse, nor are they addressed when dealing with migrant workers through legislation.

While present legislation in India, including the Labour Codes, provide entitlements for individual workers/families, they only identify individuals within their scope if they work in larger groups on construction sites. This is because they all stipulate a minimum number of workers required in order to apply to a particular unit/construction site, thus limiting their utility for circular migrants and individual migrants not moving with contractors or middlemen. In a landmark 2018 judgment in *National Campaign Committee for Central Legislation on Construction Labour v. Union of India and Others* (Writ Petition (Civil) No. 138 of 2006), the Supreme Court took cognizance of the issue of low levels of informal-worker registration and ordered the provision of Universal Access Numbers for registered workers, ensuring their movement does not hinder access to social security provisions. Both the Model Welfare Scheme for Building and Other Construction Workers and the Action Plan for Strengthening Implementation Machinery (2019), drafted by a committee on the Court's orders in the same case, suggested including provision for self-certification by the worker regarding the number of days worked (Ministry of Labour and Employment), whereby they could give full details of the sites, employers, and number of days' work performed in their passbook/ID card. Some of these measures will ease the access of migrant workers to entitlements. However, they may be insufficient and prove difficult to enforce in informal work environments.

The Proposed Worker-centric Framework

We argue that employability at the destination – that is, the type of work individuals can hope to secure – is deeply dependent on the origin of the worker. Hence, we propose a *worker-centric* framework (Figure 9.4) that should not only pay attention to the destination and the movement/migration but also focus on the origin of the labour force and the transitions that occur when individuals migrate for work to different locations.

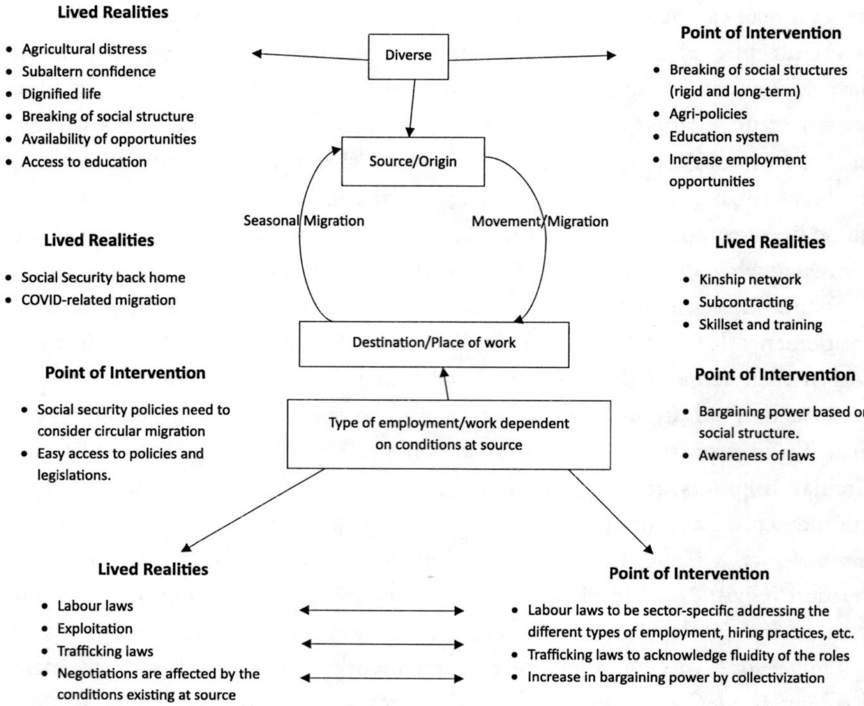

Figure 9.4 The proposed worker-centric framework of the DVC of a sector dependent on circular migrants.

Source: The authors.

This worker-centric framework acknowledges that most migration in India and the subcontinent is circular. Starting out from this premise, we attempt to understand the lived realities of workers at every stage of their movement from source to destination and back. This marks our departure from the literature discussed in this chapter. At the source, we saw multiple factors influencing migration. In this heavily agriculture-dependent society, farm fragmentation and agricultural distress commonly drive migration. Additionally, caste-specific migration occurs, where people migrate for work traditional to their caste group. Furthermore, caste and other social structures such as gender hierarchies are often reflected in landholdings and the exploitative treatment of landless agricultural labourers. Attempts to break these norms often lead to a lack of social support and the impetus to seek a dignified living elsewhere. These factors were also identified in our research into construction workers. We propose that one locus of intervention can be here, at the source itself, where policies focusing on education, agriculture, and employment opportunities can enable the breaking of social hierarchies and moves towards dignified living. In the absence of such intervention, there can be various other points of intervention to address the peculiarity of such a sector, as shown in Figure 9.4.

The kinship networks and layers of subcontracting become ripe venues for exploitation, mirroring social structures. Yet laws in India, including labour and trafficking laws, remain ill-equipped to address these stratified complexities. Trafficking laws, for instance, lack a fundamental understanding of the fluidity of roles surrounding the trafficked–trafficker–subcontractor–employee. Labour laws, too, overlook the fragmented nature of hiring, the small work units, circular movement, and sector-specific responses needed. Accessing social security measures is challenging due to continuous movement and the lack of a universal identity card system for accrediting scheme eligibility, thus disadvantaging workers. Collectivization as an intervention strategy has seen limited success, as evidenced by the identity cards discussed earlier. While we also propose collectivization, its reach in the fragmented DVC to unskilled and unaware workers has been limited. Policy intervention seeking to address the issue of lower bargaining power among such workers thus needs to ensure a larger membership of these collectives. This could be achieved through some sort of membership/registration at the source of migration itself where knowledge can be more easily accessed by the workers in a familiar setting, as opposed to membership after migration to the city, where the migrant has to grapple with another set of challenges for mere survival. Further, to address the circular nature of migration, policies addressing social security need to have universal applicability.

Recent commentary (Srivastava, 2020a) underscores the need for NREGS-like schemes for urban informal workers, whose vulnerabilities were exacerbated during the COVID-19 lockdown. The pandemic exposed structural issues, with migrants losing jobs, suffering wage losses, and undertaking arduous journeys home without sufficient state support. The precariousness of informal job contracts was laid bare. While the anti-trafficking community hoped the plight of migrant workers during the pandemic would prompt state action, the state response was simply to ease restrictions on employers hiring migrant labour, thus allowing for longer hours of work without necessarily higher wages. This is where the third point of intervention is proposed, at the destination of employment. These policy interventions need to take into consideration the fluidity of the roles in the construction sector or similar sectors; hence, a one-size-fits-all approach should be replaced with sector-specific laws and policies.

In this chapter, we have sought to expand our understanding of movement, labour, value chains, and trafficking, informed by the lived experiences of workers, to bring often-excluded groups into conversation with policy frameworks and entitlements. The worker-centric framework we propose is intended to unpack a sector-specific response to exploitation in the construction of DVCs/GVCs. We argue for a bottom-up approach to policy intervention that is grounded in the insight that workers and contractors are uniquely placed to share, to understand the true nature of their relationships and the power dynamics at play. This proposed framework can be further developed for other specific sectors.

Notes

1. The term 'circular migration' has numerous meanings in different contexts. In this study, we see circular migration as people's repetitive movement away from home and back for temporary work. This movement can be inter-state or intra-state.
2. The term 'contractor' in the present chapter refers to an individual or small company that oversees the hiring of labourers in the construction sector for any particular project. They are the 'middlemen' who mediate the flow of work and payment between the labourers and the principal hiring organisation/industry/company/person/employer.
3. The Contract Labour (Regulation and Abolition) Act, 1970. Available at: https://clc.gov.in/clc/acts-rules/contract-labour-regulation-abolition-act-1970.
4. The Bonded Labour System (Abolition) Act, 1976. Available at: www.indiacode.nic.in/bitstream/123456789/1491/1/197619.pdf.
5. The Inter-state Migrant Workmen (Regulation of Employment and Conditions of Service) Act, 1979. Available at: www.indiacode.nic.in/bitstream/123456789/7735/1/the_inter-state_migrant_workmen_%28regulation_of_employment.pdf.
6. Explanation from Section 1(4): 'For the purposes of this sub-section, the building workers employed in different relays [shifts] in a day either by the employer or the contractor shall be taken into account in computing the number of building workers employed in the establishment.' See https://clc.gov.in/clc/acts-rules/building-and-other-construction-workers#:~:text=Explanation.,workers%20employed%20in%20the%20establishment.
7. The Building and Other Construction Workers' Welfare Cess Act, 1996. Available at: www.indiacode.nic.in/bitstream/123456789/1948/1/A1996__28.pdf.

8. Research interview with construction worker, 5 October 2019.
9. Research interview with construction worker, 5 October 2019.
10. Research interviews with construction worker, 7 and 9 October 2019.
11. Research interview with construction worker, 11 October 2019.
12. Research interview with construction worker, 15 October 2019.
13. Research interview with construction worker, 11 October 2019.

References

Bonnet, F., J. Vanek, and M. Chen (2019). *Women and Men in the Informal Economy: A Statistical Brief.* Manchester, UK: WIEGO. Available at: www.ilo.org/wcmsp5/groups/public/---ed_protect/---protrav/---travail/documents/publication/wcms_711798.pdf.

Bourdieu, P. (1977). *Outline of a Theory of Practice.* Translated by R. Nice. Cambridge, UK: Cambridge University Press.

Bowers, R. (2019). 'Navigating the City and the Workplace: Migrant Female Construction Workers and Urban (Im)Mobilities'. *Global Labour Journal* 10(1): 20–36.

Carbon Pricing Leadership Coalition and International Finance Corporation (2018). *Construction Industry Value Chain: How Companies Are Using Carbon Pricing to Address Climate Risk and Find New Opportunities.* Washington, DC: IFC. Available at: https://tinyurl.com/mrx8624p.

Chen, M. (2007). *Skills, Employability and Social Inclusion: Women in the Construction Industry.* Cambridge, MA: WIEGO Network, Harvard University. Available at: www.un.org/esa/socdev/social/meetings/egm5/papers/Skills-Martha_Chen.ppt.

Chuang, J. (2010). 'Rescuing Trafficking from Ideological Capture: Prostitution Reform and Anti-Trafficking Law and Policy'. *University of Pennsylvania Law Review* 158(6): 1655–728.

Clarke, L. and G. Herrman. (2004). 'Cost vs. Production: Disparities in Social Housing Construction in Britain and Germany'. *Construction Management and Economics* 22(5): 521–32.

Connell, J., B. Dasgupta, R. Laishley, and M. Lipton (1976). *Migration from Rural Areas: The Evidence from Village Studies.* Delhi: Oxford University Press.

Crane, A., G. LeBaron, J. Allain, and L. Behbahani (2019). 'Governance Gaps in Eradicating Forced Labour: From Global to Domestic Supply Chains'. *Regulation and Governance* 13(1): 86–106.

Danailova-Trainor, G. and F. Laczko (2010). 'Trafficking in Persons and Development: towards Greater Policy Coherence'. *International Migration* 48(4): 38–83. Available at: https://onlinelibrary.wiley.com/doi/abs/10.1111/j.1468-2435.2010.00625.x.

Deshingkar, P. (2009). 'Extending Labour Inspections to the Informal Sector and Agriculture'. Chronic Poverty Research Centre Working Paper No. 154, Overseas Development Institute, London. Available at: https://papers.ssrn.com/sol3/papers.cfm?abstract_id=1524722.

Deshingkar, P. and S. Akter (2009). 'Human Development Research Paper 2009/13: Migration and Human Development in India'. United Nations Development Programme, New York. Available at: https://hdr.undp.org/system/files/documents/hdrp200913.pdf.

Ethiraj, G. (2020). 'How Migrant Exodus Has Hit Construction Industry'. IndiaSpend, 20 May. Available at: www.indiaspend.com/how-migrant-exodus-has-hit-construction-industry.

GlobalData (2019). *Construction in India: Key Trends and Opportunities to 2023.* GlobalData PLC. Available at: www.globaldata.com/store/report/construction-in-india-key-trends-and-opportunities-to-2023.

Gordon, J. (2017). 'Regulating the Human Supply Chain'. *Iowa Law Review* 102(2): 445–503.

Kotiswaran, P. (2019). 'Trafficking: A Development Approach'. *Current Legal Problems* 72(1): 375–416.

Ministry of Housing and Urban Poverty Alleviation, Government of India (2017). *Report of the Working Group on Migration*. Available at: http://mohua.gov.in/upload/uploadfiles/files/1566.pdf.

Ministry of Statistics and Programme Implementation, Government of India (2010). *Migration in India 2007–2008: NSS 64th Round (July 2007–June 2008)*. Available at: www.thehinducentre.com/resources/67093877-533_final_compressed.pdf.

——— (2019). *Annual Report: Periodic Labour Force Survey (PLFS) July 2017–June 2018.* Available at: dge.gov.in/dge/sites/default/files/2022-11/Annual_Report_PLFS_2017-18.pdf.

Nathan, D. (2020). 'Knowledge, Oligopoly and Labour in Global Value Chains'. *Global Labour Journal* 11(2): 134–51.

National Campaign Committee for Central Legislation on Construction Labour vs. Union of India and Ors. (Writ Petition (Civil) No. 138 of 2006).

Pattenden, J. (2012). 'Migrating between Rural Raichur and Boomtown Bangalore: Class Relations and the Circulation of Labour in South India'. *Global Labour Journal* 3(1): 163–90.

Picherit, D. (2009). '"Workers, Trust Us!" Labour Middlemen and the Rise of the Lower Castes in Andhra Pradesh'. In *India's Unfree Workforce: Of Bondage Old and New*, edited by J. Breman, I. Guerin, and A. Prakash, 259–83. New Delhi: Oxford University Press.

Registrar General of India (2011a). 'Census of India, D Series-D-02: Migrants Classified by Place of Last Residence, Sex and Duration of Residence in the Place of Enumeration – 2011'. Office of the RGI and Census Commissioner. Available at: https://censusindia.gov.in/census.website/data/census-tables.

——— (2011b). 'Drop-in-Article on Census No. 8: Migration'. Available at: https://censusindia.gov.in/nada/index.php/catalog/40447/download/44081/DROP_IN_ARTICLE-08.pdf.

Roy, I. (2019). *Denied the Right to Have Rights: Social and Political Exclusion of Internal Circular Migrants*. New Delhi: Centre for Equity Studies.

Roy, S. N., Manish, and M. Naik (2017). 'Migrants in Construction Work: Evaluating Their Welfare Framework'. Policy brief. Centre for Policy Research, New Delhi. Available at: https://tinyurl.com/58v2bb6y.

Saha, S., K. Peer, and S. Saha (2021), 'India's Migrant Construction Workers: An Analysis of Their Welfare Framework'. *Down to Earth*, 6 October. Available at: www.downtoearth.org.in/news/governance/india-s-migrant-construction-workers-an-analysis-of-their-welfare-framework-79551.

Shamir, H. (2012). 'A Labor Paradigm for Human Trafficking'. *UCLA Law Review* 60(1): 76–136.

Shetye, S. (2020). 'Prevention of Trafficking at Source: A Study of Osmanabad District'. Unpublished Ph.D. thesis. Tata Institute of Social Sciences, Mumbai, India.

Shivakumar, M. S., Y. K. Sheng, and K. E. Weber (1991). 'Recruitment and Employment Practices in Construction Industry: A Case Study of Bangalore'. *Economic and Political Weekly* 26(8): M27–40.

Srivastava, R. (2011). 'Labour Migration in India: Recent Trends, Patterns and Policy Issues'. *Indian Journal of Labour Economics* 54(3): 411–40.

——— (2020a). 'COVID-19 and Circular Migration in India'. *Review of Agrarian Studies* 10(1): 164–80.

——— (2020b). 'The Plight of Migrant Workers in India at the Time of COVID-19'. Tata Institute of Social Sciences, webinar 10 April 2020. Available at: www.youtube.com/watch?v=vjfppixq0Qw&t=29s.

Srivastava, R. and A. Jha (2016). *Capital and Labour Standards in the Organised Construction Industry in India: A Study Based on Fieldwork in the National Capital Region of Delhi*. New Delhi: Centre for the Study of Regional Development,

Jawaharlal Nehru University. Available at: https://eprints.soas.ac.uk/34259/1/Capital%20and%20Labour%20Standards%20in%20the%20Organised%20Construction%20Industry%20in%20India.pdf.

Srivastava, R, R. Sutradhar, C. R. Abrar, S. Reza, J. Adhikari, and G. Gurung (2014). 'Internal Labour Migration to the Construction Sector in South Asia and Its Impact on Poverty and Wellbeing'. Paper presented at the Conference on Internal Migration and Urbanization, University of Dhaka, 30 April–1 May. Available at: www.knomad.org/sites/default/files/2018-01/Dr.%20Ravi%20S.%20Srivastava.pdf.

10

Child Labour in Value Chains

Regulating Demand and Ending Supply

Varsha Joshi and Dev Nathan

This chapter deals with child labour in value chains, whether global value chains (GVCs) or domestic value chains (DVCs). This chapter goes beyond the usual question of the regulation of child labour in value chains to consider the conditions necessary for the elimination of child labour. This chapter is the product of many years of research on this topic by the two authors, sometimes jointly and at times along with other researchers. The empirical base of the analysis in this chapter comprises the various studies carried out by the authors, jointly or separately, of child labour in the garment GVCs in Delhi (Bhaskaran et al., 2010); in the global and DVCs of handicrafts in Jaipur, matches in Sivakasi, stone quarries in Rajasthan, brick kilns in Malda, West Bengal, knitwear and fireworks in Tirupur, Tamil Nadu (Nathan and George, 2012); cotton production in Punjab and Haryana (IHD and Save the Children, 2014); and of gems, lac bangles, and embroidered garments in Jaipur (The Freedom Fund, 2018). One of the authors (Varsha Joshi) led the Child Helpline, which is the key agency in the identification and rescue of child labour in Jaipur, so we were able to use the insights gathered in the course of her work in rescuing child labourers. While the data leading to the chapter's analysis are mainly from Indian cases, the analysis itself is applicable to other, developing countries in the Global South where child labour still exists in serious dimensions. The chapter's policy prescription of combining higher adult earnings at the base of the labour force pyramid with compulsory and quality education is relevant to all developing countries of the Global South.

After this introduction, the next section deals with types of child labour and the implications for different types of interventions. This is followed by a summary of the different types of interventions of both public and private regulation that have been undertaken to eliminate child labour in value chains, both global and domestic. The elimination of child labour involves a change in the business strategy of both the lead firm or principal employer and the supplier. The next section discusses what brings about such changes in business strategy. This is followed by a discussion of the incompleteness of actions to eliminate child labour in value chains and the necessity of supplementing such actions with development interventions; that is, moving from dealing with the demand side of child labour in GVCs to the supply side of the very existence of children in the labour market; or, from regulation, both public and private, to development interventions. The next section discusses the dimensions and nature of development interventions to end the supply of child labour. This is followed by a concluding section that discusses the analysis in the chapter.

Forms of Child Labour

The non-employment of child labour forms part of the Core Labour Standards of the International Labour Organization (ILO) (ILO, 2022). These Core Labour Standards have a different status from other labour standards in that very membership in the ILO implies or means acceptance of the Core Standards, without the need for any further measures of ratification by the member states' governments. The ILO's Core Labour Standards were formulated in the wake of the 1990s debate about labour standards in GVCs, with the consensus that the ILO should be the organization with responsibility for dealing with labour standards in trade issues.

What kind of exploitation does child labour in GVCs involve? Here it is necessary to introduce a distinction between two forms of child labour. One is that where the child is employed as a wage worker or employee, however low that wage may actually be. The other is where the child works as an unpaid family worker. These two forms of child labour, even when they are part of GVCs, need to be dealt with in different ways, as will be seen later on in the chapter. Children working as family workers can be further divided into two groups: child labour as involved in economic activities within the family and child labour as carrying out domestic work. The main distinction is between child labour as *employees* and as *unpaid family workers*. The latter can also be referred to as child homeworkers since they work within the home.

Boys form a higher portion of child labour as employees (ILO–UNICEF, 2017), and, as would be expected, girls predominate in child labour in carrying out domestic work. It is interesting to note that this category of girls engaged in domestic work is not measured in child labour statistics, as pointed out in the ILO's regular compendium of child labour statistics. This leaves a gap in the statistical account, as there are a large number of children, mainly girls, who are neither at work nor in school. They have been called the 'nowhere children' (Rustagi and Leiten, 2008) or 'idle' children. Eric Edmonds and Nina Pavcnik (2005: 202) say that these 'idle' children are not 'well understood'. Terms such as 'nowhere' or 'idle' children are misnomers. As the study by Preet Rustagi and Christophel Leiten revealed, these 'nowhere' or 'idle' girls actually carried out the tasks of looking after younger siblings and the house, which allowed both parents to carry out forms of income-earning work.

There would be little disagreement that child labour as wage labour is a form of extreme exploitation of children since it usually involves little payment besides minimal amounts of food to keep the child able to work. There is usually bondage and deception along with extreme exploitation. Parents may be given an advance and promised that the children will be paid some kind of wage. There is also often deception in that the parents, and even the children, may be told that the children will be sent to school. Child workers may or may not be allowed to communicate with their parents; though nowadays with mobile phones, we find that child workers are often allowed some, say, weekly, communication with their families. Further, these children are unequivocally unable to leave their particular employers.

Child workers as wage employees are thus (*a*) bonded, (*b*) unable to leave an employer, (*c*) paid little more than with minimal food, (*d*) often unable to communicate with their families, and (*e*) along with their families, often subject to deception – all of which would qualify such child workers to be categorized as subject to a form of slavery. Since the slavery is usually for a limited period, it could be called 'modern slavery', as distinguished from traditional slavery, which was lifelong and even transmitted from generation to generation. In a specific manner, we could refer to 'child slavery' where the child workers are wage employees with the conditions summarized above.

We use the term 'modern slavery' to refer to child workers who are wage employees. What about child labour as unpaid or contributing family workers? There are three situations in which children work as unpaid family workers: (*a*) to supplement adult labour in home-based production; (*b*) to care for younger siblings while the parents, especially the mother, are busy earning an income; and (*c*) to learn a trade or a skill. The first two situations of child homeworkers can be attributed to household economic compulsions, for example, the extreme poverty of the families concerned. Adult earnings, whether as homeworkers or wage employees, may be too low to meet basic household needs, such as food, shelter, and clothing. In this situation, the parents decide that their earnings from work in the home need to be supplemented by their children. Or, in the absence of free childcare services, parents may decide to keep an older daughter out of school to look after the younger non-school-age children. The third type of child homework, or unpaid family work, is that where the child learns and acquires the knowledge and skills of a family-based agriculture, craft, or domestic and care work. Such method of family apprenticeship has been the traditional way of generational transmission of craft knowledge, particularly in caste-based divisions of labour.

It is generally accepted that children have limited agency and that parents can decide certain things on behalf of their children. However, states do set limits for some of the decisions that parents can make on behalf of their children, which is why there exist laws regarding child labour. Indian law allows parents to have children work with them on economic, that is, income-earning, activities, but does not allow parents to have their children work as employees, whether bonded or not.

Overall, one cannot fit child homeworkers in any of the categories of slave, bonded, or forced labour. Those categories can, however, be used in the context of children as wage employees. As a result of these differences in the manner of recruitment and in the nature of work relations, these two types of child labour, as wage employees and as contributing family labour, have different implications for the type of actions that may be taken to deal with child labour.

In the case of child wage employees, there is a case for state action to rescue the children involved. Child homeworkers, however, would not be the subjects of 'rescue and rehabilitation' missions since they remain within their homes and with their families. Rescue of children could be considered in cases of gross mistreatment, but not for what is either undertaken under extreme economic compulsion or considered a way of passing on family-based knowledge and skills. Thus, with regard to child homeworkers, it would be necessary to consider going beyond legal interventions and regulation to include development interventions as necessary to end the circumstances that push children and their families towards child labour. However, development interventions, which include labour market matters, are not required only for dealing with child homeworkers but even for child labour in general, a point which we will discuss in more detail later on in this chapter.

Before proceeding, we will take up one point which is often made with regard to child labour – that child labour is part of certain cultures and does not need to be ended since it is the manner in which craft skills are transmitted. In Bolivia, for instance, it was argued that children working with parents was part of the indigenous system and should be continued (Stewart, 2017). In India, it is argued – and the child labour law is based on this notion of tradition – that children should be allowed to work with their parents or relatives, whether in agriculture or various types of home-based work, including that of handicrafts (Nathan, 2023). It should be noted that such a provision is open to and often is misused to conceal the employment of child labourers as wage employees. We have seen this in the lac bangle and embroidery trades in Jaipur. Employers are quite aware of the provisions of the Child Labour Act and try to pass off all children as being some sort of relatives, but the very alienated manner in which we have observed the children relate to the so-called 'relatives' shows the deceptions involved. Discussions with rescued children also reveal the deceptions involved in passing them off as relatives.

Taking up the broader question – is it necessary to end child labour? In economies based on household production, whether in agriculture or various handicrafts, children have worked with their parents and families and, in the course of such work, have acquired the knowledge and skills required for them to carry on their family's business or economic activities. Literacy in those societies was restricted to a handful, the upper castes or upper classes. The transmission of traditional knowledge did not require the acquisition of literacy.

Working with parents is the manner in which knowledge is transmitted between generations in pre-industrial economies (Nieuwenhuys, 1996). This is part of the pre-industrial knowledge economy (Nathan et al., 2022). However, with industrialization and associated new forms of knowledge access requiring literacy and a minimum school education, the older familial transmission of knowledge has generally been replaced by the formal school system.

Literacy and formal education are needed in most jobs. Even employment as a garment worker in an export factory requires a minimal primary education. The task of tailoring does not itself require literacy, since colour coding could convey instructions about size or style. But, as a garment factory manager in Bangladesh pointed out, they want workers who have acquired the discipline of working in one spot for several hours at a time. This is Foucault's capitalist discipline established through the school system.

In addition, literacy is needed even for getting around on modern transportation. As a woman from the Chenchu community, a former hunter-gatherer people in India, said to one of us, she wanted her daughter to be educated, saying that she faced humiliation in not being able to read the destinations on bus signs. Engineering factories require workers who are able to read and follow instructional pamphlets. In fact, engineering and metallurgy factories now want workers with some post-secondary education, such as a post-school technical diploma.

It has been argued that school education can be combined with working at home. Such children, however, have to sacrifice time that could be spent on schoolwork in order to perform labour. This leads to a deterioration in educational performance. Such child labourers are the ones who then drop out of school, as was noted among child labour in the garment GVC in Delhi (Bhaskaran et al. 2010) and in Jaipur (The Freedom Fund, 2018).

As Edmonds and Pavcnik point out, 'Several studies have documented a negative correlation between working and grade advances, years of schooling and test scores. Even though most working children attend school, work may still have substantial consequences for schooling attainment' (2005: 206-7). And as the ILO–United Nations Children's Fund (ILO–UNICEF) report points out, 'Child labour is frequently associated with educational marginalization' (ILO-UNICEF, 2017: 12).

There is a benefit in learning craft skills. This, however, can be done as part of the school curriculum and not have to depend on caste-based education done by parents. One school in Jaipur has included various crafts, for which Jaipur is famous, as part of its curriculum. The skilled craftworkers themselves can be instructors in such school courses, keeping the craft knowledge and skills alive. This allows the transmission of craft skills without jeopardizing children's broader, modern education.

GVC Analysis and Child Labour

The presence of child labour in GVCs has been an enduring feature of exposure of poor labour conditions in GVCs, starting with the Students Against Sweatshops and similar campus-based campaigns. These exposures have led to the formation of codes of conduct by brands, specifying the labour conditions that are expected to be enforced in GVCs. These codes of conduct are supposed to be monitored by third-party agencies. But as many studies have shown, the efficacy of the codes of conduct and auditing process are quite limited (Barrientos et al., 2010; Vaughan-Whitehead, 2014). One area of success, however, has been that of eliminating child labour in factories. Garment factories in India, for instance, usually have a sign prohibiting children from entering the facilities. This, however, has not ended child labour in the value chains. Rather, child labour has been pushed into locations away from the clusters and, particularly, into homes. This displacement of child labour has been a concern in various analyses. There are studies of Bangladesh (Khanam, 2006) and India (Sharma et al., 2004) that have documented such displacement, though a survey by Ugarte, Olarreaga, and Saiovici (2020) points out that macro data do not show such displacement effects. It is possible that the numbers are too small to be reflected in such macro data.

With the concentration of attention on codes and their implementation in value chains, mainly as to Tier-1 suppliers, there has been a neglect of the wider processes by which child labour is incorporated into GVCs. This amounts, in the terms that are being used in this chapter, to neglect in addressing the creation of the supply of child labour. The literature on global production shares some responsibility, having traditionally prioritized highly firm-centric modes of analyses and, until recently, paying rather little attention to the social and labour foundations in which global production networks (GPNs) rest (Phillips et al., 2014: 429) or, in other words, to the embedding of global production in social conditions. Thus, it is necessary to pay attention to the social situations and factors that lead to the creation of child labour and to the measures aimed at eliminating the supply of child labour.

Private Regulation and Supplier Business Strategies

We now turn to measures aimed at eliminating child labour in value chains, both global and domestic. The measures can be of two types dealing with the demand for and supply of child labour, respectively. The child labour law forbids the employment of child labour, other than as part of a household enterprise. Employment as a wage employee, for example, within a factory, is forbidden. The regulatory mechanism usually taken is that of the state, that is, public regulation. But GVCs have seen the rise of a new form of regulation, private regulation. This is carried out by lead firms in GVCs that establish codes of conduct that supplier firms must comply with in their factories. In pursuance of these codes of conduct, the lead firms also contract with third-party firms to conduct compliance audits.

In ending the employment of child labour in their factories, suppliers would carry out some change in their ways of organizing production and in their business strategies. These changes in business strategies have been the subject of studies, for example, ILO–International Programme on the Elimination of Child Labour (ILO–IPEC) (2013). From the various case studies, we identify the features of the interventions to eliminate child labour from the value chains.

Banning Child Labour from Factories

A straightforward step is to ban children from the factory. Large firms that are the immediate exporters in GVCs, Tier-1 firms, usually have a signboard on the gate stating that 'Persons below 18 years not allowed'. Not only are workers under 18 prohibited, even children of workers are not allowed to visit them in the factories. As one factory manager explained, there is a fear that buyers' compliance or audit teams may visit the factory at any time, and they do not want to have to explain that the children on the factory premises are not workers. Though Indian law allows the employment of children above 14 years of age in non-hazardous occupations, the GVC suppliers are required by buyers' compliance codes to prohibit work for those below 18 years of age (Bhaskaran et al., 2010).

The elimination of child labour results in the substitution of higher-wage adult labour for low-wage child labour. Without changes to methods of production, this would lead to higher costs and, with output prices unchanged, a reduction in profits. To cover the increase in wage costs, the elimination of child labour in the factory is often accompanied by a change in technology and/or in the organization of production. Handcraft exporter, Dileep Industries, Jaipur, shifted the production method from artisanal production to an assembly line system, which reduced unit costs below those of artisanal production (ILO–IPEC, 2013). In the Sivakasi match-firework cluster, which largely caters to the domestic market, the factories adopted some forms of mechanization. Such changes in technology and the organization of production are to be expected as firms try to reduce the impact of a higher wage bill on their profits.

Shifting to Remote Locations

There have been instances of units not actually eliminating child labour but instead shifting location in order to escape regulatory gaze. This often occurred in the case of carpet manufacture in Jaipur. Production was carried out in small units, often placed in homesteads. These units often relocated, away from cities, such as Jaipur, to rural or peri-urban locations, which would be more difficult to monitor. This, of course, is not a way of eliminating child labour but of escaping regulation, whether private regulation through compliance audits or governmental regulation through labour inspections.

Child labour is often employed not in the main or Tier-1 production units but in households to which some production tasks are outsourced through contractors. This includes both workshops that largely employed children and also women who worked along with their children. Particularly after the media exposure of children in a household workshop in the National Capital Region (NCR) working on garments with Gap labels (ABC News, 2007), there have been some moves to end such household-based handiwork, including the making of embroidery and finishing garments. Many factories, in Delhi and the adjoining regions, brought these production processes within the factory. In many instances the work was mechanized, as in embroidery logos and other such standardized embroidery. In some cases, as with more complex embroidery, the women were brought to work within the factory. The mechanization of embroidery reduces unit costs and thus pays for itself. Hand embroidery by former homeworkers, now working in the factory, may not have reduced costs. But remaining as outsourced, home-based work continued the risk of child labour with the attendant risk of losing business, as buyers cannot afford the damage to their reputation. This increased the pressure to bring in all processes into in-house, factory-located operations. Discussions with homeworkers in Delhi and the NCR make it clear that there has been a substantial reduction of outsourcing to homeworkers. At the same time, those studying GVCs point out that there has been substantial shifting of hand embroidery work to distant centres, such as Bareilly, a traditional centre for hand embroidery. This eliminates child labour at the factory level, by shifting to other, difficult–to-monitor locations of homework.

Community Centres

Another way of eliminating child labour is through the establishment of community centres, where women can work under centralized supervision and without children. This was done in the Mewat project (Bhaskaran et al., 2010; Tewari, 2016). Neerja Blue Potteries in Jaipur also brought former home-based work into community centres. Such a step was also carried out on a large scale in the Siallkot, Pakistan, football stitching cluster (Lund-Thompsen et al., 2012) and is reported to have been successful in eliminating child labour in the cluster.

The Sialkot experience of successful elimination of child labour should be contrasted with the Indian, Jullundur, where child labour in home-based hand-stitching of footballs has continued to be a feature of the production landscape.

Increasing Adult Wages

A novel way of ending child labour was seen in some brick-kilns in West Bengal, where the owner compensated the adults for the corresponding household income loss (Sarkar, 2010). Adult wages were increased to cover households for the loss of earnings by children. This, however, is quite unusual, and we have not seen any other examples of employers paying for the elimination of child labour by absorbing an increase in adult wages through a cut in profits.

To summarize, the methods of eliminating child labour from GVCs and DVCs involved changes in the factory and in homeworking. Within the factory it led to changing the technology and methods of production either (*a*) by adopting mechanization, or (*b*) through changing the production process, by replacing artisanal with an Adam Smith–style division of labour. The change in homeworking did not involve a change in technology or the production process but the shifting of outsourced production from homes to community centres.

What Brought About the Change in Business Strategies

Eliminating child labour from value chains has involved some change in business strategies, the substitution of low-wage child labour by higher-wage adult labour, often accompanied by a change in technology or the organization of the production process. Analysis of the elimination of child labour in the UK (Frey, 2019) and in the USA (Udry, 2003) both point out that the decline in child labour in the 19th century was driven by changes in technology and the increase in real wages, along with immigration in the USA.

Why did the Indian GVC suppliers change their business strategies? An answer to this question will help in developing ways of eliminating child labour in value chains. The factors that worked to eliminate child labour can be grouped into two categories – pressures that led to private and/or public regulation of labour conditions in value chains and development. By 'development' we refer to those non-value chain developments that had an impact on value chains, such as an increase in market wages and earnings in the economy as a whole.

Pressure has been of various types, all having an impact on the market for the GVC suppliers and the lead firms. In the GVC period, the elimination of child labour started with the pressure of morally concerned consumers, initially students on US campuses, who demanded that their university supplies not be secured from brands whose value chains involved child labour. Initially, the brands, such as Nike, denied any connection with labour conditions in their supplier factories. Given that brands profited from the resulting low prices of suppliers' products, this argument of non-involvement could not hold. With the pressure of mounting media exposures of the employment of child labour in various brands' supply chains, the brands came up with 'codes of conduct' for their suppliers. What worked to make brands take the stand of requiring not just technical and quality control but also labour standards was the pressure that consumer-facing sellers faced from morally concerned consumers.

The pressure on brands was transmitted to suppliers, who faced the threat of losing their supply contracts if child labour was found in their own or subcontracted factories. With the spread of manufacturing capabilities around Asia, it was not difficult for brands to switch suppliers, making threats credible. As some garment suppliers from Bangladesh admitted, it was this threat of losing their contracts that forced them to conform to compliance standards and eliminate child labour from their factories (Nathan and George, 2012).

In the GVC cases there is responsibility not just of lead firms but also of suppliers. The lead firms, however, have greater responsibility. They are akin to principal employers, a category in the Indian law on contract labour. The lead firm distributes tasks within the GVC, governs the production of the final product and earns the profit from its sales. The greater the benefit, the greater the responsibility, as has been argued in the literature on justice. There is a manner of not just joint but also several responsibility in value chains (Kotiswaran, 2019). The notion of principal responsibility of the lead firm that secures monopoly-cum-monopsony profits (Nathan et al., 2022), however, does place main responsibility on the lead firm in the GVC.

In the DVC of matches and fireworks, there was no pressure from external or, for that matter, domestic consumers or buyers. But there had been a lot of media publicity about the high incidence of child labour in the Sivakasi cluster, where children were employed in hazardous work in fireworks factories or workshops (Nathan and George, 2012). This was clearly illegal. The matter of child labour in hazardous occupations became an election issue, and the state government took action against the employment of child labour in these factories. Many factories or workshops were threatened with closure. The employers' association then took action to secure the elimination of child labour from these factories. This was achieved by the adoption of mechanized technology, which required some measure of skill and reduced, if not eliminated, the employment of low-wage, low-skilled child labour. With the employers' association itself promoting this measure, it was more or less implemented, though there have been reports that units in peri-urban areas continued to employ child labour.

In looking at electoral pressure we have already introduced the next set of actions – that of public regulation, that is, actions by the state, by governments and administrations to implement child labour laws, working through some form of punishment, either fines or imprisonment, for violations of the law.

Limits of Private Governance

Some analyses of labour conditions in GVCs have used the term 'private regulation' to refer to lead firms' actions of market pressures or threats to market positions, either in sales of final products or in loss of contracts/markets of suppliers (Locke, 2013). It is useful to distinguish regulation working through market mechanisms from regulatory threats working through carceral methods or punishment. These are interventions by two different sets of actors, those of the corporate sector and those of the state, and, for that reason, need to be distinguished from each other and not clubbed together. This distinction becomes even more important in the case of DVCs, where there have not been moral consumer movements in supplier countries (developing economies) to pressure brands and suppliers to clean up their value chains. Eliminating child labour in value chains supplying to domestic markets has very much resulted from public regulation and, as we will see further on, from broader economic developments.

Legal regulation of child labour has been of two types. The first is through 'rescue and rehabilitation' of child workers. The second is through fines levied on employers responsible for employing child workers. The child labour law in India is not part of the Indian Penal Code (IPC) or the Code of Criminal Procedure (CPC), but the police carry out the rescue of child workers and prosecute the responsible employers. Given that the employment of child workers with all the features of modern slavery that we listed above is a form of extreme exploitation, there definitely is a role not just for the rescue of child labourers but also for subsequent criminal prosecution of their employers.

Children working along with their parents or genuine families face another form of exploitation. As pointed out earlier, such child labour mainly arises from the poverty of parents or the incorrect notion that this is the only way in which to pass on traditional craft skills, as in a caste system. Here the action required is that of creating the conditions where children are not denied full participation in education through interventions outside the value chain, or what can be called 'development interventions'; certainly not a situation calling for 'raid and rescue' missions.

The second set of factors that seem to have worked in eliminating child labour from even DVCs is that of economic development in a broad sense. The exceptional case of the brick kiln owner who increased adult wages to cover the loss of children's earnings shows that an increase in adult wages could reduce the supply of child labour and thus eliminate its use in production. This was noted by Mahenda Dev (2011), where child labour was reduced by India's rural employment guarantee. The other economic development is that of technological change. This could work either by reducing the advantage of low-paid and low-skilled labour, such as child labour. Or it could work by introducing machinery that is too difficult or complicated for children to operate and end the advantage of child over adult labour, as argued for by the UK's experience (Frey, 2019). Overall economic development may be important not just at the level of forcing a change in business strategies but even in reducing or even ending the supply of child labour, a point which we take up in the next section.

The Incompleteness of Eliminating Child Labour from Value Chains

Lead firms and suppliers in value chains may see the objective of eliminating child labour from value chains as limited strictly to the elimination of child labour from their own value chains in order to reduce or even eliminate the possibility of reputational or regulatory loss. But from a social angle, the objective must be broader. The reason for eliminating child labour from employment, whether in value chains or elsewhere, is to increase the child's well-being. If this broader view is accepted, then what happens after the child leaves employment in a GVC is as important as the fact of leaving employment itself. That is also the reason why the rescue of child labour is followed by the attempt to rehabilitate the child worker through 'bridge schools' and other such programmes that are expected to enable the child to return to school education and reintegrate with both the family and community.

A socially responsible child labour policy would continue to follow the child post-employment. Merely removing the child from the value chain can often lead to a deterioration in the child's well-being if the child is forced into worse types of employment. The elimination of child labour from garment factories in Bangladesh was reported to have led to some of the children ending up in worse forms of employment, such as in the unorganized sector or even the sex trade (Khanam, 2006). This led to the child labour elimination programme being followed up by an ILO programme that sought to prevent this deterioration in their well-being.

The above implies that (*a*) it is insufficient to deal only with the demand for child labour, for employment in GVCs or other value chains; (*b*) it is also necessary to deal with the supply of child labour; and (*c*) in order to deal with the supply of child labour, it is necessary to examine development interventions that affect the supply side. We will address the question of supply-side issues and then deal with development matters.

The issue of the supply of child labour is problematic not only at the micro or enterprise level but also at the macro level of the labour market. We observed that the removal of child workers from GVC employment could lead to their being pushed into worse forms of employment in the unorganized sector or even in the sex trade. At a macro level, time-bound interventions on the demand for child labour have proved to be of limited benefit. As one cohort of child labour was removed from employment in auto workshops and eateries in the state of Andhra Pradesh, the project implementers were made aware that they were being replaced by a new cohort of children (Nathan and George, 2012). If the supply at source is not eliminated, the elimination at destination is, at best, temporary. A comprehensive policy to end child labour needs to complement the elimination of child labour from GVCs and other value chains with ending the supply of child labour through the transformation of conditions that continuously create a supply of child labour.

Supply of Child Labour

What are the conditions that create a supply of child labour? Kaushik Basu (1999) had identified low adult wages as a key factor in pushing families to put their children to work. When household consumption is well below poverty levels, there is an obvious pressure for children to work in order to support the household in surviving. Conversely, an increase in adult wages should lead to a reduction in the supply of child labour. This proposition is corroborated by evidence that the increase in earnings of agricultural labourers through the rural employment guarantee scheme, MGNREGA, led to a decline in the supply of child labour (Dev, 2011).

Making education available and compulsory is another factor that would affect the supply of child labour. In discussions with employers, schoolteachers, and non-governmental organizations (NGOs) in Sivakasi, researchers were told that the extension of education through the Sarva Siksha Abhiyan (SSA) and the accompanying mid-day meal scheme was a major factor in reducing the supply of child labour into the match-cum-fireworks factories (ILO–IPEC, 2013). The importance of the mid-day meal in increasing children's school attendance is seen even in other countries, such as Chad in Africa, where a poverty alleviation project of the Islamic Development Bank (IsDB) reported an increase in school attendance after the introduction of a mid-day meal at school (ISFD, 2021).

Nevertheless, even with almost universal school enrolment below the age of 14, the end of child labour is not complete. Even in the better-off states, such as Punjab and Haryana, it was found that children of agricultural labourers, who are also Dalits, skipped school during the cotton-picking season in order to maximize household earnings (IHD and Save the Children, 2014). Skipping classes would result in the children falling behind in their schoolwork. As pointed out earlier, children who fall behind their class are the ones who then drop out of school or attend it as a formality, particularly under the pressure of low wages.

Thus, making education available does not mean that parents will consistently send their children to school. For poor parents to do so, they must have the aspiration for their children to be something different from what they themselves are. The importance of aspirations in driving development has been brought out in Appadurai (2005) and Nathan (2005). In the case of child labour, we see it in the woman worker in a brick kiln in West Bengal who said, 'We do not want our children to be *murkho* (fools) like us' (quoted in Sarkar, 2010: 19). Discussions around child labour sites lead us to conclude that such aspirations can be said to be universal, at least in the various states in which we have done field work on various issues, and not necessarily related to child labour. Nevertheless, there is the deficiency in the capacity to aspire (Appadurai, 2005), as a result of which people are not able to meet either their own aspirations or those for their children. This requires state interventions and market development to increase adult wages so that children can consistently attend school. But we should not underestimate the importance of the cultural factor of aspirations. A study of industrializing Japan points out that peasant families highly valued children's education and that this is what ended child labour in Japan, rather than state policies or regulation (Saito, 1996).

School Education as Development Intervention to End the Supply of Child Labour

In India, education is universal and compulsory education until age 14, after which children may work legally. However, it is the internationally accepted position, in accordance with that of the ILO, that children should not work until the age of 18. Even if we accept the Indian Government's determination of age 14 as the age up to which education should be universal and compulsory, there is another problem with the official data on child labour. The National Sample Survey Office (NSSO) carries out periodic surveys of labour and households. The definition of child labour used by the NSSO is that of children who are working for a wage or in independent, own-account work. This excludes those who work with their families, as in agriculture; those who irregularly work as employees; and those, mainly girls, who look after younger siblings or otherwise participate in domestic work without attending school. They have been referred to as the 'nowhere children', meaning that they are neither at school nor employed. But, as argued in Rustagi and Leiten (2008), these children are actually at work. They do various kinds of small jobs within the household, such as looking after animals, minding the house when both parents are away, looking after younger siblings, and the like. All of these tasks are part of the household economy and should be considered work. When we consider the question of child labour from the rights' perspective as a violation of a child's right to education, this is the correct measure – all those out of school, whether working as wage employees or as contributing family workers, should be considered as child labourers.

Adding the two categories of child workers as wage employees or independent own-account workers, together with that of children neither at school nor formally at work, gives a fuller estimate of the extent of child labour. The former is a restricted definition of child labour, while the latter provides the full definition. As shown in Table 10.1, the numbers reflecting the full definition of child labour are about four times greater than those under the restricted definition. Further, the phenomenon of being neither at school nor formally employed outside of the

Table 10.1 Child labour in India, 1993–94 to 2007–08 (percentage of children 5–14 years old).

	1993–94		2007–08	
	Restricted Definition	**Full Definition**	**Restricted Definition**	**Full Definition**
Boys	6.2	26.0	2.7	13.8
Girls	6.0	38.3	2.0	17.1
Children	6.2	31.8	2.4	15.4

Source: Based on IAMR (2011), *India Human Development Report*, Tables 8.1i, 8.2, and Figure 8.1.

Note: 'Restricted' definition is as per the workforce participation definition of NSSO, that is, those who are either wage employees or independent own-account workers. 'Full definition' adds to this those who are 'neither at school, nor in the workforce', that is, those who are either working at home or elsewhere with the family.

home or with the family is largely a rural phenomenon. Thus, the bulk of India's child labour is in agriculture and related sectors in the rural areas. This is so not only for India but also globally, where agriculture accounts for 70 per cent of child labour (UNICEF and ILO, 2020).

It is notable that while the number of girls as workers or employees is about the same as that of boys, there is a big difference in the proportion of girls, as compared to boys, who are contributing family workers. Given the preponderance of contributing family workers, ending child labour mainly requires removing children from the category of contributing family workers and of supposed 'nowhere' children.

Although there has been noted improvement in school enrollment, studies, for example, in Bihar, one of the poorest states in India, show that attendance falls well below enrolment (IHD, 2011). Further, as we saw earlier, even in the highest per capita income states of Punjab and Haryana, children of Dalit agricultural labourers regularly miss school during the cotton-picking season. Filling the gap between enrolment and attendance will be reflected in a reduction in the incidence of child labour.

Conclusion

In this chapter we made a number of distinctions concerning child labour in GVCs, distinctions that have a bearing on policy with regard to child labour. One is between child labour as wage employees, usually in conditions that can be deemed 'modern slavery', and child labour as homeworkers, participating with their families as contributing to family labour or in domestic work. To combat the case of child labourers as wage employees would require 'search and rescue' missions to locate those children, as well as criminal prosecution of employers, actions that would be completely out of place in the case of child homeworkers. In contrast, the latter case requires interventions outside the area of child labour, which we have referred to as 'development interventions', such as measures to increase adult wages, increase school attendance, include craft instruction in schools, and provide child care facilities.

Another distinction is between interventions or changes to corporate policy to *eliminate* child labour from GVCs or DVCs and policies to *end* child labour completely. This distinction is akin to that between demand for and supply of child labour. Eliminating child labour from GVCs is itself incomplete as far as the well-being of the child workers is concerned, since such elimination may end up with the children moving to other, even more dangerous or exploitative employments. This is acknowledged in the addition of rehabilitation packages to 'search and rescue' missions. However, that still does not remedy the continuing supply of child labour. Ending the supply of child labour depends on changes in the poverty and other conditions of children and their families. As pointed out by Christopher Udry (2003: 14), child labour as a mass phenomenon disappears when the population moves out of poverty. Consequently, it is necessary to add development measures to end the supply of child labour to corporate interventions, which deal with the demand for child labour, in order to move from eliminating child labour in GVCs to actually ending child labour.

What has succeeded in reducing or ending child labour in GVCs? The first factor is that of pressures, such as by moral consumers on consumer-facing brands and the resultant pressure that lead firms put on suppliers to remove child labour from the GVCs with the threat of losing business if they do not. This is part of a private regulatory system set up by lead firms in GVCs in response to actual or threatened market pressures. It usually requires supplier firms to change their business strategies, adopting mechanized or on-site production. However, without other complementary measures, these changes may result in the transfer of child labour to more difficult to reach locales in order to escape the regulatory gaze.

The second factor working towards removing child labour from GVCs is that of public regulation. This can be a combination of legal prosecution, following search and rescue missions where children are employed as wage employees in conditions of modern slavery. The third factor is that of development interventions, such as increases in adult wages, compulsory school education, and introduction of craft courses in schools and childcare. A fourth factor is that of development of aspirations that children be educated, by supporting the capacity to aspire through state intervention and market development to increase adult wages.

A combination of private and public regulation, along with development measures and development of aspirations, is needed to move from eliminating child labour from GVCs or DVCs to altogether ending child labour. Private regulation by itself is quite insufficient to end child labour within value chains. Further, this chapter shows that, at an analytical level, it is necessary to embed value chains in the social context within which they exist. Much of the analysis of value chains confines itself to the value chain alone, but this chapter demonstrates that the social context or embedding of GVCs is essential for the framing of policies to end child labour.

References

ABC News (2007). 'Gap under Fire: Reports Allege Child Labour'. 28 October. Available at: https://abcnews.go.com/GMA/story?id=3786371&page=1.

Appadurai, A. (2005). 'The Capacity to Aspire'. In *Culture and Public Action*, edited by M. Walton and V. Rao, Stanford, CA: Stanford University Press.

Barrientos, S., M. Kanchan, and S. Atul (2010). 'Decent Work in Global Production Networks: Challenges for Vulnerable Workers in the Indian Garments Sector'. In *Labour in Global Production Networks in India*, edited by A. Posthuma and D. Nathan, 127–45. New Delhi: Oxford University Press.

Basu, K. (1999). 'Child labour: Cause, Consequence, and Cure'. *Journal of Economic Literature* 37: 1083–119.

Bhaskaran, R., C. Upendranadh, D. Nathan, and N. Phillips (2010). 'Home-Based Child Labour in Delhi's Garment Production: Contemporary Forms of Unfree Labour in Global Production'. *The Indian Journal of Labour Economics* 53(4): 6072–74.

Dev, S. M. (2011). 'NREGA and Child Well-being'. IHD-UNICEF Working Paper Series, No. 10, Institute for Human Development, New Delhi.

Frey, C. (2019). *The Technology Trap*. Princeton, NJ: Princeton University Press.

IAMR (Institute for Applied Manpower Research) (2011). *India Human Development Report, 2011*. Delhi: IAMR.

IHD (Institute for Human Development) (2011). *Inclusive Development for Bihar: A Study for the UNDP*. New Delhi: IHD.

IHD and Save the Children (2014). *Child Labour in Cotton Harvesting in Punjab.* New Delhi: IHD.

ILO (2022). *ILO Declaration on Fundamental Principles and Rights at Work.* Geneva: ILO.

ILO–IPEC (2013). *Businesses and the Fight against Child Labour: Experience from India, Brazil and South Africa.* Geneva: ILO.

ILO–UNICEF (2017). *Global Estimates of Child Labour.* Geneva: ILO.

ISFD (Islamic Solidarity and Development Fund) (2021). *Development Effectiveness Report.* Jeddah: ISFD (mimeo).

Khanam, R. (2006). 'Child Labour in Bangladesh'. *Asian Profile* 34(6): 593–608.

Kotiswaran, P. (2019). 'Trafficking: A Development Approach'. UCL Working Paper Series 4/2019. UCL, Faculty of Laws.

Locke, R. (2013). *The Promise and Limits of Private Power: Promoting Labor Standards in a Global Economy.* New York: Cambridge University Press.

Lund-Thomsen, P., K. Nadvi, A. Chan, N. Khara, and H. Xue (2012). 'Labour in Global Value Chains: Work Conditions in Football Manufacturing in China, India and Pakistan'. *Development and Change* 43(6): 1211–37.

Nathan, D. (2005). 'Capabilities and Aspirations'. *Economic and Political Weekly* 40(1): 36–40.

——— (2023). 'Child Labour'. In *Elgar Encyclopedia of Development*, edited by M. Clarke and X. Zhao, 83–87. London: Edward Elgar.

Nathan, D., S. S. Bhattacharjee, S. Rahul, P. Kumar, I. Dahaghani, S. Singh, and P. Swaminathan (2022). *Reverse Subsidies in Global Monopsony Capitalism: Gender, Labour, and Environmental Injustice in Garment Value Chains.* Cambridge, UK: Cambridge University Press.

Nathan, D. and A. George (2012). 'Corporate Governance and Child Labour: Role and Limits'. *Economic and Political Weekly* 47(50): 50–57.

Nieuwenhuys, O. (1996). 'The Paradox of Child Labor and Anthropology'. *Annual Review of Anthropology* 25: 237–51.

Phillips, N., R. Bhaskaran, D. Nathan, and C. Upendranadh (2014). 'The Social Foundation of Global Production Networks: Towards a Global Political Economy of Child Labour'. *Third World Quarterly* 35(3): 428–46.

Saito, O. (1996). 'Children's Work, Industrialism and the Family Economy in Japan, 1872–1926'. In *Child Labour in Historical Perspective 1800-1985: Case Studies from Europe, Japan and Colombia*, edited by H. Cunningham and P. P. Viazzo, 73–90. Florence: UNICEF, International Child Development Centre.

Sarkar, I. (2010). *Assessment of Child Labour Free Brick Kilns in Malda District, West Bengal.* Kolkota: Save the Children/Bal Raksha Bharat.

Sharma, A., R. Sharma, and R. Nikhil (2004). *Child Labour in Carpet Industry.* New Delhi: Institute for Human Development.

Stewart, K. (2017). 'Is Child Labour Always Wrong? A View from Bolivia'. *The Guardian*, 24 February. Available at: www.theguardian.com/global-development/2017/feb/24/is-child-labour-always-wrong-the-view-from-bolivia-podcast-transcript.

Tewari, M. (2016). 'Diffusing Labour Standards Down and Beyond the Value Chain: Lessons from the Mewat Experience'. In *Labour in Global Value Chains in Asia*, edited by D. Nathan, M. Tewari and S. Sarkar, 286–314. Cambridge, UK: Cambridge University Press.

The Freedom Fund (2018). *Business Strategies for a Child Labour Free Jaipur.* London: The Freedom Fund.

Udry, C. (2003). 'Child Labor'. Center Discussion Paper No. 856, Yale University, Economic Growth Center.

Ugarte, C., M. Olarreaga, and G. Saiovici (2020). 'Child Labour and Global Value Chains'. Discussion Paper DP 15426.,Centre for Economic Policy Research.

UNICEF and ILO (2020). *Covid-19 and Child Labour.* New York: UNICEF.

Vaughan-Whitehead, D. (2014). 'How Fair Are Wage Practices along the Supply Chain?' In *Towards Better Work: Understanding Labour in Apparel Global Value Chains*, edited by A. Rossi, A. Luinstra and J. Pickles, 58–102. London: Palgrave Macmillan.

About the Contributors

Lorena Arocha, PhD, is an Assistant Professor in the Department of Social Sciences at Northumbria University, UK. Her research interests critically examine the impact in policy and practice of the use of the umbrella term of 'modern slavery' and all the related practices, such as human trafficking, forced labour, and bonded labour. Her projects to date include evaluation of the implementation of child sexual exploitation and trafficking policy in the UK, exploring the roles of organizations in anti-trafficking work in South Asia, the role of migrant and refugee community organizations in the development of modern slavery policy in the UK, the role of 'modern slavery' in efforts to address female labour exploitation in agricultural sectors across a variety of contexts (that is, South Asia and southern Spain), and conducting student-led evaluations of non-governmental services, including provisions for asylum-seeking young people and women in sex work. Her research has been funded by both academic and non-academic institutions, including the British Academy, the HEI, the ESRC Festival for Social Sciences, and Comic Relief.

The late **Bimal Arora** was the founding CEO of Centre for Responsible Business (CRB) which he established to facilitate participation of Indian actors in voluntary global governance for sustainability. Having handed over the executive leadership, he served as the Honorary Chairperson of CRB. He was Reader in Enterprise at the Centre for Enterprise at Manchester Metropolitan University, UK, and Adjunct Faculty at Alliance Manchester Business School (AMBS), the University of Manchester, UK. He also held a Visiting Research Fellow position at the International

Centre for Corporate Social Responsibility (ICCSR) at Nottingham University Business School, and at Copenhagen Business School. He was a sustainability, CSR, and ethical trade expert with extensive experience working in practice and research with diverse sectors. With extensive experience of over 30 years across diverse sectors, his work has been published in several academic journals and business magazines. He obtained his Master's degree from London School of Economics and PhD in CSR and Sustainability from ICCSR, Nottingham University Business School.

Shilpi Banerjee is a Research Fellow at Hult International Business School in Dubai, UAE. Her research examines the changing roles and responsibilities of business in the global economy, with a particular focus on CSR communication, modern slavery, and inequality. She holds a PhD in Business Management from Royal Holloway, University of London, UK.

Tamar Barkay is a senior lecturer and the head of the Sociology and Anthropology Programme in the Department of Multidisciplinary Studies at Tel-Hai College. She is also affiliated with ChainGE Lab (ERC) at Tel Aviv University. Tamar holds a PhD and MA in Sociology and Anthropology from Tel Aviv University. Her research focuses on economic sociology, particularly the social and political implications of CSR and labour governance in supply chains. In this context, she has explored the emergence of new forms of non-state governance, examining how the popularization of 'corporate responsibility' intersects with the decline of organized labour.

Roshni Chattopadhyay is a PhD candidate in the Department of Anthropology at Emory University, USA. Concurrently, she is pursuing a certification from the Department of Women's, Gender, and Sexuality Studies. Her broader research interests encompass the themes: anthropology of gender, anthropology of law, anthropology of state and state formations, anthropology of indigeneity/Adivasis in South Asia, extractive industries, feminist ethnography, and contemporary politics in South Asia, with a particular regional focus on India. Her PhD research project is supported by American Ethnological Society, Halle Institute for Global Research in Emory, and Wenner-Gren Foundation. Before joining grad school, Roshni worked on three different research projects in diverse capacities in India. The projects examined the practices of early and child marriage in India, the various forms of discrimination faced by individuals from non-normative gender and sexualities, and workers' experiences in informal labour sectors in India. Roshni has also actively volunteered with Bebaak Collective: Voices of the Fearless, Muslim women's advocacy group in Mumbai, India. Roshni has extensive experiences of doing fieldwork in various parts of India often marred by economic inequalities and ethnic tensions including Maharashtra, Gujarat, Rajasthan, West Bengal, Telangana, and Uttar Pradesh.

Franz Christian Ebert is a Research Officer at the International Labour Organization (ILO). At the ILO, his research focuses on the interplay between trade law, supply chain governance, and labour standards. Previously, he worked as a researcher at the Max Planck Institute for Comparative Public Law and International Law in Heidelberg and served as a visiting professional at the Inter-American Court of Human Rights. Franz was also a visiting researcher at Columbia Law School and at the Lauterpacht Centre for International Law at the University of Cambridge. In his previous roles, Franz has advised several international organizations, governments, and civil society organizations and has appeared before committees of the European Parliament and the German Parliament. He is also an Associate Member of the Centre for Law at Work at the University of Bristol.

Klaas Hendrik Eller is an Assistant Professor at Amsterdam Law School. His research interests are centred around the spatial and distributive effects of private and economic law. His work explores how law co-constitutes and connects sites of the global economy, such as along global value chains, commercial infrastructures, and in financialized real estate. Klaas received his legal education in Germany and France and passed the German bar exam (Referendariat) at the High Court of Berlin with secondments inter alia at the Supreme Court of the State of Israel (Justice Daphne Barak-Erez) and at an international arbitration boutique. He earned his PhD from the University of Cologne, Germany (2019), and later was a Fellow both at Tel Aviv University's and Harvard University's Edmond J. Safra Center for Ethics. He is a co-editor-in-chief of the *German Law Journal* and a member of the Amsterdam Young Academy.

Francesca Francavilla is a senior economist at the International Labour Organization (ILO) with nearly 25 years of experience in employment, inclusion, gender, and impact evaluation. At the ILO's Fundamental Principles and Rights at Work branch, she leads the workstream on the economics of forced labour. She led the publications *Profits and Poverty and Acting against Forced Labour* (2024), and contributed to the 2022 *Global Estimates of Modern Slavery.* Francesca has developed innovative methods to measure decent work violations in supply chains—including in the electronics and fisheries sectors—and is currently working on a methodology for assessing forced labour risks in supply chains. Before joining the ILO, she worked with organizations such as UNICEF, UNFPA, EBRD, ADB, WHO, UNDP, UN Women, and OECD. She holds a PhD in Development Economics and an MSc in Economics, and has published widely in academic journals and policy reports.

Sahiba Gill is the Deputy Legal Director at Global Labor Justice, where she helps to build worker power in the global economy. She holds a JD from New York University School of Law and is admitted to practice law in New York. Her writing has previously been published in the *European Journal of International Law.*

Meena Gopal is currently on lien from the Tata Institute of Social Sciences, Mumbai, teaching at the Centre for Women's Studies in Pondicherry University. Her research interests are in the areas of labour, sexuality, bodily cultures such as sports, and women's movements. She recently co-edited two publications, *Women in the Worlds of Labour: Interdisciplinary and Intersectional Perspectives* (Orient BlackSwan, 2021) and *Sports Studies in India: Expanding the Field* (Oxford University Press, 2021)

Lorenzo Guarcello is a project manager and senior researcher in the area of statistics and empirical analysis within the Research and Evaluation unit of ILO-FUNDAMENTALS. He was previously the lead researcher for the 'Understanding Children's Work' (UCW) project, an inter-agency research initiative on child labour involving the International Labor Organization (ILO), UNICEF and the World Bank. In addition to his research endeavours, Lorenzo is actively engaged in sharing his knowledge and expertise. He teaches in the Master in Development Economics and International Cooperation (MESCI) programme at the University of Rome, and is key resource person in capacity-building trainings on child labour and forced labour organized by the ILO. He received a Master's in Economics from the University of Salerno, and a BA in Statistics from the Faculty of Economics, University of Palermo. His research interests include labour economics, household economics, and development economics.

Varsha Joshi was a historian and social scientist at the Institute for Development Studies, Jaipur. Besides carrying out numerous studies on child labour, she was also active in setting up and running the Child Help Line in Jaipur.

Ioannis Kampourakis is an Associate Professor in Law and Markets at Erasmus School of Law, Erasmus University Rotterdam. Ioannis' research focuses on the legal foundations of capitalism and private power. Drawing from legal theory, political economy, and international and EU law, he explores how law constitutes markets and under which conditions it could function as a vehicle for socio-economic transformation. His current project is on the law and political economy of the green transition and the legal architecture of green capitalism. In 2023, he was awarded the three-year NWO Veni grant to research the implications of the EU regulation of Critical Raw Materials and the shift to industrial policy and market instrumentalism in the context of the EU Green Deal. Ioannis is a co-PI of the network 'Law and Political Economy in Europe' and serves as a member of the editorial board of the *Journal of Law and Political Economy*.

Ingrid Landau is a Senior Lecturer at Monash Business School, Monash University. She holds a PhD in Law from Melbourne University, and Bachelor degrees in Asian Studies and Law from the Australian National University. She teaches and researches in the areas of employment law, transnational labour regulation, and business and human rights. She also works regularly as a consultant for the International Labour Organization (ILO), mostly on projects within the Asia Pacific. Her recent book *Human Rights Due Diligence and Labour Governance*, published by Oxford University Press, examines human rights due diligence as a mechanism of transnational labour law.

Shelley Marshall is Professor of Law at RMIT University. She has advised and published on corporate accountability and business and human rights for 25 years, with a focus on the labour conditions of vulnerable workers and modern slavery. Shelley left legal practice in 2001 to join the team setting up Ethical Clothing Australia. Her research has informed labour law reform in several countries and the policies of the International Labour Organization (ILO). For example, over 2018–19, she made frequent trips to Thailand to advise the Thai Ministry of Labour on how to enforce labour laws for homeworkers. In 2023, she co-drafted the text for an ILO Convention on Decent Work in Global Supply Chains with Ingrid Landau. Her book *Living Wage*, published by Oxford University Press in 2019, proposed a new architecture for international labour law. An Australian Research Council DECRA Fellowship, 2020–23, allowed Shelley to examine the deployment of digital technologies to address modern slavery.

Dev Nathan is a social scientist with the Southern Centre for Inequality Studies at the University of the Witwatersrand, Johannesburg; the Institute for Human Development, Delhi; and GevDev Centre for Research and Innovation, Gurgaon. His recent book, *Knowledge and Global Inequality Since 1800*, is open access at Cambridge-UNU WIDER Elements in Development Economics. Besides various studies of global value chains, he is also co-author of *Witch Hunts: Culture, Patriarchy and Structural Transformation*.

Bindhulakshmi Pattadath is an independent academic and researcher based in Mumbai, India. She previously served as Associate Professor and Chairperson at the Advanced Centre for Women's Studies, Tata Institute of Social Sciences (TISS), Mumbai, and was a postdoctoral fellow at the Amsterdam School for Social Science Research, University of Amsterdam. Her research explores intersections of gender, labour, migration, mental health, and disability studies.

Divya Priyadarshini has a PhD in Sociology from Delhi School of Economics, India. Currently she is a freelance urban researcher working on the urban scenario of Delhi. Previously she has worked with the Indian government's apex think tank, NITI Aayog, as a social policy researcher. She also has the experience of working in numerous non-profit organizations working on right to adequate housing, homelessness, and migration. Divya has keen interest in policy making and planning.

Roseanne Russell is Senior Lecturer in Law at the University of Bristol Law School in the UK . Her research interests lie at the intersection of labour law, corporate governance, and feminist legal theory. She was formerly co-editor-in-chief of the *Common Law World Review*, a member of the Law Society of England and Wales Employment Law Committee from 2008 to 2018, and co-convenor of the Society of Legal Scholars Company Law Stream from 2015 to 2018. Before entering academia, Roseanne practised as a solicitor in Edinburgh and London and from 2005 to 2007 was Principal Legal Officer at the former Equal Opportunities Commission. She holds a LLB (Honours) in Scots Law from the University of Glasgow and MPhil and PhD from the University of Bristol.

Hila Shamir is a Professor of Law at Tel Aviv University, where she previously served as Associate Dean. She is an expert in employment, labour, immigration, and welfare law, with a particular focus on issues affecting workers in global value chains, human trafficking, and gender equality. Shamir has held visiting appointments at

Harvard Law School, the University of Toronto Faculty of Law, Georgetown Law, Cornell Law School, and UC Berkeley.

She received a European Research Council (ERC) grant to lead the project 'TraffLab: A Labor Approach to Human Trafficking' (2018–23), which was a finalist for the ERC Public Engagement with Research Award in 2022. In 2024, she was awarded a second ERC grant for the project 'A New Labor Law for Supply Chain Capitalism' (ChainGE Lab, 2024–29).

Saie Shetye completed her PhD from the Tata Institute of Social Sciences, Mumbai, India, in 2020. She presently works with the Migration and Asylum Project in New Delhi where she works on legal representation for asylum seekers and refugees. She has previously worked with various non-profit organizations in India working on migration, trafficking, forced displacement, and incarceration.

Index